Borland C++ Programmer's

Guide to Graphics

Borland C++ Programmer's
Guide to Graphics

James W. McCord

SAMS

A Division of Macmillan Computer Publishing

11711 North College, Carmel, Indiana 46032 USA

Trademarks

Publisher:

Richard K. Swadley

Publishing Manager:

Joseph Wikert

Managing Editor:

Neweleen A. Trebnik

Acquisitions Editor:

Gregory Croy

Development Editor:

Ella M. Davis

Production Editor:

Kathy Grider-Carlyle

Copy Editor:

Lori L. Cates

Technical Reviewer:

Derrel Blain

Cover Design:

Tracy Rea

Illustrator:

Don Clemons

Production Assistance:

Scott Boucher
Brad Chinn
Martin Coleman
Joelynn Gifford
Sandy Grieshop
Howard Peircc
Joe Ramon
Tad Ringo
Dennis Sheehan
Mary Beth Wakefield
Lisa Wilson

Indexer:

Hilary Adams

Contents

2   Reference Guide

10   Video BIOS Services   241

11   Turbo C++ Graphics Reference   269

Introduction

The field of graphics programming can be the most fun, yet challenging, area of computer programming. The graphics programmer must be able to visualize, create, and develop graphics-based applications in specialized environments. These applications must meet the constraints of speed, functionality, and portability. This book is designed to introduce the concepts and principles of graphics programming for the IBM personal computers, and their compatibles, using the Borland C++ Compiler.

This book provides all the information you will need to get "up and running" with graphics and Borland C++. The book contains two parts.

Part I—Computer Graphics with Borland C++

This section contains eight chapters that discuss a variety of topics ranging from video hardware to animation techniques. The following paragraphs briefly describe each chapter in Section I.

Chapter 1—Introduction to IBM PCs and Compatibles

This chapter discusses the fundamentals of the IBM PC and its compatibles. The hardware devices it describes include microprocessors, operating systems, graphics cards, monitors, and input devices.

Chapter 2—C, C++, and Object-Oriented Programming

This chapter outlines the advantages and code structure of the C language, along with a brief discussion of C++ and object-oriented programming.

Chapter 3—Text-Based Graphics

This chapter describes the methods for using the ASCII and IBM extended character sets for basic graphics while in text mode.

Chapter 4—Graphics Techniques

This chapter is dedicated to the presentation of the basic drawing capabilities of the Borland C++ graphics library. It presents concepts of coordinate systems, drawing, area fills, and viewports.

Chapter 5—Text and Graphics

Chapter 5 presents the methods for combining text with graphics. The focus of this chapter is the introduction of the Borland fonts. It also covers methods for creating your own character set.

Chapter 6—Presentation Graphics

This chapter presents several methods for creating presentation graphics charts with the Borland C++ graphics library. Examples for creating pie, line, bar, column, and scatter charts are provided.

Chapter 7—Animation

This chapter introduces the art of animation. The basics of animation, as well as the use of hidden pages, are described along with numerous examples that demonstrate these techniques.

Chapter 8—Two- and Three-Dimensional Drawing

The concepts used to develop both two- and three-dimensional drawings are presented in this chapter. This chapter provides examples that use the concepts discussed.

Chapter 9—Developing a Graphical User Interface

This chapter introduces a fundamental approach to developing a graphical user interface. The topics of mouse input, pop-up menus, dialog boxes, and scroll bars are discussed.

Part II—Reference Guide

This section contains two chapters that provide extensive documentation on the use of the video BIOS services and the Borland C++ graphics library.

Chapter 10—Video BIOS Services

This chapter describes the Video ROM BIOS Services. For each video service and subservice, the chapter provides inputs, outputs, and a description.

Chapter 11—Borland C++ Graphics Functions

This chapter contains detailed information on each function provided in the graphics library. For each function, the following information is provided:

Syntax:

The syntax for each function is provided in this section. A brief description of each argument is also included.

Function:

This section contains a very brief description of the function.

File(s) to Include:

The `include` file needed for the function described is listed in this section.

Description:

This section provides a full description of the function.

Value(s) Returned:

The return values of the function are discussed here.

Related Function(s):

This section describes some of the Borland C++ functions that are used with, or similar to, the function described.

Similar Microsoft C Function(s):

Microsoft C functions used for similar purposes are described in this section.

Example:

This section briefly describes an example that uses the function. The code for the example is also listed.

The information in this book is designed to provide all the information needed to develop graphics-based programs. By using the techniques and information described, you can develop graphics programs of all types and complexities.

About the Author

James W. McCord, a captain in the United States Air Force, is a Computer Research Scientist at the Avionics Directorate, Wright Laboratory, Wright-Patterson Air Force Base. He has a bachelor's degree in electrical engineering from Auburn University and a master's of science degree from Central Michigan University. He is the author of *The C Programmer's Guide to Graphics*, *Borland C++ Programmer's Reference*, and numerous technical reports and papers on software development and engineering. Capt. McCord has programmed extensively in the C, Lisp, and Ada languages.

Acknowledgments

I would like to thank the staff at SAMS for the opportunity to write this book. I would also like to thank my wife, Jill, son, Joshua, and daughter, Jamie, for making my life great. Special thanks to T.B.T.

I

Computer Graphics
with Borland C++

1

Introduction to IBM PCs and Compatibles

E ffective graphics programming requires a basic understanding of computer hardware. The physical limitations of the *host system* (the system that will run the developed graphics software) will have an effect on the design of the graphics software. For example, the video adapter and monitor will determine the range of resolution and the colors available for the application. Other hardware factors, such as the microprocessor, the memory, and operating speeds, play important roles in setting requirements and specifications for the graphics product.

Microprocessors

The *microprocessor* is the heart of the computer system. Sometimes called the *central processing unit* (CPU), the microprocessor executes the program by performing a series of computations, data transfers, and numeric comparisons. All of the computer's basic operations are controlled by the CPU. Data of all types are sent to the CPU via the *buses* (pathways for signals). The buses connect the CPU to various input/output (I/O) ports.

All IBM PCs (and compatibles), Personal System (PS)/1 models, and PS/2 models use a microprocessor from the Intel 8086 family, as shown in the following table. The following sections describe the current microprocessors in the Intel 8086 family.

Table 1.1. *Microprocessors used in IBM PCs, ATs, PS/1s, and PS/2s*

Model	Microprocessor
PC	8088
PC XT	8088
AT	80286
PS/1	80286
PS/2 25	8086
PS/2 30	8086
PS/2 50	80286
PS/2 60	80286
PS/2 80	80386
PS/2 90	80486
PS/2 95	80486

8086/8088

The 8086 microprocessor, used in PS/2 models 25 and 30, is a 16-bit microprocessor with a 16-bit data bus. Fourteen registers are used to transfer, process, and store data. The registers also store memory addresses, status and control flags, and instruction pointers. The 8086 can access one megabyte of memory.

The 8088 microprocessor, used for the IBM PC, PCjr, and PC/XT, is a 16-bit microprocessor with an 8-bit data bus. The major difference between the 8088 and the 8086 is that the 8088 has an 8-bit data bus, while the 8086 has a 16-bit data bus. For programming purposes, the 8088 is identical to the 8086 in all other respects.

80286

The 80286, used in the IBM PC/AT, the IBM PS/1, and PS/2 Models 50 and 60, is compatible with the 8086/8088. The most important feature added to the 808286 is its *multitasking* ability. Multitasking is best described as the ability to perform several tasks at one time. The 80286 accomplishes multitasking by switching its processing between the two tasks at hand. An example of multitasking would be editing one document on a word processor while printing another document.

The 80286 microprocessor operates in two modes. The *real mode* forces the 80286 to behave and respond exactly like the 8086. The *protected mode* reserves a predetermined amount of memory for program execution. This memory is protected from use by any other program. This protected mode is where the multitasking abilities originate. By using this protected mode, several programs can run concurrently without affecting one another.

80386

The 80386 microprocessor is used in the PS/2 Model 80, and in many IBM PC compatibles. The 80386 is a powerful 32-bit microprocessor that includes 32-bit registers. Although the 80386 microprocessor supports the 8086 functions and the 80286 protected memory mode, it offers more flexible memory management than either of these CPUs.

80486

The 80486 microprocessor is the newest release in the line of 80X86 CPUs. The IBM PS/2 Models 90 and 95 use the 80486. In addition, several manufacturers have released IBM compatibles that use the 80486. Although these systems are, at present, the most expensive IBM compatibles on the market, they offer the latest technology. The 80486 is faster and more integrated than any other member of the 8086 family of microprocessors. It combines the capabilities of an enhanced 80386 microprocessor with an equally fast 80387 math coprocessor, a sophisticated cache controller, and, usually, 8K of supporting cache memory.

Operating Systems

Every computer has an operating system. The operating system is a set of machine language computer programs that manages the variety of functions, including peripheral operations, required of the hardware system. For the IBM series of personal computers, two principle operating systems, MS-DOS and OS/2, are used.

MS-DOS

MS-DOS, or the *disk operating system*, began as QDOS, an operating system for an S-100 bus-designed system that used an 8086 microprocessor. QDOS, which become 86-DOS, was developed by Seattle Computer Products and purchased by The Microsoft Corporation in 1980. Microsoft was one of the software development teams chosen by IBM to develop the operating system for its new computer. The resulting product was MS-DOS, which became the standard operating system for the IBM PC and its compatibles. MS-DOS has been revised several times, and continues to be the dominant operating system for personal computers.

OS/2

When IBM introduced its Personal System/2 (PS/2) models, a new operating system came with it. The new OS/2 operating system functioned similarly to MS-DOS versions 3.2 and 3.3. However, OS/2 was designed to run on the newer microprocessors and take advantage of them.

To support the newer microprocessors, OS/2 operates in two modes. The real mode responds in a manner almost identical to MS-DOS. Therefore, almost all applications designed for MS-DOS are supported by OS/2. Multitasking, however, is not supported in the real mode.

OS/2 also operates in protected mode. Although this mode appears to operate like MS-DOS, it is much more powerful and flexible. The major advantage of OS/2 is its support of multitasking while in the protected mode. In addition, OS/2 in the protected mode does not limit the size of the application to 640K of RAM, as the real mode does.

While DOS is presently the dominant operating system, the features and capabilities of OS/2 make it appealing for future development. Unfortunately for the graphics programmer, the graphic features provided by Borland C++ are not supported by OS/2.

Video Subsystems

The video subsystem produces the screen images for the computer system. Most of the IBM series of personal computers (PC, PC/XT, PC/AT) and their compatibles require the installation of a *video display adapter*. This adapter is a special video circuit board that is plugged into one of the system's expansion slots. The IBM Personal Systems (PS) series comes with its own built-in video circuitry.

The *adapter boards,* or video circuitry, contain a block of dedicated memory which holds the display information. This information is transformed by the video subsystem into signals that drive the video display. The video subsystems designed for the PCs are the Monochrome Display Adapter (MDA), the Color Graphics Adapter (CGA), and the Enhanced Graphics Adapter. The Multi-Color Graphics Array (MCGA) and the Video Graphics Array (VGA) were developed for the PS/2 series. A VGA adapter is also made to fit the PC series.

CGA

The color graphics adapter (CGA) is the oldest of the series of IBM-compatible graphics adapters. Although the CGA adapter is still very common for use with home computers, the VGA adapter has become the standard for business computers. Even with this trend toward using the VGA, nearly all applications software is made to be compatible with the CGA. The CGA, as well as all of the video subsystems, can operate in either of two general modes. Each of these general modes, text and graphics, have many specific modes that support a predefined number of colors and screen resolution. Inside the graphics mode there are several screen resolution and color options.

The CGA graphics driver is provided by Borland C++ to use the graphics modes of the CGA adapter. The graphics modes supported by the CGA driver include the CGAC0, CGAC1, CGAC2, CGAC3, and CGAHI modes. In the CGAHI mode, only foreground and background colors are available. The background color can be changed with the use of the setbkcolor function. On the positive side, the CGAHI mode has a higher resolution (640 pixels wide by 200 pixels high) than the other CGA modes.

The CGAC0, CGAC1, CGAC2, and CGAC3 modes each have a resolution of 320 pixels wide by 200 pixels high. These modes are designed for use with color monitors, and they display four colors. The background color is selectable from the predefined sixteen-color palette. The other three colors are defined according to the default palette for the mode. Table 1.2 lists the palettes for these modes.

Table 1.2. *CGA color constants and values*

Palette Number	Color 1	Color 2	Color 3
0	CGA_LIGHTGREEN	CGA_LIGHTRED	CGA_YELLOW
1	CGA_LIGHTCYAN	CGA_LIGHTMAGENTA	CGA_WHITE
2	CGA_GREEN	CGA_RED	CGA_BROWN
3	CGA_CYAN	CGA_MAGENTA	CGA_LIGHTGRAY

NOTE: Color 0 is set by the setbkcolor function.

The Enhanced Graphics Adapter

The Enhanced Graphics Adapter (EGA) supports all graphics and text modes of the CGA. The EGA supports the EGALO, EGAHI, EGA64LO, EGA64HI, and EGAMONOHI modes, in addition to the CGA graphics modes. In EGAMONOHI, foreground and background colors with a resolution of 640 by 350 pixels are available. In EGAHI mode, the user can choose from sixteen colors with a screen resolution of 640 by 350 pixels. In EGALO mode, sixteen colors are available; however, the screen resolution is limited to 320 by 200 pixels. The EGA64LO mode shares the same limitations with the EGALO mode. The EGA64HI mode offers a screen resolution of 640 by 350 pixels, and uses four colors.

MCGA

The MultiColor Graphics Array (MCGA) is found in the 8086-based models of the IBM Personal System/2 computers. The MCGA is an extension of the CGA adapter and supports all CGA modes. In addition to the standard CGA modes (called MCGAC0, MCGAC1, MCGAC2, and MCGAC3), the MCGA supports a 640 by 480 pixel two-color mode and a 320 by 200 pixel two-color mode. These modes are the MCGAHI mode and the MCGAMED mode, respectively.

VGA

The Video Graphics Array (VGA) is the current standard for IBM personal computers. The VGA is the video subsystem for the 80286-through 80486-based IBM Personal System/2 series. The VGA is available in adapter form for the IBM personal computer series and compatibles. The VGA supports all CGA, MCGA, and EGA modes. In addition, three sixteen-color modes are supported. These modes are the VGALO, VGAMED, and VGAHI. The VGALO mode supports 16 colors at a resolution of 640 by 200 pixels. The VGAMED mode supports 16 colors at a resolution of 640 by 350 pixels, while the VGAHI mode supports 16 colors at a 640 by 480 pixels resolution.

Table 1.3 lists the available modes for the graphics drivers provided by Borland. As these figures illustrate, several adapters and modes are provided outside the CGA, MCGA, EGA, and VGA adapters.

Table 1.3. *Graphics modes*

Driver	Mode	Value	Description
CGA	CGAC0	0	320 by 200 – 4-color
	CGAC1	1	320 by 200 – 4-color
	CGAC2	2	320 by 200 – 4-color
	CGAC3	3	320 by 200 – 4-color
	CGAHI	4	640 by 200 – 2-color
MCGA	MCGAC0	0	320 by 200 – 4-color
	MCGAC1	1	320 by 200 – 4-color
	MCGAC2	2	320 by 200 – 4-color
	MCGAC3	3	320 by 200 – 4-color
	MCGAMED	4	640 by 200 – 2-color
	MCGAHI	5	640 by 480 – 2-color
EGA	EGALO	0	640 by 200 – 16-color
	EGAHI	1	640 by 350 – 16-color

Driver	Mode	Value	Description
EGA64	EGA64LO	0	640 by 200 – 16-color
	EGA64HI	1	640 by 350 – 4-color
EGAMONO	EGAMONOHI	3	640 by 350 – 2-color
VGA	VGALO	0	640 by 200 – 16-color
	VGAMED	1	640 by 350 – 16-color
	VGAHI	2	640 by 480 – 16-color
ATT400	ATT400C0	0	320 by 200 – 4-color
	ATT400C1	1	320 by 200 – 4-color
	ATT400C2	2	320 by 200 – 4-color
	ATT400C3	3	320 by 200 – 4-color
	ATT400MED	4	640 by 200 – 2-color
	ATT400HI	5	640 by 400 – 2-color
HERC	HERCMONOHI	0	720 by 348 – 2-color
PC3270	PC3270HI	0	720 by 350 – 2-color
IBM8514	IBM8514LO	0	640 by 480 – 256-color
	IBM8514HI	1	1024 by 768 – 256-color

Monitors

For each type of video subsystem, there is at least one compatible monitor. When you are selecting a hardware configuration, the monitor is just as important to consider as the display adapter is. There are basically five types of monitors, which are discussed in the following paragraphs.

Direct-drive Monochrome Monitors

Direct-drive monochrome monitors are used with the Monochrome Display Adapter (MDA) and the Enhanced Graphics Adapter. These monitors provide only foreground and background colors.

Composite Monochrome Monitors

Composite monochrome monitors are used with the CGA's composite video output. These monitors provide one-color foreground displays, and cannot be used with any adapter other than the CGA.

Composite Color Monitors

The composite color monitors use the CGA's composite video signal to produce color text and graphics. The resolution of CGA output with composite color monitors is often poor; however, simple graphics and text are readable.

Red-Green-Blue Color Monitor

The red-green-blue (RGB) color monitor is used with the CGA's video signal. The RGB monitor produces better results than the composite color monitor because it processes red, green, and blue signals separately. This monitor can display high-resolution color graphics and color text.

Variable-Frequency Monitors

Because different video subsystems may produce different signals, some monitors cannot be used with certain adapters. For this reason, variable-frequency monitors, which can be used with several video subsystems, were created. Although these monitors cost more, they are often more practical, because they allow the user to upgrade to newer technologies without having to buy a new monitor.

Input Devices

Input devices can be very useful to the graphics programmer. Graphics programming can be tedious and time-consuming; therefore, alternate input devices (other than the traditional keyboard) offer some relief from the boredom of inputting points manually.

But this relief does not come without a price. To use alternate input devices, device drivers and user interfaces must be created. For the graphics programmer, commercial packages range from complete "paintbrush" programs to simple device drivers that output a series of coordinates to a data file. But for most uses, these packages are not exactly what is needed. For example, when using the functions provided by the Borland Graphics Library, the user must obtain coordinate points by drawing the desired image on graph paper, and reading the desired coordinates off the graph paper. Although this method is simple and straightforward, it is not very efficient.

The following sections introduce the capabilities of the keyboard and various alternate input devices. When the user understands these devices, there are many ways they can be used to gather data.

The Keyboard

The keyboard, which is the primary input device, is very flexible and accepts input through any of its alphanumeric, cursor control, or function keys. The keyboard is a one-dimensional input device. The sequence (or order) of the input is important in one-dimensional devices. For text, the one-dimensional, sequential input of data is satisfactory. Effective graphics, however, require two dimensions. Thus, the keyboard is not a good device for the input of spatial, graphics-oriented data.

Many of the keyboard's features attempt to add a second dimension. The cursor control keys, as well as the special function keys, are examples of this attempt at achieving two-dimensional input from a keyboard by permitting both row and column manipulation.

The Mouse

The mouse is probably the most commonly-used alternate input device. For the most part, the mouse is used to simply manipulate the graphics or text cursor. This is accomplished through monitoring of the mouse's internal sensors. As the user moves the mouse, positional (directional) information is input into the computer. This directional information is then used to position the on-screen cursor. The mouse also comes with one, two, or three buttons, depending on the manufacturer. These buttons provide additional, non-directional, user input.

The one-button mouse is the simplest mouse to use because there are no key sequences to remember. This simplistic approach forces the user to input multiple clicks to make a menu selection. However, the two button mouse offers more input options than the one button mouse. By using the left button, the right button, or a combination of the two, the user is offered a wider range of input from the mouse. The three-button mouse increases the number of possible button combinations to seven. The increased number of combinations often makes the mouse more difficult to use.

The mouse is available in mechanical and optical forms, as shown in Figure 1.1. The mechanical mouse uses a roller ball. As the mouse is moved, the roller ball turns, moving internal sensors in the mouse. These sensors translate the input into directional information. This directional information is used to move the cursor.

The optical mouse uses two light emitting diodes (LEDs) and two phototransistors to detect motion. The optical mouse is used with a special pad that alters the light from the LEDs. One LED emits red light and the other produces infrared light. The pad contains a grid made up of perpendicular lines. When the mouse is moved in one direction, the red light is absorbed by the lines. In the other direction, the infrared light is absorbed by the lines. The color and number of light breaks determine the direction and distance of the mouse movement.

Figure 1.1. Two- and three-button versions of the mouse, along with mechanical and optical versions of the mouse

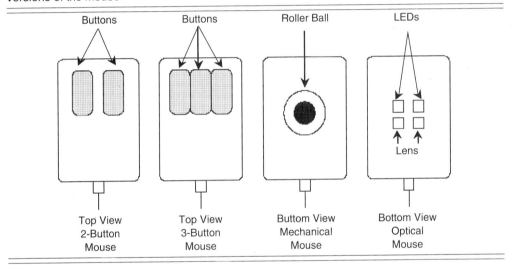

The Trackball

The trackball is used primarily for the same functions as the mouse. The main difference is the configuration of the device (see Figure 1.2). With a mouse, the entire device is moved to provide directional information. With a trackball, however, the body of the device remains in place while the palm of the hand or a finger moves the trackball, thus providing directional input. The trackball was designed with limited desk space in mind. Where the mouse requires a good bit of free space for use (several times its own physical dimensions), the trackball requires only the space of its physical dimensions. As on the mouse, buttons permit additional, non-directional input.

Figure 1.2. The typical trackball

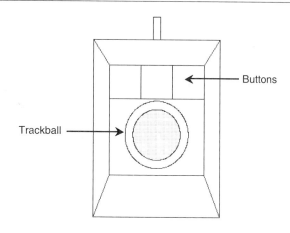

The Digitizer Tablet

The *digitizer tablet*, often called a graphics tablet, is useful for precise coordinate input. Most uses of the graphics tablet fall in the range of computer-aided design (CAD) or PC painting and drawing applications. The resolution of the graphics tablet is, in general, higher than that of a trackball or mouse, making it ideal for precision tracing, drawing, and design.

Most tablets are of the electronic/magnetic type. The pointing device, a pen or a cursor, generates an electromagnetic field that is sensed by the screen-like wire grid embedded in the tablet (see Figure 1.3). Through the use of this grid and cursor combination, precise directional and coordinate information is determined. Other tablets use sound waves or resistive touch pads to provide information.

The pointing devices most typically used with graphics tablets include the *pen*, the *stylus*, and the *cursor* (see Figure 1.4). The pen and stylus are pen-like pointers used to provide input. The pen contains ink to provide feedback, while the stylus contains only a blunt point. The stylus is used for tracing existing drawings, while the pen is used for freehand drawing. The cursor is a hand-held device similar in appearance to a mouse, with the addition of a lens, or reticle, with wire crosshairs. The crosshairs are used to trace drawings, while the buttons provide non-directional input to the computer. Most cursors contain either four or sixteen buttons.

Figure 1.3. The digitizer tablet

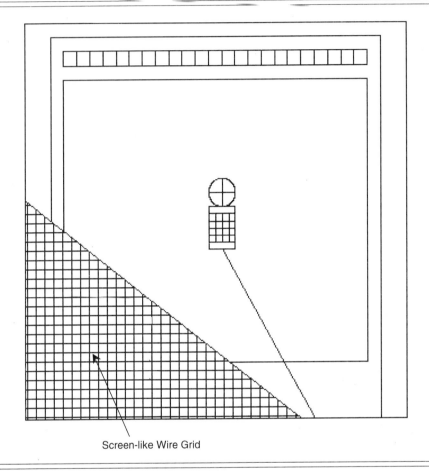

Screen-like Wire Grid

Light Pens

Light pens are useful as both drawing and point-and-shoot devices. Light pens work by monitoring the time interval between the time the screen's electron beam begins its refresh cycle, and the time the location of the light pen is illuminated (see Figure 1.5). The x and y screen coordinates are then determined and passed to the computer through the graphics adapter. The following illustration shows the basics of how the light pen works.

Figure 1.4. Digitizer input devices

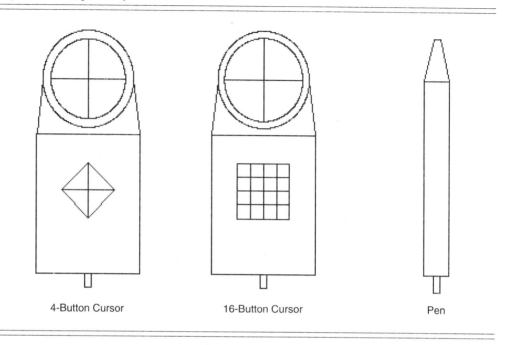

4-Button Cursor   16-Button Cursor   Pen

Figure 1.5. Information transfer in a typical light pen

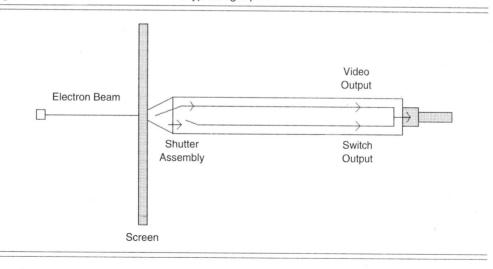

Electron Beam

Video
Output

Shutter
Assembly

Switch
Output

Screen

Summary

Graphics programming requires a fundamental understanding of the hardware configuration of the host computer system. This chapter described the various microprocessors, operating systems, monitors, graphics adapters, and input devices used with the IBM personal computers and their compatibles. By understanding the hardware configuration of the host system, you will be able to optimize the graphics software for speed and appearance.

2
C and C++

The C and C++ languages have, in recent years, become some of the most popular and powerful development languages. There are many reasons for this; however, the primary reason is that these languages produce fast, compact code. This chapter introduces the power of the C and C++ languages.

Advantages of C and C++

The C language has become very popular over the past few years, largely due to its compact, fast, and portable code. Although C is considered a high-level language, it is often called a mid-level language because the programmer has the ability to program near machine level.

Borland C++ is an extension and an enhancement of the C language, and it is fully compatible with the features of AT&T C++ Version 2.0. In addition, C++ provides object-oriented features. Because C++ is an enhancement of the C language, the C and C++ languages share the same basic advantages. Borland C++ is also fully compatible with the ANSI C standard. For this reason, Borland C++ can meet the needs of the programmer who likes to program using traditional C styles and the programmer who prefers object-oriented C++ programming.

Power

The C and C++ languages are considered high-level languages. However, these languages have many of the characteristics of a low-level language. The syntax and structure of many of the standard C functions closely resemble the actual operations of the computer's internal registers; therefore, the C and C++ languages offer the ability to gain machine-level control over the actual operations of the computer.

The C and C++ languages also have the characteristics of a mid-level language. Source code written with a mid-level language is easier to read than code written with a low-level language, but it still resembles the operation of the computer's internal registers.

In addition to the characteristics of low- and mid-level languages, the C and C++ languages contain the characteristics of a high-level language by offering ease of use. A high-level language offers source code that is easier to develop and maintain because it more closely resembles the design *pseudocode.*

Because the C and C++ languages have the characteristics of low-, mid-, and high-level languages, the programmer has the flexibility of optimizing the code structure relative to the requirements of the application. For example, if speed is important, the low-level characteristics can be used for the most important functions. Similarly, if maintainability and rapid development are most important, the high-level characteristics are available.

The low- and mid-level characteristics are most commonly used by the hard-line ANSI C programmers, while the high-level features are used in support of the object-oriented design by the C++ programmers. Because Borland C++ supports both ANSI C and AT&T C++ standards, the programmer has a great deal of power and flexibility in design and implementation.

Speed

The C and C++ languages produce fast, executable code. As described in the previous section, the flexibility of the C and C++ languages allows the programmer to optimize the design by using specialized, low- and mid-level functions. Because most high-level languages trade efficiency in the executable code for ease in programming and maintainability, the low-level characteristics of the C language, plus the support of in-line assembly, allow C code to run more efficiently and quickly.

Versatility

The C and C++ languages are very versatile. They provide many functions that offer flexibility in software system design and implementation. Therefore, the programmer/designer has the ability to optimize the design to meet the specific needs of the application. The many methods for memory management provided in the C and C++ languages (such as the use of pointers, structures, classes, and so on) offer ways to meet the needs of specific applications, ranging from database management to graphics and statistical applications. The range of functions given by the C and C++ languages, when combined with the libraries included with the Borland C++ compiler, provides an excellent environment for the development of almost any type of software application.

The C Language

When using Borland C++ without using the recently added object-oriented features, the structure of every program will be generally the same. As with other modular languages, such as PASCAL and Ada, there is one main function that is recognized by the operating system as the controlling function. For the C language, this controlling function is referred to as the `main()` function.

The `main()` function, in normal operations, is the beginning and endpoint of every C program. Other functions, often referred to as *subroutines* in other languages, are often called from the main program. These functions, in turn, can then call other functions, and so on. When each function has completed its intended task, control is returned to the calling function. In this way, control always returns to the `main()` function. Figure 2.1 illustrates one relationship between the `main()` function and its supporting functions.

Figure 2.1. The C program structure

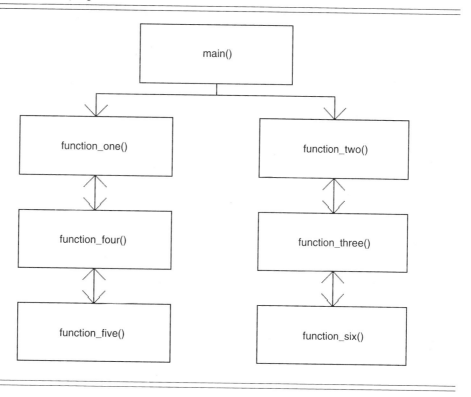

As mentioned previously, C is designed to be a modular language. This means that sections of code that are designed to perform a specific task are usually removed from the `main()` function and placed inside their own functions. For example, suppose that is it necessary to draw a circular image several times during the execution of the program. Because this is a specific and repetitive task, a function that creates the image could be developed easily.

Modular design has several advantages. The first is that modular design eliminates redundancy of code. It is easier and more efficient to produce a function that can be called to perform a particular task than it is to add the required lines of code every time that task is needed. Secondly, code that is modular in design is easier to read and understand. By giving functions names that accurately reflect their designed task, the interpretation of the program's operation is a simple matter. Lastly, modular code is easier to maintain because it is easier to read and understand. Maintainability is not especially important to the casual programmer. However, it is a very important consideration when designing code for professional applications because this code will, most likely, have to be enhanced and updated in the future.

The examples in this book are developed using traditional C programming methods. The purpose of this book is to introduce the capabilities of the Borland graphics library. Therefore, examples are short and to the point. The features of the Borland graphics library can easily be implemented using C or C++ programming techniques. Because the examples are short, there is really no need to use the features of the C++ language. Since the examples use C programming methods, it is important to understand the basic structure of C programs. The following paragraphs describe the main features of the C program structure.

Preprocessor Directives

A *preprocessor directive* is a command to the C preprocessor. One commonly used preprocessor directive is the `#include` directive. This directive allows external text files to be incorporated into a C program. The `#include` directive instructs the preprocessor to substitute the contents of the specified file for the `#include` statement.

The `#include` statement is often used to include header files. The header files contain common variable and function declarations for the proper use of certain functions. For example, the header file `graphics.h` must be included to use the graphics functions. Without the inclusion of the header file, the required definitions, declarations, and constants are not available for use.

The format of the `#include` directive determines the search path for the specified file. The three formats shown in the following paragraphs are used with the `#include` statement.

```
#include <graphics.h>
```

In the preceding format, the computer searches for the `graphics.h` file in the standard directories. The working directory is not searched.

```
#include "graphics.h"
```

In this format, the search for the `graphics.h` file begins in the current directory, then moves to the standard directories, if necessary.

```
#include "c:\tc\include\graphics.h"
```

In this format, the computer searches for the `graphics.h` file in only the specified path.

Declarations

A declaration establishes the names and attributes of variables, functions, and types used in the program. The declaration also specifies the visibility of the variable. When declaring variables and functions, there is a set of standard data types used by the C language. Table 2.1 lists these available data types.

Table 2.1. *Data types*

Type	Number of bits	Range
unsigned char	8	0 to 255
char	8	−128 to 127
enum	16	−32,768 to 32,767
unsigned int	16	0 to 65,535
short int	16	−32,768 to 32,767
int	16	−32,768 to 32,767
unsigned long	32	0 to 4,294,967,295
long	32	−2,147,483,648 to 2,147,483,647
float	32	3.4×10^{-38} to 3.4×10^{38}
double	64	1.7×10^{-308} to 1.7×10^{308}
long double	80	3.4×10^{-4932} to 1.1×10^{4932}
near pointer	16	
far pointer	32	

The *visibility* of a variable is determined by the location of the declaration. Visibility can be defined as the availability of that variable to the various functions in the program. Global variables are declared prior to the `main()` function and are visible to all functions. Local variables are declared inside the function and, thus, are visible only inside the function.

A function declaration consists of a return-type list, the function name, and an argument-type list (if any), and is used to define the characteristics of the function.

Definitions

A *definition* is used to assign the contents of a variable or function and allocate storage for that variable or function. A function definition contains a function header and body. The function header contains the type of data returned by the function, the function name, and the list of formal parameters required by the function. The body of the function definition consists of local declarations and a compound statement that describes the operation of the function.

Expressions

An *expression* can be defined as the combination of operators and operands which yields a single value. The *operand* is a constant or variable value which is manipulated in an expression. The operator defines the method by which its operands will interact. Table 2.2 lists the operators defined in the C language.

Table 2.2. *Operators for the C language*

Operator	Name	Use	Meaning
		Arithmetic operators	
*	Multiplication	x*y	Multiply x and y
/	Division	x/y	Divide x by y
%	Modulo	x%y	Divide x remainder by y
+	Addition	x+y	Add x and y
-	Subtraction	x-y	Subtract y from x
++	Increment	x++	Increment x
--	Decrement	--x	Decrement x
-	Negation	-x	Negate x

Operator	Name	Use	Meaning
Relational and logical operators			
>	Greater than	x>y	1 if x is greater than y
>=	Greater than or equal to	x>=y	1 if x is greater than or equal to y
<	Less than	x<y	1 if x is less than y
<=	Less than or equal to	x<=y	1 if x is less than or equal to y
==	Equal to	x==y	1 if x equals y
!=	Not equal to	x!=y	1 if x is not equal to y
!	Logical NOT	!x	1 if x is 0
&&	Logical AND	x&&y	0 if both x or y are 0
||	Logical OR	x||y	0 if either x or y is 0

NOTE: 1 indicates true, 0 indicates false

Operator	Name	Use	Meaning
Assignment operators			
=	Assignment	x=y	Set x to y value
?=	Compound Assignment	x?=y	Same as x=x?y where ? is one of the following: + - * / % << >> & ^ |

Operator	Name	Use	Meaning
Data access and size operators			
[]	Array element	x[0]	First element of x
.	Select member	y.x	Member x in structure y
->	Select member	p->x	Member x in structure p
*	Indirection	*p	Contents of address p
&	Address of	&x	Address of x
sizeof	Size in bytes	sizeof(x)	Size of x in bytes

Operator	Name	Use	Meaning
Bitwise operators			
~	Bitwise Complement	~x	Switches 1s and 0s
&	Bitwise AND	x&y	Bitwise AND of x and y

Table 2.2. *continues*

Table 2.2. cont.   *Operators for the C language*

Operator	Name	Usc	Meaning
		Bitwise operators	
|	Bitwise OR	x | y	Bitwise OR of x and y
^	Bitwise exclusive OR	x^y	Exclusive OR of x and y
<<	Left shift	x<<2	Shift x left 2 bits
>>	Right shift	x>>2	Shift x right 2 bits
		Miscellaneous operators	
()	Function	malloc(x)	Call malloc function
(type)	Type cast	(int)x	Set x to type int
?:	Conditional	x1?x2:x3	If x1 is not 0, x2 is evaluated; else x3
,	Sequential evaluation	x++,y++	Increment x, then y

Statements

Statements control the order of execution of a C program. A statement ends in a semicolon and contains keywords, expressions, and other statements. The following paragraphs briefly describe the C statements.

The `assignment` statement (=) is used to assign the value of the expression on the right to the variable on the left.

```
z = 1000;
```

The `break` statement (`break;`) ends the innermost `do`, `for`, `switch`, or `while` statement.

```
while (x < 1000)
{
     if (x == 123)
          break;
     x = x + 1;
}
```

The `continue` statement (`continue;`) begins the next iteration of the innermost `do`, `for`, or `while` statement in which it appears, skipping the loop body.

```
while (x < 1000)
{
    if (x == 123)
        continue;
    x = x + 1;
}
```

The `do-while` loop executes a block of statements until the expression in the `while` statement fails.

```
do
{
    x = x + 1;
} while (x < 1000);
```

The `for` loop evaluates the first of its three expressions once. The third expression is then evaluated after each pass through the loop until the second expression becomes false.

```
for (x = 1; x < 100; x = x + 10)
{
    y = y + x;
}
```

The `goto` statement transfers program control to the statement defined by the label.

```
    if (x == 200)
        goto X;
    x == x - 1;
X:    x == x + 1;
```

The `if` statement executes the following statements (enclosed in brackets) or the next statement (if no brackets) if the expression is true; otherwise, the second expression is executed.

```
if (x == 0)
    y = 10;
else
    y = 0;
```

The `null` statement is used to indicate that nothing is to happen.

```
if (x == 100)
    ;                    /* do nothing */
```

The `return` statement stops the execution of the current function and returns control to the calling function. A single value can be returned.

```
if (z == 500)
    return (y);
```

The `switch` statement evaluates an expression and attempts to match it to a set of case statements. If there is no match, the default statement is executed.

```
switch (x)
{
    case BUY:    buy();
                 break;
    case SELL:   sell();
                 break;
    default:     do_nothing();
                 break;
}
```

The `while` loop executes a statement or block of statements as long as the expression evaluates to a true (non-zero) value.

```
while (x > 1000)
{
    y = y + x;
}
```

Functions

A *function* is a set of declarations, definitions, expressions, and statements that performs a specific job. The function is combined with the preprocessor directives, definitions, expressions, and statements to form the code structure.

The following code structure illustrates the use of the preprocessor directives, declarations, definitions, expressions, statements, and functions:

```
#include <stdio.h>         /* preprocessor directives */
#include <graphics.h>      /* include header files    */

#define TRUE 1             /* define a constant */

short radius;              /* declare a global variables */
short diameter_main;

int calc_diameter (int); /* function definition */


int main ()
{                          /* begin main function */
```

```
      int x, y;                    /* declare local variables */
      int gdriver = VGA;
      int gmode = VGAHI;

      registerbgidriver (EGAVGA_driver);
      registerbgifont (sansserif_font);

      initgraph (&gdriver,&gmode,"");
                    .
                    .
                    .
      radius = 10;
      diameter_main = calc_diameter (x);
                    .
                    .
                    .
      getch ();
      closegraph ();
      return 0;
    }                              /* end main function */


    int calc_diameter (radius)   /* function head */
    {
      int diameter;              /* declare local variable */

      diameter = 2 * radius;
      return (diameter);         /* return value */
    }                            /* end calc_diameter */
```

The first lines of any C program are the *preprocessor directives*. The preprocessor directives are commands to the C preprocessor that are invoked before compiling the program. In the preceding code structure, the #define and #include statements are the preprocessor directives.

The other statements prior to the main() function are often *declaration statements*. A declaration statement establishes the name and attributes of variables, functions, and types used in the program. Global variables are declared outside the main() function, and are visible to all functions in the current process.

The main() function is next. When inside the main() function, local variables are declared. Local variables are declared inside the function and are visible only inside the function. When these variables are declared, the graphics and font drivers are loaded and the graphics mode is initialized. When the graphics mode is set, the body of the graphics program can be developed and executed.

For the most part, the examples in this book do not use functions other than the main() function. This is due primarily to the short length of the programs. Although the examples in this book are not always as efficiently structured as possible, they are designed to be simple to understand.

The previous code structure includes a call to the getch, closegraph, and return functions. These functions are used to delay the program, close the graphics system, and return a value, respectively. These functions are used in almost all of the examples in this book.

The simple code structure illustrated is followed throughout the book and should provide a simple, yet effective, framework for the interpretation of the enclosed programming examples.

C++ and Object-Oriented Programming

The C++ language is an extension of the C language. The purpose of the C++ language is to add features to the standard ANSI C language that support the use of object-oriented techniques to develop computer applications.

Object-oriented programming (OOP) is a design philosophy that allows the programmer to classify and generalize objects. For example, just knowing what an object is gives us a lot of information. If you were told to go find a ball in a room, certain images would come to mind. Most balls are round and usually less than one foot in diameter. Therefore, we are able to classify a variety of balls under this description. Just knowing this information would give you a good chance of finding the ball. C++ provides language features that support the classification and abstraction of objects.

Object-oriented programming has several characteristics and advantages. First of all, since objects contain properties and behaviors, objects support modular programming. Modular programming supports ease of development and maintainability of code. Object-oriented programming is characterized by encapsulation, inheritance, and polymorphism.

Encapsulation

Very simply defined, *encapsulation* is the practice of using classes to link data and the code used to manipulate the data. In the traditional C programming style, data is usually kept in data structures; functions are then created to manipulate the data. This style is shown as follows:

```
struct data_items
    {
    int a;
    int b;
    int c;
    };
void manipulate_data (int x, int y, int z)
{
data_items.a = data_items.a + x;
data_items.b = data_items.b + y;
data_items.c = data_items.c + z;
}
```

This structure and function would then be put into a source file, compiled separately, and treated as a module. The problem with this method is that even though the structure and function are created to be used together, the data can be accessed without using the described function.

The property of encapsulation solves this problem. Encapsulation is provided in C++ by the `struct`, `union`, and `class` keywords. These keywords allow you to combine data and functions into a *class entity*. The data items are called *data members* while the functions are called *member functions*.

An example of a class follows:

```
class Circle {
    int x;
    int y;
    int radius;
    int DrawCircle (int a, int b, int rad);
    int DeleteCircle (int a, int b, int rad);
};
```

The data members of the class are `x`, `y`, and `radius`. The member functions of the class are `DrawCircle` and `DeleteCircle`.

By defining the class `Circle`, the properties of the object cannnot be directly accessed from outside the object. Only the behaviors of the object, `DrawCircle` and `DeleteCircle`, can manipulate the data. The behaviors of the object can only be invoked by sending a message to the object. By defining an object in this way, the implementation details of the object are not visible to, or accessible by, the outside.

Inheritance

Inheritance is the ability to create a class which has the properties and behaviors of another class. For example, suppose you start with a class called `Dog`. This class has several properties including four legs, a tail, two eyes, two ears, a mouth, and a nose. Under this class you can add classes which provide more specific information. For our purposes, we'll add the `BigDog` class and the `LittleDog` class. The `BigDog` class has the properties of heavy and tall. The `LittleDog` class has the properties of light and short. More classes could be added to provide even more detail. For example, `LongHairBigDog`, `ShortHairBigDog`, `LongHairLittleDog`, and `ShortHairLittleDog` could provide even more detail. The `LongHairLittleDog` and `LongHairBigDog` classes add the property of long hair. The `ShortHairBigDog` and `ShortHairLittleDog` classes add the property of short hair. Additional classes, again, could be added. The `IrishSetter` class adds the property of red hair. The `Chihuahua` class adds the properties of very small and nervous. By developing a hierarchy, it is possible to classify and inherit properties of objects.

Let's now look at applying this hierarchy. An Irish Setter, for example, has the propery of red hair as determined from the *derived class* `IrishSetter`. Derived classes inherit properties from other classes called *base classes*. Therefore, the Irish Setter also has the property of the `LongHairBigDog` class which is long hair. The `LongHairBigDog` class also inherits properties for the `BigDog` class which, in turn, inherits properties from

29

the `Dog` class. Therefore, we can determine that the Irish Setter has long red hair, is heavy and tall, and has two ears, two eyes, a tail, a mouth, a nose, and four legs.

Although this is a simple illustration of inheritance, it provides a basic understanding of the power of inheritance. Through inheritance, you can generalize data and properties and, thus, improve programmer efficiency and reduce redundancy in code.

Polymorphism

Very simply stated, *polymorphism*, in C++, is the ability to create several versions of the same function or operator. The Borland C++ run-time library contains several functions which have been "overloaded" to work with various data types. Let's look, for example, at the following function prototypes.

```
int square (int value);
float square (float value);
double square (double value);
```

Each function is designed to accept and return a particular data type; however, each function is called *square*. In C, you can only have one function with a given name. In C++, on the other hand, function overloading is supported as long the argument lists differ between function declarations. Therefore, if you call square while passing an integer value, the proper function will be called and an integer value will be returned. Similarly, if you call square with a float or double value, a float or double value, respectively, will be returned.

Summary

The C++ language is designed to help reduce the complexity of large applications. By using the encapsulation, inheritance, and polymorphism features of the C++ language, the developed code is more modular, thus, it is more reusable and maintainable.

3

Text-Based Graphics

Many programs, including the Borland C++ environment, use the IBM extended character set to create simple graphics, such as boxes and rectangles, while operating in a text mode. Using the extended character set allows the programmer to develop pop-up menus, windows, and dialog boxes for applications that are to run in text mode.

The standard ASCII character set contains 128 characters, with values 0 to 127. The IBM extended character set adds another 128 characters, with values 128 to 255. The standard ASCII character set and the IBM extended character set are shown in Table 3.1.

Table 3.1. *The standard ASCII and IBM extended character set*

Decimal	Hexadecimal	Octal	Character or Code
0	00	0	NUL
1	01	1	SOH
2	02	2	STX
3	03	3	ETX
4	04	4	EOT
5	05	5	ENQ
6	06	6	ACK
7	07	7	BEL

Table 3.1. *continues*

Table 3.1. cont. *The standard ASCII and IBM extended character set*

Decimal	Hexadecimal	Octal	Character or Code
8	08	10	BS
9	09	11	HT
10	0A	12	LF
11	0B	13	VT
12	0C	14	FF
13	0D	15	CR
14	0E	16	SO
15	0F	17	SI
16	10	20	DLE
17	11	21	DC1
18	12	22	DC2
19	13	23	DC3
20	14	24	DC4
21	15	25	NAK
22	16	26	SYN
23	17	27	ETB
24	18	30	CAN
25	19	31	EM
26	1A	32	SUB
27	1B	33	ESC
28	1C	34	FS
29	1D	35	GS
30	1E	36	RS
31	1F	37	US
32	20	40	SPACE
33	21	41	!
34	22	42	"
35	23	43	#
36	24	44	$

Decimal	Hexadecimal	Octal	Character or Code
37	25	45	%
38	26	46	&
39	27	47	'
40	28	50	(
41	29	51	)
42	2A	52	*
43	2B	53	+
44	2C	54	,
45	2D	55	-
46	2E	56	.
47	2F	57	/
48	30	60	0
49	31	61	1
50	32	62	2
51	33	63	3
52	34	64	4
53	35	65	5
54	36	66	6
55	37	67	7
56	38	70	8
57	39	71	9
58	3A	72	:
59	3B	73	;
60	3C	74	<
61	3D	75	=
62	3E	76	>
63	3F	77	?
64	40	100	@
65	41	101	A

Listing 3.1. *continues*

Table 3.1. cont. *The standard ASCII and IBM extended character set*

Decimal	Hexadecimal	Octal	Character or Code
66	42	102	B
67	43	103	C
68	44	104	D
69	45	105	E
70	46	106	F
71	47	107	G
72	48	110	H
73	49	111	I
74	4A	112	J
75	4B	113	K
76	4C	114	L
77	4D	115	M
78	4E	116	N
79	4F	117	O
80	50	120	P
81	51	121	Q
82	52	122	R
83	53	123	S
84	54	124	T
85	55	125	U
86	56	126	V
87	57	127	W
88	58	130	X
89	59	131	Y
90	5A	132	Z
91	5B	133	[
92	5C	134	\
93	5D	135	]
94	5E	136	^

Decimal	Hexadecimal	Octal	Character or Code
95	5F	137	_
96	60	140	`
97	61	141	a
98	62	142	b
99	63	143	c
100	64	144	d
101	65	145	e
102	66	146	f
103	67	147	g
104	68	150	h
105	69	151	i
106	6A	152	j
107	6B	153	k
108	6C	154	l
109	6D	155	m
110	6E	156	n
111	6F	157	o
112	70	160	p
113	71	161	q
114	72	162	r
115	73	163	s
116	74	164	t
117	75	165	u
118	76	166	v
119	77	167	w
120	78	170	x
121	79	171	y
122	7A	172	z
123	7B	173	{
124	7C	174	¦

Table 3.1. *continues*

Table 3.1. cont.   *The standard ASCII and IBM extended character set*

Decimal	Hexadecimal	Octal	Character or Code
125	7D	175	}
126	7E	176	~
127	7F	177	DEL
128	80	200	Ç
129	81	201	ü
130	82	202	é
131	83	203	â
132	84	204	ä
133	85	205	à
134	86	206	å
135	87	207	ç
136	88	210	ê
137	89	211	ë
138	8A	212	è
139	8B	213	ï
140	8C	214	î
141	8D	215	ì
142	8E	216	Ä
143	8F	217	Å
144	90	220	É
145	91	221	æ
146	92	222	Æ
147	93	223	ô
148	94	224	ö
149	95	225	ò
150	96	226	û
151	97	227	ù
152	98	230	ÿ
153	99	231	Ö

Decimal	Hexadecimal	Octal	Character or Code
154	9A	232	Ü
155	9B	233	¢
156	9C	234	£
157	9D	235	¥
158	9E	236	Pt
159	9F	237	ƒ
160	A0	240	á
161	A1	241	í
162	A2	242	ó
163	A3	243	ú
164	A4	244	ñ
165	A5	245	Ñ
166	A6	246	a
167	A7	247	o
168	A8	250	¿
169	A9	251	⌐
170	AA	252	¬
171	AB	253	1/2
172	AC	254	1/4
173	AD	255	¡
174	AE	256	«
175	AF	257	»
176	B0	260	▓
177	B1	261	▒
178	B2	262	█
179	B3	263	│
180	B4	264	┤
181	B5	265	╡
182	B6	266	╢
183	B7	267	╖

Table 3.1. *continues*

Table 3.1. cont.   *The standard ASCII and IBM extended character set*

Decimal	Hexadecimal	Octal	Character or Code
184	B8	270	╕
185	B9	271	╣
186	BA	272	║
187	BB	273	╗
188	BC	274	╝
189	BD	275	╜
190	BE	276	╛
191	BF	277	┐
192	C0	300	└
193	C1	301	┴
194	C2	302	┬
195	C3	303	├
196	C4	304	─
197	C5	305	+
198	C6	306	╞
199	C7	307	╟
200	C8	310	╚
201	C9	311	╔
202	CA	312	╩
203	CB	313	╦
204	CC	314	╠
205	CD	315	=
206	CE	316	╬
207	CF	317	╧
208	D0	320	╨
209	D1	321	╤
210	D2	322	╥
211	D3	323	╙
212	D4	324	╘

Decimal	Hexadecimal	Octal	Character or Code
213	D5	325	╞
214	D6	326	╥
215	D7	327	╫
216	D8	330	╪
217	D9	331	┘
218	DA	332	┌
219	DB	333	█
220	DC	334	▄
221	DD	335	▌
222	DE	336	▐
223	DF	337	▀
224	E0	340	α
225	E1	341	β
226	E2	342	Γ
227	E3	343	π
228	E4	344	Σ
229	E5	345	σ
230	E6	346	μ
231	E7	347	τ
232	E8	350	Φ
233	E9	351	θ
234	EA	352	Ω
235	EB	353	δ
236	EC	354	∞
237	ED	355	$\emptyset$
238	EE	356	$\in$
239	EF	357	$\cap$
240	F0	360	$\equiv$
241	F1	361	$\pm$
242	F2	362	$\geq$

Table 3.1. *continues*

Table 3.1. cont.   *The standard ASCII and IBM extended character set*

Decimal	Hexadecimal	Octal	Character or Code
243	F3	363	≤
244	F4	364	⌠
245	F5	365	⌡
246	F6	366	÷
247	F7	367	≈
248	F8	370	°
249	F9	371	•
250	FA	372	•
251	FB	373	√
252	FC	374	η
253	FD	375	2
254	FE	376	■
255	FF	377	

Listing 3.1 and Figure 3.1 show how you can use the extended character set to create a frame around the screen and then display the ASCII and IBM extended character set.

Listing 3.1.   Displaying the ASCII and IBM extended character sets

```
#include <stdio.h>
#include <stdlib.h>
#include <conio.h>

int main (void)
{
int x, y;
int ch;

    /* Note : This program is designed  */
    /* for VGA monitors in 50-line mode */

textmode (C4350);
clrscr();

    /* draw the four corners */

gotoxy (1,1);
printf ("%c",201);
gotoxy (79,1);
```

```
printf ("%c",187);
gotoxy (1,50);
printf ("%c",200);
gotoxy (79,50);
printf("%c",188);

      /* draw the borders */

for (x=2; x <79; x=x+1)
{
      gotoxy (x,1);
      printf ("%c",205);
      gotoxy (x,50);
      printf ("%c",205);
}

for (y=2; y<50; y=y+1)
{
      gotoxy (1,y);
      printf ("%c",186);
      gotoxy (79,y);
      printf ("%c",186);
}

      /* print all the characters */

y = 9;
for (ch=0; ch<32; ch=ch+1)
{
      gotoxy (8,y);
      printf ("%3d %c",ch,ch);
      gotoxy (16,y);
      printf ("%3d %c",ch+32,ch+32);
      gotoxy (24,y);
      printf ("%3d %c",ch+64,ch+64);
      gotoxy (32,y);
      printf ("%3d %c",ch+96,ch+96);
      gotoxy (40,y);
      printf ("%3d %c",ch+128,ch+128);
      gotoxy (48,y);
      printf ("%3d %c",ch+160,ch+160);
      gotoxy (56,y);
      printf ("%3d %c",ch+192,ch+192);
      gotoxy (64,y);
      printf ("%3d %c",ch+224,ch+224);
      y = y+1;
}


gotoxy (79,50);
textmode (LASTMODE);
return 0;
}
```

Figure 3.1. Screen output for Listing 3.1

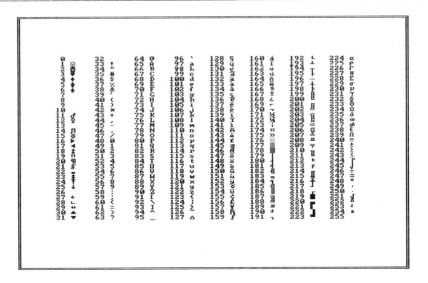

Drawing Boxes Using the Extended Character Set

The extended character set can be used, as in the previous example, to create boxes. There are four primary types of characters used for drawing boxes.

Double-Line Boxes

The first group of characters is used to create boxes with double lines. The characters of this type include the following:

Decimal Value	Character
185	╣
186	║
187	╗
188	╝
200	╚
201	╔

Decimal Value	Character
202	⊥⊥
203	⊤⊤
204	╠
205	=
206	╬

These characters are used to create frames and borders as follows:

╔ (201) = (205) ╦ (203) ╗ (187)

║ (186

╠ (204)   ╬ (206)   ╣ (185)

╚ (200)   ╩ (202)   ╝ (188)

Listing 3.2 and Figure 3.2 demonstrate how these characters can be used to create borders, frames, or boxes:

Listing 3.2.   Creating double-lined borders and boxes

```
#include <stdio.h>
#include <stdlib.h>
#include <conio.h>

int main (void)
{
int x, y;
int ch;

clrscr();

    /* draw the four corners */
gotoxy (1,1);
printf ("%c",201);
gotoxy (79,1);
printf ("%c",187);
gotoxy (1,25);
printf ("%c",200);
gotoxy (79,25);
printf ("%c",188);

    /* draw the intersections */
```

Listing 3.2. *continues*

Listing 3.2. cont. Creating double-lined borders and boxes

```
gotoxy (39,1);
printf ("%c",203);
gotoxy (39,13);
printf ("%c",206);
gotoxy (39,25);
printf ("%c",202);
gotoxy (1,13);
printf ("%c",204);
gotoxy (79,13);
printf ("%c",185);

        /* draw the borders */

for (x=2; x <39; x=x+1)
{
        gotoxy (x,1);
        printf ("%c",205);
        gotoxy (x,13);
        printf ("%c",205);
        gotoxy (x,25);
        printf ("%c",205);
}

for (x=40; x<79; x=x+1)
{
        gotoxy (x,1);
        printf ("%c",205);
        gotoxy (x,13);
        printf ("%c",205);
        gotoxy (x,25);
        printf ("%c",205);
}

for (y=2; y<13; y=y+1)
{
        gotoxy (1,y);
        printf ("%c",186);
        gotoxy (39,y);
        printf ("%c",186);
        gotoxy (79,y);
        printf ("%c",186);
}

for (y=14; y<25; y=y+1)
{
        gotoxy (1,y);
        printf ("%c",186);
        gotoxy (39,y);
        printf ("%c",186);
        gotoxy (79,y);
        printf ("%c",186);
}

gotoxy (5,6);
printf ("Double Line Box Example");
return 0;
}
```

Figure 3.2. Screen output from Listing 3.2

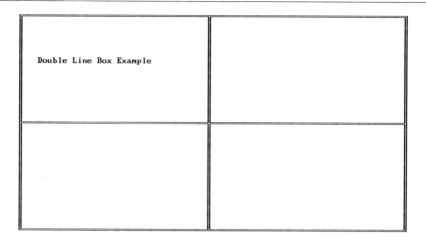

Single-Line Boxes

A different group of characters is used to create boxes with single lines. The characters used to create single-line boxes are shown next:

Decimal Value	Character
179	|
180	┤
191	┐
192	L
193	⊥
194	┬
195	├
196	—
197	+
217	┘
218	┌

These characters are used in the following manner to create boxes and borders:

┌ (218) ─ (196) ┬ (194)   ┐ (191)

│ (179)

├ (195)   ┼ (197)   ┤ (180)

└ (192)   ┴ (193)   ┘ (217)

Listing 3.3 and Figure 3.3 demonstrate how these characters can be used to create single-line boxes and borders:

Listing 3.3. Creating single-line boxes and borders

```
#include <stdio.h>
#include <stdlib.h>
#include <conio.h>

int main (void)
{
int x, y;
int ch;

clrscr();

    /* draw the four corners */

gotoxy (1,1);
printf ("%c",218);
gotoxy (79,1);
printf ("%c",191);
gotoxy (1,25);
printf ("%c",192);
gotoxy (79,25);
printf ("%c",217);

    /* draw the intersections */

gotoxy (39,1);
printf ("%c",194);
gotoxy (39,13);
printf ("%c",197);
gotoxy (39,25);
printf ("%c",193);
gotoxy (1,13);
printf ("%c",195);
gotoxy (79,13);
printf ("%c",180);

    /* draw the borders */
```

```
for (x=2; x <39; x=x+1)
{
     gotoxy (x,1);
     printf ("%c",196);
     gotoxy (x,13);
   printf ("%c",196);
     gotoxy (x,25);
     printf ("%c",196);
}

for (x=40; x<79; x=x+1)
{
     gotoxy (x,1);
     printf ("%c",196);
     gotoxy (x,13);
     printf ("%c",196);
     gotoxy (x,25);
     printf ("%c",196);
}

for (y=2; y<13; y=y+1)
{
     gotoxy (1,y);
     printf ("%c",179);
     gotoxy (39,y);
     printf ("%c",179);
     gotoxy (79,y);
   printf ("%c",179);
}

for (y=14; y<25; y=y+1)
{
     gotoxy (1,y);
     printf ("%c",179);
   gotoxy (39,y);
     printf ("%c",179);
     gotoxy (79,y);
     printf ("%c",179);
}

gotoxy (5,6);
printf ("Single Line Box Example");
return 0;
}
```

Mixing Single and Double Lines for Boxes

Two groups of characters can be used to create mixed single- and double-line boxes. The first creates single vertical lines and double horizontal lines. The second creates single horizontal lines and double vertical lines.

Figure 3.3. Screen output for Listing 3.3

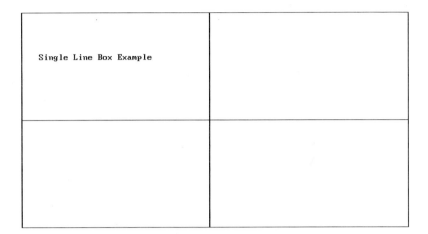

The group of characters used to create boxes with single vertical lines and double horizontal lines follows:

Decimal Value	Character
179	|
181	⊣
184	⊓
190	⊒
198	⊢
205	=
207	⊥
209	⊤
212	⊢
213	⊏
216	±

These characters are used in the following manner to create borders and boxes:

╔ (213) = (205) ╦ (209)   ╗ (184)

| (179)

╠ (198)   ╬ (216)   ╣ (181)

╚ (212)   ╩ (207)   ╝ (190)

Listing 3.4 and Figure 3.4 demonstrate the use of these characters for drawing boxes and borders:

Listing 3.4.   Drawing boxes with single/double lines

```
#include <stdio.h>
#include <stdlib.h>
#include <conio.h>

int main (void)
{
int x, y;
int ch;

clrscr();

        /* draw the four corners */
gotoxy (1,1);
printf ("%c",213);
gotoxy (79,1);
printf ("%c",184);
gotoxy (1,25);
printf ("%c",212);
gotoxy (79,25);
printf ("%c",190);

        /* draw the intersections */
gotoxy (39,1);
printf ("%c",209);
gotoxy (39,13);
printf ("%c",216);
gotoxy (39,25);
printf ("%c",207);
gotoxy (1,13);
printf ("%c",198);
gotoxy (79,13);
printf ("%c",181);

        /* draw the borders */
```

Listing 3.4.   *continues*

Listing 3.4. cont. Drawing boxes with single/double lines

```
for (x=2; x <39; x=x+1)
{
     gotoxy (x,1);
     printf ("%c",205);
     gotoxy (x,13);
     printf ("%c",205);
     gotoxy (x,25);
     printf ("%c",205);
}

for (x=40; x<79; x=x+1)
{
     gotoxy (x,1);
     printf ("%c",205);
     gotoxy (x,13);
     printf ("%c",205);
     gotoxy (x,25);
     printf ("%c",205);
}

for (y=2; y<13; y=y+1)
{
     gotoxy (1,y);
     printf ("%c",179);
     gotoxy (39,y);
     printf ("%c",179);
     gotoxy (79,y);
     printf ("%c",179);
}

for (y=14; y<25; y=y+1)
{
     gotoxy (1,y);
     printf ("%c",179);
     gotoxy (39,y);
     printf ("%c",179);
     gotoxy (79,y);
     printf ("%c",179);
}

gotoxy (5,6);
printf ("Single/Double Line Box Example");
return 0;
}
```

Figure 3.4. Screen output for Listing 3.4

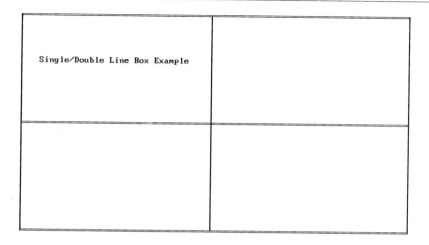

The other group of characters creates boxes and borders with double vertical lines and single horizontal lines. The characters used to draw this type of box or border are:

Decimal Value	Character
182	╢
183	╖
186	║
189	╜
196	─
199	╟
208	╨
210	╥
211	╙
214	╓
215	╫

These characters are used in the manner shown next to create boxes and borders with single horizontal lines and double vertical lines:

⌐ (214)   − (196)   ╥ (210)   ╖ (183)

‖ (186)

╟ (199)   ╫ (215)   ╢ (182)

╙ (211)   ╨ (208)   ╜ (189)

Listing 3.5 and Figure 3.5 demonstrate the use of these characters to create boxes and borders:

Listing 3.5.   Drawing boxes with double/single lines

```
#include <stdio.h>
#include <stdlib.h>
#include <conio.h>

int main (void)
{
int x, y;
int ch;

clrscr();

        /* draw the four corners */

gotoxy (1,1);
printf ("%c",214);
gotoxy (79,1);
printf ("%c",183);
gotoxy (1,25);
printf("%c",211);
gotoxy (79,25);
printf ("%c",189);

        /* draw the intersections */

gotoxy (39,1);
printf ("%c",210);
gotoxy (39,13);
printf ("%c",215);
gotoxy (39,25);
printf ("%c",208);
gotoxy (1,13);
printf ("%c",199);
gotoxy (79,13);
printf ("%c",182);
```

```
      /* draw the borders */

for (x=2; x <39; x=x+1)
{
     gotoxy (x,1);
     printf ("%c",196);
     gotoxy (x,13);
     printf ("%c",196);
     gotoxy (x,25);
     printf ("%c",196);
}

for (x=40; x<79; x=x+1)
{
     gotoxy (x,1);
     printf ("%c",196);
     gotoxy (x,13);
     printf ("%c",196);
     gotoxy (x,25);
     printf ("%c",196);
}

for (y=2; y<13; y=y+1)
{
     gotoxy (1,y);
     printf ("%c",186);
     gotoxy (39,y);
     printf ("%c",186);
     gotoxy (79,y);
     printf ("%c",186);
}

for (y=14; y<25; y=y+1)
{
     gotoxy (1,y);
     printf ("%c",186);
     gotoxy (39,y);
     printf ("%c",186);
     gotoxy (79,y);
     printf ("%c",186);
}

gotoxy (5,6);
printf ("Double/Single Line Box Example");
getch();
return 0;
}
```

Figure 3.5. Screen output for Listing 3.5

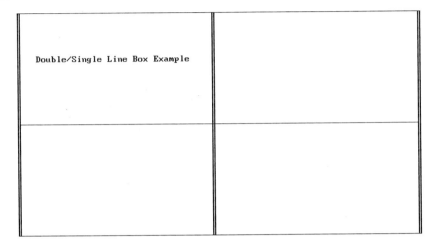

Listing 3.6 and Figure 3.6 demonstrate the use of the extended character set to implement a windowed environment. This example begins by creating a main window, a message window, and a menu bar. The extended character set is used to frame the message and main windows. The keyboard is then monitored. If an 'f' is input, the first menu pops up. The menu is framed using the extended character set. Similarly, when an 's' is input, the second menu pops up. Although this example does not go into all the details of creating a full-featured, text-based windowing system, it does demonstrate how the extended character set can be used to frame various windows and menus.

Listing 3.6. Developing pop-up menus

```
#include <stdio.h>
#include <stdlib.h>
#include <conio.h>

int main()
{
int x, y;
int in_char;

clrscr();

   /* draw the main window */

textbackground(1);
textcolor(7);
gotoxy (1,2);
cprintf ("%c",201);
```

```
gotoxy (1,20);
cprintf ("%c",200);
gotoxy (79,2);
cprintf ("%c",187);
gotoxy (79,20);
cprintf ("%c",188);

for (x=2; x<79; x=x+1)
{
   gotoxy (x,2);
   cprintf ("%c",205);
   gotoxy (x,20);
   cprintf ("%c",205);
}

for (y=3; y<20; y=y+1)
{
   gotoxy (1,y);
   cprintf ("%c",186);
   gotoxy (79,y);
   cprintf ("%c",186);
}

for (x=2; x<79; x=x+1)
{
   for (y=3; y<20; y=y+1)
   {
   gotoxy (x,y);
   cprintf (" ");
   }
}

gotoxy (3,2);
cprintf ("[*]");
gotoxy (35,2);
cprintf ("Main Window");

   /* draw the message window */

textbackground(4);
gotoxy (1,21);
cprintf ("%c",218);
gotoxy (1,24);
cprintf ("%c",192);
gotoxy (79,21);
cprintf ("%c",191);
gotoxy (79,24);
cprintf ("%c",217);

for (x=2; x<79; x=x+1)
{
   gotoxy (x,21);
   cprintf ("%c",196);
   gotoxy (x,24);
   cprintf ("%c",196);
}
```

Listing 3.6. *continues*

Listing 3.6. cont.   Developing pop-up menus

```
for (y=22; y<24; y=y+1)
{
   gotoxy (1,y);
   cprintf ("%c",179);
   gotoxy (79,y);
   cprintf ("%c",179);
}

for (x=2; x<79; x=x+1)
{
   for (y=22; y<24; y=y+1)
   {
   gotoxy (x,y);
   cprintf (" ");
   }
}

gotoxy (3,21);
cprintf ("[*]");
gotoxy (33,21);
cprintf ("Message Window");
gotoxy (15,22);
cprintf ("Press 'f' for first menu or 's' for second menu");
gotoxy (15,23);
cprintf ("Press ESC to exit");

   /* draw menu bar */

textbackground(7);
textcolor(0);
for (x=1; x<80; x=x+1)
{
   gotoxy (x,1);
   cprintf (" ");
}
gotoxy (15,1);
cprintf ("First Menu");
gotoxy (55,1);
cprintf ("Second Menu");
gotoxy (2,3);

   /* monitor keyboard for f, s, or ESC */

do
{
   in_char = getch();
   if (in_char == 's')
   {
   gotoxy (55,2);
   cprintf ("%c%c%c%c%c%c%c%c%c%c%c",213,205,205,205,
     205,205,205,205,205,184);
   gotoxy (55,3);
   cprintf ("%c ONE     %c",179,179);
   gotoxy (55,4);
   cprintf ("%c TWO     %c",179,179);
```

```
  gotoxy (55,5);
  cprintf ("%c%c%c%c%c%c%c%c%c%c%c",198,205,205,205,
    205,205,205,205,205,181);
  gotoxy (55,6);
  cprintf ("%c THREE  %c",179,179);
  gotoxy (55,7);
  cprintf ("%c FOUR  %c",179,179);
  gotoxy (55,8);
  cprintf ("%c%c%c%c%c%c%c%c%c%c%c",212,205,205,205,
    205,205,205,205,205,190);
  }

  if (in_char == 'f')
  {
  gotoxy (15,2);
  cprintf ("%c%c%c%c%c%c%c%c%c%c%c",214,196,196,196,
    196,196,196,196,196,183);
  gotoxy (15,3);
  cprintf ("%c ONE     %c",186,186);
  gotoxy (15,4);
  cprintf ("%c TWO     %c",186,186);
  gotoxy (15,5);
  cprintf ("%c%c%c%c%c%c%c%c%c%c%c",199,196,196,196,
    196,196,196,196,196,182);
  gotoxy (15,6);
  cprintf ("%c THREE   %c",186,186);
  gotoxy (15,7);
  cprintf ("%c FOUR  %c",186,186);
  gotoxy (15,8);
  cprintf ("%c%c%c%c%c%c%c%c%c%c%c",211,196,196,196,
    196,196,196,196,196,189);
  }

  gotoxy (2,3);
} while (in_char != 27);

textcolor(7);
return 0;
}
```

The characters in the ASCII and IBM extended character sets offer flexibility in the development of text-based graphics such as pop-up menus, dialog boxes, and windows. However, text-based graphics are extremely limited and will not be discussed any further in this book. The graphics routines in the Borland C++ run-time library offer a wide variety of tools for developing graphics programs for graphics modes. The focus of this book is on programming in the graphics modes.

Figure 3.6. Screen output for Listing 3.6

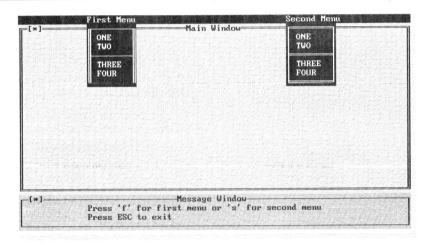

Summary

This chapter briefly described text-based graphics programming using the extended character set. The remainder of this book describes programming applications for graphics modes.

4

Graphics Techniques

This chapter introduces the basic concepts behind graphics programming with Borland C++. The Borland C++ functions used for drawing are presented, and full explanations of each function are provided. It is important to understand the functions and techniques described in this chapter, because these principles are the foundation for all graphics programs.

Coordinate Systems

The IBM personal computers have two basic video operating modes. The first, the default, is the text mode. In text mode, the screen is divided into character cells, usually 80 character cells wide by 25 character cells high. The second operating mode is the graphics mode. In graphics mode, the screen is divided into pixels. The graphics mode is the focus of this book.

When in graphics mode, there are two coordinate systems recognized by the Borland C++ graphics library. These are the physical and viewport coordinate systems. From this point on, the viewport coordinate system will be referred to as the *view coordinate system.*

The Physical Coordinate System

The dimensions of the physical coordinate system are determined by the hardware, display configuration, and video mode in use. The physical coordinate system has its origin (0,0) in the upper left-hand corner of the screen as shown in Figure 4.1. The positive x-axis extends toward the right of the screen, while the positive y-axis extends toward the bottom of the screen. The maximum x value is determined by the number of pixels in the horizontal direction of the screen (considering the video mode in use). Similarly, the maximum y value is determined by the number of pixels in the vertical direction. For example, when using the Enhanced Graphics Adapter driver and EGAHI mode, there are 640 pixels in the horizontal direction (ranging from 0 to 639) and 350 pixels in the vertical direction (ranging from 0 to 349).

The physical coordinate system does not change, even when the user shifts the view coordinate system. As a default, the physical and view coordinate systems are identical.

Figure 4.1.   The physical coordinate system

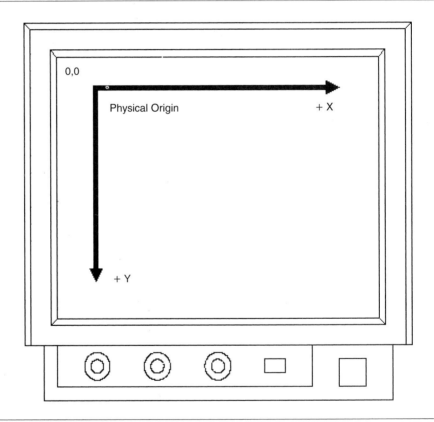

The View Coordinate System

The view coordinate system is based on the current *viewport*. A viewport can be described best as a rectangular region of the screen. All graphics output is drawn relative to the location of the viewport. As mentioned previously, the view coordinate system is, by default, the same as the physical coordinate system. This is due to the fact that the default viewport is set to the entire physical dimensions of the screen.

The difference between the view coordinate system and the physical coordinate system is that the view coordinate system can be moved by specifying a viewport. When a viewport is specified, the origin of the view coordinate system is placed in the upper left-hand corner of the viewport.

The viewport, thus the origin of the view coordinate system, is defined in physical coordinates. Therefore, the physical coordinate system is used only as a reference coordinate system for defining the viewport.

The view coordinate system has the same resolution as the physical coordinate system. Therefore, if there are 640 by 350 pixels available in the current video mode, this physical limitation applies to both the view coordinate system and the physical coordinate system since the view coordinate system is a subset of the physical coordinate system. The only difference is in the way each pixel is labeled. Figure 4.2 illustrates the axes of the view coordinate system.

The Graphics Cursor

The Borland C++ graphics library routines maintain an internal reference point from which most of the actions of the drawing routines originate. This point is called the *graphics cursor*. You can move the graphics cursor about the screen with the `moveto` function, the `moverel` function, and several of the drawing routines.

Use the `moveto` function to place the graphics cursor at a specified point that is defined in the view coordinates. The syntax for the `moveto` function is as follows:

```
void far moveto(int x, int y);

int x, y;     View coordinates of new cursor position
```

Figure 4.3 illustrates the use of the `moveto` function.

Figure 4.2. The view coordinate system

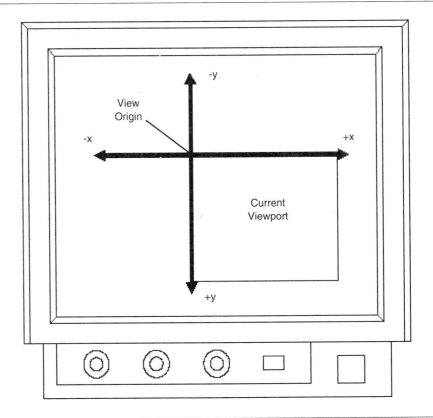

Figure 4.3. The moveto function

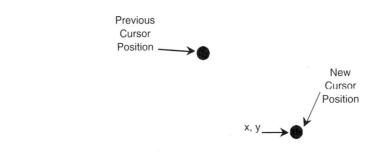

The `moverel` function is used to move the graphics cursor a relative distance from its current location. The syntax for the `moverel` function is as follows:

```
void far moverel(int dx, int dy);

int dx, dy;     Relative distances to move.
```

Figure 4.4 illustrates the use of the `moverel` function.

Figure 4.4. The `moverel` function

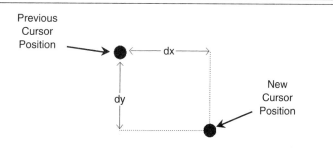

The `moveto` and `moverel` functions merely alter the location of the graphics cursor. When these functions are called, no drawing takes place.

The Borland C++ graphics library provides two functions that can be used to retrieve the view coordinates of the current graphics cursor position. These functions are the `getx` and the `gety` functions.

The `getx` function is used to retrieve the horizontal, or x, view coordinate of the graphics cursor. The syntax for this function is:

```
int far getx(void);
```

The `gety` function is used to retrieve the vertical, or y, view coordinate of the graphics cursor. The syntax for this function is:

```
int far gety(void);
```

Together, these functions provide the current position of the graphics cursor.

Aspect Ratios

The easiest and most common way to create simple graphics on the screen is to draw the desired shape on graph paper, mark all relevant points, and then transfer these points into coordinates for use in the graphics program. Because engineering graph paper is easy to obtain and uses a square grid, it is most commonly used for sketching simple graphics. However, there is a problem with using a square grid to sketch a graphic. The pixels in most video modes are not square (VGA modes are the exception to this rule). Therefore, when the program is run, the image is often distorted. In order to create the desired image, you must consider the *aspect ratio* of the video configuration.

The aspect ratio of the video configuration is the ratio of the number of pixels along a vertical line on the screen compared to the number of pixels along a horizontal line of the same length. When the aspect ratio is 1, for example, a vertical line of 20 pixels will have the same length as a horizontal line of 20 pixels. In order for the desired image to appear undistorted, when using square graph paper for drawing, the vertical (y) dimension must be multiplied by the aspect ratio. The image will then appear on the screen as you have drawn it on the paper.

You can use the following formula to determine the aspect ratio of the video configuration:

```
aspect ratio = (width of screen/height of screen) *
               (number of y pixels/number of x pixels)
```

The width and height of the screen refer to the actual physical dimensions of the usable screen. You can find these dimensions in the monitor's technical manual, or you can simply measure the screen. The number of pixels on the x and y axes depends on the video mode in use. You can determine the number of pixels on the axes by referring to Chapter 11—the `initgraph` function.

Fortunately, the Borland C++ graphics library provides many of the functions you need to manipulate the aspect ratio. These functions include the `getaspectratio` function and the `setaspectratio` functions. Use the aspect ratio, as set by the graphics library, to ensure roundness when calculating and drawing circles and arcs.

The `getaspectratio` function is used to retrieve the current aspect ratio given the current video configuration and mode in use. This information is useful for drawing undistorted images. The syntax for the `getaspectratio` function is:

```
void far getaspectratio (int far *xasp, int far *yasp);

int far *xasp;        x aspect factor
int far *yasp;        y aspect factor
```

The `setaspectratio` function is used to alter the default settings of the aspect ratio. Altering the aspect ratio will result in circles that do not appear to be round. The syntax for the `setaspectratio` function is as follows:

```
void far setaspectratio(int xasp, int yasp);

int xasp;        New x aspect factor
int yasp;        New y aspect factor
```

Pixels

The smallest part of a screen is known as a pixel. For most modes, the pixel is not square. The pixel size of a screen depends on the graphics mode in use. The size of the pixel also relates to the resolution of the screen. The bigger the pixel, the lower the resolution, and vice versa.

You can set each pixel on the screen to one and only one color. The choice of colors is, of course, limited by the video mode and palette in use. Because the pixel can be set to only one color, the pixel represents the most fundamental drawing element.

The Borland C++ graphics library provides a function that can be used to set a particular pixel to the specified color. This function, the `putpixel` function, is:

```
void far putpixel(int x, int y, int color);

int x, y;               Coordinates of pixel
int color;              Desired color
```

The `putpixel` function sets the pixel specified by the x and y arguments to the designated color.

The Borland C++ library also includes a function for retrieving the color, or pixel value, of a specified pixel. This function is the `getpixel` function. The syntax is:

```
unsigned far getpixel(int x, int y);

int x, y;               Coordinates of pixel
```

The `getpixel` function is useful for determining the status of a pixel before setting it to a color.

Lines

The line is perhaps the most important feature of any graphics library. With the line, you can create an image of almost any level of complexity. The line is primarily used to connect two points. You can also use it to create boxes and other geometric figures, approximate curves, or outline complex images and shapes. Although its function is simple, the line is very versatile.

The Borland C++ graphics library provides three functions for drawing lines. These functions are the `line`, `linerel`, and `lineto` functions. Each of these functions connects two points, expressed in view coordinates, with a straight line. These functions differ slightly.

Use the `line` function to draw a line between two specified points. Both points are expressed in view coordinates. When the line is drawn, the current position of the graphics cursor is not changed. The syntax for the `line` function is as follows:

```
void far line(int x1, int y1, int x2, int y2);

int x1, y1;          Coordinates of first point
int x2, y2;          Coordinates of second point
```

You can use the `linerel` function to draw a line a relative distance from the current position of the graphics cursor. The `dx` and `dy` arguments, as listed in the following syntax, describe the relative distance to draw the line. When you draw the line, the current position of the graphics cursor is updated to the point described by `dx` and `dy`.

```
void far linerel(int dx, int dy);

int dx;              Relative x distance
int dy;              Relative y distance
```

You can use the `lineto` function to draw a line from the current position of the graphics cursor to the point specified by the x and y arguments, as shown in the following syntax. When you draw the line, the current position of the graphics cursor is updated to the point specified by x and y.

```
void far lineto(int x, int y);

int x,y;             Coordinates of line's endpoint
```

The lines created by these functions are drawn in the current color. You can define the current color with the `setcolor` function. The number of colors available depends on the video hardware configuration and the video mode in use. In Chapter 11, the `setcolor` function documentation explains the availability of colors given the video mode in use.

These functions also use the current line style and thickness. You can define these with the `setlinestyle` function. The syntax for the `setlinestyle` function is:

```
void far setlinestyle(int linestyle, unsigned upattern,
                      int thickness);

int linestyle;       Predefined pattern number (0-4)
unsigned upattern;   16-bit user-defined pattern
int thickness;       Predefined line thickness (1 or 3)
```

The `linestyle` argument ranges from 0 to 4 and is used to select a predefined line pattern. Table 4.1 lists the options for the `linestyle` argument.

Table 4.1. *Predefined line styles and thicknesses*

Constant	Value	Meaning
Line Styles		
SOLID_LINE	0	Solid line
DOTTED_LINE	1	Dotted line
CENTER_LINE	2	Centered line
DASHED_LINE	3	Dashed line
USERBIT_LINE	4	User-defined line
Line thicknesses		
NORM_WIDTH	1	Line width of 1 pixel
THICK_WIDTH	3	Line width of 3 pixels

The upattern argument defines a line pattern that will be used when the linestyle argument is set to 4, or USERBIT_LINE.

When the linestyle argument is set to 4, the setlinestyle function sets the current line pattern to the 16-bit line pattern defined in the upattern argument.

The 16-bit line pattern, specified in the upattern argument, represents the line pattern. Each bit of the 16-bit line pattern corresponds to one bit on the line. A 1 bit in the line pattern indicates that the corresponding pixel on the line will be set to the current color. A 0 bit indicates that the corresponding pixel will remain unchanged. The 16-bit line pattern is repeated over the entire length of the line.

An example of a line pattern is 1111111111111111 binary, or 0xFFFF hex. This line pattern indicates that every bit on the line will be set to the current color (a solid line). Other patterns can be set and used easily. Appendix A contains numerous line patterns that you can define and use in any graphics application to create dashed and dotted lines.

You can use the thickness argument of the setlinestyle function to select a predefined thickness for the line. Table 4.1 lists the predefined line thicknesses.

Listing 4.1 and Figure 4.5 demonstrate the use of the line function to create a complex image of an F-4 fighter aircraft. You could also use the linerel and lineto functions to create this display.

Listing 4.1. F-4 fighter aircraft example

```c
#include <graphics.h>
#include <stdio.h>
#include <stdlib.h>
#include <conio.h>

int main ()
{
int gdriver = EGA;
int gmode = EGAHI;

     /* register EGAVGA_driver and sansserif_font */
     /* ... these have been added to graphics.lib */
     /* as described in UTIL.DOC                  */

registerbgidriver (EGAVGA_driver);
registerbgifont (sansserif_font);

     /* set EGA 16-color high resolution video mode  */

initgraph (&gdriver,&gmode,"");
rectangle (0,0,639,349);

     /* draw F-4 fighter */

setlinestyle(SOLID_LINE,0xFFFF,NORM_WIDTH);

line (120,240,120,270);
line (120,270,120,275);
line (120,275,118,288);
line (118,288,130,288);
line (130,288,175,273);
line (153,282,195,293);
line (195,293,195,296);
line (195,296,230,296);
line (230,296,445,296);
line (445,296,490,298);
line (490,298,505,296);
line (505,296,520,292);
line (520,292,490,282);
line (490,282,454,278);
line (454,278,440,275);
line (440,275,430,272);
line (430,272,415,268);
line (415,268,400,266);
line (400,266,385,264);
line (385,264,350,266);
line (350,266,240,266);
line (240,266,150,240);
line (150,240,120,240);
line (175,273,195,278);
line (195,278,200,272);
line (200,272,360,272);
line (360,272,375,274);
line (375,274,415,278);
line (415,278,410,296);
```

```
line (240,266,140,260);
line (140,260,120,270);
line (175,273,120,275);
line (120,240,140,260);
line (153,282,195,278);
line (195,278,215,278);
line (195,278,195,296);
line (210,278,210,296);
line (215,278,215,296);
line (400,276,394,296);
line (405,277,399,296);
line (230,296,215,285);
line (215,285,250,285);
line (250,285,305,296);
line (275,290,360,290);
line (360,290,355,296);
line (490,282,490,302);
line (410,296,490,302);
line (490,302,500,303);
line (500,303,510,300);
line (510,300,511,299);
line (511,299,505,296);
line (350,266,393,272);
line (393,272,425,278);
line (425,278,448,277);
line (400,266,405,274);
line (399,266,395,272);

        /* Draw Title */

line (220,83,260,30);
line (260,30,300,30);
line (300,30,290,43);
line (290,43,270,43);
line (270,43,260,56);
line (260,56,280,56);
line (280,56,270,70);
line (270,70,250,70);
line (250,70,240,83);
line (240,83,220,83);
line (290,70,300,56);
line (300,56,340,56);
line (340,56,330,70);
line (330,70,290,70);
line (380,83,390,70);
line (390,70,350,70);
line (350,70,380,30);
line (380,30,400,30);
line (400,30,380,56);
line (380,56,400,56);
line (400,56,420,30);
line (420,30,440,30);
line (440,30,400,83);
line (400,83,380,83);
line (180,153,220,100);
```

Listing 4.1.   *continues*

Listing 4.1. cont. F-4 fighter aircraft example

```
line (220,100,240,100);
line (240,100,210,140);
line (210,140,220,140);
line (220,140,230,126);
line (230,126,250,126);
line (250,126,240,140);
line (240,140,250,140);
line (250,140,280,100);
line (280,100,300,100);
line (300,100,260,153);
line (260,153,180,153);
line (280,153,320,100);
line (320,100,340,100);
line (340,100,300,153);
line (300,153,280,153);
line (320,153,360,100);
line (360,100,380,100);
line (380,100,350,140);
line (350,140,370,140);
line (370,140,360,153);
line (360,153,320,153);
line (380,153,420,100);
line (420,100,470,100);
line (470,100,430,153);
line (430,153,380,153);
line (410,140,430,113);
line (430,113,440,113);
line (440,113,420,140);
line (420,140,410,140);
line (120,223,160,170);
line (160,170,180,170);
line (180,170,150,210);
line (150,210,160,210);
line (160,210,170,196);
line (170,196,190,196);
line (190,196,180,210);
line (180,210,190,210);
line (190,210,220,170);
line (220,170,240,170);
line (240,170,200,223);
line (200,223,120,223);
line (220,223,260,170);
line (260,170,300,170);
line (300,170,290,183);
line (290,183,270,183);
line (270,183,265,189);
line (265,189,285,189);
line (285,189,275,203);
line (275,203,255,203);
line (255,203,250,210);
line (250,210,270,210);
line (270,210,260,223);
line (260,223,220,223);
```

```
line (280,223,320,170);
line (320,170,365,170);
line (365,170,330,223);
line (330,223,310,223);
line (310,223,320,210);
line (320,210,310,210);
line (310,210,300,223);
line (300,223,280,223);
line (320,196,330,183);
line (330,183,340,183);
line (340,183,330,196);
line (330,196,320,196);
line (340,223,350,210);
line (350,210,380,210);
line (380,210,385,203);
line (385,203,355,203);
line (355,203,380,170);
line (380,170,430,170);
line (430,170,420,183);
line (420,183,390,183);
line (390,183,385,189);
line (385,189,415,189);
line (415,189,390,223);
line (390,223,340,223);
line (410,223,450,170);
line (450,170,490,170);
line (490,170,480,183);
line (480,183,460,183);
line (460,183,455,189);
line (455,189,475,189);
line (475,189,465,203);
line (465,203,445,203);
line (445,203,440,210);
line (440,210,460,210);
line (460,210,450,223);
line (450,223,410,223);
line (470,223,510,170);
line (510,170,530,170);
line (530,170,500,210);
line (500,210,520,210);
line (520,210,510,223);
line (510,223,470,223);

        /* Delay and Exit */

settextjustify(CENTER_TEXT,BOTTOM_TEXT);
outtextxy (320,320,"Press Any Key To Exit");

getch ();

closegraph();
return 0;
}
```

Figure 4.5. Screen output for Listing 4.1

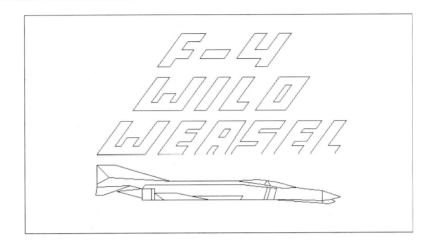

Rectangles and Bars

The Borland C++ graphics library contains several functions that you can use to create bars and rectangles. These functions include the bar, bar3d, and rectangle functions.

The bar function is used to draw a rectangular bar. The bar is filled with the current *fill pattern* (the bit map used to fill the figure) and *fill color* (the color used to fill the figure) and is not drawn with a border. As the following syntax shows, the bar function uses four arguments to define the bar. The left and top arguments define the upper left-hand corner of the bar, while the right and bottom arguments define the lower right-hand corner of the bar (see Figure 4.6).

```
void far bar(int left, int top, int right, int bottom);

int left, top;          Upper left corner of bar
int right, bottom;      Lower right corner of bar
```

Figure 4.6. The bar function

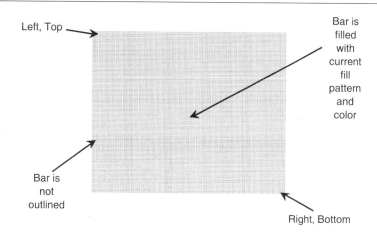

Left, Top

Bar is
filled
with
current
fill
pattern
and
color

Bar is
not
outlined

Right, Bottom

The bar3d function is used to create a three-dimensional rectangular bar (see Figure 4.7). The front face of the bar is filled with the current fill color and fill pattern. The bar is outlined, in all three dimensions, with the current line style and color. The following syntax is used for the bar3d function.

```
void far bar3d(int left, int top, int right, int bottom,
               int depth, int topflag);

int left, top;       Upper left corner of 3-d bar
int right, bottom;   Lower right corner of 3-d bar
int depth;           Depth of bar in pixels
int topflag;         Top indicator
```

As with the bar function, the left and top arguments define the upper left-hand corner of the bar, while the right and bottom arguments define the lower right-hand corner of the bar. The depth argument defines the depth, in pixels, of the three-dimensional portion of the bar. Use the topflag argument to specify whether or not you want a top to be placed on the bar. If topflag is 0, no top is placed on the bar, making it possible for you to stack several bars on top of each other. Otherwise, a top is placed on the bar.

Figure 4.7. The bar3d function

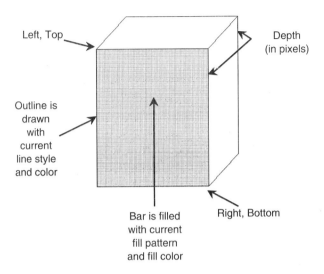

Left, Top

Depth
(in pixels)

Outline is
drawn
with
current
line style
and color

Bar is filled
with current
fill pattern
and fill color

Right, Bottom

You can use the rectangle function to create an unfilled rectangle with the current line style and color. The following syntax is used with the rectangle function:

```
void far rectangle(int left, int top, int right,
                   int bottom);

int left, top;        Upper left corner of rectangle
int right, bottom;    Lower right corner of rectangle
```

As with the bar and bar3d functions, the left and top arguments define the upper left-hand corner of the rectangle, while the right and bottom arguments define the lower right-hand corner (see Figure 4.8).

The outlines of the rectangle and bar3d functions are drawn using the current line style and current color. The current color is set by the setcolor function, while the current line style is set by the setlinestyle function. Chapter 11 provides a full explanation of the setcolor and setlinestyle functions.

The bar and bar3d functions are filled with the current fill pattern and fill color. You can define the fill pattern and fill color with the setfillstyle and setfillpattern functions.

The setfillstyle function is most commonly used because it selects a predefined fill pattern from the graphics library. The syntax is:

```
void far setfillstyle(int pattern, int color);

int pattern;        Fill pattern
int color;          Fill color
```

Figure 4.8. The rectangle function

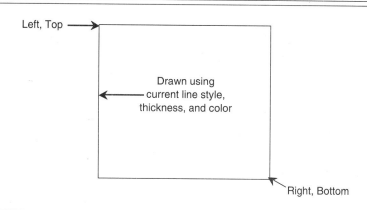

The pattern argument is a constant, or value, selected from Table 4.2 (which lists the available fill patterns). The color argument specifies the desired fill color from the current palette.

Table 4.2. *Predefined fill patterns*

Constant	Value	Meaning
EMPTY_FILL	0	Fill with background color
SOLID_FILL	1	Solid fill
LINE_FILL	2	Horizontal line fill
LTSLASH_FILL	3	Light slash fill
SLASH_FILL	4	Heavy slash fill
BKSLASH_FILL	5	Heavy backslash fill
LTBKSLASH_FILL	6	Light backslash fill
HATCH_FILL	7	Light hatch fill
XHATCH_FILL	8	Heavy hatch fill
INTERLEAVE_FILL	9	Interleaving fill
WIDE_DOT_FILL	10	Wide dot fill
CLOSE_DOT_FILL	11	Close dot fill
USER_FILL	12	User-defined pattern

The setfillpattern function is similar to the setfillstyle function except that the fill pattern is defined by the user. The syntax for the setfillpattern function follows.

```
void far setfillpattern(char far *upattern, int color);

char far *upattern;        8x8-bit user-defined fill pattern
int color;                 Fill color
```

The upattern argument defines the fill pattern. When using the setfillpattern function, you must define the fill pattern. The fill pattern is an 8-by-8 bit map that repeats over the entire area to be filled. Each bit in the pattern corresponds to one pixel on the screen. For each bit in the pattern, a 1 bit sets the corresponding screen pixel to the current color, while a 0 bit leaves the corresponding pixel unchanged. Therefore, a solid fill pattern would be eight rows of 11111111 binary, or xFF\xFF\xFF\xFF\xFF\xFF\xFF\xFF hex. The color argument sets the fill color.

The setfillstyle function requires less planning than the setfillpattern function, but it also provides less flexibility.

Listing 4.2 and Figure 4.9 demonstrate the use of the bar, bar3d, and rectangle functions using the same fill pattern, fill color, line style, and current color.

Listing 4.2. Using the bar, bar3d, and rectangle functions

```
#include <graphics.h>
#include <stdio.h>
#include <stdlib.h>
#include <conio.h>

int main ()
{
int gdriver = EGA;
int gmode = EGAHI;

    /* register EGAVGA_driver and sansserif_font */
    /* ... these have been added to graphics.lib */
    /* as described in UTIL.DOC                   */

registerbgidriver (EGAVGA_driver);
registerbgifont (sansserif_font);

    /* set EGA 16-color high resolution video mode  */

initgraph (&gdriver,&gmode,"");
rectangle (0,0,639,349);

    /* set fill color, fill pattern, line style */
    /* and current color                        */

setfillstyle (WIDE_DOT_FILL,15);
setcolor (15);
setlinestyle (DASHED_LINE,0xFFFF,1);

    /* draw bar */
```

```
bar (50,50,150,300);

     /* draw 3-d bar */

bar3d (270,50,370,300,20,1);

     /* draw rectangle */

rectangle (590,50,490,300);

     /* Delay and Exit */

settextjustify(CENTER_TEXT,BOTTOM_TEXT);
outtextxy (320,320,"Press Any Key To Exit");

getch ();

closegraph();
return 0;
}
```

Figure 4.9. Screen output for Listing 4.2

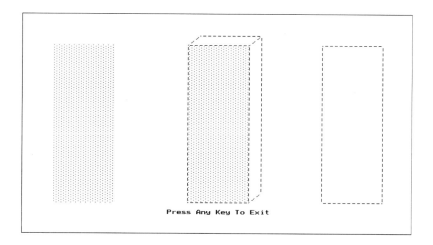

As demonstrated in this example, the bar, bar3d, and rectangle functions each offer unique features. You can produce an almost unlimited combination of rectangular figures with these three functions in combination, and with various fill patterns, line styles, and colors.

Polygons

Borland C++ provides two functions for drawing polygons—the `drawpoly` and `fillpoly` functions. These functions create multisided, filled, or unfilled images.

Use the `drawpoly` function to draw the border of the specified polygon with the current line style and current color. The figure is not filled with this function. As the following syntax shows, there are two arguments for the `drawpoly` function. The `numpoints` argument defines the number of points in the polygon. This number is equal to the actual number of points in the figure plus one. For example, an octagon (8 sides) would require `numpoints` to be set to 9. The reason for this is that the `drawpoly` function does not automatically close the figure. Therefore, in order to create a closed figure, the last point must be equal to the first.

The `*polypoints` argument contains the x and y values of the points. The length of this array is two times the `numpoints` argument. For example, the octagon with 9 points would require the `*polypoints` array to contain 18 values. The first two values represent the x and y values, respectively, of the first point. Similarly, the third and fourth values represent the x and y values of the second point, and so forth.

```
void far drawpoly(int numpoints, int far *polypoints);

int numpoints;              Number of points + 1
int far *polypoints;        The x and y values of the points
```

You can use the `fillpoly` function to display a polygon outlined in the current color and line style and filled with the current fill pattern and fill color. The syntax for the `fillpoly` function is similar to that of the `drawpoly` function. However, the arguments are defined in a different manner.

```
void far fillpoly(int numpoints, int far *polypoints);

int numpoints;              Number of points
int far *polypoints;        The x and y values of the points
```

The `numpoints` argument is used to specify the number of points in the polygon. This number should be *equal* to the number of sides, or points, in the polygon. For example, `numpoints` should equal 8 for an octagon. Note that this is different from the `drawpoly` function, in that the `fillpoly` function automatically closes the figure. Therefore, there is no need to set the last point equal to the first. The `*polypoints` array contains the x and y values of the polygon's points and should be two times the number of points in length. It is used in exactly the same manner as with the `drawpoly` function.

You can use the following functions with the `drawpoly` and `fillpoly` functions to create a variety of fill and outline combinations. The `setcolor` function defines the current color, thus the color of the polygon's border. The `setlinestyle` function is used to define border's style (dashed, dotted, etc.). The `setfillpattern` function or the `setfillstyle` function is used to set the current fill pattern and current fill color.

Listing 4.3 produces two triangles using the `drawpoly` and `fillpoly` functions (see Figure 4.10).

Listing 4.3. Drawing triangles with drawpoly and fillpoly

```
#include <graphics.h>
#include <stdio.h>
#include <stdlib.h>
#include <conio.h>

int main ()
{
int gdriver = EGA;
int gmode = EGAHI;
int triangle1[8];   /* for the drawpoly function */
int triangle2[6];   /* for the fillpoly function */

     /* register EGAVGA_driver and sansserif_font */
     /* ... these have been added to graphics.lib */
     /* as described in UTIL.DOC                  */

registerbgidriver (EGAVGA_driver);
registerbgifont (sansserif_font);

     /* set EGA 16-color high resolution video mode  */

initgraph (&gdriver,&gmode,"");
rectangle (0,0,639,349);

     /* set fill pattern and color, current color, line style */

setlinestyle (DASHED_LINE,0xFFFF,NORM_WIDTH);
setcolor (15);
setfillstyle (WIDE_DOT_FILL,15);

     /* define and draw triangle 1 - use drawpoly */

triangle1 [0] = 200;
triangle1 [1] = 50;
triangle1 [2] = 300;
triangle1 [3] = 300;
triangle1 [4] = 100;
triangle1 [5] = 300;
triangle1 [6] = 200;
triangle1 [7] = 50;

drawpoly (4,triangle1);

     /* define and draw triangle 2 - use fillpoly */

triangle2 [0] = 440;
triangle2 [1] = 50;
triangle2 [2] = 540;
triangle2 [3] = 300;
triangle2 [4] = 340;
triangle2 [5] = 300;
```

Listing 4.3. *continues*

Listing 4.3. cont.   Drawing triangles with `drawpoly` and `fillpoly`

```
fillpoly (3,triangle2);

    /* Delay and Exit */

settextjustify(CENTER_TEXT,BOTTOM_TEXT);
outtextxy (320,320,"Press Any Key To Exit");

getch ();

closegraph();
return 0;
}
```

Figure 4.10.   Screen output from Listing 4.3

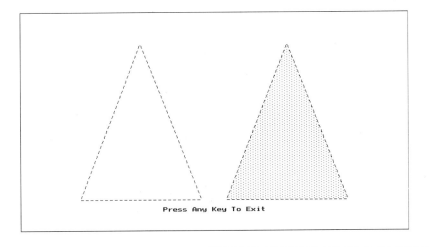

Arcs

The Borland C++ graphics library provides two functions for creating arcs. The first, the `arc` function, is used to create a circular arc. The second, the `ellipse` function, is used to create an elliptical arc.

The arc function displays a circular arc. As the following syntax shows, there are five arguments passed. The x and y arguments define the center of the circular arc. The arc begins at the angle specified by the startangle argument, extends in a counterclockwise direction, and ends at the angle specified by the endangle argument. These angles are defined in reference to 0 degrees being equal to the 3 o'clock position, 90 degrees to the 12 o'clock position, and so forth. The radius argument defines the horizontal radius of the circular arc. The aspect ratio, as defined by the graphics library, is used to ensure that the arc is circular.

The arc is drawn in the current color, as set by the setcolor function, and current line thickness, as defined by the setlinestyle function. The arc function ignores the linestyle argument of the setlinestyle function. Figure 4.11 illustrates the use of the arc function.

```
void far arc(int x, int y, int startangle, int endangle,
            int radius);

int x, y;               Center of arc
int startangle;         Starting angle for arc
int endangle;           Ending angle for arc
int radius;             Horizontal radius for arc
```

Figure 4.11. The arc function

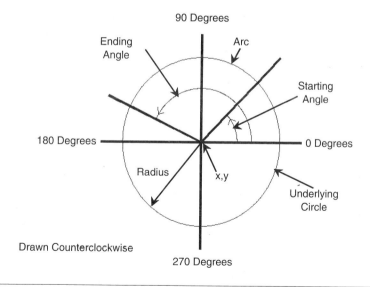

The `ellipse` function is similar to the `arc` function except that it produces an elliptical arc rather than a circular one. There are six arguments passed to the `ellipse` function as shown in the following syntax.

```
void far ellipse(int x, int y, int startangle, int endangle,
                 int xradius, int yradius);
```

```
int x, y;              Center of elliptical arc
int startangle;        Starting angle
int endangle;          Ending angle
int xradius;           Horizontal radius of arc
int yradius;           Vertical radius of arc
```

The x and y arguments define the center of the elliptical arc. The arc begins at the angle defined by the `startangle` argument, extends in a counterclockwise direction, and ends at the angle defined by the `endangle` argument. The `xradius` argument defines the horizontal radius of the arc, while the `yradius` argument defines the arc's vertical radius.

As with the `arc` function, the arc is drawn in the current color, as set by the `setcolor` function, and current line thickness, as set by the `setlinestyle` function. The `ellipse` function ignores the `linestyle` argument of the `setlinestyle` function. Figure 4.12 illustrates the use of the `ellipse` function.

Figure 4.12. The `ellipse` function

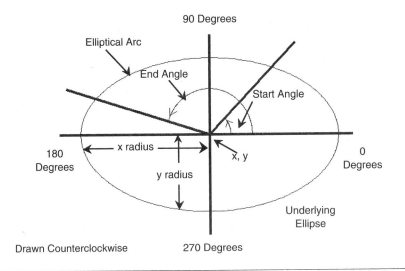

The following example demonstrates the use of arc and ellipse functions.

Listing 4.4. Using the arc and ellipse functions

```c
#include <graphics.h>
#include <stdio.h>
#include <stdlib.h>
#include <conio.h>

int main ()
{
int gdriver = EGA;
int gmode = EGAHI;

    /* register EGAVGA_driver and sansserif_font */
    /* ... these have been added to graphics.lib */
    /* as described in UTIL.DOC                   */

registerbgidriver (EGAVGA_driver);
registerbgifont (sansserif_font);

    /* set EGA 16-color high resolution video mode  */

initgraph (&gdriver,&gmode,"");
rectangle (0,0,639,349);

    /* define current line thickness and current color */

setlinestyle (SOLID_LINE,0xFFFF,THICK_WIDTH);
setcolor (15);

    /* draw half of two arcs with thick lines */

arc (320,175,0,180,75);
ellipse (320,175,0,180,250,75);

    /* draw other half of arcs with thin lines */

setlinestyle (SOLID_LINE,0xFFFF,NORM_WIDTH);
arc (320,175,180,360,75);
ellipse (320,175,180,360,250,75);

    /* Delay and Exit */

settextjustify(CENTER_TEXT,BOTTOM_TEXT);
outtextxy (320,320,"Press Any Key To Exit");

getch ();
closegraph();
return 0;
}
```

Figure 4.13. Screen output from Listing 4.4

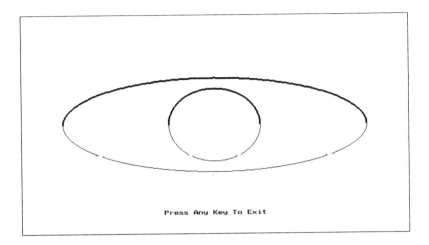

Circles and Ellipses
===================

There are several functions in the Borland C++ graphics library that you can use to create circles and ellipses. These functions include the `circle`, `ellipse`, and `fillellipse` functions.

The `circle` function is used to draw a circle (see the following syntax). The circle is centered on the point defined by the x and y arguments. The `radius` argument defines the horizontal, or x, radius. The aspect ratio, as determined by the graphics library, is considered when calculating the circle to make sure that the circle is round. The circle is not filled by this function. The border of the circle is drawn using the current color, as set by the `setcolor` function, and the current line thickness, as set by the `setlinestyle` function. Only the thickness parameter of the `setlinestyle` function is used by the `circle` function.

```
void far circle(int x, int y, int radius);

int x, y;        Center of circle
int radius;      Radius of circle
```

Figure 4.14 illustrates the use of the `circle` function.

Figure 4.14. The `circle` function

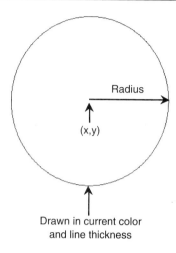

Radius

(x,y)

Drawn in current color
and line thickness

The `ellipse` function, as the following syntax shows, is similar to the `arc` function, with the exception that it produces an elliptical arc. The elliptical arc is centered at the point specified by the x and y arguments. It begins at the angle defined by `startangle` and ends at the angle defined by `endangle`. The `xradius` argument specifies the length of the radius (in pixels) of the arc in the horizontal direction, while the `yradius` argument specifies the length of the radius of the arc (in pixels) in the vertical direction. By setting `startangle` to 0 and `endangle` to 360, you can draw an ellipse. However, the main purpose of the `ellipse` function is to create elliptical arcs. Therefore, the `ellipse` function is described in detail in the following section.

```
void far ellipse(int x, int y, int startangle, int endangle,
                 int xradius, int yradius);

int x, y;           Center of elliptical arc
int startangle;     Starting angle of arc
int endangle;       Ending angle of arc
int xradius;        Horizontal radius of arc
int yradius;        Vertical radius of arc
```

The `fillellipse` function is used draw a filled ellipse. The following syntax is used for this function.

```
void far fillellipse(int x, int y, int xradius,
                     int yradius);

int x, y;           Center of ellipse
int xradius;        Horizontal radius of ellipse
int yradius;        Vertical radius of ellipse
```

The ellipse is centered on the point defined by the x and y arguments. The xradius argument defines the radius of the ellipse in the horizontal direction, while the yradius argument defines the radius in the vertical direction.

The border of the ellipse is drawn in the current color, as set by the setcolor function. The ellipse is filled with the current fill color and fill pattern, as set by either the setfillpattern or setfillstyle function. Figure 4.15 illustrates the use of the fillellipse function.

Figure 4.15. The fillellipse function

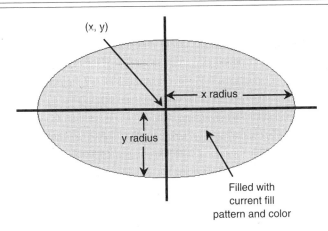

Listing 4.5 and Figure 4.16 illustrate the use of the arc, circle, ellipse, and fillellipse functions.

Listing 4.5. Using arc, circle, ellipse, and fillellipse

```
#include <graphics.h>
#include <stdio.h>
#include <stdlib.h>
#include <conio.h>

int main ()
{
int gdriver = EGA;
int gmode = EGAHI;

        /* register EGAVGA_driver and sansserif_font */
        /* ... these have been added to graphics.lib */
        /* as described in UTIL.DOC                   */
```

```
registerbgidriver (EGAVGA_driver);
registerbgifont (sansserif_font);

     /* set EGA 16-color high resolution video mode  */

initgraph (&gdriver,&gmode,"");
rectangle (0,0,639,349);

     /* define the current color, fill pattern, fill color */
     /* and line thickness                                 */

setcolor (15);
setlinestyle (SOLID_LINE,0xFFFF,NORM_WIDTH);
setfillstyle (WIDE_DOT_FILL,15);

     /* draw circle with arc function */

arc (200,100,0,360,50);

     /* draw circle with circle function */

circle (200,250,50);

     /* draw ellipse with ellipse function */

ellipse (440,100,0,360,75,25);

     /* draw filled ellipse with fillellipse function */

fillellipse (440,250,75,25);

     /* Delay and Exit */

settextjustify(CENTER_TEXT,BOTTOM_TEXT);
outtextxy (320,320,"Press Any Key To Exit");
getch ();
closegraph();
return 0;
}
```

Complex Curves

Other than the arc and ellipse functions, there are no provisions for creating complex
curves in the Borland C++ libraries. Therefore, here are several methods for creating
complex curves.

Figure 4.16. Screen output from Listing 4.5

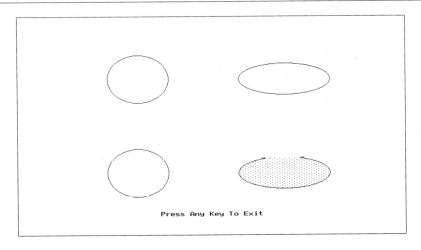

Press Any Key To Exit

Curves Using the arc and ellipse Functions

The arc and ellipse functions provide an easy way to create simple circular and elliptical arcs. However, displaying complex curves and waveforms with these functions requires a great deal of design and planning.

The following paragraphs describe the methods used to create complex curves with the arc and ellipse functions.

The simplest complex curve you can create with the arc and ellipse functions is the *sinusoidal waveform*. In order to create this waveform, you must complete several steps. First, sketch the waveform. It is important to remember that the aspect ratio of most modes is not 1 (square pixels). Therefore, when you are drawing either the grid on the graph paper should reflect the pixel dimensions, or the y values of each point should be multiplied by the aspect ratio. Figure 4.17 illustrates the sinusoidal waveform.

After you draw the waveform, you should identify all the points you plotted to draw the waveform and label their coordinates. When all the points are identified, place them into the appropriate functions to display the curve.

The following code implements the arc and ellipse functions to display overlying sinusoidal waves.

Figure 4.17. The sinusoidal waveform

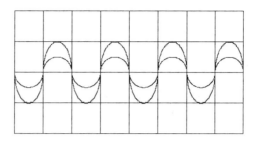

Listing 4.6. Sinusoidal wave example

```c
#include <graphics.h>
#include <stdio.h>
#include <stdlib.h>
#include <conio.h>

int main ()
{
int gdriver = EGA;
int gmode = EGAHI;

      /* register EGAVGA_driver and sansserif_font */
      /* ... these have been added to graphics.lib */
      /* as described in UTIL.DOC                   */

registerbgidriver (EGAVGA_driver);
registerbgifont (sansserif_font);

      /* set EGA 16-color high resolution video mode  */

initgraph (&gdriver,&gmode,"");
rectangle (0,0,639,349);

      /* define the current color and line thickness */

setcolor (15);
setlinestyle (SOLID_LINE,0xFFFF,THICK_WIDTH);

      /* draw sinusoidal wave */

line (0,175,639,175);
arc(40,175,180,360,40);
ellipse(40,175,180,360,40,100);

arc(120,175,0,180,40);
ellipse(120,175,0,180,40,100);
```

Listing 4.6. *continues*

89

Listing 4.6. cont. Sinusoidal wave example

```
arc(200,175,180,360,40);
ellipse(200,175,180,360,40,100);

arc(280,175,0,180,40);
ellipse(280,175,0,180,40,100);

arc(360,175,180,360,40);
ellipse(360,175,180,360,40,100);

arc(440,175,0,180,40);
ellipse(440,175,0,180,40,100);

arc(520,175,180,360,40);
ellipse(520,175,180,360,40,100);

arc(600,175,0,180,40);
ellipse(600,175,0,180,40,100);

      /* Delay and Exit */

settextjustify(CENTER_TEXT,BOTTOM_TEXT);
outtextxy (320,320,"Press Any Key To Exit");

getch ();
closegraph();
return 0;
}
```

Figure 4.18. Screen output from Listing 4.6

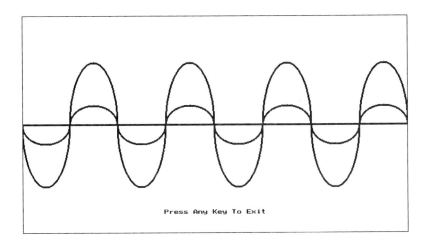

The Straight-Line Approximation Method

The easiest way to create a curve is to simply connect a series of short lines that approximate the shape of the curve. This method produces good results with small curves, as long as the lines are very short. However, this method requires a lot of time and patience. The straight-line approximation method is especially useful with small curves, which require the entry of only a few points. Figure 4.19 illustrates the principle behind the straight-line approximation method. Again, the key to successful implementation of this method is keeping the lines short and using only small curves.

Figure 4.19. The straight-line approximation

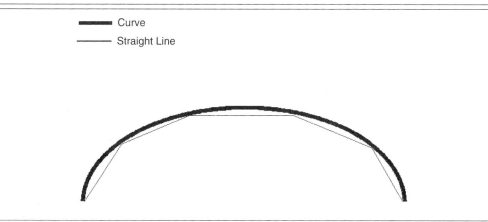

The following example (see Listing 4.7 and Figure 4.20) illustrates the use of straight-line approximation for creating an outline of the MIG-29 fighter aircraft. If the straight-line approximation method was not used in this example for the creation of the curves, but instead the curve drawing functions were used, the demonstration would have required a great deal more planning and careful sketching.

Listing 4.7. MIG-29 fighter aircraft example

```
#include <graphics.h>
#include <stdio.h>
#include <stdlib.h>
#include <conio.h>

int main ()
{
int gdriver = EGA;
int gmode = EGAHI;
```

Listing 4.7. *continues*

Listing 4.7. cont.   MIG-29 fighter aircraft example

```
        /* register EGAVGA_driver and sansserif_font */
        /* ... these have been added to graphics.lib */
        /* as described in UTIL.DOC                   */

registerbgidriver (EGAVGA_driver);
registerbgifont (sansserif_font);

        /* set EGA 16-color high resolution video mode  */

initgraph (&gdriver,&gmode,"");
rectangle (0,0,639,349);
rectangle (210,25,610,325);

        /* draw MIG-29 */

moveto (240,255);
lineto (260,250);
lineto (275,248);
lineto (289,245);
lineto (300,244);
lineto (310,239);
lineto (318,236);
lineto (328,234);
lineto (335,234);
lineto (345,234);
lineto (360,236);
lineto (375,240);
lineto (465,250);
lineto (498,240);
lineto (530,215);
lineto (540,220);
lineto (530,252);
lineto (542,252);
lineto (542,266);
lineto (530,266);
lineto (467,270);
lineto (390,270);
lineto (381,260);
lineto (290,260);
lineto (275,259);
lineto (260,258);
lineto (240,255);

moveto (290,260);
lineto (290,245);

moveto (300,244);
lineto (320,245);
lineto (340,245);
lineto (375,240);
```

```
moveto (300,244);
lineto (320,245);
lineto (340,245);
lineto (375,240);

moveto (318,236);
lineto (320,245);

moveto (345,234);
lineto (340,245);

moveto (530,266);
lineto (530,252);

moveto (538,225);
lineto (533,225);
lineto (520,250);
lineto (531,250);

moveto (465,250);
lineto (452,255);
lineto (310,255);
lineto (500,260);
lineto (490,255);

moveto (452,255);
lineto (530,253);

moveto (381,260);
lineto (391,260);
lineto (400,270);

moveto (510,258);
lineto (559,258);
lineto (575,262);
lineto (540,262);
lineto (510,258);

moveto (479,270);
lineto (482,272);
lineto (525,270);
lineto (525,267);

settextstyle (SANS_SERIF_FONT,VERT_DIR,0);
settextjustify (CENTER_TEXT,CENTER_TEXT);
outtextxy (105,175,"SOVIET FIGHTER");
settextstyle (SANS_SERIF_FONT,HORIZ_DIR,0);
outtextxy (410,100,"MIG 29");

    /* Delay and Exit */

getch ();
closegraph();
return 0;
}
```

Figure 4.20. Screen output from Listing 4.7

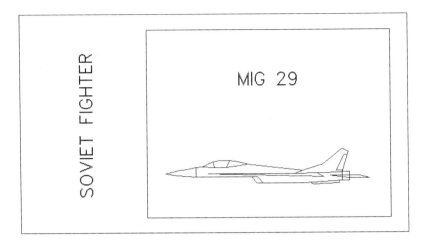

The Bézier Curve

The *Bézier curve* was developed by the French mathematician Pierre Bézier for use in automobile design. This curve is generally defined by four points. The four points consist of two end points and two control points. The curve begins at one end point and terminates at the other. The two control points are used to determine the curvature of the line.

Figure 4.21 illustrates, in geometric terms, the principle behind the Bézier curve. The first step to reproducing the curve geometrically is to draw the end and control points. Then draw three lines to connect **1)** the control and end points and **2)** the control points. From these lines, you should draw two more lines to connect the midpoints of the lines. Next, from the four inner line segments, you should draw more lines to connect the midpoints of the line segments. This process, if repeated, gives the basic shape of the expected curve.

The mathematical derivation of the Bézier curve is not trivial. For most users, however, there is really no need to derive the equations. Just knowing how to use the equations to implement the curve is sufficient. The Bézier curve uses parametric cubic equations, which use variables raised to the third power. These equations are described in the following equations, where t represents a variable that ranges from 0 to 1. In order to understand the equations, some notation needs to be made. The x0 and y0 parameters define the initial point of the curve. The x1 and y1 parameters define the first control point, while x2 and y2 define the second control point. The ending point is defined by x3 and y3. In these equations, a, b, c, and d are constants.

```
x(t) = axt3 + bxt2 + cxt + dx

y(t) = ayt3 + byt2 + cyt + dy
```

Figure 4.21. The geometric form of the Bézier curve

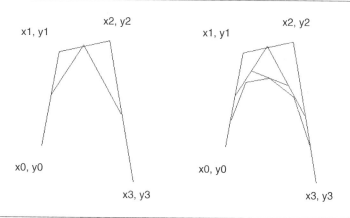

The mathematical representation of the Bézier curve makes several assumptions. The first of these assumptions is that the curve passes through the point (x0,y0) when t equals 0. The second assumption is that the curve passes through the point (x3,y3) when t equals 1. The other assumptions deal with the slope of the lines at the initial and ending points.

```
1)  when t=0:      x(0) = x0
                   y(0) = y0

2)  when t=1:      x(1) = x3
                   y(1) = y3

3)  initial slope:  x(0)' = 3(x1-x0)
                    y(0)' = 3(y1-y0)

4)  ending slope:   x(1)' = 3(x3-x2)
                    y(1)' = 3(y3-y2)
```

The final form of the Bézier curve formulas is:

```
x(t) = (1-t)3x0 + 3t(1-t)2x1 + 3t2(1-t)x2 + t3x3

y(t) = (1-t)3y0 + 3t(1-t)2y1 + 3t2(1-t)y2 + t3y3
```

95

You can easily incorporate these formulas into a function that creates the curve. The resolution of the curve can be adjusted by the variable t. As t gets bigger (keeping in mind that t must be between 0 and 1), the curve becomes less smooth. Similarly, as t gets smaller, the curve becomes more smooth but requires more processing time for calculation and drawing. Listing 4.8 and figure 4.22 demonstrate the implementation of the Bézier curve using four points.

Listing 4.8. Bézier curve example

```
#include <graphics.h>
#include <stdio.h>
#include <stdlib.h>
#include <conio.h>

int main ()
{
int gdriver = EGA;
int gmode = EGAHI;

    /* register EGAVGA_driver and sansserif_font */
    /* ... these have been added to graphics.lib */
    /* as described in UTIL.DOC                  */

registerbgidriver (EGAVGA_driver);
registerbgifont (sansserif_font);

    /* set EGA 16-color high resolution video mode  */

initgraph (&gdriver,&gmode,"");
rectangle (0,0,639,349);

    /* draw B zier curve and mark the four points */

circle (50,300,10);     /* point 1 */
circle (430,50,10);     /* point 2 */
circle (610,100,10);    /* point 3 */
circle (320,250,10);    /* point 4 */

Bézier (50,300,430,50,610,100,320,250);

    /* Delay and Exit */

settextjustify(CENTER_TEXT,BOTTOM_TEXT);
outtextxy (320,320,"Press Any Key To Exit");

getch ();

closegraph();
return 0;
}
```

```
int Bézier (int x0, int y0, int x1, int y1,
        int x2, int y2, int x3, int y3)
{
float x, y;
int x_temp, y_temp;
float i, t;

t = .01;  /* corresponds to 100 line segment in the curve */

moveto (x0,y0);

i = 0.0;

do {

    x = (((1-i)*(1-i)*(1-i))*x0)+(3*i*((1-i)*(1-i))*x1)+
        (3*(i*i)*(1-i)*x2)+((i*i*i)*x3);

    y = (((1-i)*(1-i)*(1-i))*y0)+(3*i*((1-i)*(1-i))*y1)+
        (3*(i*i)*(1-i)*y2)+((i*i*i)*y3);

    x_temp = (int)x;
    y_temp = (int)y;

    lineto (x_temp,y_temp);
    i = i + t;

    } while (i <= 1.0);

return 0;
}
```

Figure 4.22. Screen output from Listing 4.8

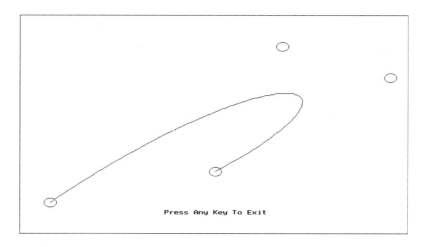

Press Any Key To Exit

Area Fills

The `floodfill` function gives you the ability to fill a bound area with the current fill color and fill pattern. The `floodfill` function adds to the previous drawing functions' capabilities by allowing the programmer to add various colors and fill patterns to figures. The following syntax is used for the `floodfill` function:

```
void far floodfill(int x, int y, int border);

int x, y;          Starting point for fill routine
int border;        Border color of bound area
```

The `floodfill` function uses the current fill color and fill pattern to fill an area surrounded by the border color specified in the border argument. The x and y arguments define the point at which the fill will begin. If the point defined by the x and y arguments lies within the bound area, the inside of the area is filled. If the point lies outside the area, the outside will be filled.

You can set the current fill pattern and fill color with either the `setfillpattern` function or the `setfillstyle` function. These functions accept two arguments. The first argument defines the fill pattern. For the `setfillpattern` function, the pattern is an 8-by-8 bit map that is defined by the user. For the `setfillstyle` function, the fill pattern is selected from the predefined fill patterns shown in Table 4.2. The second argument identifies the color value of the fill color.

In order to use the `setfillpattern` function, you must define a fill pattern. The fill pattern consists of eight rows of eight bits each. Each bit in the pattern corresponds to one pixel on the screen. If the pattern bit is 1, the corresponding screen pixel is set to the current fill color. If the bit is 0, the screen pixel remains unchanged.

An example fill pattern would be eight rows of 11111111 binary or xFF hex. With this pattern every pixel in the fill area would be set to the current fill color—a solid fill pattern. The corresponding fill pattern would be \xFF\xFF\xFF\xFF\xFF\xFF\xFF\xFF.

Appendix B contains a series of fill patterns that can be used to define fill patterns ranging from three percent to 100 percent.

Listing 4.9 and Figure 4.23 demonstrate the use of the `setfillstyle` function and the `floodfill` function to create several filled rectangles.

Listing 4.9. Using `floodfill` and `setfillstyle` for area fills

```
#include <graphics.h>
#include <stdio.h>
#include <stdlib.h>
#include <conio.h>
```

```c
int main ()
{
int gdriver = EGA;
int gmode = EGAHI;
int x;
int pattern = 0;

    /* register EGAVGA_driver and sansserif_font */
    /* ... these have been added to graphics.lib */
    /* as described in UTIL.DOC                   */

registerbgidriver (EGAVGA_driver);
registerbgifont (sansserif_font);

    /* set EGA 16-color high resolution video mode  */

initgraph (&gdriver,&gmode,"");
rectangle (0,0,639,349);

    /* draw 12 rectangles */

for (x=15; x<550; x=x+106)
    {
    rectangle (x,20,x+80,150);
    rectangle (x,170,x+80,300);
    }

    /* fill top rectangles   */

for (x=16; x<550; x=x+106)
    {
    setfillstyle(pattern,15);
    floodfill(x,21,15);
    pattern = pattern + 1;
    }

    /* fill bottom rectangles */

for (x=16; x<550; x=x+106)
    {
    setfillstyle(pattern,15);
    floodfill(x,171,15);
    pattern = pattern + 1;
    }

    /* Delay and Exit */

settextjustify(CENTER_TEXT,BOTTOM_TEXT);
outtextxy (320,320,"Press Any Key To Exit");

getch ();
closegraph();
return 0;
}
```

Figure 4.23. Screen output from Listing 4.9

Listing 4.10 and Figure 4.24 demonstrate the use of the setfillpattern and floodfill functions to create a series of filled rectangles.

Listing 4.10. Using floodfill and setfillpattern for area fills

```
#include <graphics.h>
#include <stdio.h>
#include <stdlib.h>
#include <conio.h>

unsigned char *(fillpattern [12]) =
   {"\x00\x20\x00\x00\x00\x02\x00\x00",
    "\x20\x00\x02\x00\x80\x00\x08\x00",
    "\x20\x02\x80\x08\x20\x02\x80\x08",
    "\x44\x11\x44\x11\x44\x11\x44\x11",
    "\xAA\x44\xAA\x11\xAA\x44\xAA\x11",
    "\x55\xAA\x55\xAA\x55\xAA\x55\xAA",
    "\x55\xBB\x55\xEE\x55\xBB\x55\xEE",
    "\xBB\xEE\xBB\xEE\xBB\xEE\xBB\xEE",
    "\xDF\xFF\x7F\xF7\xDF\xFD\x7F\xF7",
    "\xDF\xFF\xFD\xFF\x7F\xFF\xF7\xFF",
    "\xFF\xDF\xFF\xFF\xFF\xFD\xFF\xFF",
    "\xFF\xFF\xFF\xFF\xFF\xFF\xFF\xFF"};

int main ()
{
int gdriver = EGA;
```

```
int gmode = EGAHI;
int x;
int pattern = 0;

     /* register EGAVGA_driver and sansserif_font */
     /* ... these have been added to graphics.lib */
     /* as described in UTIL.DOC                   */

registerbgidriver (EGAVGA_driver);
registerbgifont (sansserif_font);

     /* set EGA 16-color high resolution video mode  */

initgraph (&gdriver,&gmode,"");
rectangle (0,0,639,349);

     /* draw 12 rectangles */

for (x=15; x<550; x=x+106)
     {
     rectangle (x,20,x+80,150);
     rectangle (x,170,x+80,300);
     }

     /* fill top rectangles  */

for (x=16; x<550; x=x+106)
     {
     setfillpattern((char far *)(fillpattern[pattern]),15);
     floodfill(x,21,15);
     pattern = pattern + 1;
     }

     /* fill bottom rectangles */

for (x=16; x<550; x=x+106)
     {
     setfillpattern((char far *)(fillpattern[pattern]),15);
     floodfill(x,171,15);
     pattern = pattern + 1;
     }

     /* Delay and Exit */

settextjustify(CENTER_TEXT,BOTTOM_TEXT);
outtextxy (320,320,"Press Any Key To Exit");

getch ();

closegraph();
return 0;
}
```

Figure 4.24. Screen output from Listing 4.10

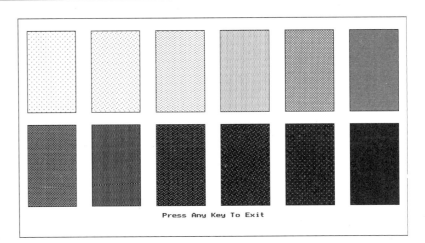

Halftoning and Shading

As described in the previous section, you can use fill patterns to create various shades and half-toning effects. These effects are created by partially filling a specified area. For example, using black and white, and the fill patterns provided in Appendix B, you can create thirteen shades of gray.

The ability to shade and half-tone allows the programmer to make the most of limited colors. This is especially important in two-color and four-color modes. One of the effects that shading and halftoning can create is the airbrushed image. Instead of distinct lines, an airbrushed image contains indistinct edges—the edges seem to blend together smoothly. By dividing the image into smaller images and filling the smaller images with increasing or decreasing fill patterns, you can obtain some spectacular airbrushed effects.

Listing 4.11 and Figure 4.25 demonstrate the use of various fill patterns, as defined in Appendix B, to create an airbrushed horizon.

Listing 4.11. Horizon example

```
#include <graphics.h>
#include <stdio.h>
#include <stdlib.h>
#include <conio.h>

unsigned char *(fillpattern [12]) =
   {"\x00\x20\x00\x00\x00\x02\x00\x00",
    "\x20\x00\x02\x00\x80\x00\x08\x00",
```

```
                     "\x20\x02\x80\x08\x20\x02\x80\x08",
                     "\x44\x11\x44\x11\x44\x11\x44\x11",
                     "\xAA\x44\xAA\x11\xAA\x44\xAA\x11",
                     "\x55\xAA\x55\xAA\x55\xAA\x55\xAA",
                     "\x55\xBB\x55\xEE\x55\xBB\x55\xEE",
                     "\xBB\xEE\xBB\xEE\xBB\xEE\xBB\xEE",
                     "\xDF\xFF\x7F\xF7\xDF\xFD\x7F\xF7",
                     "\xDF\xFF\xFD\xFF\x7F\xFF\xF7\xFF",
                     "\xFF\xDF\xFF\xFF\xFF\xFD\xFF\xFF",
                     "\xFF\xFF\xFF\xFF\xFF\xFF\xFF\xFF"};

int main ()
{
int gdriver = EGA;
int gmode = EGAHI;
int y;
int pattern = 0;

     /* register EGAVGA_driver and sansserif_font */
     /* ... these have been added to graphics.lib */
     /* as described in UTIL.DOC                  */

registerbgidriver (EGAVGA_driver);
registerbgifont (sansserif_font);

     /* set EGA 16-color high resolution video mode  */

initgraph (&gdriver,&gmode,"");
rectangle (0,0,639,349);

     /* draw horizon */

for (y=150; y<210; y=y+5)
     {
     setfillpattern((char far *)(fillpattern[pattern]),15);
     bar(1,y,638,y+10);
     pattern = pattern + 1;
     }

     /* fill bottom of screen */

setfillpattern ((char far *)(fillpattern[11]),15);
bar (1,215,638,349);

     /* Delay and Exit */

setcolor (0);
settextjustify(CENTER_TEXT,BOTTOM_TEXT);
outtextxy (320,320,"Press Any Key To Exit");

getch ();
closegraph();
return 0;
}
```

Figure 4.25. Screen output from Listing 4.11

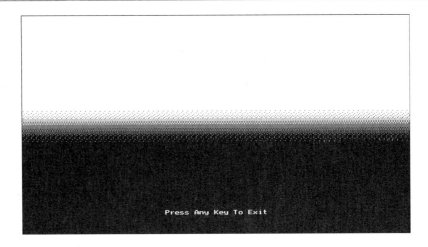

Listing 4.12 and Figure 4.26 demonstrate the use of airbrushed effects. These examples enlarge the airbrushed areas so that it is obvious how the fill patterns are being used. For most purposes, the area to be airbrushed will be much smaller.

Listing 4.12. Airbrushed effects

```
#include <graphics.h>
#include <stdio.h>
#include <stdlib.h>
#include <conio.h>

unsigned char *(fillpattern [12]) =
  {"\x00\x20\x00\x00\x00\x02\x00\x00",
   "\x20\x00\x02\x00\x80\x00\x08\x00",
   "\x20\x02\x80\x08\x20\x02\x80\x08",
   "\x44\x11\x44\x11\x44\x11\x44\x11",
   "\xAA\x44\xAA\x11\xAA\x44\xAA\x11",
   "\x55\xAA\x55\xAA\x55\xAA\x55\xAA",
   "\x55\xBB\x55\xEE\x55\xBB\x55\xEE",
   "\xBB\xEE\xBB\xEE\xBB\xEE\xBB\xEE",
   "\xDF\xFF\x7F\xF7\xDF\xFD\x7F\xF7",
   "\xDF\xFF\xFD\xFF\x7F\xFF\xF7\xFF",
   "\xFF\xDF\xFF\xFF\xFF\xFD\xFF\xFF",
   "\xFF\xFF\xFF\xFF\xFF\xFF\xFF\xFF"};
```

```
int main ()
{
int gdriver = EGA;
int gmode = EGAHI;
int x1, y1, x2, y2;
int pattern = 0;

x1 = 150;
x2 = 490;
y1 = 50;
y2 = 275;


    /* register EGAVGA_driver and sansserif_font */
    /* ... these have been added to graphics.lib */
    /* as described in UTIL.DOC                  */

registerbgidriver (EGAVGA_driver);
registerbgifont (sansserif_font);

    /* set EGA 16-color high resolution video mode  */

initgraph (&gdriver,&gmode,"");
rectangle (0,0,639,349);

    /* draw bars */
do
  {
  setfillpattern((char far *)(fillpattern[pattern]),15);
  bar(x1,y1,x2,y2);
  x1 = x1+5;
  x2 = x2-5;
  y1 = y1+3;
  y2 = y2-3;
  pattern = pattern + 1;
  } while (pattern != 12);

    /* Delay and Exit */

settextjustify(CENTER_TEXT,BOTTOM_TEXT);
outtextxy (320,320,"Press Any Key To Exit");

getch ();
closegraph();
return 0;
}
```

Figure 4.26. Screen output from Listing 4.12

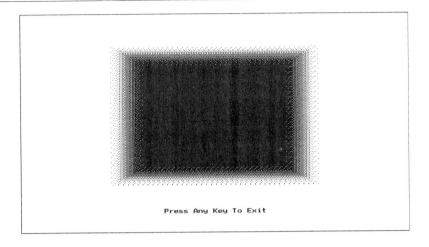

Pie Slices and Sectors

You can create both elliptical and circular wedges with Borland C++. The functions that create these images are the `pieslice` and `sector` functions. The syntax for the `pieslice` function is shown next, followed by Figure 4.27, which illustrates the `pieslice` function.

```
void far pieslice(int x, int y, int startangle,
                  int endangle, int radius);

int x, y;           Center of circular wedge
int startangle;     Starting angle for wedge
int endangle;       Ending angle for wedge
int radius;         Horizontal radius
```

The syntax for the `sector` function is given next, followed by an illustration of the `sector` function in Figure 4.28.

```
void far sector(int x, int y, int startangle,
                int endangle, int xradius, int yradius);

int x, y;           Center of elliptical wedge
int startangle;     Starting angle for wedge
int endangle;       Ending angle for wedge
int xradius;        Horizontal radius
int yradius;        Vertical radius
```

Figure 4.27. The pieslice function

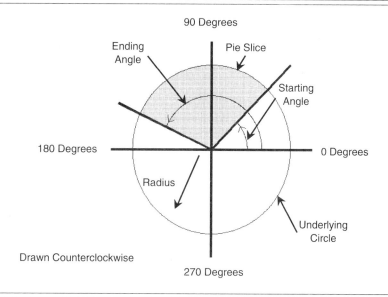

Figure 4.28. The sector function

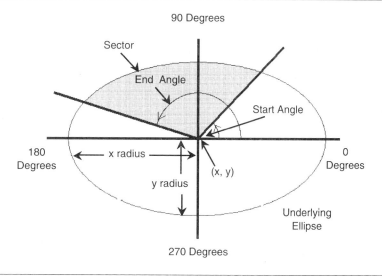

The main difference between these functions is that the `pieslice` function produces a circular wedge, while the `sector` function produces an elliptical wedge. The x and y arguments of these functions specify the center of the wedge. The arc of the wedge begins at the angle defined by the starting angle arguments, extends counterclockwise, and ends at the angle specified by the `endangle` arguments. The `pieslice` function uses the horizontal radius—as defined by the `radius` argument—and the aspect ratio to calculate and display the circular arc. The `sector` function uses the `xradius` and `yradius` arguments to calculate and display the elliptical arc.

Both functions use the current color to outline the wedge and the current fill pattern and fill color to fill the wedge. The most common use for these functions is to create circular and elliptical pie charts.

Listing 4.13 and Figure 4.29 use the `pieslice` function to create a circular ten-wedge pie chart with one wedge set apart from the rest of the chart. Chapter 6 introduces a more generic method of using the `pieslice` function for full-featured pie charts.

Listing 4.13. Using `pieslice` to create a pie chart

```
#include <graphics.h>
#include <stdio.h>
#include <stdlib.h>
#include <conio.h>


int main ()
{
int gdriver = VGA;
int gmode = VGAHI;

    /* register EGAVGA_driver and sansserif_font */
    /* ... these have been added to graphics.lib */
    /* as described in UTIL.DOC                   */

registerbgidriver (EGAVGA_driver);
registerbgifont (sansserif_font);

    /* set VGA 16-color high resolution video mode  */

initgraph (&gdriver,&gmode,"");
rectangle (0,0,639,479);

    /* draw pie */

setfillstyle (0,15);                    /* wedge 1 */
pieslice (320,240,0,15,180);

setfillstyle (11,15);                   /* wedge 2 */
pieslice (320,240,15,30,180);

setfillstyle (6,15);                    /* wedge 3 */
pieslice (320,240,30,80,180);
```

```
setfillstyle (10,15);                    /* wedge 4 */
pieslice (320,200,80,100,180);

setfillstyle (2,15);                     /* wedge 5 */
pieslice (320,240,100,145,180);

setfillstyle (9,15);                     /* wedge 6 */
pieslice (320,240,145,200,180);

setfillstyle (3,15);                     /* wedge 7 */
pieslice (320,240,200,240,180);

setfillstyle (8,15);                     /* wedge 8 */
pieslice (320,240,240,290,180);

setfillstyle (4,15);                     /* wedge 9 */
pieslice (320,240,290,320,180);

setfillstyle (7,15);                     /* wedge 10 */
pieslice (320,240,320,360,180);

     /* Delay and Exit */

settextjustify(CENTER_TEXT,BOTTOM_TEXT);
outtextxy (320,460,"Press Any Key To Exit");

getch ();

closegraph();
return 0;
}
```

Listing 4.14 and Figure 4.30 use the sector function to create a six-wedge, elliptical pie chart with one wedge set apart from the rest of the chart.

Listing 4.14.   Using sector to create a pie chart

```
#include <graphics.h>
#include <stdio.h>
#include <stdlib.h>
#include <conio.h>


int main ()
{
int gdriver = VGA;
int gmode = VGAHI;

     /* register EGAVGA_driver and sansserif_font */
     /* ... these have been added to graphics.lib */
     /* as described in UTIL.DOC                  */

registerbgidriver (EGAVGA_driver);
```

Listing 4.14.   *continues*

Listing 4.14. cont.   Using sector to create a pie chart

```
registerbgifont (sansserif_font);

     /* set VGA 16-color high resolution video mode  */

initgraph (&gdriver,&gmode,"");
rectangle (0,0,639,479);

     /* draw pie */

setfillstyle (0,15);                  /* wedge 1 */
sector (320,240,0,70,280,100);

cctfillstyle (11,15);                 /* wedge 2 */
sector (320,200,70,110,280,100);

setfillstyle (6,15);                  /* wedge 3 */
sector (320,240,110,190,280,100);

setfillstyle (10,15);                 /* wedge 4 */
sector (320,240,190,250,280,100);

setfillstyle (2,15);                  /* wedge 5 */
sector (320,240,250,300,280,100);

setfillstyle (9,15);                  /* wedge 6 */
sector (320,240,300,360,280,100);


     /* Delay and Exit */

settextjustify(CENTER_TEXT,BOTTOM_TEXT);
outtextxy (320,460,"Press Any Key To Exit");

getch ();

closegraph();
return 0;
}
```

Figure 4.29. Screen output from Listing 4.13

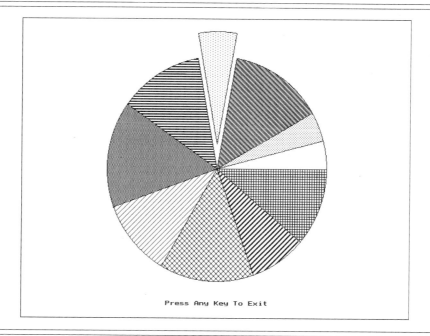

Figure 4.30. Screen output from Listing 4.14

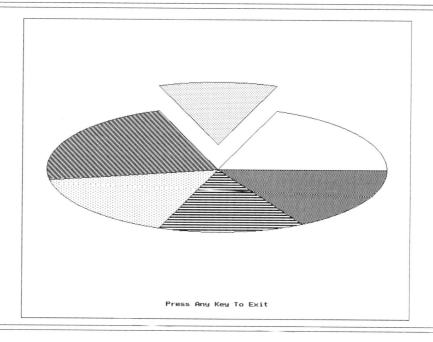

Color and Palette Selection

The colors and palettes available when using the Borland C++ graphics library depend on the video hardware configuration and the video mode selected. This section addresses the selection of colors and palettes in graphics modes.

There are basically two predefined color palettes available in the C++ graphics library. These palettes are shown in Tables 4.3 and 4.4.

Table 4.3 lists the four available color palettes for the CGA. For each palette there are four colors. Color 0 is the background color and can be set to any of the 16 available background colors with the setbkcolor function. The other three colors are predefined.

Table 4.3. *CGA color palettes*

Palette Number	Color 1	Color 2	Color 3
0	CGA_LIGHTGREEN	CGA_LIGHTRED	CGA_YELLOW
1	CGA_LIGHTCYAN	CGA_LIGHTMAGENTA	CGA_WHITE
2	CGA_GREEN	CGA_RED	CGA_BROWN
3	CGA_CYAN	CGA_MAGENTA	CGA_LIGHTGRAY

NOTE: Color 0 is set by the setcolor function.

Table 4.4 lists the 16 predefined colors available with 16-color modes.

Table 4.4. *16-color palette*

Constant	Value
BLACK	0
BLUE	1
GREEN	2
CYAN	3
RED	4
MAGENTA	5
BROWN	6
LIGHTGRAY	7
DARKGRAY	8
LIGHTBLUE	9
LIGHTGREEN	10

Constant	Value
LIGHTCYAN	11
LIGHTRED	12
LIGHTMAGENTA	13
YELLOW	14
WHITE	15

You can set the current color to any of the colors in the current palette. For the CGA modes, colors range from Color 0 to Color 3. For EGA modes, colors range from Color 0 to Color 15. The current color is selected with the setcolor function. The syntax for the setcolor function is:

```
void far setcolor (int color);

int color;              Color value
```

The color argument specifies the integer color value or the defined constant that represents the desired color.

As mentioned earlier, for CGA color modes, Color 0 can be selected with the setbkcolor function. The 16 available color values and constants for background color selection are shown in Table 4.5.

The setbkcolor function can also be used to alter the first entry of the 16-color palette in EGA modes.

The 16-color palettes can be modified with the setallpalette and setpalette functions. The syntax for each of these functions is shown next.

```
void far setallpalette (struct palettetype far *palette);
struct palettetype far *palette;  New palette values

void far setpalette (int colornum, int color);
int colornum;                     Palette member to change
int color;                        New color value
```

The setallpalette function is used to change the entire color palette. The values in the palettetype structure, as pointed to by the palette argument, are assigned as the current palette when the setallpalette function is called. All changes made to the palette are reflected on the screen immediately.

The setpalette function is used to change only one color in the palette. The color argument defines the new color value assigned to the palette member described by the colornum argument.

Table 4.5. *Background colors*

Constant	Value
BLACK	0
BLUE	1
GREEN	2
CYAN	3
RED	4
MAGENTA	5
BROWN	6
LIGHTGRAY	7
DARKGRAY	8
LIGHTBLUE	9
LIGHTGREEN	10
LIGHTCYAN	11
LIGHTRED	12
LIGHTMAGENTA	13
YELLOW	14
WHITE	15

Viewports

All graphics output is drawn relative to a rectangular region of the screen known as a *viewport*. By default, the viewport covers the entire screen. However, the viewport can be defined to cover any physical portion of the screen. The location of the viewport is defined by the `setviewport` function in terms of the physical coordinates of the screen. The upper left-hand corner of the viewport is expressed in physical coordinates. It is defined by the left and top arguments of the `setviewport` function. The syntax is:

```
void far setviewport (int left,int top,int right,int bottom,
                      int clip);
int left, top;          Upper left corner of viewport
int right, bottom;      Lower right corner of viewport
int clip;               Clipping region flag
```

The physical coordinates of the lower right-hand corner of the viewport (see Figure 4.31) are defined in the `bottom` and `right` arguments. The `clip` argument is used to express the characteristics of the viewport. If the `clip` argument is a nonzero value, all graphics output that extends beyond the borders of the viewport will be clipped at the viewport's border. If the `clip` argument is 0, graphics output can extend beyond the border of the viewport.

Figure 4.31. The viewport

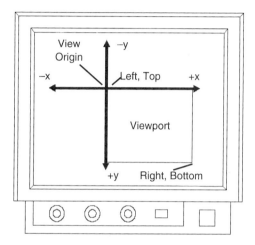

When the viewport is defined, the origin of the view coordinate system (as described earlier in the chapter) is set to the upper left corner of the viewport. Thus, the creation of a viewport redefines the view coordinate system. All subsequent graphics output is drawn relative to the location of the viewport and the new location of the view coordinate system.

The viewport is commonly used to define a region that binds graphics output. When the viewport is used in this manner, the resulting viewport is often called a *clipping region*. Another use of the viewport involves the movement of the view coordinate system origin. It is necessary to move the view coordinate origin to achieve two- and three-dimensional rotations. The rotation of two- and three-dimensional objects will be discussed in Chapter 8.

Summary

This chapter introduced the basic graphics functions provided in the Borland C++ graphics library. With these basic functions you can create graphical interfaces, animation, or two- and three-dimensional drawings as presented in the following chapters.

5

Text and Graphics

This chapter explains the use of text with graphics modes. The Borland C++ graphics library provides several fonts, text styles, and text settings that you can use in graphics modes. The programmer must understand the fundamental principles of combining text with graphics to achieve the optimum combination of graphics and text.

Text and Graphics Cursors

As mentioned previously in this book, there are two basic operating modes in the IBM and compatible computers. These modes are the text modes and the graphics modes. In text modes, the screen is divided into character cells that are processed and displayed. In graphics modes, the screen is divided into pixels. The pixel is the most fundamental screen element. The pixel can be used to create images and characters. In summary, text modes offer the programmer control over character cells, while graphics modes offer control at the pixel level.

While in text modes, the current text position is maintained internally. This text position is often referred to as the *text cursor*. The text cursor is used to identify the row and column coordinates where the next display character will be placed. Almost everyone familiar with computers understands the basic principles behind a text cursor because the text cursor is used extensively in all text-based programs (word processors, editors, etc). It is important to understand, however, that the row and column positioning of the text cursor only works in text modes.

In graphics modes, the current position of the internal cursor is maintained relative to an (x, y) coordinate pair. This current position is called the *graphics cursor*. The graphics cursor is used as the starting point for almost all drawing routines and for all font text output.

117

It is very important to understand the distinction between font text output and text output. Text output includes those text handling functions defined in the `stdio.h`, `conio.h`, and other header files. These functions include `printf`, `cprintf`, and `puts`. These functions are for use only with text modes. Font text output functions are for displaying text while in graphics modes. These functions are defined in the `graphics.h` header file and include the `outtext` and `outtextxy` functions.

To reiterate, font text is used in graphics modes. The graphics cursor is used as the reference point for placing font text on a graphics screen. Font text works only in graphics modes. Traditional text output functions, such as `printf`, do not work in graphics modes.

Use of Font Text in Graphics

There are four basic steps to follow when using font text for the first time in a program. These steps are as follows:

1. Register any font(s) needed.
2. Set the text style, direction, and size.
3. Set the text justification.
4. Display the text.

To register the fonts, it is suggested that the font file(s) be added, or "linked in," to the `graphics.lib` file. The method for adding font files to the graphics library is described under the `BGIOBJ` heading in `UTIL.DOC`, which is a text file included on the Borland C++ distribution disks. By adding the font files to the graphics library, the executable program will not depend on outside programs for proper execution. The desired font files, as shown in Table 5.1, should be added to the graphics library.

Table 5.1. *Font files and registration constants*

File Name	Type Font	Registration Constant
SANS.CHR	Stroked sans-serif	sansserif_font
TRIP.CHR	Stroked triplex	triplex_font
LITT.CHR	Stroked small	small_font
GOTH.CHR	Stroked gothic	gothic_font

When these fonts have been "linked in," the `registerbgifont` function can be used to register the font. The `registerbgifont` function checks all linked-in code for the font specified in the `font` argument (see the following syntax). If the code is found and is valid, the code is registered (or loaded) into internal font tables. Several fonts can be registered into these internal font tables. If the font specified in the font argument is not valid, the font cannot be registered, and a graphics error code is returned. The registration constants listed in Table 5.1 should be used for the font argument to register the "linked-in" Borland fonts.

```
int registerbgifont(void(*font)(void));
void(*font)(void);                  Font to register
```

The second step involves setting the text style, direction, and size. This is done with the settextstyle function. The syntax for the settextstyle function is:

```
void far settextstyle(int font, int direction,
                      int charsize);
int font;                 Font to use
int direction;            Text direction
int charsize;             Character size
```

The font argument is used to specify the type of font desired. The desired font must be registered as in the first step. The default for the font argument is DEFAULT_FONT. Table 5.2 lists the available fonts and their values.

Table 5.2. *Borland fonts*

Constant	Value	Meaning
DEFAULT_FONT	0	8-by-8 bit-mapped font
TRIPLEX_FONT	1	Stroked triplex font
SMALL_FONT	2	Stroked small font
SANS_SERIF_FONT	3	Stroked sans serif font
GOTHIC_FONT	4	Stroked gothic font

The DEFAULT_FONT is a *bit-mapped* font. Each character in a bit-mapped font is defined by a pattern of pixels. Bit-mapped fonts provide good output for small text; however, these fonts do not provide good output for larger scales.

The other fonts are *stroked* fonts. Characters in a stroked font are described in terms of vectors. Therefore, stroked fonts provide excellent output for both large and small characters.

The direction argument is used to specify the desired direction of font text output. There are two choices, as shown in Table 5.3. The HORIZ_DIR constant indicates that the font will be displayed horizontally in an upright position. The VERT_DIR constant is used to display text drawn in a vertical direction. This option produces text that appears to have rotated 90 degrees counterclockwise from its horizontal position.

Table 5.3. *Text direction*

Constant	Value	Meaning
HORIZ_DIR	0	Horizontal text
VERT_DIR	1	Vertical text

The `charsize` argument defines the magnification factor of the default character. A nonzero `charsize` argument can be used with either bit-mapped or stroked fonts. However, if charsize is 0, it only affects stroked fonts. When `charsize` is 0, the stroked font output is enlarged by a default magnification of 4. However, this default magnification factor can be altered with the `setusercharsize` function.

The third step is to set the text justification. You can accomplish this with a call to the `settextjustify` function. Text justification refers to the location of the text relative to the current position of the graphics cursor. The default settings are `LEFT_TEXT`, for horizontal, and `TOP_TEXT`, for vertical.

```
void far settextjustify(int horiz, int vert);
int horiz;              Horizontal justification
int vert;               Vertical justification
```

The `horiz` argument is used to specify the horizontal justification. The constants shown in Table 5.4 are used for horizontal justifications.

Table 5.4. *Horizontal justification*

Constant	Value	Meaning
LEFT_TEXT	0	Left justification
CENTER_TEXT	1	Center text
RIGHT_TEXT	2	Right justification

The `vert` argument specifies the vertical justification. Table 5.5 lists the constants used for the `vert` argument.

Table 5.5. *Vertical justification*

Constant	Value	Meaning
BOTTOM_TEXT	0	Justify from bottom
CENTER_TEXT	1	Center text
TOP_TEXT	2	Justify from top

The last step is to display the desired text using the settings described in the previous two steps. This can be accomplished with either the `outtext` or `outtextxy` functions. Their syntaxes are:

```
void far outtext(char far *textstring);
char far *textstring;           Text to display

void far outtextxy(int x, int y, char far *textstring);
char far *textstring;           Text to display
```

The `outtext` and `outtextxy` functions display the text string using the current color, font, text direction, and justifications. The `outtext` function places the text relative to the current position of the graphics cursor. The `outtextxy` function places the text relative to the coordinates passed in the x and y arguments.

These steps describe the initial process for displaying text. There is no need to follow this procedure each time text is to be output. Steps 2, 3, and 4 can be repeated in unison or independently, depending on the required changes to text output.

Listing 5.1 and Figure 5.1 demonstrate this four-step process to display text using the sans serif font.

Listing 5.1. Using font text

```
#include <graphics.h>
#include <stdio.h>
#include <stdlib.h>
#include <conio.h>

int main ()
{
int gdriver = VGA;
int gmode = VGAHI;

    /* register EGAVGA_driver and sansserif_font */
    /* ... these have been added to graphics.lib */
    /* as described in UTIL.DOC               */

registerbgidriver (EGAVGA_driver);
registerbgifont (sansserif_font);      /* step 1 */

    /* set VGA 16-color high resolution video mode  */

initgraph (&gdriver,&gmode,"");
rectangle (0,0,639,479);

    /* complete steps 2, 3, and 4 */

settextstyle (SANS_SERIF_FONT,HORIZ_DIR,6);
settextjustify (CENTER_TEXT,CENTER_TEXT);
outtextxy (320,200,"Sans-serif font example");

    /* Delay and Exit */
```

Listing 5.1. *continues*

121

Listing 5.1. cont. Using font text

```
settextstyle (DEFAULT_FONT,HORIZ_DIR,1);
settextjustify(CENTER_TEXT,BOTTOM_TEXT);
outtextxy (320,320,"Press Any Key To Exit");

getch ();
closegraph();
return 0;
}
```

Figure 5.1. Screen output from Listing 5.1

Text Colors

The text displayed with the outtext and outtextxy functions is drawn in the current color. You can set the current color with the setcolor function. The current color is limited to the colors available in the current palette. For CGA four-color modes, there are four palettes available. These palettes are shown in Table 5.6.

Table 5.6. *CGA colors*

Palette Number	Color 1	Color 2	Color 3
0	CGA_LIGHTGREEN	CGA_LIGHTRED	CGA_YELLOW
1	CGA_LIGHTCYAN	CGA_LIGHTMAGENTA	CGA_WHITE
2	CGA_GREEN	CGA_RED	CGA_BROWN
3	CGA_CYAN	CGA_MAGENTA	CGA_LIGHTGRAY

NOTE: Color 0 is selected with the `setcolor` function

In the 16-color modes available with EGA/VGA, there are 16 predefined constants available for use. These are listed in Table 5.7.

Table 5.7. *16-color palette*

Constant	Value
BLACK	0
BLUE	1
GREEN	2
CYAN	3
RED	4
MAGENTA	5
BROWN	6
LIGHTGRAY	7
DARKGRAY	8
LIGHTBLUE	9
LIGHTGREEN	10
LIGHTCYAN	11
LIGHTRED	12
LIGHTMAGENTA	13
YELLOW	14
WHITE	15

The section on colors and palettes in Chapter 4 explains the availability of colors and palettes in more detail.

Creating a Character Set

The fonts provided by Borland are sufficient for most simple text output. However, these character sets are not really sufficient for graphics screens that require large text, such as title screens. As Listing 5.1 demonstrates, the large characters displayed with the Borland fonts produce unimpressive results. For advanced graphics text output, it is often necessary to create a character set. If there are only a few characters that need printing, it may not be worth the effort to create an entire set. However, if you plan to do much graphics programming, creating a character set that is flexible enough to display multicolored, scaled, and shadowed text will save time in the long run. This section describes the methods used to create a character set. The methods used are simple in design, but provide flexibility in use.

The first step in developing a character set is to determine the use of the character set. For small text, characters that are created with single lines are sufficient (see Figure 5.2). However, larger text requires the use of hollow, or skeleton characters (see Figure 5.3).

Figure 5.2. Model for small characters

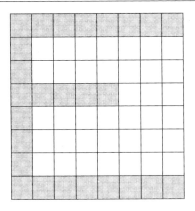

Figure 5.3. Model for large characters

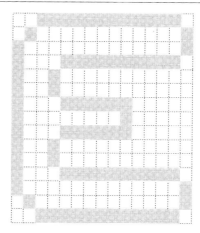

When you determine the use of the character set, you must also determine a minimum character size. The character set described in the remainder of this chapter is designed for the EGA video system (it will work with any graphics system, but it was designed with the EGA aspect ratio in mind) and with a minimum character size of 15-by-15 pixels.

After you define the minimum character size, a character type must be identified. The character set in this chapter (and continued in Appendix C) is not based on any commercially available font. It was simply created by using straight lines. Many arts, crafts, and business supply stores carry rub-on letters that can be used as a model for a character set. Be aware, however, that many of these fonts are difficult to duplicate because they generally use curved letters.

The next step is to draw each character of the selected character set on a grid of the minimum character size. For the character set in this chapter, this is a 15-by-15 grid. After you draw the characters, you must write the actual code that will display the character. The best way to do this is to break the character into simple curves and lines that can be described in relationship to the upper left corner of the grid, (x,y). In other words, the lower right-hand corner of the grid could be described by (x+14, y+14) on a 15-by-15 grid. By carefully describing the character, as shown in the following function, you can create a character set that can be scaled larger. The following character (Figure 5.4) and code illustrate the manner by which a character should be described.

Figure 5.4. Model character

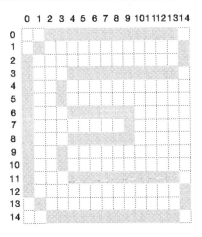

```
void e ()
{
    moveto (x+fraction[2],y);
    lineto (x+fraction[13],y);
    lineto (x+fraction[14],y+fraction[1]);
    lineto (x+fraction[14],y+fraction[2]);
    lineto (x+fraction[13],y+fraction[3]);
    lineto (x+fraction[4],y+fraction[3]);
    lineto (x+fraction[3],y+fraction[4]);
    lineto (x+fraction[3],y+fraction[5]);
    lineto (x+fraction[4],y+fraction[6]);
    lineto (x+fraction[9],y+fraction[6]);
    lineto (x+fraction[9],y+fraction[8]);
    lineto (x+fraction[4],y+fraction[8]);
    lineto (x+fraction[3],y+fraction[9]);
    lineto (x+fraction[3],y+fraction[10]);
    lineto (x+fraction[4],y+fraction[11]);
    lineto (x+fraction[13],y+fraction[11]);
    lineto (x+fraction[14],y+fraction[12]);
    lineto (x+fraction[14],y+fraction[13]);
    lineto (x+fraction[13],y+fraction[14]);
    lineto (x+fraction[2],y+fraction[14]);
    lineto (x,y+fraction[12]);
    lineto (x,y+fraction[2]);
    lineto (x+fraction[2],y);
}
```

This code is made scalable by the method in which the character is defined. The beginning and endpoints of each line are described in relationship to a fraction of the overall size of the grid. The for loop in Listing 5.2 (and shown in Figure 5.5) defines the components of an array called fraction that contains all the possible starting and stopping x and y values on the grid. The scale argument identifies the size of the grid

(15 indicates 15-by-15, 100 indicates 100-by-100, etc). The factor argument is similar to a counter for the 15 arguments in the array. In a minimum-sized character, with scale = 15, the fifteen components of the array would be 0, 1, 2, 3, 4, 5, 6, 7, 8, 9, 10, 11, 12, 13, and 14. Therefore, lineto(x, y+fraction[14]) would draw a line from the current position of the graphics cursor to x, y+((14*scale)/15). By describing the character in this manner, any size text down to the minimum size is possible.

Listing 5.2. Scalable character example

```
#include <graphics.h>
#include <stdio.h>
#include <stdlib.h>
#include <conio.h>

int x,y;
div_t result;
int fraction[15];
int scale;
int factor;
int i;
void e();

int main ()
{
int gdriver = EGA;
int gmode = EGAHI;

     /* register EGAVGA_driver and sansserif_font */
     /* ... these have been added to graphics.lib */
     /* as described in UTIL.DOC                   */

registerbgidriver (EGAVGA_driver);
registerbgifont (sansserif_font);

     /* set EGA 16-color high resolution video mode   */

initgraph (&gdriver,&gmode,"");
rectangle (0,0,639,349);

     /* draw first character - scale 20 */

scale = 20;
x = 50;
y = 150;
factor = 0;

for (i=0; i<15; i=i+1)
     {
     result = div ((factor*scale),15);
     fraction[i] = result.quot;
     factor = factor + 1;
     }
```

Listing 5.2. *continues*

Listing 5.2. cont. Scalable character example

```
setcolor (15);
e ();

      /* draw second character - scale 40 */

scale = 40;
x = 240;
y = 150;
factor = 0;

for (i=0; i<15; i = i+1)
      {
      result = div((factor*scale),15);
      fraction[i] = result.quot;
      factor = factor + 1;
      }
e();

      /* draw third character - scale 80 */

scale = 80;
x = 440;
y = 150;
factor = 0;

for (i=0; i<15; i=i+1)
      {
      result = div((factor*scale),15);
      fraction[i] = result.quot;
      factor = factor + 1;
      }
e();

      /* Delay and Exit */

settextjustify(CENTER_TEXT,BOTTOM_TEXT);
outtextxy (320,320,"Press Any Key To Exit");

getch ();

closegraph();
return 0;
}

void e ()
{
moveto (x+fraction[2],y);
lineto (x+fraction[13],y);
lineto (x+fraction[14],y+fraction[1]);
lineto (x+fraction[14],y+fraction[2]);
lineto (x+fraction[13],y+fraction[3]);
lineto (x+fraction[4],y+fraction[3]);
lineto (x+fraction[3],y+fraction[4]);
lineto (x+fraction[3],y+fraction[5]);
lineto (x+fraction[4],y+fraction[6]);
```

```
lineto (x+fraction[9],y+fraction[6]);
lineto (x+fraction[9],y+fraction[8]);
lineto (x+fraction[4],y+fraction[8]);
lineto (x+fraction[3],y+fraction[9]);
lineto (x+fraction[3],y+fraction[10]);
lineto (x+fraction[4],y+fraction[11]);
lineto (x+fraction[13],y+fraction[11]);
lineto (x+fraction[14],y+fraction[12]);
lineto (x+fraction[14],y+fraction[13]);
lineto (x+fraction[13],y+fraction[14]);
lineto (x+fraction[2],y+fraction[14]);
lineto (x,y+fraction[12]);
lineto (x,y+fraction[2]);
lineto (x+fraction[2],y);
}
```

Figure 5.5. Screen output from Listing 5.2

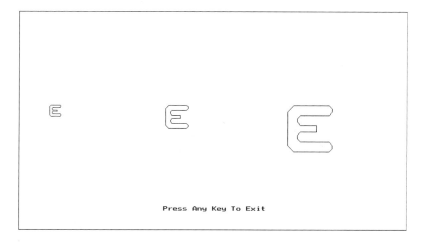

The for loop in Listing 5.2 needs to be implemented only once in the program, assuming that the scale of the text remains the same. Any change in the scale requires that the array be redefined. The array is redefined when the loop is executed. There is no need to change the character's code when the scale changes.

Unfilled Characters

Assuming that the characters have been created in a manner similar to those described in this chapter, it is easy to generate characters that are not filled. By using the for loop described in the previous example, setting a scaling factor, and identifying the upper left

129

corner of the rectangular region where the character is to be drawn (the x and y variables), you can display an unfilled character. Listing 5.3 and Figure 5.6 demonstrate the method by which the letter "E" can be placed on the screen with a scale of 105. The setcolor function can be used prior to calling the e() function to specify the border color of the character.

Listing 5.3. Example of an unfilled character

```
#include <graphics.h>
#include <stdio.h>
#include <stdlib.h>
#include <conio.h>

int x,y;
div_t result;
int fraction[15];
int scale;
int factor;
int i;
void e();

int main ()
{
int gdriver = EGA;
int gmode = EGAHI;

        /* register EGAVGA_driver and sansserif_font */
        /* ... these have been added to graphics.lib */
        /* as described in UTIL.DOC                   */

registerbgidriver (EGAVGA_driver);
registerbgifont (sansserif_font);

        /* set EGA 16-color high resolution video mode  */

initgraph (&gdriver,&gmode,"");
rectangle (0,0,639,349);

        /* define dimensions and draw character */

scale = 105;
x = 270;
y = 125;
factor = 0;

for (i=0; i<15; i=i+1)
    {
    result = div ((factor*scale),15);
    fraction[i] = result.quot;
    factor = factor + 1;
    }
```

```
setcolor (15);
e ();

    /* Delay and Exit */

settextjustify(CENTER_TEXT,BOTTOM_TEXT);
outtextxy (320,320,"Press Any Key To Exit");

getch ();

closegraph();
return 0;
}

void e ()
{
moveto (x+fraction[2],y);
lineto (x+fraction[13],y);
lineto (x+fraction[14],y+fraction[1]);
lineto (x+fraction[14],y+fraction[2]);
lineto (x+fraction[13],y+fraction[3]);
lineto (x+fraction[4],y+fraction[3]);
lineto (x+fraction[3],y+fraction[4]);
lineto (x+fraction[3],y+fraction[5]);
lineto (x+fraction[4],y+fraction[6]);
lineto (x+fraction[9],y+fraction[6]);
lineto (x+fraction[9],y+fraction[8]);
lineto (x+fraction[4],y+fraction[8]);
lineto (x+fraction[3],y+fraction[9]);
lineto (x+fraction[3],y+fraction[10]);
lineto (x+fraction[4],y+fraction[11]);
lineto (x+fraction[13],y+fraction[11]);
lineto (x+fraction[14],y+fraction[12]);
lineto (x+fraction[14],y+fraction[13]);
lineto (x+fraction[13],y+fraction[14]);
lineto (x+fraction[2],y+fraction[14]);
lineto (x,y+fraction[12]);
lineto (x,y+fraction[2]);
lineto (x+fraction[2],y);
}
```

Filled Characters

Creating filled characters is a simple extension of creating unfilled characters. The only difference is that you will add a call to the floodfill function. The floodfill function requires a starting point and the color of the character's border. The starting point should be defined in relationship to the dimensions of the character's overall size, just like the character's border. The border color is entered manually, but it could easily be a local or global parameter. Listing 5.4 code creates a character that is 105-by-105 pixels in size and is filled with the same color as its border (as shown in Figure 5.7).

Figure 5.6. Screen output from Listing 5.3

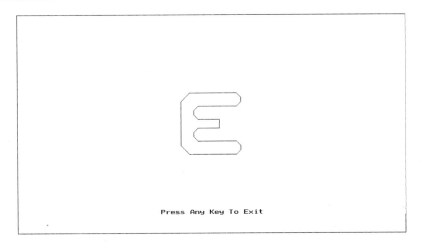

Press Any Key To Exit

Listing 5.4. Example of a filled character

```
#include <graphics.h>
#include <stdio.h>
#include <stdlib.h>
#include <conio.h>

int x,y;
div_t result;
int fraction[15];
int scale;
int factor;
int i;
void e();

int main ()
{
int gdriver = EGA;
int gmode = EGAHI;

     /* register EGAVGA_driver and sansserif_font */
     /* ... these have been added to graphics.lib */
     /* as described in UTIL.DOC                   */

registerbgidriver (EGAVGA_driver);
registerbgifont (sansserif_font);

     /* set EGA 16-color high resolution video mode   */

initgraph (&gdriver,&gmode,"");
rectangle (0,0,639,349);

     /* define dimensions and draw character */
```

```
scale = 105;
x = 270;
y = 125;
factor = 0;

for (i=0; i<15; i=i+1)
    {
    result = div ((factor*scale),15);
    fraction[i] = result.quot;
    factor = factor + 1;
    }

setcolor (15);
e ();
setfillstyle (SOLID_FILL,15);
floodfill (x+fraction[7],y+fraction[1],15);

    /* Delay and Exit */

settextjustify(CENTER_TEXT,BOTTOM_TEXT);
outtextxy (320,320,"Press Any Key To Exit");

getch ();

closegraph();
return 0;
}

void e ()
{
moveto (x+fraction[2],y);
lineto (x+fraction[13],y);
lineto (x+fraction[14],y+fraction[1]);
lineto (x+fraction[14],y+fraction[2]);
lineto (x+fraction[13],y+fraction[3]);
lineto (x+fraction[4],y+fraction[3]);
lineto (x+fraction[3],y+fraction[4]);
lineto (x+fraction[3],y+fraction[5]);
lineto (x+fraction[4],y+fraction[6]);
lineto (x+fraction[9],y+fraction[6]);
lineto (x+fraction[9],y+fraction[8]);
lineto (x+fraction[4],y+fraction[8]);
lineto (x+fraction[3],y+fraction[9]);
lineto (x+fraction[3],y+fraction[10]);
lineto (x+fraction[4],y+fraction[11]);
lineto (x+fraction[13],y+fraction[11]);
lineto (x+fraction[14],y+fraction[12]);
lineto (x+fraction[14],y+fraction[13]);
lineto (x+fraction[13],y+fraction[14]);
lineto (x+fraction[2],y+fraction[14]);
lineto (x,y+fraction[12]);
lineto (x,y+fraction[2]);
lineto (x+fraction[2],y);
}
```

Figure 5.7. Screen output from Listing 5.4

Press Any Key To Exit

Shaded Characters

One effect that you can add easily to the previous capabilities is shading the inside of the character. The previous method used a solid fill pattern to create a filled character. A more flexible method is to fill the character with a nonsolid fill pattern. The pattern in Listing 5.5 (and shown in Figure 5.8) uses the `setfillstyle` function to specify a backslash fill pattern.

Listing 5.5. Shaded character example

```
#include <graphics.h>
#include <stdio.h>
#include <stdlib.h>
#include <conio.h>

int x,y;
div_t result;
int fraction[15];
int scale;
int factor;
int i;
void e();

int main ()
{
int gdriver = EGA;
int gmode = EGAHI;
```

```
      /* register EGAVGA_driver and sansserif_font */
      /* ... these have been added to graphics.lib */
      /* as described in UTIL.DOC                  */

registerbgidriver (EGAVGA_driver);
registerbgifont (sansserif_font);

      /* set EGA 16-color high resolution video mode  */

initgraph (&gdriver,&gmode,"");
rectangle (0,0,639,349);

      /* define dimensions and draw character */

scale = 105;
x = 270;
y = 125;
factor = 0;

for (i=0; i<15; i=i+1)
      {
      result = div ((factor*scale),15);
      fraction[i] = result.quot;
      factor = factor + 1;
      }

setcolor (15);
e ();
setfillstyle(BKSLASH_FILL,15);
floodfill(x+fraction[7],y+fraction[1],15);

      /* Delay and Exit */

settextjustify(CENTER_TEXT,BOTTOM_TEXT);
outtextxy (320,320,"Press Any Key To Exit");

getch ();

closegraph();
return 0;
}

void e ()
{
moveto (x+fraction[2],y);
lineto (x+fraction[13],y);
lineto (x+fraction[14],y+fraction[1]);
lineto (x+fraction[14],y+fraction[2]);
lineto (x+fraction[13],y+fraction[3]);
lineto (x+fraction[4],y+fraction[3]);
lineto (x+fraction[3],y+fraction[4]);
lineto (x+fraction[3],y+fraction[5]);
lineto (x+fraction[4],y+fraction[6]);
lineto (x+fraction[9],y+fraction[6]);
lineto (x+fraction[9],y+fraction[8]);
lineto (x+fraction[4],y+fraction[8]);
lineto (x+fraction[3],y+fraction[9]);
```

Listing 5.5. *continues*

Listing 5.5. cont.   Shaded character example

```
lineto (x+fraction[3],y+fraction[10]);
lineto (x+fraction[4],y+fraction[11]);
lineto (x+fraction[13],y+fraction[11]);
lineto (x+fraction[14],y+fraction[12]);
lineto (x+fraction[14],y+fraction[13]);
lineto (x+fraction[13],y+fraction[14]);
lineto (x+fraction[2],y+fraction[14]);
lineto (x,y+fraction[12]);
lineto (x,y+fraction[2]);
lineto (x+fraction[2],y);
}
```

Figure 5.8.   Screen output from Listing 5.5

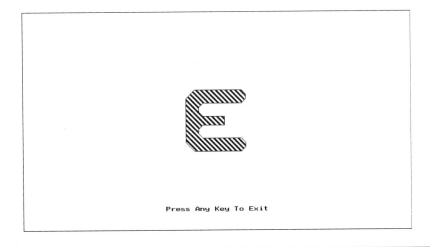

Press Any Key To Exit

Multicolored Characters

You can make the previous effects of shading and filling the character more spectacular by adding the variations of border colors and fill colors. The combination of border and fill colors adds to the overall visual effect of the text. The task of creating multicolored characters is a simple one, provided by an extra call to the setcolor function. The following code demonstrates the generation of a multicolored character.

Listing 5.6. Multicolored character example

```
#include <graphics.h>
#include <stdio.h>
#include <stdlib.h>
#include <conio.h>

int x,y;
div_t result;
int fraction[15];
int scale;
int factor;
int i;
void e();

int main ()
{
int gdriver = EGA;
int gmode = EGAHI;

        /* register EGAVGA_driver and sansserif_font */
        /* ... these have been added to graphics.lib */
        /* as described in UTIL.DOC                   */

registerbgidriver (EGAVGA_driver);
registerbgifont (sansserif_font);

        /* set EGA 16-color high resolution video mode   */

initgraph (&gdriver,&gmode,"");
rectangle (0,0,639,349);

        /* define dimensions and draw character */

scale = 105;
x = 270;
y = 125;
factor = 0;

for (i=0; i<15; i=i+1)
    {
    result = div ((factor*scale),15);
    fraction[i] = result.quot;
    factor = factor + 1;
    }

setcolor (15);
e ();
setfillstyle (SOLID_FILL,3);
floodfill (x+fraction[7],y+fraction[1],15);

        /* Delay and Exit */

settextjustify(CENTER_TEXT,BOTTOM_TEXT);
outtextxy (320,320,"Press Any Key To Exit");
```

Listing 5.6. continues

Listing 5.6. cont.   Multicolored character example

```
getch ();

closegraph();
return 0;
}

void e ()
{
moveto (x+fraction[2],y);
lineto (x+fraction[13],y);
lineto (x+fraction[14],y+fraction[1]);
lineto (x+fraction[14],y+fraction[2]);
lineto (x+fraction[13],y+fraction[3]);
lineto (x+fraction[4],y+fraction[3]);
lineto (x+fraction[3],y+fraction[4]);
lineto (x+fraction[3],y+fraction[5]);
lineto (x+fraction[4],y+fraction[6]);
lineto (x+fraction[9],y+fraction[6]);
lineto (x+fraction[9],y+fraction[8]);
lineto (x+fraction[4],y+fraction[8]);
lineto (x+fraction[3],y+fraction[9]);
lineto (x+fraction[3],y+fraction[10]);
lineto (x+fraction[4],y+fraction[11]);
lineto (x+fraction[13],y+fraction[11]);
lineto (x+fraction[14],y+fraction[12]);
lineto (x+fraction[14],y+fraction[13]);
lineto (x+fraction[13],y+fraction[14]);
lineto (x+fraction[2],y+fraction[14]);
lineto (x,y+fraction[12]);
lineto (x,y+fraction[2]);
lineto (x+fraction[2],y);
}
```

Shadowed Characters

Another effect that can be used with filled characters is shadowing the character. The best effects come from a dark-colored, solid-filled shadow character with a light-colored, solid-filled top character. All of the combinations of colors and fill patterns are available, but non-solid fill patterns, especially on the top character, allow the background and shadow letter colors to show through. Trial and error is often needed when using non-solid fill patterns. The following code demonstrates the shadowing effect.

Figure 5.9. Screen output from Listing 5.6

Press Any Key To Exit

Listing 5.7. Shadowed character example

```
#include <graphics.h>
#include <stdio.h>
#include <stdlib.h>
#include <conio.h>

int x,y;
div_t result;
int fraction[15];
int scale;
int factor;
int i;
void e();

int main ()
{
int gdriver = EGA;
int gmode = EGAHI;

      /* register EGAVGA_driver and sansserif_font */
      /* ... these have been added to graphics.lib */
      /* as described in UTIL.DOC                  */
```

Listing 5.7. *continues*

Listing 5.7. cont. Shadowed character example

```
registerbgidriver (EGAVGA_driver);
registerbgifont (sansserif_font);

     /* set EGA 16-color high resolution video mode  */

initgraph (&gdriver,&gmode,"");
rectangle (0,0,639,349);

scale = 105;
x = 275;
y = 130;
factor = 0;

     /* grid calculations */

for (i=0; i<15; i=i+1)
     {
     result = div ((factor*scale),15);
     fraction[i] = result.quot;
     factor = factor + 1;
     }

     /* draw and fill shadow character */

setcolor (15);
e ();
setfillstyle (SOLID_FILL,15);
floodfill (x+fraction[7],y+fraction[1],15);

     /* draw and fill top character */

x=270;
y=125;
setcolor (1);
e ();
setfillstyle (SOLID_FILL,1);
floodfill (x+fraction[7],y+fraction[1],1);

     /* Delay and Exit */

setcolor (15);
settextjustify(CENTER_TEXT,BOTTOM_TEXT);
outtextxy (320,320,"Press Any Key To Exit");

getch ();

closegraph();
return 0;
}

void e ()
{
moveto (x+fraction[2],y);
lineto (x+fraction[13],y);
lineto (x+fraction[14],y+fraction[1]);
```

```
lineto (x+fraction[14],y+fraction[2]);
lineto (x+fraction[13],y+fraction[3]);
lineto (x+fraction[4],y+fraction[3]);
lineto (x+fraction[3],y+fraction[4]);
lineto (x+fraction[3],y+fraction[5]);
lineto (x+fraction[4],y+fraction[6]);
lineto (x+fraction[9],y+fraction[6]);
lineto (x+fraction[9],y+fraction[8]);
lineto (x+fraction[4],y+fraction[8]);
lineto (x+fraction[3],y+fraction[9]);
lineto (x+fraction[3],y+fraction[10]);
lineto (x+fraction[4],y+fraction[11]);
lineto (x+fraction[13],y+fraction[11]);
lineto (x+fraction[14],y+fraction[12]);
lineto (x+fraction[14],y+fraction[13]);
lineto (x+fraction[13],y+fraction[14]);
lineto (x+fraction[2],y+fraction[14]);
lineto (x,y+fraction[12]);
lineto (x,y+fraction[2]);
lineto (x+fraction[2],y);
}
```

Figure 5.10. Screen output from Listing 5.7

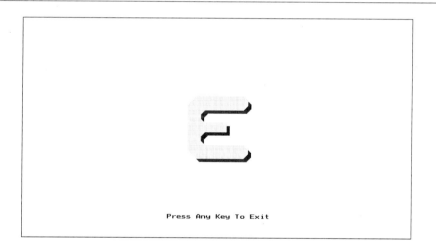

Appendix C contains the code listings for the remainder of the character set.

Summary

The Borland C++ graphics library provides flexible text support for graphics applications. This text support, when combined with a user-defined character set, such as the one presented in this chapter, offers you a wide range of text and graphics combinations which can be implemented into software programs such as graphical user interfaces or animation.

6

Presentation Graphics

O ne important part of graphics programming is the ability to display a series of information, or data, in a manner that makes it easy to understand. This displaying of information is often called *presentation graphics*. Presentation graphics output is usually in the form of bar, pie, column, line, or scatter charts.

The Borland C++ graphics library does not provide any direct means to create these types of charts. However it does provide all of the basic drawing capabilities. This chapter will demonstrate programming methods to create charts. These methods present the fundamentals of creating generic programs for the development of presentation graphics charts.

Bar Charts

The bar chart is one of the most common forms used to represent data. With the bar chart, each member of a data series, displayed with a horizontal bar, can be represented relative to the others. The scales on the chart's axes are used for a true comparison of each member of the data series.

The Borland C++ library includes many functions that make it possible to create simple bar charts. The following example (see Listing 6.1 and Figure 6.1) demonstrates a method for creating a "generic" bar chart program.

This program is designed to display a data series with up to 10 members in bar chart form. In addition, several parameters are initiated for use later in the program. These parameters include four title parameters. These character strings, the `maintitle`, `subtitle`, `xtitle`, and `ytitle`, are used to label the chart and x/y axes. The `members` and `values` arrays are used to define the length of the bars and their associated names.

When the parameters are initialized, the program displays the titles, draws a grid for the chart, and displays the bars. This demonstration uses only two colors; however, it could easily be modified to include multiple colors. Furthermore, the maxvalue parameter is set to the highest value in the values array. The result is that the highest-valued member maximizes the scale. To avoid this, the maxvalue parameter could be set to a proportional value higher than the maximum value in the values array.

Listing 6.1. Bar chart example with 10 members

```
#include <graphics.h>
#include <stdio.h>
#include <stdlib.h>
#include <conio.h>

#define MAXNUM 10        /* maximum number of bars */

int main ()
{
int gdriver = VGA;
int gmode = VGAHI;

int numbars = 10;              /* number of bars in chart */
char maintitle[80];            /* main title of chart     */
char subtitle[80];             /* subtitle of chart       */
char xtitle[80];               /* title of x axis         */
char ytitle[80];               /* title of y axis         */
char *members[] = {"John","Jill","Tom","Jane","Gary","Kim",
               "Peter","Mary","Jim","Sue"};
int values[MAXNUM];            /* values for bars         */
int maxvalue;                  /* max value in values     */
int yspace;                    /* spacing in y direction  */
int ymarker;                   /* y marker                */
char buffer[40];
div_t a;
int i, x;
int holder;

        /* register EGAVGA_driver and sansserif_font */
        /* ... these have been added to graphics.lib */
        /* as described in UTIL.DOC                   */

registerbgidriver (EGAVGA_driver);
registerbgifont (sansserif_font);

        /* set VGA 16-color high resolution video mode  */

initgraph (&gdriver,&gmode,"");
rectangle (0,0,639,479);

        /* make sure no more than 10 bars are drawn */

if (numbars > MAXNUM)
    numbars = MAXNUM;
```

```
        /* define titles and values */

sprintf (maintitle,"Annual Sales Report");
sprintf (subtitle,"Total Sales");
sprintf (xtitle,"Sales $Thousands x 10");
sprintf (ytitle,"Employee");

values[0] = 60;
values[1] = 52;
values[2] = 48;
values[3] = 40;
values[4] = 40;
values[5] = 36;
values[6] = 36;
values[7] = 32;
values[8] = 28;
values[9] = 28;
maxvalue = 60;

        /* display titles */

settextstyle (DEFAULT_FONT,HORIZ_DIR,2);
settextjustify(CENTER_TEXT,CENTER_TEXT);
outtextxy (320,40,maintitle);
outtextxy (320,70,subtitle);
settextstyle (DEFAULT_FONT,HORIZ_DIR,1);
outtextxy (320,470,xtitle);
settextstyle (DEFAULT_FONT,VERT_DIR,1);
outtextxy (10,240,ytitle);

        /* draw box and scales for bars */

rectangle (60,90,620,440);
line (200,90,200,440);
line (340,90,340,440);
line (480,90,480,440);

settextstyle (DEFAULT_FONT,HORIZ_DIR,1);
settextjustify (CENTER_TEXT,TOP_TEXT);
sprintf (buffer,"%d",maxvalue);
outtextxy (620,443,buffer);

a = div (maxvalue * 3,4);
sprintf (buffer,"%d",a.quot);
outtextxy (480,443,buffer);

a = div (maxvalue,2);
sprintf (buffer,"%d",a.quot);
outtextxy (340,443,buffer);

a = div (maxvalue,4);
sprintf (buffer,"%d",a.quot);
outtextxy (200,443,buffer);

outtextxy (60,443,"0");
```

Listing 6.1.   *continues*

145

Listing 6.1. cont. Bar chart example with 10 members

```
      /* draw and title bars */

a = div(350,numbars + 1);
yspace = a.quot;
ymarker = 90;

setfillstyle (CLOSE_DOT_FILL,15);
settextjustify (RIGHT_TEXT,CENTER_TEXT);
for (i = 0; i < numbars; i = i + 1)
    {
    ymarker = ymarker + yspace;
    outtextxy (57,ymarker,members[i]);
    holder = 56 * values[i];
    a = div (holder,maxvalue);
    x = a.quot * 10;
    bar3d (60,ymarker + 10,60 + x,ymarker - 10,5,1);
    }

      /* Delay and Exit */

getch ();
closegraph();
return 0;
}
```

Figure 6.1. Screen output from Listing 6.1

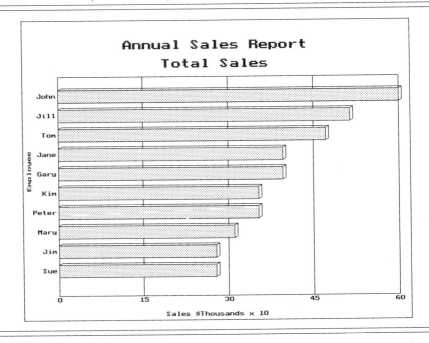

Listing 6.2, as shown in Figure 6.2, is similar to the previous example. However, with this example there are only seven members in the data series. Note that only seven bars are displayed, which demonstrates the code's ability to handle varying numbers of data series.

Listing 6.2. Bar chart example with seven members

```
#include <graphics.h>
#include <stdio.h>
#include <stdlib.h>
#include <conio.h>

#define MAXNUM 10        /* maximum number of bars */

int main ()
{
int gdriver = VGA;
int gmode = VGAHI;

int numbars = 7;                  /* number of bars in chart */
char maintitle[80];               /* main title of chart    */
char subtitle[80];                /* subtitle of chart       */
char xtitle[80];                  /* title of x axis         */
char ytitle[80];                  /* title of y axis         */
char *members[] = {"#1","#2","#3","#4","#5","#6","#7"};
int values[MAXNUM];               /* values for bars         */
int maxvalue;                     /* max value in values     */
int yspace;                       /* spacing in y direction  */
int ymarker;                      /* y marker                */
char buffer[40];
div_t a;
int i, x;
int holder;

    /* register EGAVGA_driver and sansserif_font */
    /* ... these have been added to graphics.lib */
    /* as described in UTIL.DOC                   */

registerbgidriver (EGAVGA_driver);
registerbgifont (sansserif_font);

    /* set VGA 16-color high resolution video mode  */

initgraph (&gdriver,&gmode,"");
rectangle (0,0,639,479);

    /* make sure no more than 10 bars are drawn */

if (numbars > MAXNUM)
     numbars = MAXNUM;
```

Listing 6.2. *continues*

Listing 6.2. cont. Bar chart example with seven members

```
      /* define titles and values */

sprintf (maintitle,"Gross Sales");
sprintf (subtitle,"Sales Per Store");
sprintf (xtitle,"Gross Sales $Millions");
sprintf (ytitle,"Store Number");

values[0] = 42;
values[1] = 14;
values[2] = 20;
values[3] = 30;
values[4] = 20;
values[5] = 40;
values[6] = 34;
maxvalue = 42;

      /* display titles */

settextstyle (DEFAULT_FONT,HORIZ_DIR,2);
settextjustify(CENTER_TEXT,CENTER_TEXT);
outtextxy (320,40,maintitle);
outtextxy (320,70,subtitle);
settextstyle (DEFAULT_FONT,HORIZ_DIR,1);
outtextxy (320,470,xtitle);
settextstyle (DEFAULT_FONT,VERT_DIR,1);
outtextxy (10,240,ytitle);

      /* draw box and scales for bars */

rectangle (60,90,620,440);
line (200,90,200,440);
line (340,90,340,440);
line (480,90,480,440);

settextstyle (DEFAULT_FONT,HORIZ_DIR,1);
settextjustify (CENTER_TEXT,TOP_TEXT);
sprintf (buffer,"%d",maxvalue);
outtextxy (620,443,buffer);

a = div (maxvalue * 3,4);
sprintf (buffer,"%d",a.quot);
outtextxy (480,443,buffer);

a = div (maxvalue,2);
sprintf (buffer,"%d",a.quot);
outtextxy (340,443,buffer);

a = div (maxvalue,4);
sprintf (buffer,"%d",a.quot);
outtextxy (200,443,buffer);
```

```
outtextxy (60,443,"0");

    /* draw and title bars */

a = div(350,numbars + 1);
yspace = a.quot;
ymarker = 90;

setfillstyle (CLOSE_DOT_FILL,15);
settextjustify (RIGHT_TEXT,CENTER_TEXT);
for (i = 0; i < numbars; i = i + 1)
    {
    ymarker = ymarker + yspace;
    outtextxy (57,ymarker,members[i]);
    holder = 56 * values[i];
    a = div (holder,maxvalue);
    x = a.quot * 10;
    bar3d (60,ymarker + 10,60 + x,ymarker - 10,5,1);
    }

    /* Delay and Exit */

getch ();
closegraph();
return 0;
}
```

Figure 6.2. Screen output from Listing 6.2

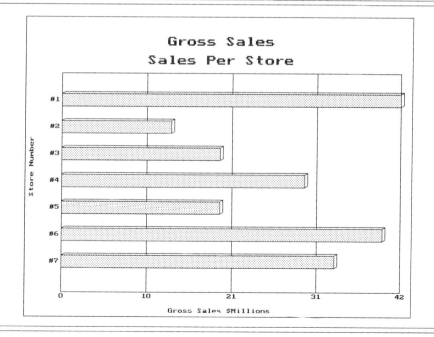

Column Charts

The column chart is similar to the bar chart, except that it uses vertical bars rather than horizontal bars to represent the members of the data series. Like the bar chart, the column chart is used to compare the members in a data series, and to illustrate data variations over time.

The following program (see Listing 6.3 and Figure 6.3) is similar to the previous bar chart examples. The main difference is that the displayed bars are vertical. As before, there is a 10-member limit on the size of the data series, and several parameters are initiated for use later in the program. These parameters include the maintitle, subtitle, xtitle, and ytitle parameters, which are used to label the chart. The values and members arrays are used to define the height of the columns and their associated names, respectively.

When all the parameters are defined, the program displays the titles, draws a grid for the chart, and displays the columns. This program uses only two colors, but it could be modified easily to use a variety of colors. Furthermore, the maxvalue parameter is set to the highest value in the values array. This causes the highest-valued member to be displayed at the maximum position on the chart. To avoid this, the maxvalue parameter could be set to a proportional value higher than the maximum value in the values array.

Listing 6.3. Column chart example with 10 members

```
#include <graphics.h>
#include <stdio.h>
#include <stdlib.h>
#include <conio.h>

#define MAXNUM 10       /* maximum number of bars */

int main ()
{
int gdriver = VGA;
int gmode = VGAHI;

int numbars = 10;               /* number of bars in chart */
char maintitle[80];             /* main title of chart     */
char subtitle[80];              /* subtitle of chart       */
char xtitle[80];                /* title of x axis         */
char ytitle[80];                /* title of y axis         */
char *members[] =
{"John","Jill","Tom","Jane","Gary","Kim","Peter",
          "Mary","Jim","Sue"};
int values[MAXNUM];             /* values for bars         */
int maxvalue;                   /* max value in values     */
int xspace;                     /* spacing in x direction  */
int xmarker;                    /* x marker                */
char buffer[40];
div_t a;
```

```
int i, y;
int holder;

    /* register EGAVGA_driver and sansserif_font */
    /* ... these have been added to graphics.lib */
    /* as described in UTIL.DOC                  */

registerbgidriver (EGAVGA_driver);
registerbgifont (sansserif_font);

    /* set VGA 16-color high resolution video mode  */

initgraph (&gdriver,&gmode,"");
rectangle (0,0,639,479);

    /* make sure no more than 10 bars are drawn */

if (numbars > MAXNUM)
    numbars = MAXNUM;

    /* define titles and values */

sprintf (maintitle,"Annual Sales Report");
sprintf (subtitle,"Total Sales");
sprintf (xtitle,"Employee");
sprintf (ytitle,"Sales $Thousands x 10");

values[0] = 60;
values[1] = 52;
values[2] = 48;
values[3] = 40;
values[4] = 40;
values[5] = 36;
values[6] = 36;
values[7] = 32;
values[8] = 28;
values[9] = 28;
maxvalue = 60;


    /* display titles */

settextstyle (DEFAULT_FONT,HORIZ_DIR,2);
settextjustify(CENTER_TEXT,CENTER_TEXT);
outtextxy (320,40,maintitle);
outtextxy (320,70,subtitle);
settextstyle (DEFAULT_FONT,HORIZ_DIR,1);
outtextxy (320,470,xtitle);
settextstyle (DEFAULT_FONT,VERT_DIR,1);
outtextxy (10,240,ytitle);

    /* draw box and scales for bars */

rectangle (60,90,620,440);
line (60,354,620,354);
line (60,265,620,265);
line (60,178,620,178);
```

Listing 6.3. *continues*

151

Listing 6.3. cont. Column chart example with 10 members

```
settextstyle (DEFAULT_FONT,HORIZ_DIR,1);
settextjustify (RIGHT_TEXT,CENTER_TEXT);
sprintf (buffer,"%d",maxvalue);
outtextxy (55,90,buffer);

a = div (maxvalue * 3,4);
sprintf (buffer,"%d",a.quot);
outtextxy (55,178,buffer);

a = div (maxvalue,2);
sprintf (buffer,"%d",a.quot);
outtextxy (55,265,buffer);

a = div (maxvalue,4);
sprintf (buffer,"%d",a.quot);
outtextxy (55,354,buffer);

    /* draw and title bars */

a = div(560,numbars + 1);
xspace = a.quot;
xmarker = 60;

setfillstyle (CLOSE_DOT_FILL,15);
settextjustify (CENTER_TEXT,TOP_TEXT);
for (i = 0; i < numbars; i = i + 1)
    {
    xmarker = xmarker + xspace;
    outtextxy (xmarker,445,members[i]);
    holder = 35 * values[i];
    a = div (holder,maxvalue);
    y = a.quot * 10;
    bar3d (xmarker - 10,440 - y,xmarker + 10,440,5,1);
    }

    /* Delay and Exit */

getch ();
closegraph();
return 0;
}
```

The next example (see Listing 6.4 and Figure 6.4) is similar to the previous column chart example, with the exception that the data series contains only seven members. By displaying only seven members, the generic characteristics of the program structure are demonstrated. Note that no matter how many bars are displayed (with a maximum of 10), they will be evenly spaced on the horizontal axis.

Listing 6.4. Column chart example with seven members

```
#include <graphics.h>
#include <stdio.h>
```

```
#include <stdlib.h>
#include <conio.h>

#define MAXNUM 10          /* maximum number of bars */

int main ()
{
int gdriver = VGA;
int gmode = VGAHI;

int numbars = 7;                    /* number of bars in chart */
char maintitle[80];                 /* main title of chart      */
char subtitle[80];                  /* subtitle of chart        */
char xtitle[80];                    /* title of x axis          */
char ytitle[80];                    /* title of y axis          */
char *members[] = {"#1","#2","#3","#4","#5","#6","#7"};
int values[MAXNUM];                 /* values for bars          */
int maxvalue;                       /* max value in values      */
int xspace;                         /* spacing in x direction   */
int xmarker;                        /* x marker                 */
char buffer[40];
div_t a;
int i, y;
int holder;

        /* register EGAVGA_driver and sansserif_font */
        /* ... these have been added to graphics.lib */
        /* as described in UTIL.DOC                   */

registerbgidriver (EGAVGA_driver);
registerbgifont (sansserif_font);

        /* set VGA 16-color high resolution video mode  */

initgraph (&gdriver,&gmode,"");
rectangle (0,0,639,479);

        /* make sure no more than 10 bars are drawn */

if (numbars > MAXNUM)
        numbars = MAXNUM;

        /* define titles and values */

sprintf (maintitle,"Gross Sales");
sprintf (subtitle,"Sales Per Store");
sprintf (xtitle,"Store Number");
sprintf (ytitle,"Gross Sales $Millions");

values[0] = 42;
values[1] = 14;
values[2] = 20;
values[3] = 30;
values[4] = 20;
values[5] = 40;
values[6] = 34;
maxvalue = 42;

        /* display titles */
```

Listing 6.4.   *continues*

Listing 6.4. cont.   Column chart example with seven members

```
settextstyle (DEFAULT_FONT,HORIZ_DIR,2);
settextjustify(CENTER_TEXT,CENTER_TEXT);
outtextxy (320,40,maintitle);
outtextxy (320,70,subtitle);
settextstyle (DEFAULT_FONT,HORIZ_DIR,1);
outtextxy (320,470,xtitle);
settextstyle (DEFAULT_FONT,VERT_DIR,1);
outtextxy (10,240,ytitle);

    /* draw box and scales for bars */

rectangle (60,90,620,440);
line (60,354,620,354);
line (60,265,620,265);
line (60,178,620,178);

settextstyle (DEFAULT_FONT,HORIZ_DIR,1);
settextjustify (RIGHT_TEXT,CENTER_TEXT);
sprintf (buffer,"%d",maxvalue);
outtextxy (55,90,buffer);

a = div (maxvalue * 3,4);
sprintf (buffer,"%d",a.quot);
outtextxy (55,178,buffer);

a = div (maxvalue,2);
sprintf (buffer,"%d",a.quot);
outtextxy (55,265,buffer);

a = div (maxvalue,4);
sprintf (buffer,"%d",a.quot);
outtextxy (55,354,buffer);

    /* draw and title bars */

a = div(560,numbars + 1);
xspace = a.quot;
xmarker = 60;

setfillstyle (CLOSE_DOT_FILL,15);
settextjustify (CENTER_TEXT,TOP_TEXT);
for (i = 0; i < numbars; i = i + 1)
    {
    xmarker = xmarker + xspace;
    outtextxy (xmarker,445,members[i]);
    holder = 35 * values[i];
    a = div (holder,maxvalue);
    y = a.quot * 10;
    bar3d (xmarker - 10,440 - y,xmarker + 10,440,5,1);
    }

    /* Delay and Exit */

getch ();
closegraph();
return 0;
}
```

Figure 6.3. Screen output from Listing 6.3

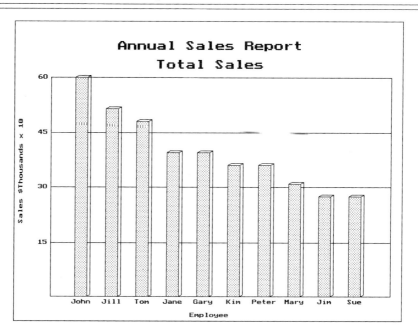

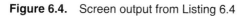

Figure 6.4. Screen output from Listing 6.4

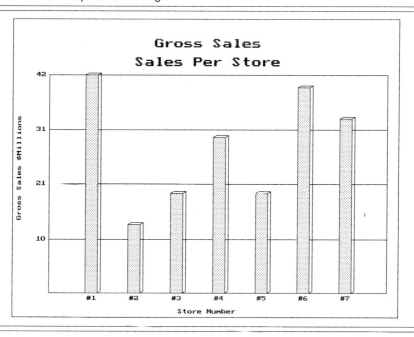

Line Charts

The line chart is used to show changes in a data series, usually relative to time. Because the line chart is generally used to illustrate trends, it is very important that you list the data in the order it is to be displayed. In the line chart, there is usually an option to connect the points that represent the data with lines.

The following example (see Listing 6.5 and Figure 6.5) demonstrates the methods for creating a line chart that displays a variable number of values from a data series. This code structure is similar to the column chart code structure. The main difference between the two code structures is that instead of drawing columns, as with the column chart, this code structure plots points to represent the members of the data series. Furthermore, each point is stored in the xpoints and ypoints arrays so that a line can be used to connect each point at a later time. This program includes the option of connecting the displayed points with a line by using the lineflag parameter. If the lineflag parameter is set to 0, the points are not connected. Similarly, if the lineflag parameter is set to 1, the points are connected.

Like the previous examples, the maintitle, subtitle, xtitle, and ytitle parameters define the character strings that provide the appropriate chart or axis title. The members and values arrays contain the name and value of each member of the data series.

This design is limited by the fact that it uses only two colors, and the fact that the maxvalue argument is equal to the maximum value in the values array. The setcolor function could be used anywhere the user desires to change the color of the grid, titles, etc. In addition, the maxvalue argument could be set to a value higher than the maximum value of the values array to avoid plotting that point at the maximum range of the display grid.

Listing 6.5. Line chart example with 10 members

```
#include <graphics.h>
#include <stdio.h>
#include <stdlib.h>
#include <conio.h>

#define MAXNUM 10        /* maximum number of points */

int main ()
{
int gdriver = VGA;
int gmode = VGAHI;

int numpoints = 10;             /* number of points in chart  */
char maintitle[80];             /* main title of chart        */
char subtitle[80];              /* subtitle of chart          */
char xtitle[80];                /* title of x axis            */
char ytitle[80];                /* title of y axis            */
```

```
char *members[] =
{"John","Jill","Tom","Jane","Gary","Kim","Peter",
          "Mary","Jim","Sue"};
int values[MAXNUM];             /* values for points          */
int xpoints[MAXNUM];            /* x values for drawing lines */
int ypoints[MAXNUM];            /* y values for drawing lines */
int maxvalue;                   /* max value in values        */
int xspace;                     /* spacing in x direction     */
int xmarker;                    /* x marker                   */
int lineflag=1;                 /* 0-no connection, 1-connect */
char buffer[40];
div_t a;
int i, y;
int holder;

        /* register EGAVGA_driver and sansserif_font */
        /* ... these have been added to graphics.lib */
        /* as described in UTIL.DOC                  */

registerbgidriver (EGAVGA_driver);
registerbgifont (sansserif_font);

        /* set VGA 16-color high resolution video mode  */

initgraph (&gdriver,&gmode,"");
rectangle (0,0,639,479);

        /* make sure no more than 10 points are drawn */

if (numpoints > MAXNUM)
        numpoints = MAXNUM;

        /* define titles and values */

sprintf (maintitle,"Annual Sales Report");
sprintf (subtitle,"Total Sales");
sprintf (xtitle,"Employee");
sprintf (ytitle,"Sales $Thousands x 10");

values[0] = 60;
values[1] = 52;
values[2] = 48;
values[3] = 40;
values[4] = 40;
values[5] = 36;
values[6] = 36;
values[7] = 32;
values[8] = 28;
values[9] = 28;
maxvalue = 60;

        /* display titles */

settextstyle (DEFAULT_FONT,HORIZ_DIR,2);
settextjustify(CENTER_TEXT,CENTER_TEXT);
outtextxy (320,40,maintitle);
```

Listing 6.5. *continues*

Listing 6.5. cont.   Line chart example with 10 members

```
outtextxy (320,70,subtitle);
settextstyle (DEFAULT_FONT,HORIZ_DIR,1);
outtextxy (320,470,xtitle);
settextstyle (DEFAULT_FONT,VERT_DIR,1);
outtextxy (10,240,ytitle);

      /* draw box and scales for chart */

rectangle (60,90,620,440);
line (60,354,620,354);
line (60,265,620,265);
line (60,178,620,178);

settextstyle (DEFAULT_FONT,HORIZ_DIR,1);
settextjustify (RIGHT_TEXT,CENTER_TEXT);
sprintf (buffer,"%d",maxvalue);
outtextxy (55,90,buffer);

a = div (maxvalue * 3,4);
sprintf (buffer,"%d",a.quot);
outtextxy (55,178,buffer);

a = div (maxvalue,2);
sprintf (buffer,"%d",a.quot);
outtextxy (55,265,buffer);

a = div (maxvalue,4);
sprintf (buffer,"%d",a.quot);
outtextxy (55,354,buffer);

      /* draw and title chart points */

a = div(560,numpoints + 1);
xspace = a.quot;
xmarker = 60;

settextjustify (CENTER_TEXT,TOP_TEXT);
for (i = 0; i < numpoints; i = i + 1)
    {
    xmarker = xmarker + xspace;
    outtextxy (xmarker,445,members[i]);
    holder = 35 * values[i];
    a = div (holder,maxvalue);
    y = a.quot * 10;
    circle (xmarker,440 - y,5);
    xpoints[i] = xmarker;
    ypoints[i] = 440-y;
    }
```

```
lineflag = 1;
if (lineflag == 1)
    {
    for (i = 0; i<numpoints - 1; i = i + 1)
        {
        line (xpoints[i],ypoints[i],xpoints[i+1],ypoints[i+1]);
        }
    };

    /* Delay and Exit */

getch ();
closegraph();
return 0;
}
```

Figure 6.5.   Screen output from Listing 6.5

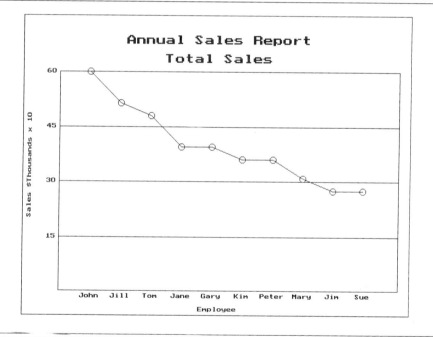

This example (see Listing 6.6 and Figure 6.6) demonstrates a seven-point line chart. The code is almost identical to the previous example; however, this example demonstrates the generic qualities of the code structure because the data series contains only seven points. Note that the lineflag parameter is set to 1, which indicates that the displayed points will be connected by lines.

159

Listing 6.6. Line chart example with seven members

```
#include <graphics.h>
#include <stdio.h>
#include <stdlib.h>
#include <conio.h>

#define MAXNUM 10        /* maximum number of points */

int main ()
{
int gdriver = VGA;
int gmode = VGAHI;

int numpoints = 7;                  /* number of points in chart */
char maintitle[80];                 /* main title of chart       */
char subtitle[80];                  /* subtitle of chart         */
char xtitle[80];                    /* title of x axis           */
char ytitle[80];                    /* title of y axis           */
char *members[] = {"#1","#2","#3","#4","#5","#6","#7"};
int values[MAXNUM];                 /* values for points         */
int xpoints[MAXNUM];                /* x values for drawing lines */
int ypoints[MAXNUM];                /* y values for drawing lines */
int maxvalue;                       /* max value in values       */
int xspace;                         /* spacing in x direction    */
int xmarker;                        /* x marker                  */
int lineflag=1;                     /* 0-no connection, 1-connect */
char buffer[40];
div_t a;
int i, y;
int holder;

        /* register EGAVGA_driver and sansserif_font */
        /* ... these have been added to graphics.lib */
        /* as described in UTIL.DOC                   */

registerbgidriver (EGAVGA_driver);
registerbgifont (sansserif_font);

        /* set VGA 16-color high resolution video mode   */

initgraph (&gdriver,&gmode,"");
rectangle (0,0,639,479);

        /* make sure no more than 10 points are drawn */

if (numpoints > MAXNUM)
        numpoints = MAXNUM;

        /* define titles and values */

sprintf (maintitle,"Gross Sales");
sprintf (subtitle,"Sales Per Store");
sprintf (xtitle,"Store Number");
sprintf (ytitle,"Gross Sales $Millions");
```

```
values[0] = 42;
values[1] = 14;
values[2] = 20;
values[3] = 30;
values[4] = 20;
values[5] = 40;
values[6] = 34;
maxvalue = 42;

        /* display titles */

settextstyle (DEFAULT_FONT,HORIZ_DIR,2);
settextjustify(CENTER_TEXT,CENTER_TEXT);
outtextxy (320,40,maintitle);
outtextxy (320,70,subtitle);
settextstyle (DEFAULT_FONT,HORIZ_DIR,1);
outtextxy (320,470,xtitle);
settextstyle (DEFAULT_FONT,VERT_DIR,1);
outtextxy (10,240,ytitle);

        /* draw box and scales for chart */

rectangle (60,90,620,440);
line (60,354,620,354);
line (60,265,620,265);
line (60,178,620,178);

settextstyle (DEFAULT_FONT,HORIZ_DIR,1);
settextjustify (RIGHT_TEXT,CENTER_TEXT);
sprintf (buffer,"%d",maxvalue);
outtextxy (55,90,buffer);

a = div (maxvalue * 3,4);
sprintf (buffer,"%d",a.quot);
outtextxy (55,178,buffer);

a = div (maxvalue,2);
sprintf (buffer,"%d",a.quot);
outtextxy (55,265,buffer);

a = div (maxvalue,4);
sprintf (buffer,"%d",a.quot);
outtextxy (55,354,buffer);

        /* draw and title chart points */

a = div(560,numpoints + 1);
xspace = a.quot;
xmarker = 60;

settextjustify (CENTER_TEXT,TOP_TEXT);
for (i = 0; i < numpoints; i = i + 1)
    {
    xmarker = xmarker + xspace;
    outtextxy (xmarker,445,members[i]);
    holder = 35 * values[i];
```

Listing 6.6. *continues*

Listing 6.6. cont.   Line chart example with seven members

```
        a = div (holder,maxvalue);
        y = a.quot * 10;
        circle (xmarker,440 - y,5);
        xpoints[i] = xmarker;
        ypoints[i] = 440-y;
        }

lineflag = 1;
if (lineflag == 1)
    {
    for (i = 0; i<numpoints - 1; i = i + 1)
      {
      line (xpoints[i],ypoints[i],xpoints[i+1],ypoints[i+1]);
      }
    };

    /* Delay and Exit */

getch ();
closegraph();
return 0;
}
```

Figure 6.6.   Screen output from Listing 6.6

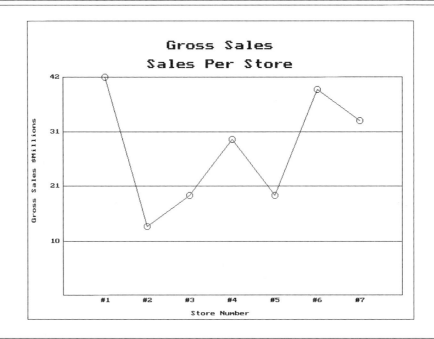

Scatter Diagrams

The *scatter diagram* illustrates the direct relationship between two values (x and y). For each pair of values (x and y), a point is plotted on the chart. The scatter diagram is used to illustrate trends or correlations in the data series. Although most scatter diagrams allow the plotted points to be connected with a line, you should do this only when the points are drawn in such a manner that the plotted line has meaning.

The following example (see Listing 6.7 and Figure 6.7) demonstrates the code structure that produces a scatter diagram. All previous examples in this chapter have used one fixed axis, and one variable axis. However, the scatter diagram, because it illustrates the relationship between two values, requires both the x and y axes to be variable.

The structure of this program is designed so that the maintitle, subtitle, xtitle, and ytitle parameters are defined and used as in the previous examples in this chapter. However, this example requires you to calculate and plot both the vertical and horizontal grids. In addition, each point must be calculated relative to the grid. For this reason, this example is the most complicated example in the chapter.

The lineflag parameter is used to allow the programmer the option of connecting the displayed points. However, if the points are to be connected, the values of the points should be arranged carefully so that the connecting lines have some relative meaning.

This program has the same limitations as the previous examples in this chapter. For example, the maxxvalue and maxyvalue arguments are set to the maximum values in the xpoints and ypoints arrays, respectively. The result is that the maximum x and y values lie on borders of the display grid. By making maxxvalue and maxyvalue a value higher than the maximum values of the xpoints and ypoints arrays, you could avoid plotting points on the chart's borders.

Listing 6.7. Scatter diagram example with 10 members

```
#include <graphics.h>
#include <stdio.h>
#include <stdlib.h>
#include <conio.h>

#define MAXNUM 10        /* maximum number of points */

int main ()
{
int gdriver = VGA;
int gmode = VGAHI;

int numpoints = 10;          /* number of points in chart */
char maintitle[80];          /* main title of chart       */
char subtitle[80];           /* subtitle of chart         */
char xtitle[80];             /* title of x axis           */
char ytitle[80];             /* title of y axis           */
int xpoints[MAXNUM];         /* x values for points       */
int ypoints[MAXNUM];         /* y values for points       */
```

Listing 6.7. *continues*

Listing 6.7. cont.   Scatter diagram example with 10 members

```
int xplot[MAXNUM];          /* x plot values              */
int yplot[MAXNUM];          /* y plot values              */
int maxxvalue;              /* max x value                */
int maxyvalue;              /* max y value                */
int lineflag = 1;           /* 0-no connection, 1-connect */
char buffer[40];
div_t a;
int i,x,y;
int holder;

        /* register EGAVGA_driver and sansserif_font */
        /* ... these have been added to graphics.lib */
        /* as described in UTIL.DOC                   */

registerbgidriver (EGAVGA_driver);
registerbgifont (sansserif_font);

        /* set VGA 16-color high resolution video mode  */

initgraph (&gdriver,&gmode,"");
rectangle (0,0,639,479);

        /* make sure no more than 10 points are drawn */

if (numpoints > MAXNUM)
        numpoints = MAXNUM;

        /* define titles and values */

sprintf (maintitle,"Sales Report");
sprintf (subtitle,"Total Sales vs. Experience");
sprintf (ytitle,"Sales Person Experience (Years)");
sprintf (xtitle,"Sales $Thousands x 10");

xpoints[0] = 15;    ypoints[0] = 60;
xpoints[1] = 9;     ypoints[1] = 52;
xpoints[2] = 11;    ypoints[2] = 48;
xpoints[3] = 7;     ypoints[3] = 40;
xpoints[4] = 8;     ypoints[4] = 40;
xpoints[5] = 5;     ypoints[5] = 36;
xpoints[6] = 8;     ypoints[6] = 36;
xpoints[7] = 4;     ypoints[7] = 32;
xpoints[8] = 5;     ypoints[8] = 28;
xpoints[9] = 2;     ypoints[9] = 28;
maxxvalue = 15;
maxyvalue = 60;

        /* display titles */

settextstyle (DEFAULT_FONT,HORIZ_DIR,2);
settextjustify(CENTER_TEXT,CENTER_TEXT);
outtextxy (320,40,maintitle);
outtextxy (320,70,subtitle);
settextstyle (DEFAULT_FONT,HORIZ_DIR,1);
outtextxy (320,470,xtitle);
settextstyle (DEFAULT_FONT,VERT_DIR,1);
outtextxy (10,240,ytitle);
```

```
      /* draw box and scales for chart */

rectangle (60,90,620,440);
line (60,354,620,354);
line (60,265,620,265);
line (60,178,620,178);

settextstyle (DEFAULT_FONT,HORIZ_DIR,1);
settextjustify (RIGHT_TEXT,CENTER_TEXT);
sprintf (buffer,"%d",maxxvalue);
outtextxy (55,90,buffer);

a = div (maxxvalue * 3,4);
sprintf (buffer,"%d",a.quot);
outtextxy (55,178,buffer);

a = div (maxxvalue,2);
sprintf (buffer,"%d",a.quot);
outtextxy (55,265,buffer);

a = div (maxxvalue,4);
sprintf (buffer,"%d",a.quot);
outtextxy (55,354,buffer);

outtextxy (55,440,"0");

line (200,90,200,440);
line (340,90,340,440);
line (480,90,480,440);

settextstyle (DEFAULT_FONT,HORIZ_DIR,1);
settextjustify (CENTER_TEXT,TOP_TEXT);
sprintf (buffer,"%d",maxyvalue);
outtextxy (620,443,buffer);

a = div (maxyvalue * 3,4);
sprintf (buffer,"%d",a.quot);
outtextxy (480,443,buffer);

a = div (maxyvalue,2);
sprintf (buffer,"%d",a.quot);
outtextxy (340,443,buffer);

a = div (maxyvalue,4);
sprintf (buffer,"%d",a.quot);
outtextxy (200,443,buffer);

outtextxy (60,443,"0");

      /* draw and title chart points */

settextjustify (CENTER_TEXT,TOP_TEXT);
for (i = 0; i < numpoints; i = i + 1)
    {
    holder = 35 * xpoints[i];
    a = div(holder,maxxvalue);
```

Listing 6.7. *continues*

165

Listing 6.7. cont.   Scatter diagram example with 10 members

```
          y = 440 - (a.quot * 10);
          holder = 56 * ypoints[i];
          a = div(holder,maxyvalue);
          x = 60 + (a.quot * 10);
          circle (x,y,5);
          xplot[i] = x;
          yplot[i] = y;
          }

if (lineflag == 1)
     {
     for (i = 0; i<numpoints - 1; i = i + 1)
          {
          line (xplot[i],yplot[i],xplot[i+1],yplot[i+1]);
          }
     }
     /* Delay and Exit */

getch ();
closegraph();
return 0;
}
```

Figure 6.7.   Screen output from Listing 6.7

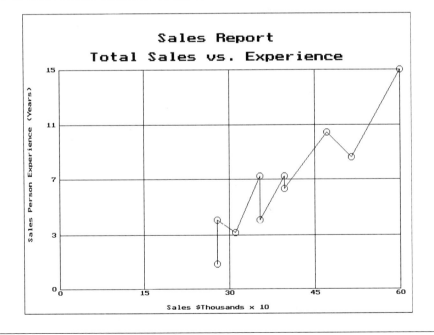

This example (see Listing 6.8 and Figure 6.8) is similar to the previous scatter diagram example. However, only seven points are plotted and no line is used to connect the points.

Listing 6.8. Scatter diagram example with seven members

```
#include <graphics.h>
#include <stdio.h>
#include <stdlib.h>
#include <conio.h>

#define MAXNUM 10        /* maximum number of points */

int main ()
{
int gdriver = VGA;
int gmode = VGAHI;

int numpoints = 7;             /* number of points in chart  */
char maintitle[80];            /* main title of chart        */
char subtitle[80];             /* subtitle of chart          */
char xtitle[80];               /* title of x axis            */
char ytitle[80];               /* title of y axis            */
int xpoints[MAXNUM];           /* x values for points        */
int ypoints[MAXNUM];           /* y values for points        */
int xplot[MAXNUM];             /* x plot values              */
int yplot[MAXNUM];             /* y plot values              */
int maxxvalue;                 /* max x value                */
int maxyvalue;                 /* max y value                */
int lineflag = 0;              /* 0-no connection, 1-connect */
char buffer[40];
div_t a;
int i,x,y;
int holder;

        /* register EGAVGA_driver and sansserif_font */
        /* ... these have been added to graphics.lib */
        /* as described in UTIL.DOC                   */

registerbgidriver (EGAVGA_driver);
registerbgifont (sansserif_font);

        /* set VGA 16-color high resolution video mode  */

initgraph (&gdriver,&gmode,"");
rectangle (0,0,639,479);

        /* make sure no more than 10 points are drawn */

if (numpoints > MAXNUM)
    numpoints = MAXNUM;

        /* define titles and values */

sprintf (maintitle,"Gross Sales");
```

Listing 6.8. *continues*

167

Listing 6.8. cont.   Scatter diagram example with seven members

```
sprintf (subtitle,"Gross Sales vs. Customers");
sprintf (ytitle,"Number of Customers (Millions)");
sprintf (xtitle,"Gross Sales $Millions");

xpoints[0] = 42;        ypoints[0] = 23;
xpoints[1] = 14;        ypoints[1] = 9;
xpoints[2] = 20;        ypoints[2] = 11;
xpoints[3] = 30;        ypoints[3] = 7;
xpoints[4] = 20;        ypoints[4] = 17;
xpoints[5] = 40;        ypoints[5] = 26;
xpoints[6] = 34;        ypoints[6] = 16;
maxxvalue = 42;
maxyvalue = 26;

      /* display titles */

settextstyle (DEFAULT_FONT,HORIZ_DIR,2);
settextjustify(CENTER_TEXT,CENTER_TEXT);
outtextxy (320,40,maintitle);
outtextxy (320,70,subtitle);
settextstyle (DEFAULT_FONT,HORIZ_DIR,1);
outtextxy (320,470,xtitle);
settextstyle (DEFAULT_FONT,VERT_DIR,1);
outtextxy (10,240,ytitle);

      /* draw box and scales for chart */

rectangle (60,90,620,440);
line (60,354,620,354);
line (60,265,620,265);
line (60,178,620,178);

settextstyle (DEFAULT_FONT,HORIZ_DIR,1);
settextjustify (RIGHT_TEXT,CENTER_TEXT);
sprintf (buffer,"%d",maxxvalue);
outtextxy (55,90,buffer);

a = div (maxxvalue * 3,4);
sprintf (buffer,"%d",a.quot);
outtextxy (55,178,buffer);

a = div (maxxvalue,2);
sprintf (buffer,"%d",a.quot);
outtextxy (55,265,buffer);

a = div (maxxvalue,4);
sprintf (buffer,"%d",a.quot);
outtextxy (55,354,buffer);

outtextxy (55,440,"0");
```

```
line (200,90,200,440);
line (340,90,340,440);
line (480,90,480,440);

settextstyle (DEFAULT_FONT,HORIZ_DIR,1);
settextjustify (CENTER_TEXT,TOP_TEXT);
sprintf (buffer,"%d",maxyvalue);
outtextxy (620,443,buffer);

a = div (maxyvalue * 3,4);
sprintf (buffer,"%d",a.quot);
outtextxy (480,443,buffer);

a = div (maxyvalue,2);
sprintf (buffer,"%d",a.quot);
outtextxy (340,443,buffer);

a = div (maxyvalue,4);
sprintf (buffer,"%d",a.quot);
outtextxy (200,443,buffer);

outtextxy (60,443,"0");

      /* draw and title chart points */

settextjustify (CENTER_TEXT,TOP_TEXT);
for (i = 0; i < numpoints; i = i + 1)
     {
     holder = 35 * xpoints[i];
     a = div(holder,maxxvalue);
     y = 440 - (a.quot * 10);
     holder = 56 * ypoints[i];
     a = div(holder,maxyvalue);
     x = 60 + (a.quot * 10);
     circle (x,y,5);
     xplot[i] = x;
     yplot[i] = y;
     }

if (lineflag == 1)
     {
     for (i = 0; i<numpoints - 1; i = i + 1)
         {
         line (xplot[i],yplot[i],xplot[i+1],yplot[i+1]);
         }
     }
     /* Delay and Exit */

getch ();
closegraph();
return 0;
}
```

Figure 6.8. Screen output from Listing 6.8.

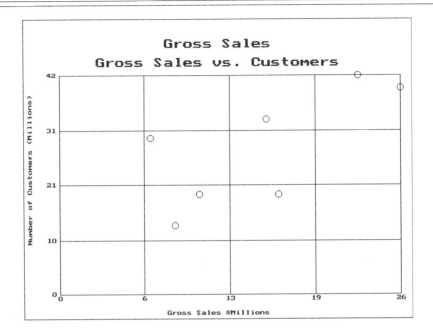

Pie Charts

The *pie chart* illustrates the relationship of a member of the data series relative to the whole. In other words, the size of the pie piece reflects its percentage of the whole, or contribution to the whole.

The following example (see Listing 6.9 and Figure 6.9) demonstrates the use of the Borland C++ graphics library to create a code structure that displays a pie chart with up to 10 slices. In this example, the `maintitle` and `subtitle` parameters define the character strings for the chart titles. In addition, the members and values arrays contain the name and corresponding percentage of each member in the data series.

When all values are defined, the pie chart is drawn using a different fill pattern for each pie slice. The example also creates a legend that lists the corresponding fill pattern, value, and name for each member. You should keep member names short to avoid extending beyond the legend's border.

Listing 6.9. Pie chart example with 10 members

```
#include <graphics.h>
#include <stdio.h>
#include <stdlib.h>
#include <conio.h>

#define MAXNUM 10              /* maximum number of pie slices */

int main ()
{
int gdriver = VGA;
int gmode = VGAHI;

int numslices = 10;              /* number of slices in pie */
char maintitle[80];              /* main title of chart      */
char subtitle[80];               /* subtitle of chart        */
char *members[] = {"John", "Jill", "Tom", "Jane", "Gary", "Kim",
          "Peter", "Mary", "Jim", "Sue"};
int values[MAXNUM];              /* percentages for slices   */
int pattern = 0;                 /* fill pattern number      */
int x,y;
int oldangle, angle;
int i;
char buffer[40];
div_t a;
int holder;

     /* register EGAVGA_driver and sansserif_font */
     /* ... these have been added to graphics.lib */
     /* as described in UTIL.DOC                   */

registerbgidriver (EGAVGA_driver);
registerbgifont (sansserif_font);

     /* set VGA 16-color high resolution video mode  */

initgraph (&gdriver,&gmode,"");
rectangle (0,0,639,479);

     /* see if numslices < MAXNUM */

if (numslices > MAXNUM)
     numslices = MAXNUM;

     /* define the titles and percentages */

sprintf (maintitle,"Annual Sales Report");
sprintf (subtitle,"Based on Percentages of Total Sales");

values[0] = 15;        /* note - sum of values should */
values[1] = 13;        /* equal 100 - although this    */
values[2] = 12;        /* program only requires the    */
values[3] = 10;        /* sum to be less than 100      */
values[4] = 10;
values[5] = 9;
```

Listing 6.9. *continues*

Listing 6.9. cont. Pie chart example with 10 members

```
values[6] = 9;
values[7] = 8;
values[8] = 7;
values[9] = 7;

      /* display titles */

settextstyle (DEFAULT_FONT,HORIZ_DIR,2);
settextjustify (CENTER_TEXT,CENTER_TEXT);
outtextxy (320,50,maintitle);
outtextxy (320,80,subtitle);

      /* create legend */

y = 170;
pattern = 0;
rectangle (400,140,620,420);
settextjustify (LEFT_TEXT,CENTER_TEXT);
for (i=0; i<numslices; i=i+1)
      {
      sprintf (buffer,"%s : %d",members[i],values[i]);
      outtextxy (460,y,buffer);
      setfillstyle (pattern,15);
      bar (410,y-10,440,y+10);
      rectangle (410,y-10,440,y+10);
      pattern = pattern + 1;
      y = y + 25;
      }

      /* create the pie */

pattern = 0;
oldangle = 0;
for (i=0; i < numslices - 1; i=i+1)
      {
      setfillstyle (pattern,15);
      holder = 360 * values[i];
      a = div(holder,100);
      angle = oldangle + a.quot;
      pieslice (205,280,oldangle,angle,175);
      oldangle = angle;
      pattern = pattern + 1;
      }
setfillstyle (pattern,15);
pieslice(205,280,oldangle,360,175);

      /* Delay and Exit */

getch ();
closegraph();
return 0;
}
```

Figure 6.9. Screen output from Listing 6.9

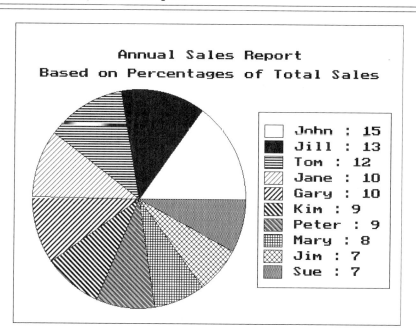

This example (see Listing 6.10 and Figure 6.10) is similar to the previous pie chart example with the exception that it creates only seven pie slices. As demonstrated, the code structure effectively handles any number of pie slices from 1 to 10.

Listing 6.10. Pie chart example with seven members

```
#include <graphics.h>
#include <stdio.h>
#include <stdlib.h>
#include <conio.h>

#define MAXNUM 10              /* maximum number of pie slices */

int main ()
{
int gdriver = VGA;
int gmode = VGAHI;

int numslices = 7;            /* number of slices in pie */
char maintitle[80];           /* main title of chart     */
char subtitle[80];            /* subtitle of chart       */
char *members[] = {"#1", "#2", "#3", "#4", "#5", "#6","#7"};
int values[MAXNUM];           /* percentages for slices  */
int pattern = 0;              /* fill pattern number     */
```

Listing 6.10. *continues*

Listing 6.10. cont.   Pie chart example with seven members

```
int x,y;
int oldangle, angle;
int i;
char buffer[40];
div_t a;
int holder;

        /* register EGAVGA_driver and sansserif_font */
        /* ... these have been added to graphics.lib */
        /* as described in UTIL.DOC                   */

registerbgidriver (EGAVGA_driver);
registerbgifont (sansserif_font);

        /* set VGA 16-color high resolution video mode  */

initgraph (&gdriver,&gmode,"");
rectangle (0,0,639,479);

        /* see if numslices < MAXNUM */

if (numslices > MAXNUM)
    numslices = MAXNUM;

        /* define the titles and percentages */

sprintf (maintitle,"Gross Sales Per Store");
sprintf (subtitle,"Based on Percentages of Corporate Sales");

values[0] = 21;       /* note - sum of values should */
values[1] = 7;        /* equal 100 - although this   */
values[2] = 10;       /* program only requires the   */
values[3] = 15;       /* sum to be less than 100     */
values[4] = 10;
values[5] = 20;
values[6] = 17;

        /* display titles */

settextstyle (DEFAULT_FONT,HORIZ_DIR,2);
settextjustify (CENTER_TEXT,CENTER_TEXT);
outtextxy (320,50,maintitle);
outtextxy (320,80,subtitle);

        /* create legend */

y = 170;
pattern = 0;
rectangle (400,140,620,420);
settextjustify (LEFT_TEXT,CENTER_TEXT);
for (i=0; i<numslices; i=i+1)
    {
    sprintf (buffer,"%s : %d",members[i],values[i]);
    outtextxy (460,y,buffer);
    setfillstyle (pattern,15);
    bar (410,y-10,440,y+10);
    rectangle (410,y-10,440,y+10);
    pattern = pattern + 1;
```

```
        y = y + 25;
        }

        /* create the pie */
pattern = 0;
oldangle = 0;
for (i=0; i < numslices - 1; i=i+1)
        {
        setfillstyle (pattern,15);
        holder = 360 * values[i];
        a = div(holder,100);
        angle = oldangle + a.quot;
        pieslice (205,280,oldangle,angle,175);
        oldangle = angle;
        pattern = pattern + 1;
        }
setfillstyle (pattern,15);
pieslice(205,280,oldangle,360,175);

        /* Delay and Exit */
getch ();
closegraph();
return 0;
}
```

Figure 6.10. Screen output from Listing 6.10

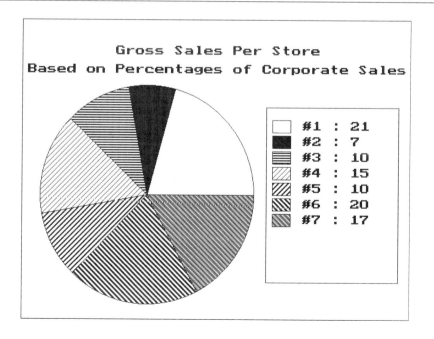

Summary

This chapter introduced some methods that could be used to develop presentation graphics, such as bar, line, scatter, column, and pie charts, using the functions of the Borland C++ graphics library. By carefully applying these methods, you can create flexible, full-featured presentation graphics applications.

7

Animation

A nimation is the art of making a series of distinct images appear to have life or motion. For computer graphics, animation is often associated with computer video games. The art of animation is both challenging and exciting for the computer graphics programmer. This chapter introduces the basic animation concepts behind advanced computer graphics. By combining the techniques introduced in this chapter with the concepts discussed in other chapters, you can produce sophisticated computer graphics packages and programs.

The Art of Animation

The key to successful animation is the artwork. If you are like the average computer programmer, however, you lack the skills to create intricate sketches. Fortunately, this is usually not a problem because you can obtain images from many sources, such as magazines and clip-art libraries. You need only to find the image, trace it onto a sheet of properly-sized graph paper (keep in mind that the aspect ratio of the target screen must be considered), and then transfer the image into coordinates that the computer can work with and display. This is the *trace-draw-transfer* method.

The trace-draw-transfer method can be very time-consuming and lengthy. For small programming examples, this process is sufficient; big projects, however, may require alternate methods. The examples in this chapter follow the trace-draw-transfer method. All applicable copyright laws should be considered when using this method.

One alternate method of creating complex screens and images for use in animation is the use of a screen capture program. Many paintbrush programs (including PC Paintbrush IV by ZSoft) create screen images that you can save as files in the .PCX file format. Then, using programs such as PCX Programmer's Toolkit, PCX Effects, and PCX Text (all by Genus Microprogramming), the .PCX images can be manipulated and included in a Borland C++ application. These programs also include a wide variety of additional functions that add to the overall graphics programming flexibility of Borland C++.

By using a paintbrush program that allows you to edit an image on-screen, you can create and edit the image much more quickly than with the trace-draw-transfer method. In addition, most paintbrush programs permit the use of alternate input devices such as mice, trackballs, and digitizer tablets, which greatly help the creation and editing process.

Animation Concepts

Basically, there are two types of animation. These types are full-screen animation and partial-screen animation. With full-screen animation, you use the entire screen to create animation. With partial-screen animation, only parts of the screen are used. Each of these methods is discussed in detail in the following sections.

Full-Screen Animation

To successfully accomplish full-screen animation with the Borland C++ functions, the video adapter must be either an EGA or a VGA and have sufficient memory to support multiple pages of graphics output. Assuming that the video adapter has sufficient memory, the setactivepage and setvisualpage functions can be used to alternate video pages in memory to simulate animation. The syntax for each is:

```
void far setactivepage(int page);
int page;                    Page number

void far setvisualpage(int page);
int page;                    Page number
```

The visual page is the page in video memory that is currently displayed on the screen. The active page is the page in video memory to which all graphics output is currently sent. These pages do not have to be the same. The default setting for both is page 0.

The following example should help you understand the method for alternating pages. Let's assume that two pages of video graphics memory are available, page 0 and page 1. Upon entering the graphics mode, both the visual page and active page are 0. Therefore, we have the following:

```
Active page = 0            Visual Page = 0
```

We now want to create a screen to accomplish the desired animation. It is a good idea to draw on a nonvisual screen when developing applications, so that the end-user doesn't actually see the lines or objects being drawn. Therefore, the active page would be set to 1 with the setactivepage (1); call. We now have the following:

Active page = 1   Visual Page = 0

Nothing is displayed presently. When you have completed the first screen, you should make it the visual page. You should also make the active screen the nonvisual page. The setvisualpage (1); and setactivepage (0); calls will do this. We now have the following:

Active page = 0   Visual Page = 1

When you have completed the nonvisual screen, you can alternate the screens (0 and 1) to produce the animation effects. You would again use the setvisualpage and setactivepage functions. The following would continue until interrupted:

Active page = 1   Visual Page = 0

Active Page = 0   Visual Page = 1

Active Page = 1   Visual Page = 0
        .   .
        .   .
        .   .

Listing 7.1 demonstrates the use of the setactivepage and setvisualpage functions for full-screen animation using two screens. The first of the two screens shows a simplistic picture of a highway blending into the horizon. The second screen is almost identical to the first, except that the center lines differ slightly between the first and second screen. When the screens are flipped, it appears as though you are traveling down the highway. This is a simple demonstration of how many video driving games are created. Figures 7.1 and 7.2 show the first and second screens. It may be necessary to alter the for loops in the program to speed up or slow down the delays between page flips to achieve good animation effects.

Figure 7.1.   The first screen used in Listing 7.1

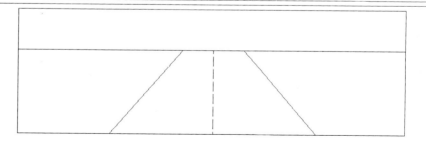

Figure 7.2. The second screen used in Listing 7.1

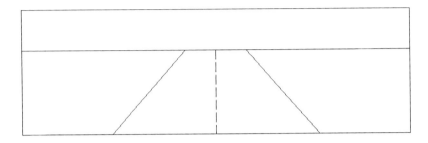

Listing 7.1. Full-screen animation example

```c
#include <graphics.h>
#include <stdio.h>
#include <stdlib.h>
#include <conio.h>

int main ()
{
int gdriver = EGA;
int gmode = EGALO;
int i,x;

        /* register EGAVGA_driver and sansserif_font */
        /* ... these have been added to graphics.lib */
        /* as described in UTIL.DOC                   */

registerbgidriver (EGAVGA_driver);
registerbgifont (sansserif_font);

        /* set EGA low resolution video mode   */

initgraph (&gdriver,&gmode,"");
rectangle (0,0,639,199);

        /* draw screen 1 */

setactivepage (1);
clearviewport ();
rectangle (0,0,639,199);
line (0,65,639,65);
line (270,65,150,199);
line (370,65,490,199);
line (320,65,320,80);
line (320,85,320,100);
line (320,105,320,120);
line (320,125,320,140);
line (320,145,320,160);
line (320,165,320,180);
line (320,185,320,199);
```

```
                /* draw screen 2 */

setvisualpage (1);
setactivepage(0);
line (0,65,639,65);
line (270,65,150,199);
line (370,65,490,199);
line (320,65,320,70);
line (320,75,320,90);
line (320,95,320,110);
line (320,115,320,130);
line (320,135,320,150);
line (320,155,320,170);
line (320,175,320,190);
line (320,195,320,199);

        /* flip pages */

do
{
setvisualpage (1);
for (i=1; i<50; i=i+1)
{
      for (x=1; x<10000; x=x+1)
           {};
}
setvisualpage (0);
for (i=1; i<50; i=i+1)
{
      for (x=1; x<10000; x=x+1)
           {};
}
} while (!kbhit());

closegraph();
return 0;
}
```

Partial-Screen Animation

In partial-screen animation, you use only a small portion of the screen to create the animation. The portion of the screen used for animation is usually saved in memory and then moved about the screen. Another possibility is to store several images and place them on top of each other to simulate motion.

The Borland C++ graphics library includes two functions for use with partial-screen animation. These are the getimage and putimage functions. The syntax for each is:

```
void far getimage (int left, int top, int right,
                   int bottom, void far *bitmap);
   int left, top;          Upper left corner of image
   int right, bottom;      Lower right corner of image
   void far *bitmap;       Image buffer
```

181

```
void far putimage (int left, int top, void far *bitmap,
                   int op);
int left, top;             Position to place image
void far *bitmap;          Image buffer
int op;                    Logical operation for placing image
```

You can use the getimage function to store a rectangular image in a buffer. The upper left and lower right corners of the rectangular image are identified and passed to the function. The specified rectangular region is then stored in the buffer identified in the bitmap argument. The getimage function is used with the view coordinate system.

The putimage function is used to place an image stored by the getimage function onto the screen (hidden or visual). The location of the upper left corner of the image is specified, along with the image to place, and the method. The method specifies exactly how the image will interact with its background. For example, the XOR_PUT action will perform an exclusive-OR between each image pixel and the background. This action is often performed because doing an exclusive-OR twice will return the background to its original state. However, as will be discussed later in this chapter, the image often is distorted. Table 7.1 lists the five op arguments for use with the putimage functions. Like the getimage function, the putimage function is used with the view coordinate system.

Table 7.1. *Logical operations for the* putimage *function*

Constant	Value	Meaning
COPY_PUT	0	Copy image "as is"
XOR_PUT	1	Exclusive OR image
OR_PUT	2	Inclusive OR image
AND_PUT	3	AND image
NOT_PUT	4	Copy inverse of image

Listing 7.2 demonstrates the concepts of the getimage and putimage functions. In this example, a circular image, or ball, bounces around the screen. The XOR_PUT action argument is used for the animation. This example is very simplistic because it uses only one page (the next example presents a method that could be used to make this example more realistic by using hidden pages with partial screens). In addition, the XOR_PUT action only works well with plain backgrounds. When using multicolored backgrounds, the background will tend to bleed through, leaving the image obscured. However, the XOR_PUT argument works well for simple animation. Other methods will be discussed later in the chapter.

Listing 7.2. Animation using exclusive-OR

```
#include <graphics.h>
#include <stdio.h>
#include <stdlib.h>
#include <conio.h>

int main ()
{
int gdriver = EGA;
int gmode = EGAHI;
void *ball;
unsigned int imsize;
short x1,y1;
short oldx, oldy;
short x_dir, y_dir;
x_dir = -5;
y_dir = 5;

     /* register EGAVGA_driver and sansserif_font */
     /* ... these have been added to graphics.lib */
     /* as described in UTIL.DOC               */

registerbgidriver (EGAVGA_driver);
registerbgifont (sansserif_font);

     /* set EGA 16-color high resolution video mode  */

initgraph (&gdriver,&gmode,"");
rectangle (0,0,639,349);

     /* draw and store circular image */

fillellipse (320,175,10,7);
imsize = imagesize(310,168,330,182);
ball = malloc(imsize);
getimage (310,168,330,182,ball);

     /* move ball around screen */

x1 = 310;
y1 = 168;
do
{
oldx = x1;
oldy = y1;
x1 = x1 + x_dir;
y1 - y1 + y_dir;

if (x1 < 0)
{
     x1 = x1 + 5;
     x_dir = 5;
}
if (x1 > 619)
{
     x1 = x1 - 5;
     x_dir = -5;
```

Listing 7.2. *continues*

Listing 7.2. cont.   Animation using `exclusive-OR`

```
}
if (y1 > 329)
{
    y1 = y1 - 5;
    y_dir = -5;
}
if (y1 < 0)
{
    y1 = y1 + 5;
    y_dir = 5;
}
putimage (oldx,oldy,ball,XOR_PUT);
putimage (x1,y1,ball,XOR_PUT);
} while (!kbhit());

closegraph();
return 0;
}
```

Hidden Pages with Partial-Screen Animation

In the previous example, one image was moved over the screen to produce motion. The output was far from optimal because the image appeared to flicker as it moved (this is a characteristic of single-page animation). The best way to overcome this flickering is to use multiple pages of graphics to store several images, each slightly different than the other, then move the object on a hidden page. Listing 7.3 is an example of this type of animation. This example uses the same basic code structure as before, but tracks two screens and ball locations. The example also uses the `pause` function to control the speed of the animation. It may be necessary to modify the example's `for` loops, which call the `pause` function to modify the speed of animation.

Listing 7.3.   Spinning ball example

```
#include <graphics.h>
#include <stdio.h>
#include <stdlib.h>
#include <conio.h>

void pause (void);

int main ()
{
int gdriver = EGA;
int gmode = EGAHI;
void *ball1;
void *ball2;
void *ball3;
void *ball4;
```

```
void *ball5;
void *ball6;
unsigned int imsize;
int i;

     /* register EGAVGA_driver and sansserif_font */
     /* ... these have been added to graphics.lib */
     /* as described in UTIL.DOC                   */

registerbgidriver (EGAVGA_driver);
registerbgifont (sansserif_font);

     /* set EGA 16-color high resolution video mode  */

initgraph (&gdriver,&gmode,"");
rectangle (0,0,639,349);

    /* draw and store ball 1 */

setcolor (15);
ellipse (70,175,0,360,40,30);
ellipse (70,175,0,360,15,30);
setfillstyle (SOLID_FILL,1);
floodfill (32,175,15);
setfillstyle (SOLID_FILL,4);
floodfill (70,175,15);
setfillstyle (SOLID_FILL,2);
floodfill (108,175,15);
imsize = imagesize(30,145,110,205);
ball1 = malloc (imsize);
getimage (30,145,110,205,ball1);

        /* draw and store ball 2 */

setcolor (15);
ellipse (170,175,0,360,40,30);
ellipse (170,175,0,360,15,30);
setfillstyle (SOLID_FILL,14);
floodfill (132,175,15);
setfillstyle (SOLID_FILL,1);
floodfill (170,175,15);
setfillstyle (SOLID_FILL,4);
floodfill (208,175,15);
imsize = imagesize(130,145,210,205);
ball2 = malloc(imsize);
getimage (130,145,210,205,ball2);

        /* draw and store ball 3 */

setcolor (15);
ellipse (270,175,0,360,40,30);
ellipse (270,175,0,360,15,30);
setfillstyle (SOLID_FILL,3);
floodfill (232,175,15);
setfillstyle (SOLID_FILL,14);
floodfill (270,175,15);
setfillstyle (SOLID_FILL,1);
floodfill (308,175,15);
```

Listing 7.3. *continues*

185

Listing 7.3. cont.   Spinning ball example

```
imsize = imagesize(230,145,310,205);
ball3 = malloc(imsize);
getimage (230,145,310,205,ball3);

        /* draw and store ball 4 */

setcolor (15);
ellipse (370,175,0,360,40,30);
ellipse (370,175,0,360,15,30);
setfillstyle (SOLID_FILL,15);
floodfill (332,175,15);
setfillstyle (SOLID_FILL,3);
floodfill (370,175,15);
setfillstyle (SOLID_FILL,14);
floodfill (408,175,15);
imsize = imagesize(330,145,410,205);
ball4 = malloc(imsize);
getimage (330,145,410,205,ball4);

        /* draw and store ball 5 */

setcolor (15);
ellipse (470,175,0,360,40,30);
ellipse (470,175,0,360,15,30);
setfillstyle (SOLID_FILL,2);
floodfill (432,175,15);
setfillstyle (SOLID_FILL,15);
floodfill (470,175,15);
setfillstyle (SOLID_FILL,3);
floodfill (508,175,15);
imsize = imagesize(430,145,510,205);
ball5 = malloc(imsize);
getimage (430,145,510,205,ball5);

        /* draw and store ball 6 */

setcolor (15);
ellipse (570,175,0,360,40,30);
ellipse (570,175,0,360,15,30);
setfillstyle (SOLID_FILL,4);
floodfill (532,175,15);
setfillstyle (SOLID_FILL,2);
floodfill (570,175,15);
setfillstyle (SOLID_FILL,15);
floodfill (608,175,15);
imsize = imagesize(530,145,610,205);
ball6 = malloc(imsize);
getimage (530,145,610,205,ball6);

settextjustify (CENTER_TEXT,CENTER_TEXT);
outtextxy (320,320,"Press Any Key to Continue");
getch();

        /* rotate ball */
```

```
clearviewport();
rectangle (0,0,639,349);
setactivepage (1);
clearviewport();
rectangle (0,0,639,349);

do
{
setactivepage(1);
putimage (280,145,ball1,COPY_PUT);
setvisualpage(1);
for (i-1; i<50; i=i+1)
     pause();

setactivepage(0);
putimage (280,145,ball2,COPY_PUT);
setvisualpage(0);
for (i=1; i<50; i=i+1)
     pause();

setactivepage(1);
putimage (280,145,ball3,COPY_PUT);
setvisualpage(1);
for (i=1; i<50; i=i+1)
     pause();

setactivepage(0);
putimage (280,145,ball4,COPY_PUT);
setvisualpage(0);
for (i=1; i<50; i=i+1)
     pause();

setactivepage(1);
putimage (280,145,ball5,COPY_PUT);
setvisualpage(1);
for (i=1; i<50; i=i+1)
     pause();

setactivepage(0);
putimage (280,145,ball6,COPY_PUT);
setvisualpage(0);
for (i=1; i<50; i=i+1)
     pause();
} while (!kbhit());


closegraph();
return 0;
}

void pause ()
{
int x = 0;
do
{
x=x+1;
} while (x!=10000);
}
```

Partial- and full-screen animation can be used in combination to generate almost any graphics application. These basic techniques are the foundation for most personal computer graphics applications.

Advanced Concepts in Animation

In order to make the most of animation, it is important to understand a few of its more complex concepts. These concepts, when applied with the previously introduced techniques, greatly enhance the flexibility and results of the graphics program.

Placing Images on Multicolored Backgrounds

The putimage function is the primary means of animation. Therefore, it is important that you fully understand this function and its corresponding arguments. For this reason, Listing 7.4 is provided. In this example, an image is created, stored, and placed on a multicolored background using each of the five action constants described in Table 7.1.

Listing 7.4. Using the putimage function

```c
#include <graphics.h>
#include <stdio.h>
#include <stdlib.h>
#include <conio.h>

int main ()
{
int gdriver = EGA;
int gmode = EGAHI;
void *image;
unsigned int imsize;
int x,y;
int color = 1;

        /* register EGAVGA_driver and sansserif_font */
        /* ... these have been added to graphics.lib */
        /* as described in UTIL.DOC                   */

registerbgidriver (EGAVGA_driver);
registerbgifont (sansserif_font);

        /* set EGA 16-color high resolution video mode  */

initgraph (&gdriver,&gmode,"");
rectangle (0,0,639,349);
setbkcolor (1);

        /* draw multicolored grid */
```

```
for (x=0; x<639; x=x+10)
{
     setcolor(color);
     moveto (x,0);
     lineto (x,349);
     color = color + 1;
     if (color > 15)
          color = 1;
}

for (y=0; y<349; y=y+10)
{
     setcolor (color);
     moveto (0,y);
     lineto (639,y);
     color = color + 1;
     if (color > 15)
          color = 1;
}

     /* store image to place on screen */

setactivepage (1);
clearviewport ();
setfillstyle (SOLID_FILL,4);
fillellipse(55,55,25,25);
imsize = imagesize (30,30,80,80);
image = malloc (imsize);
getimage(30,30,80,80,image);

     /* place image on screen */

setactivepage (0);
putimage (155,10,image,COPY_PUT);
putimage (225,80,image,XOR_PUT);
putimage (295,150,image,OR_PUT);
putimage (365,220,image,AND_PUT);
putimage (435,290,image,NOT_PUT);

setcolor (15);
settextjustify (CENTER_TEXT,CENTER_TEXT);
outtextxy (220,315,"COPY_PUT, XOR_PUT, OR_PUT, AND_PUT,
NOT_PUT");

     /* Delay and Exit */

settextjustify(CENTER_TEXT,BOTTOM_TEXT);
outtextxy (220,330,"Press Any Key To Exit");

getch ();

closegraph();
return 0;
}
```

From this example it is apparent that none of these action arguments provides a good means of placing an image on a multicolored background. Fortunately, there is a way to successfully place complex images onto complex backgrounds.

Combining Action Arguments for Complex Images

As the previous example demonstrated, no single action argument effectively places a complex image (a nonrectangular image) on a multicolored background. Fortunately, you can use a combination of action arguments to place an image cleanly on the multicolored background. This is the OR_PUT/AND_PUT combination. A preparatory image is first placed on the screen with the OR_PUT action argument. The complex image is then placed on the screen with the AND_PUT argument. The result is an image that, even if it is irregularly shaped, allows the background around the image to show while the image is undistorted. Using this combination makes it impossible to restore the background. Therefore, if the background must be restored, it should be saved prior to using this combination.

Listing 7.5 demonstrates the use of the OR_PUT/AND_PUT combination. When you press a key, the program clears the screen, draws a multicolored background, then places the preparatory and display images on the screen with the OR_PUT/AND_PUT arguments. The result is an image that is placed cleanly on the background. The preparatory image consists of a white ellipse on a black background. The preparatory image is the same shape as the image to transer. When the preparatory image is placed on the screen with the OR_PUT argument, each white pixel turns any colored background pixel white. The complex image is created as follows: pixels written over the white preparatory image are transferred "as is," meaning they retain their appearance. Pixels that aren't placed on the preparatory image allow the background color to show through unchanged. Figure 7.3 shows the final result of this example.

Listing 7.5. Example of the OR_PUT/AND_PUT combination

```
#include <graphics.h>
#include <stdio.h>
#include <stdlib.h>
#include <conio.h>

int main ()
{
int gdriver = EGA;
int gmode = EGAHI;
void *prepimage;
void *image;
unsigned int imsize;
int x,y;

        /* register EGAVGA_driver and sansserif_font */
        /* ... these have been added to graphics.lib */
        /* as described in UTIL.DOC                   */

registerbgidriver (EGAVGA_driver);
registerbgifont (sansserif_font);
```

```
        /* set EGA 16-color high resolution video mode  */

initgraph (&gdriver,&gmode,"");
rectangle (0,0,639,349);

      /* draw preparatory and complex image */

setfillstyle (SOLID_FILL,15);
fillellipse (260,150,50,50);

setfillstyle (SOLID_FILL,4);
bar (330,100,430,200);
setfillstyle (SOLID_FILL,2);
bar (350,120,410,180);
setfillstyle (SOLID_FILL,14);
bar (370,140,390,160);

      /* save images */

imsize = imagesize(210,100,310,200);
prepimage = malloc(imsize);
getimage (210,100,310,200,prepimage);

imsize = imagesize(330,100,430,200);
image = malloc(imsize);
getimage (330,100,430,200,image);

settextjustify (CENTER_TEXT,CENTER_TEXT);
outtextxy (320,320,"Press any key to continue");
getch();

      /* draw multi-colored background */

clearviewport ();
setcolor (4);
for (x=0; x<639; x=x+10)
    line (x,0,x,349);
for (y=0; y<349; y=y+10)
    line (0,y,639,y);
setcolor (15);
rectangle (0,0,639,349);

      /* place image */

putimage (270,125,prepimage,OR_PUT);
putimage (270,125,image,AND_PUT);

      /* Delay and Exit */

settextjustify(CENTER_TEXT,BOTTOM_TEXT);
outtextxy (320,320,"Press Any Key To Exit");

getch ();

closegraph();
return 0;
}
```

Figure 7.3. Screen output from Listing 7.5

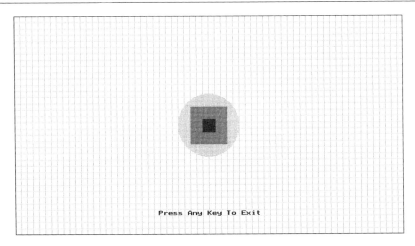

Press Any Key To Exit

Optimizing the Speed of Animation

To achieve good results, the program must have adequate speed. The programmer can influence the speed of animation through application design.

The first and foremost method for animation optimization is to create several screens in memory and flip through them. Unfortunately, this is seldom a viable alternative because a limited number of pages can be created and manipulated in video RAM. Some applications use assembly routines to save screens in computer memory. Even with this, the computer's total memory (video and computer) can be used up quickly. Therefore, you must consider other solutions.

The only other method is to use any combination of the techniques in this chapter. However, there are certain rules of thumb that you should keep in mind. The first is that you should keep the images that are manipulated with the `getimage` and `putimage` functions as small as possible. The smaller the image, the faster it is transferred. Secondly, you should carefully consider the method by which the images are placed. For example, when using the `OR_PUT`/`AND_PUT` combination for animation, you must save the background immediately behind the image (if you are required to restore to background). Then you must place the preparatory and complex images and restore the background (when required). This is a total of four placements for every animation iteration. Using the `COPY_PUT` argument could save one iteration, while using the `XOR_PUT` argument could save two iterations. The requirements of the application are the driving force behind the trade-offs between animation speed and image complexity. Lastly, it is often more efficient to move several small images than one large image. Careful planning and implementation are necessary and vital for effective graphics animation programming.

By carefully considering the application, the best combination of techniques can be selected to make the optimal trade-off between speed and graphics detail.

Summary

This chapter introduced partial- and full-page animation techniques. These techniques can be used by themselves or in combination to create animated presentations.

8

Two- and Three-Dimensional Drawing

A dvanced drawing packages, such as computer-aided design (CAD) packages, can usually operate with either two- or three-dimensional images. This chapter introduces the basic concepts and mathematical formulas behind drawing in two- and three-dimensions.

The Two-Dimensional Coordinate System

The drawing techniques discussed in the previous chapters were all based on the two-dimensional coordinate system. The two-dimensional coordinate system consists of two axes. The x axis extends horizontally. The y axis extends vertically. By labeling the axes in the manner shown in Figure 8.1, the two-dimensional coordinate system corresponds to the screen coordinates described by the Borland C++ graphics library.

The most obvious thing to note about the way this coordinate system is labeled is that the positive y axis extends downward. This can cause some initial problems with some engineers who are unfamiliar with this convention. By labeling the coordinate system in this way, however, you can transfer sketches, drawings, and other figures to the screen without transforming coordinates.

Figure 8.1. The two-dimensional coordinate system

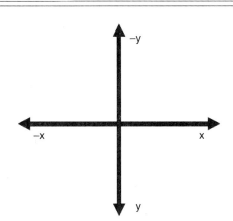

Formulas for Two-Dimensional Rotation

In a two-dimensional setting, it is easy to rotate a coordinate pair (defined by an x value and a y value) about a point. The key to two-dimensional rotation, however, is that the rotation must be about the origin of the coordinate system. Initially, this seems like a severe limitation when using Borland C++, because the upper left-hand corner of the screen is the physical origin of the screen's two-dimensional coordinate system.

Fortunately, the Borland C++ graphics environment supports two coordinate systems. These coordinate systems are the physical coordinate system and the view coordinate system, as discussed in Chapter 4. By moving the origin of the view coordinate system to the point from which rotation will occur, it is possible to rotate any coordinate pair (on or off the screen) about any physical point on the screen. The view origin, however, must remain within the physical coordinates of the screen. Figure 8.2 illustrates the relationship between the physical and view coordinate systems.

In a two-dimensional coordinate system, you can rotate coordinate pairs in either a clockwise or counterclockwise direction. Simple trigonometric algorithms are used to rotate these coordinate pairs. These formulas are as follows:

```
x = (x' * cos(angle)) + (y' * sin(angle))
y = (y' * cos(angle)) - (x' * sin(angle))
```

where x' and y' are the values of x and y prior to transformation.

Figure 8.2. The physical and view coordinate systems

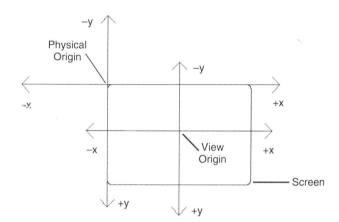

Note:

- The angle argument must be expressed as type double and in radians.
- A positive angle rotates in a counterclockwise direction.
- A negative angle rotates in a clockwise direction.

When describing the amount of rotation desired, an `angle` argument is used in the equations above. For example, if you wanted a 45-degree clockwise rotation, an `angle` parameter of –45 degrees would be used. An `angle` parameter of 45 degrees would be used for counterclockwise rotation. The trigonometric functions provided by Borland (sin, cos, etc.) require the `angle` argument to be in radians. Because it is easier and more natural to think in degrees, a simple conversion can be used to convert degrees to radians. The relationship between radians and degrees is shown in Figure 8.3.

Listing 8.1 demonstrates the simple rotation of a point about the center of the screen. In order to accomplish this demonstration successfully, you must first identify a point by its x and y coordinates and place it on the screen. In this case, the initial point is (100,0) with respect to the view origin at the center of the screen. The program is designed to then rotate this point, in 10-degree increments, about the view origin. Each time the point is moved, the program draws a circle around the point (see Figure 8.4).

Figure 8.3. Relationship between radians and degrees

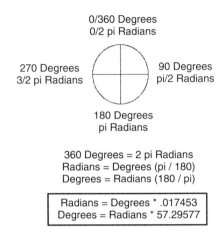

0/360 Degrees
0/2 pi Radians

270 Degrees
3/2 pi Radians

90 Degrees
pi/2 Radians

180 Degrees
pi Radians

360 Degrees = 2 pi Radians
Radians = Degrees (pi / 180)
Degrees = Radians (180 / pi)

Radians = Degrees * .017453
Degrees = Radians * 57.29577

You must consider several issues when doing this seemingly simple example. The first issue is that in order to make a circular pattern (as opposed to an elliptical pattern), you must use an aspect ratio. For the video mode in use (EGAHI), multiplying the rotated y coordinate by .75 works well. The use of .75 is due to the aspect ratio of the pixel. (Chapter 4 explains aspect ratios in more detail.) The second issue is the proper use of variable types. When using the trigonometric functions, the `angle` argument must be expressed as type double and in radians. If this is not done properly, the rotational results will be unpredictable.

Listing 8.1. Two-dimensional rotation example

```
#include <stdio.h>
#include <graphics.h>
#include <stdlib.h>
#include <conio.h>
#include <math.h>

int main ()
{
int gdriver = EGA;
int gmode = EGAHI;
float x,y;
float oldx, oldy;
double angle;
int rotation;

        /* register EGAVGA_driver and sansserif_font */
        /* ... these have been added to graphics.lib */
```

```
        /* as described in UTIL.DOC                    */

registerbgidriver (EGAVGA_driver);
registerbgifont (sansserif_font);

initgraph (&gdriver,&gmode,"");
rectangle (0,0,639,349);

x = 150.0;
y = 0.0;
rotation = 0;

setviewport (320,175,639,349,0);
putpixel ((int)x,(int)y,15);
angle = -10.0 * .017453;

            /* rotate point and draw circles */

do {
    oldx = x;
    oldy = y;
    x = (oldx * cos (angle))+(oldy * sin (angle));
    y = (oldy * cos (angle))-(oldx * sin (angle));
    putpixel ((int)x,(int)(.75 * y),15);
    circle((int)x,(int)(.75*y),15);
    rotation = rotation + 10;
    } while (rotation < 360);

getch ();
closegraph();
return 0;
}
```

Figure 8.4.   Screen output from Listing 8.1

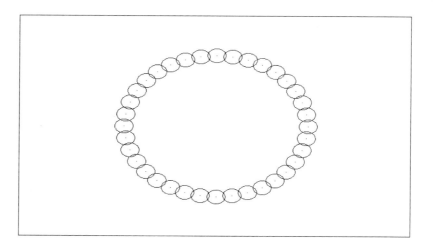

Rotating Objects

The formulas provided for two-dimensional rotation in the previous section are good for only one purpose. That purpose is to rotate a coordinate pair through a given angle. Although these formulas do an excellent job with coordinate pairs, they fall short when attempting to rotate objects.

Rotating the Rectangle

The method used to describe a rectangle when using the Borland C++ `rectangle`, `bar`, and `bar3d` functions is through the identification of the upper left-hand and lower right-hand corners of the rectangle. Because the rectangle is described by two coordinate pairs, it would appear to be an easy task to rotate those coordinate pairs and, thus, rotate the rectangle. This, unfortunately, is not the case.

The method by which the rectangle is drawn (by using two coordinate pairs) presents a problem for rotation. When the two coordinate pairs are passed to the `bar`, `rectangle`, or `bar3d` function, four line segments are created. These four line segments are described as follows:

> Line 1: High y, Low x to High y, High x
> Line 2: Low y, Low x to Low y, High x
> Line 3: Low y, High x to High y, High x
> Line 4: Low y, Low x to High y, Low x

These functions, given two corner points, calculate the other two corner points. Although these functions are easy to use, they do not provide a good way of describing a rectangle that must be rotated. This is due to the limitations in the way the other two corner points are evaluated. By looking at the preceding equations, it is obvious that only vertical and horizontal lines are generated using this method. Therefore, rotating the two corner points does no good. Figure 8.5 illustrates this point by showing what a square rotated through 45 degrees looks like. The result is a vertical line if it is rotated counterclockwise, or a horizontal line if it is rotated clockwise. Obviously, this is not the desired output.

Fortunately, there is an easy solution to this problem. By creating a rectangle with four line segments and defining all four corner points, it is easy to rotate the rectangle about any point. The following example demonstrates this method. Initially a rectangle is described by four coordinate pairs. These coordinate pairs are then rotated in a counterclockwise fashion through 360 degrees in 20-degree increments (see Figure 8.6). The view origin for this example is the center of the screen.

Figure 8.5. Rotation using `rectangle`, `bar`, and `bar3` functions

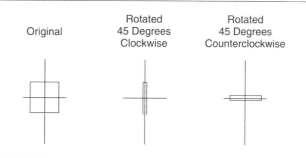

Original | Rotated 45 Degrees Clockwise | Rotated 45 Degrees Counterclockwise

Listing 8.2. Rectangle rotation example

```
#include <stdio.h>
#include <graphics.h>
#include <stdlib.h>
#include <conio.h>
#include <math.h>

int main ()
{
int gdriver = EGA;
int gmode = EGAHI;
float x1,y1;
float x2,y2;
float x3,y3;
float x4,y4;
float oldx1,oldy1;
float oldx2,oldy2;
float oldx3,oldy3;
float oldx4,oldy4;
double angle;
int rotation;

        /* register EGAVGA_driver and sansserif_font */
        /* ... these have been added to graphics.lib */
        /* as described in UTIL.DOC                   */

registerbgidriver (EGAVGA_driver);
registerbgifont (sansserif_font);

        /* set EGA 16-color high resolution video mode */

initgraph (&gdriver,&gmode,"");
rectangle (0,0,639,349);
```

Listing 8.2. *continues*

Listing 8.2. cont. Rectangle rotation example

```
x1 = -100.0;
y1 = -50.0;
x2 = 100.0;
y2 = -50.0;
x3 = 100.0;
y3 = 50.0;
x4 = -100.0;
y4 = 50.0;
angle = 20 * .017453;
rotation = 0;

setviewport (320,175,639,349,0);
moveto ((int)x1, (int)y1);
lineto ((int)x2, (int)y2);
lineto ((int)x3, (int)y3);
lineto ((int)x4, (int)y4);
lineto ((int)x1, (int)y1);
putpixel (0,0,15);

            /* rotate rectangle */

do {
    oldx1 = x1;
    oldy1 = y1;
    x1 = (oldx1 * cos (angle))+(oldy1 * sin (angle));
    y1 = (oldy1 * cos (angle))-(oldx1 * sin (angle));
    oldx2 = x2;
    oldy2 = y2;
    x2 = (oldx2 * cos (angle))+(oldy2 * sin (angle));
    y2 = (oldy2 * cos (angle))-(oldx2 * sin (angle));
    oldx3 = x3;
    oldy3 = y3;
    x3 = (oldx3 * cos (angle))+(oldy3 * sin (angle));
    y3 = (oldy3 * cos (angle))-(oldx3 * sin (angle));
    oldx4 = x4;
    oldy4 = y4;
    x4 = (oldx4 * cos (angle))+(oldy4 * sin (angle));
    y4 = (oldy4 * cos (angle))-(oldx4 * sin (angle));

    moveto ((int)x1, (int)y1);
    lineto ((int)x2, (int)y2);
    lineto ((int)x3, (int)y3);
    lineto ((int)x4, (int)y4);
    lineto ((int)x1, (int)y1);

    rotation = rotation + 20;
    } while (rotation < 360);

getch ();
closegraph();
return 0;
}
```

Figure 8.6. Screen output from Listing 8.2

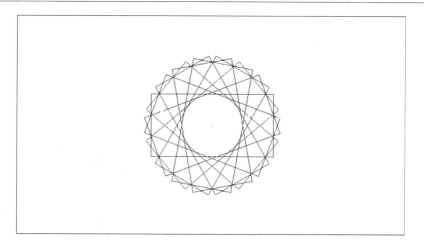

Rotating the Polygon

The two-dimensional rotation formulas work well with the `drawpoly` and `fillpoly` functions provided by Borland. Because the polygon is defined by a set of points that fully describe the object, there is no need to come up with any alternate means of defining the object. The `rectangle`, `bar`, and `bar3d` functions require an alternate drawing method because two of the figure's corners are interpreted by the function. However, this type of problem is not present in the `drawpoly` and `fillpoly` functions.

The following example demonstrates the use of the rotation algorithms for rotating a polygon. In this example, a triangle is created using the `drawpoly` function. This triangle is then rotated 360 degrees, in 90-degree increments around the view origin (see Figure 8.7). Each coordinate pair that describes a point in the polygon (in this case the triangle) is passed through the rotation algorithms.

Listing 8.3. Polygon rotation example

```
#include <stdio.h>
#include <graphics.h>
#include <math.h>
#include <stdlib.h>
#include <conio.h>

main ()
{
int gdriver = EGA;
int gmode = EGAHI;
```

Listing 8.3. *continues*

Listing 8.3. cont.   Polygon rotation example

```
int points[8];
double angle;
double ang;
int holdx;
int holdy;

      /* register EGAVGA_driver and sansserif_font */
      /* ... these have been added to graphics.lib */
      /* as described in UTIL.DOC                   */


registerbgidriver (EGAVGA_driver);
registerbgifont (sansserif_font);

      /* set EGA 16-color high resolution video mode */

initgraph (&gdriver,&gmode,"");
rectangle (0,0,639,349);
setviewport (320,175,639,349,0);

      /* define and rotate polygon */

points[0] = 0;
points[1] = 0;
points[2] = 25;
points[3] = 50;
points[4] = -25;
points[5] = 50;
points[6] = 0;
points[7] = 0;

for (angle = 0.0; angle < 360.0; angle = angle + 90.0)
{
      ang = angle * .017453;
      holdx = points[0];
      holdy = points[1];
      points[0] = (int)((holdx * cos (ang))+(holdy * sin (ang)));
      points[1] = (int)((holdy * cos (ang))-(holdx * sin (ang)));

      holdx = points[2];
      holdy = points[3];
      points[2] = (int)((holdx * cos (ang))+(holdy * sin (ang)));
      points[3] = (int)((holdy * cos (ang))-(holdx * sin (ang)));

      holdx = points[4];
      holdy = points[5];
      points[4] = (int)((holdx * cos (ang))+(holdy * sin (ang)));
      points[5] = (int)((holdy * cos (ang))-(holdx * sin (ang)));

      points[6] = points[0];
      points[7] = points[1];

      drawpoly (4,points);
}
```

```
getch ();
closegraph();
return 0;
}
```

Figure 8.7.   Screen output from Listing 8.3

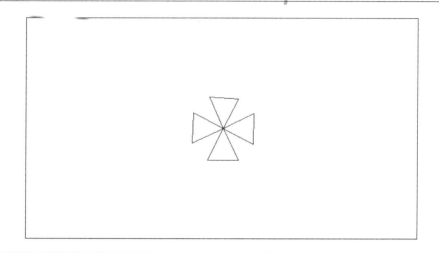

Rotating the Ellipse

The `ellipse` and `fillellipse` functions provided by Borland share the same problems as the `rectangle` function. Because each point that describes the object is not defined, the function interprets, or calculates, each point on the object. For the `ellipse` and `fillellipse` functions, the ellipse is defined using x and y radii and a center point. The ellipse is then calculated and drawn with its midlines in the vertical and horizontal directions, which makes these functions useless for rotating ellipses. Therefore, an alternate drawing method for creating the rotated ellipse must be found.

Listing 8.4 offers an effective, but slow, implementation of ellipse rotation. The rotation function listed below is based on a function found in Roger T. Stevens' *Graphics Programming in C*. This function is far from optimal, but it provides one method by which you can define the ellipse in order to accomplish the desired two-dimensional rotation. The example demonstrates the use of a `rotate_ellipse` function for ellipse rotation (see Figure 8.8). In this example, the view coordinate system is in use. In addition, the method by which the ellipse is described is not the same as with the `ellipse` and `fillellipse` functions provided by Borland. The ellipse in this example is described according to its center point (`x,y`), its radius, and its aspect ratio. The aspect ratio for this function (and this function only) is described as the ratio between the width of the ellipse and its length. An aspect ratio of .50, for this example, indicates that the ellipse is half as wide as it is long.

Listing 8.4. Ellipse rotation example

```
#include <graphics.h>
#include <stdio.h>
#include <conio.h>
#include <stdlib.h>
#include <math.h>

int main ()
{
int gdriver = EGA;
int gmode = EGAHI;

      /* register EGAVGA_driver and sansserif_font */
      /* ... these have been added to graphics.lib */
      /* as described in UTIL.DOC                  */

registerbgidriver (EGAVGA_driver);
registerbgifont (sansserif_font);

      /* set EGA 16-color high resolution mode */

initgraph (&gdriver,&gmode,"");
rectangle (0,0,639,349);
setviewport (320,175,639,349,0);

rotate_ellipse (0,0,75,0.0);
rotate_ellipse (0,0,75,45.0);
rotate_ellipse (0,0,75,90.0);
rotate_ellipse (0,0,75,135.0);

      /* delay and exit */

getch ();
closegraph();
return 0;
}

rotate_ellipse (int x, int y, int radius, double angle)
{
float aspect;
float aspect_square;
int column, row;
int i;
int x1, y1;
long one_square, two_square;
long two_one_square, two_two_square;
long four_one_square, four_two_square;
long d;
double sin_angle, cos_angle;


aspect = 0.50;
angle = (360.0 - angle) * .01754329;

sin_angle = sin (angle);
cos_angle = cos (angle);
```

```
aspect_square = aspect * aspect;

two_square = radius * radius;
one_square = two_square/aspect_square;

row = radius;
column = 0;

two_one_square = one_square << 1;
four_one_square = one_square << 2;
four_two_square = two_square << 2;
two_two_square = two_square << 1,

d = two_one_square * ((row - 1) * (row )) + one_square +
    two_two_square * (1 - one_square);

while (one_square * (row ) > two_square * (column))
{
    x1 = x + column * cos_angle - row * sin_angle;
    y1 = y + column * sin_angle + row * cos_angle;
    putpixel (x1,y1,15);

    x1 = x + column * cos_angle + row * sin_angle;
    y1 = y + column * sin_angle - row * cos_angle;
    putpixel (x1,y1,15);

    x1 = x - column * cos_angle - row * sin_angle;
    y1 = y - column * sin_angle + row * cos_angle;
    putpixel (x1,y1,15);

    x1 = x - column * cos_angle + row * sin_angle;
    y1 = y - column * sin_angle - row * cos_angle;
    putpixel (x1,y1,15);

    if (d >= 0)
    {
        row--;
        d -= four_one_square*(row);
    }
    d += two_two_square * (3 + (column << 1));
    column ++;
}

d = two_two_square * (column + 1) * column + two_one_square *
    (row * (row - 2) + 1) + (1 - two_one_square) * two_square;

while ((row) + 1)
{
    x1 = x + column * cos_angle - row * sin_angle;
    y1 = y + column * sin_angle + row * cos_angle;
    putpixel (x1,y1,15);

    x1 = x + column * cos_angle + row * sin_angle;
    y1 = y + column * sin_angle - row * cos_angle;
    putpixel (x1,y1,15);
```

Listing 8.4.   *continues*

207

Listing 8.4. cont. Ellipse rotation example

```
        x1 = x - column * cos_angle - row * sin_angle;
        y1 = y - column * sin_angle + row * cos_angle;
        putpixel (x1,y1,15);

        x1 = x - column * cos_angle + row * sin_angle;
        y1 = y - column * sin_angle - row * cos_angle;
        putpixel (x1,y1,15);

        if (d <= 0)
        {
            column++;
            d += four_two_square * column;
        }
        row--;
        d += two_one_square * (3 - (row << 1));
        }
    radius++;
}
```

Figure 8.8. Screen output from Listing 8.4

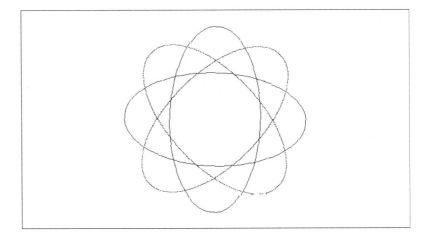

The Three-Dimensional Coordinate System

The three-dimensional coordinate system is very similar to the two-dimensional coordinate system, but it adds a third dimension. So far, we have discussed flat, or two-dimensional drawings exclusively. The remainder of this chapter focuses on drawing three-dimensional objects, or objects with depth.

The three-dimensional coordinate system, like the two-dimensional coordinate system, has a horizontal x axis and a vertical y axis. The difference in these coordinate systems, however, lies in the addition of a z axis, which adds a depth feature. The three-dimensional coordinate system is shown in Figure 8.9.

Figure 8.9. The three-dimensional coordinate system

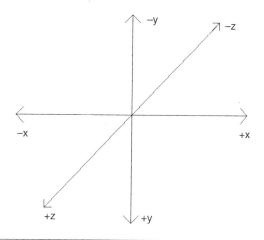

The problem with the three-dimensional coordinate system when it is used with computer graphics is that the three dimensions must be placed on the screen, which is a flat, two-dimensional surface. Fortunately, there are three primary sets of algorithms that do exactly that. These algorithm sets describe rotation about the x, y, and z axes. Note that x', y', and z' represent the values of x, y, and z, respectively, prior to transformation.

Rotation About the X Axis

The first set of algorithms is for rotation about the x axis.

```
x = x'
y = (sin(angle) * z') + (cos(angle) * y')
z = (cos(angle) * z') - (sin(angle) * y')
```

Rotation About the Y Axis

The second set of algorithms is for rotation about the y axis.

```
x = (cos(angle) * x') - (sin(angle) * z')
```

```
y = y'
z = (sin(angle) * x') + (cos(angle) * z')
```

Rotation About the z Axis

The third set of algorithms is for rotation about the z axis.

```
x = (cos(angle) * x') + (sin(angle) * y')
y = (cos(angle) * y') - (sin(angle) * x')
z = z'
```

By using these three sets of algorithms in combination, it is possible to rotate a three-dimensional object in literally any direction.

Listing 8.5 demonstrates the use of these algorithms to rotate two rectangles. These rectangles are the same size, and one initially overlays the other. The first initially exists in the positive z plane, while the other initially exists in the negative z plane. When shown in three dimensions, only one is visible. The cursor keys (with the <Num Lock> key on) are used to manipulate, or rotate, the figures about the x (4 and 6 keys) and the y (8 and 2 keys) axes. As the rectangles are rotated about the center point of the screen, the power of the three-dimensional rotation algorithms becomes apparent. The example is written so that it is easy to understand the operation of the program and its algorithms; therefore, the code is not written as efficiently as possible.

Listing 8.5. Three-dimensional rotation example

```
#include <graphics.h>
#include <stdlib.h>
#include <conio.h>
#include <stdio.h>
#include <math.h>

int main ()
{
int gdriver = EGA;
int gmode = EGAHI;
double angle;
int x1, y1, z1;
int x2, y2, z2;
int x3, y3, z3;
int x4, y4, z4;
int x5, y5, z5;
int x6, y6, z6;
int x7, y7, z7;
int x8, y8, z8;
int ch;
int oldx, oldy, oldz;

        /* register EGAVGA_driver and sansserif_font */
        /* ... these have been added to graphics.lib */
        /* as described in UTIL.DOC                   */

registerbgidriver (EGAVGA_driver);
```

```
registerbgifont (sansserif_font);

initgraph (&gdriver,&gmode,"");
setviewport (320,175,639,349,0);
x1 = 100;   y1 = 100;   z1 = -100;
x2 = 100;   y2 = -100;  z2 = -100;
x3 = -100;  y3 = -100;  z3 = -100;
x4 = -100;  y4 = 100;   z4 = -100;
x5 = 100;   y5 = 100;   z5 = 100;
x6 = 100;   y6 = -100;  z6 = 100;
x7 = -100;  y7 = -100;  z7 = 100;
x8 = -100;  y8 = 100;   z8 = 100;
setcolor (1);
moveto (x1,y1);
lineto (x2,y2);
lineto (x3,y3);
lineto (x4,y4);
lineto (x1,y1);
setcolor (4);
moveto (x5,y5);
lineto (x6,y6);
lineto (x7,y7);
lineto (x8,y8);
lineto (x5,y5);

do
{
      ch = getch ();
      if (ch == '4')
      {
            angle = (-10.0) * .017453;
        oldx = x1;
        oldy = y1;
        oldz = z1;
        x1 =(int)((cos(angle) * oldx) - (sin(angle) * oldz));
        y1 = y1;
        z1 =(int)((sin(angle) * oldx) + (cos(angle) * oldz));
        oldx = x2;
        oldy = y2;
        oldz = z2;
        x2 =(int)((cos(angle) * oldx) - (sin(angle) * oldz));
        y2 = y2;
        z2 =(int)((sin(angle) * oldx) + (cos(angle) * oldz));
        oldx = x3;
        oldy = y3;
        oldz = z3;
        x3 =(int)((cos(angle) * oldx) - (sin(angle) * oldz));
        y3 = y3;
        z3 =(int)((sin(angle) * oldx) + (cos(angle) * oldz));
        oldx = x4;          oldy = y4;          oldz = z4;
        x4 =(int)((cos(angle) * oldx) - (sin(angle) * oldz));
        y4 = y4;
        z4 =(int)((sin(angle) * oldx) + (cos(angle) * oldz));
        oldx = x5;
        oldy = y5;
```

Listing 8.5.   *continues*

211

Listing 8.5. cont.   Three-dimensional rotation example

```
        oldz = z5;
        x5 =(int)((cos(angle) * oldx) - (sin(angle) * oldz));
        y5 = y5;
        z5 =(int)((sin(angle) * oldx) + (cos(angle) * oldz));
        oldx = x6;
        oldy = y6;
        oldz = z6;
        x6 =(int)((cos(angle) * oldx) - (sin(angle) * oldz));
        y6 = y6;
        z6 =(int)((sin(angle) * oldx) + (cos(angle) * oldz));
        oldx = x7;
        oldy = y7;
        oldz = z7;
        x7 =(int)((cos(angle) * oldx) - (sin(angle) * oldz));
        y7 = y7;
        z7 =(int)((sin(angle) * oldx) + (cos(angle) * oldz));
        oldx = x8;
        oldy = y8;
        oldz = z8;
        x8 =(int)((cos(angle) * oldx) - (sin(angle) * oldz));
        y8 = y8;
        z8 =(int)((sin(angle) * oldx) + (cos(angle) * oldz));
    }
    if (ch == '6')
    {
        angle = 10.0 * .017453;
        oldx = x1;
        oldy = y1;
        oldz = z1;
        x1 =(int)((cos(angle) * oldx) - (sin(angle) * oldz));
        y1 = y1;
        z1 =(int)((sin(angle) * oldx) + (cos(angle) * oldz));
        oldx = x2;
        oldy = y2;
        oldz = z2;
        x2 =(int)((cos(angle) * oldx) - (sin(angle) * oldz));
        y2 = y2;
        z2 =(int)((sin(angle) * oldx) + (cos(angle) * oldz));
        oldx = x3;
        oldy = y3;
        oldz = z3;
        x3 =(int)((cos(angle) * oldx) - (sin(angle) * oldz));
        y3 = y3;
        z3 =(int)((sin(angle) * oldx) + (cos(angle) * oldz));
        oldx = x4;
        oldy = y4;
        oldz = z4;
        x4 =(int)((cos(angle) * oldx) - (sin(angle) * oldz));
        y4 = y4;
        z4 =(int)((sin(angle) * oldx) + (cos(angle) * oldz));
        oldx = x5;
        oldy = y5;
        oldz = z5;
        x5 =(int)((cos(angle) * oldx) - (sin(angle) * oldz));
        y5 = y5;
```

```
          z5 =(int)((sin(angle) * oldx) + (cos(angle) * oldz));
          oldx = x6;
          oldy = y6;
          oldz = z6;
          x6 =(int)((cos(angle) * oldx) - (sin(angle) * oldz));
          y6 = y6;
          z6 =(int)((sin(angle) * oldx) + (cos(angle) * oldz));
          oldx = x7;
          oldy = y7;
          oldz = z7;
          x7 =(int)((cos(angle) * oldx) - (sin(angle) * oldz));
          y7 = y7;
          z7 =(int)((sin(angle) * oldx) + (cos(angle) * oldz));
          oldx = x8;
          oldy = y8;
          oldz = z8;
          x8 =(int)((cos(angle) * oldx) - (sin(angle) * oldz));
          y8 = y8;
          z8 =(int)((sin(angle) * oldx) + (cos(angle) * oldz));
}
if (ch == '8')
{
          angle = (-10.0) * .017453;
          oldx = x1;
          oldy = y1;
          oldz = z1;
          x1 = x1;
          y1 =(int)((sin(angle) * oldz) + (cos(angle) * oldy));
          z1 =(int)((cos(angle) * oldz) - (sin(angle) * oldy));
          oldx = x2;
          oldy = y2;
          oldz = z2;
          x2 = x2;
          y2 =(int)((sin(angle) * oldz) + (cos(angle) * oldy));
          z2 =(int)((cos(angle) * oldz) - (sin(angle) * oldy));
          oldx = x3;
          oldy = y3;
          oldz = z3;
          x3 = x3;
          y3 =(int)((sin(angle) * oldz) + (cos(angle) * oldy));
          z3 =(int)((cos(angle) * oldz) - (sin(angle) * oldy));
          oldx = x4;
          oldy = y4;
          oldz = z4;
          x4 = x4;
          y4 =(int)((sin(angle) * oldz) + (cos(angle) * oldy));
          z4 =(int)((cos(angle) * oldz) - (sin(angle) * oldy));
          oldx = x5;
          oldy = y5;
          oldz = z5;
          x5 = x5;
          y5 =(int)((sin(angle) * oldz) + (cos(angle) * oldy));
          z5 =(int)((cos(angle) * oldz) - (sin(angle) * oldy));
          oldx = x6;
          oldy = y6;
```

Listing 8.5. *continues*

213

Listing 8.5. cont.   Three-dimensional rotation example

```
        oldz = z6;
        x6 = x6;
        y6 =(int)((sin(angle) * oldz) + (cos(angle) * oldy));
        z6 =(int)((cos(angle) * oldz) - (sin(angle) * oldy));
        oldx = x7;
        oldy = y7;
        oldz = z7;
        x7 = x7;
        y7 =(int)((sin(angle) * oldz) + (cos(angle) * oldy));
        z7 =(int)((cos(angle) * oldz) - (sin(angle) * oldy));
        oldx = x8;
        oldy = y8;
        oldz = z8;
        x8 = x8;
        y8 =(int)((sin(angle) * oldz) + (cos(angle) * oldy));
        z8 =(int)((cos(angle) * oldz) - (sin(angle) * oldy));
}
if (ch == '2')
{
        angle = 10.0 * .017453;
        oldx = x1;
        oldy = y1;
        oldz = z1;
        x1 = x1;
    y1 =(int)((sin(angle) * oldz) + (cos(angle) * oldy));
    z1 =(int)((cos(angle) * oldz) - (sin(angle) * oldy));
    oldx = x2;
    oldy = y2;
    oldz = z2;
    x2 = x2;
    y2 =(int)((sin(angle) * oldz) + (cos(angle) * oldy));
    z2 =(int)((cos(angle) * oldz) - (sin(angle) * oldy));
    oldx = x3;
    oldy = y3;
    oldz = z3;
    x3 = x3;
    y3 =(int)((sin(angle) * oldz) + (cos(angle) * oldy));
    z3 =(int)((cos(angle) * oldz) - (sin(angle) * oldy));
    oldx = x4;
    oldy = y4;
    oldz = z4;
    x4 = x4;
    y4 =(int)((sin(angle) * oldz) + (cos(angle) * oldy));
    z4 =(int)((cos(angle) * oldz) - (sin(angle) * oldy));
    oldx = x5;
    oldy = y5;
    oldz = z5;
    x5 = x5;
    y5 =(int)((sin(angle) * oldz) + (cos(angle) * oldy));
    z5 =(int)((cos(angle) * oldz) - (sin(angle) * oldy));
    oldx = x6;
    oldy = y6;
    oldz = z6;
    x6 = x6;
    y6 =(int)((sin(angle) * oldz) + (cos(angle) * oldy));
    z6 =(int)((cos(angle) * oldz) - (sin(angle) * oldy));
```

```
            oldx = x7;
            oldy = y7;
            oldz = z7;
            x7 = x7;
            y7 =(int)((sin(angle) * oldz) + (cos(angle) * oldy));
            z7 =(int)((cos(angle) * oldz) - (sin(angle) * oldy));
            oldx = x8;
            oldy = y8;
            oldz = z8;
            x8 = x8;
            y8 =(int)((sin(angle) * oldz) + (cos(angle) * oldy));
            z8 =(int)((cos(angle) * oldz) - (sin(angle) * oldy));
          }
          setviewport (0,0,639,349,0);
          clearviewport ();
          setviewport (320,175,639,349,0);
          setcolor (1);
          moveto (x1, y1);
          lineto (x2, y2);
          lineto (x3, y3);
          lineto (x4, y4);
          lineto (x1, y1);
          setcolor (4);
          moveto (x5, y5);
          lineto (x6, y6);
          lineto (x7, y7);
          lineto (x8, y8);
          lineto (x5, y5);
  } while (ch != 27);
  closegraph();
  return 0;
  }
```

Hidden Surface Removal for Three-Dimensional Drawing

Three-dimensional drawing can become very complex. Most three-dimensional models are created with a series of planes that represent the shell of the object. If the planes are filled, then the plane is considered to be nontransparent. Similarly, if the plane is not filled, the plane is considered to be transparent.

When rotating or moving three-dimensional objects, it is often necessary to remove parts of objects, or even entire objects, in order to provide realistic representations of the environment. The method by which these objects are altered is called *hidden surface removal*. The most common types of hidden surface removal are discussed in this section.

There are two basic types of hidden surface removal. These are object-space methods and image-space methods. Three-dimensional information is used with object-space methods to decide which surfaces should be hidden and which surfaces should overlay others. Image-space methods use two-dimensional information to determine the hidden surfaces.

The most common method of hidden surface removal for personal computers is probably the *plane equation method*, which is an object-space method. In general terms, the plane equation method determines if a point is in front of, on, or behind a specified plane. By testing each point against the viewing position, always $(0,0,0)$, the visible and hidden planes are determined.

The equation of a plane is:

```
Ax + By + Cz + D
```

where x, y, and z define a point on the surface of the plane. The A, B, C, and D values are constants and are derived as follows when three points on the plane are specified $(x1,y1,z1; x2,y2,z2; x3,y3,z3)$.

```
A = y1(z2-z3) + y2(z3-z1) + y3(z1-z2)

B = z1(x2-x3) + z2(x3-x1) + z3(x1-x2)

C = x1(y2-y3) + x2(y3-y1) + x3(y1-y2)

D = -x1(y2z3-y3z2) - x2(y3z1-y1z3) - x3(y1z2-y2z1)
```

By identifying three points on a plane, solving for A, B, C, and D, substituting A, B, C, and D into the plane equation, and passing each object point through the new plane equation, you can determine whether or not each point is on, in front of, or behind the defined plane. If the plane equation evaluates to a positive value, the point is hidden. If the plane equation evaluates to zero, the point is on the plane and is usually defined as visible. If the equation evaluates to a negative value, the point is visible.

When using this method it is important that the points used to derive the equations are plotted in a counterclockwise direction and can be viewed as a part of a *convex polyhedron*. A convex polyhedron is a figure that has many faces and is curved outward, such as a cube.

Summary

The techniques of two- and three-dimensional drawing are powerful tools for the graphics programmer. The basic principles presented in this chapter provide the foundation for creating complex graphics interfaces and routines for drawing packages. Chapter 9 introduces the concepts of developing a graphical user interface.

9

Developing a Graphical User Interface

G raphical User Interfaces (GUIs) have become extremely popular over the past few years. Once found only in paintbrush and drawing programs, GUIs are now used for everything from databases to word processors. The popularity of Microsoft Windows has proven that GUIs are here to stay. Almost daily, popular applications are released that offer new GUIs to older, established products.

GUIs offer the user distinct advantages over old, text-based programming styles. "What-you-see-is-what-you-get" (WYSIWYG) is one of these advantages. Text-based programs generally use the ROM BIOS character sets. Therefore, even if you have chosen a proportional font, the characters on the screen still appear as the standard, non-proportional font. With GUIs, characters are graphical objects created with bit-map or vector fonts. Therefore, the program has the capability to display the text in the font style and size that you choose. Thus, what you see on the screen is what you will get in the printout. In addition, you can directly import and display graphical images on the screen.

Another advantage of GUIs is the use of features like pop up menus, dialog boxes, and radio buttons. These features offer greater ease and flexibility when navigating through complex and sophisticated applications. It is important for you to realize that these features are not limited to GUIs programmed in graphics modes. Many applications use these features while operating solely in text modes. One example of the use of these features while in text modes is the IDE for Borland C++.

This chapter introduces some basic concepts behind developing a functional graphical user interface using the graphics modes. It presents basics such as the mouse interface, pop-up menus, dialog boxes, radio buttons, drawing tools, and scroll bars. This chapter is not intended to "walk you through" the entire process of developing a complete GUI. That process, in itself, could fill volumes of text. The intent of this chapter is to present ideas that will get you started on the right track to developing useful, full-featured GUIs. An example which demonstrates the principles of graphical user interface development is presented at the end of this chapter.

The Mouse Interface

The two primary input devices used with GUIs are the keyboard and the mouse. The mouse is the input device of choice for many users because it offers greater flexibility and movement than manual keyboard input.

The mouse is very easy to access and control. Because most mice are compatible with the Microsoft mouse, I will discuss only the use of the Microsoft mouse and its compatibles. The mouse system consists of the mouse and the *mouse driver*. The mouse is the device manipulated by the user to provide directional input to the program. The mouse driver is the memory-resident program that provides communication between the mouse and the computer. The mouse driver maintains the cursor position of the mouse and the status of the mouse buttons. You can access the cursor position and the button status with any application.

You can access the mouse and the mouse driver from within an application through software `interrupt 33h`. The Borland C++ function `int86` can be used to generate the software `interrupt 33h`. The mouse driver has several functions (see Table 9.1). You can select the appropriate function by specifying the function number in the `AX` register when calling `interrupt 33h`. The `BX`, `CX`, and `DX` registers are used to pass parameters to the mouse functions.

Table 9.1. *Functions for the Microsoft mouse and compatibles*

Function	Meaning
0	Resets the mouse and retrieves the mouse status
1	Displays the mouse cursor
2	Hides the mouse cursor
3	Retrieves the mouse cursor position and the status of the mouse buttons
4	Places the mouse at a specified location
5	Retrieves the number of times a button was pressed since the last call

Function	Meaning
6	Retrieves the number of times a button was released since the last call
7	Specifies the horizontal limits for the cursor
8	Specifies the vertical limits for the cursor
9	Specifies the cursor to use for graphics modes
10	Specifies the cursor to use for text modes
11	Reads the counters for mouse movement
12	Sets an interrupt routine
13	Sets light pen emulation to on
14	Sets light pen emulation to off
15	Sets mouse movement ratio
16	Hides the mouse when it is within a particular region
19	Allows quicker mouse movement
20	Swaps interrupt routines
21	Gets the status of the mouse driver
22	Saves the status of the mouse driver
23	Restores the status of the mouse driver
29	Sets the page number for the mouse cursor
30	Gets the page number for the mouse cursor

Because all of these mouse functions are generated using `interrupt 33h`, you should create a function, such as the one in Listing 9.1, to generate the interrupt with the specified `AX`, `BX`, `CX`, and `DX` register values. The function can also retrieve and store the resulting `AX`, `BX`, `CX`, and `DX` register values. The following function accepts the four register values, generates the interrupt, and stores the retrieved register values in global variables `globax`, `globbx`, `globcx`, and `globdx`. This `mouse_call` function is used in the GUI demonstration in Listing 9.1.

```
/* This function is used to communicate with the */
/* mouse via interrupt 0x33h.                     */

void mouse_call(regax, regbx, regcx, regdx)
{
union REGS inregs, outregs;

inregs.x.ax = regax;
inregs.x.bx = regbx;
inregs.x.cx = regcx;
inregs.x.dx = regdx;
```

```
int86(0x33,&inregs,&outregs);

globax = outregs.x.ax;
globbx = outregs.x.bx;
globcx = outregs.x.cx;
globdx = outregs.x.dx;
}
```

The following sections describe a few of the mouse functions and explain how you can use these functions to implement a GUI.

Initializing the Mouse

The first step in using the mouse is to reset the mouse driver. This is accomplished by generating interrupt 33h with 0 (for mouse function 0) in the AX register. The values in the BX, CX, and DX registers are ignored. Function 0 returns -1 in the AX register when the mouse hardware and driver are detected. Zero is returned if no mouse or mouse driver is found. The following line of code will reset the mouse by calling the mouse_call function described earlier in this chapter.

```
mouse_call(0,0,0,0);
```

Displaying and Hiding the Mouse Cursor

The next step in using the mouse is to display the mouse cursor. This is accomplished by generating the interrupt 33h with 1 (to initiate mouse function 1) in the AX register. The BX, CX, and DX registers are ignored. By using the mouse_call function, it is easy to display the mouse cursor.

```
mouse_call(1,0,0,0);
```

Hiding the cursor is just as easy as displaying it. By generating interrupt 33h with 2 in the AX register (to initiate mouse function 2), the mouse cursor is hidden. Again, the BX, CX, and DX registers are ignored. The following call to the mouse_call function will hide the cursor.

```
mouse_call(2,0,0,0);
```

Monitoring the Mouse Position

The mouse driver maintains the position of the mouse cursor. You can retrieve the position of the mouse cursor by generating interrupt 33h with 3 in the AX register (to initiate mouse function 3). The BX, CX, and DX registers are ignored. The x coordinate of the cursor is returned in the CX register. The y coordinate of the cursor is returned in the DX register. The returned values correspond to the screen coordinates. The only exception is in graphics modes that are only 320 pixels wide. For these modes, the x coordinate returned in the CX register should be divided by two to reflect the actual screen coordinates of the mouse cursor. The following call to mouse_call will retrieve the position of the mouse cursor.

```
mouse_call(3,0,0,0);
```

Monitoring the Mouse Buttons

The Microsoft mouse has two buttons. The most common method of monitoring these buttons is to check each button to see whether or not it has been pressed or released. By calling interrupt 33h with 5 in the AX register (to initiate mouse function 5), you can check to see if a particular button has been pressed. In order to test the right button, 1 is placed in the BX register. To test the left button, 0 is placed in the BX register. CX and DX are ignored. Mouse function 5 returns the number of times the button has been pressed in the BX register. The cursor position where the last button was pressed is returned in CX and DX. CX holds the horizontal cursor position. DX holds the vertical cursor position. The following call to mouse_call will test to see if the left button has been pressed.

```
mouse_call(5,0,0,0);
```

Calling interrupt 33h with 6 in the AX register (to initiate mouse function 6) allows you to see if a particular button has been released. The BX register should be set to 1 to test the right button. The BX register should be set to 0 to test the left button. CX and DX are ignored by mouse function 6. Mouse function 6 returns the number of times the button has been pressed in the BX register. The cursor position where the last button was released is returned in CX and DX. CX holds the horizontal cursor position, while DX holds the vertical cursor position. The following call to the mouse_call function will test whether or not the left button has been released.

```
mouse_call(6,0,0,0);
```

Confining the Mouse

For many applications it may be desirable to confine the mouse position to a particular rectangular region. Mouse functions 7 and 8 are used to set the horizontal and vertical limits, respectively, of the confining rectangular region.

For mouse function 7, a 7 is placed in the AX register. The x coordinate for the left side of the confining rectangle is specified in the CX register. The x coordinate of the right side of the confining rectangle is specified in the DX register. The following call to mouse_call would set the horizontal limits of the mouse to between 50 and 150.

```
mouse_call(7,0,50,150);
```

For mouse function 8, an *8* is placed in the AX register. The y coordinate for the top of the confining rectangle is specified in the CX register. The y coordinate for the bottom of the confining rectangle is specified in the DX register. The following call to mouse_call would set the vertical limits of the mouse to between 100 and 200.

```
mouse_call(8,0,100,200);
```

Pop-up Menus, Scroll Bars, Dialog Boxes, and Buttons

Pop-up menus offer the user easy access to many program options with only one or two clicks of the mouse. The most common method of implementing pop-up menus is:

1. Create the pop-up menu on a hidden page using the low-level graphics functions provided by Borland C++. Some of the functions required to create the menu might include bar, outtextxy, floodfill, and setfillstyle. You can use the setactivepage and setvisualpage functions to switch between hidden and visual pages.
2. Save the pop-up menu. The getimage and imagesize functions will be used to save the image into an allocated memory block.
3. Create a menu bar in the application on the active page. Again, you can use the low-level graphics functions to create this menu bar.
4. Wait for the menu to be selected from the menu bar. This is usually accomplished by monitoring the status of the mouse buttons as well as the mouse position. When you click the button in the rectangular region of the menu name, the menu opens.
5. Save the part of the screen where the menu will be placed. The getimage function accomplishes this action, which is necessary to restore the screen after a menu item has been selected.
6. Place the menu on the active page. The putimage function is used to place the stored image on the screen.
7. Monitor the mouse for menu item selection.
8. Restore the screen by placing the image back on the screen that you stored prior to positioning the menu. This is done with the putimage function.

This procedure is a simple, yet effective, way to implement pop-up menus. It may be to your best advantage to save the menus to disk and pull them from the disk when you need them, to conserve computer memory.

The procedure for implementing scroll bars, dialog boxes, buttons, and so on is basically the same as the procedure just described for implementing pop-up menus. The important thing to remember to do when implementing these features is to choose an interface type that best fits the needs of the application. Menus work well for some situations, but dialog boxes are better for others. A poorly-designed GUI is often worse than no interface at all.

A Simple GUI Demonstration

Listing 9.1 provides the code for a simple GUI. This interface is very fundamental, but it provides the ideas behind the implementation of GUIs. This example begins by creating the menus, dialog box, radio buttons, and scrolling window on a visual page. Usually, these would be created on a hidden page; however, they are created on a visual page to allow you to see the items prior to creating the main interface screen. Figure 9.1 provides the screen output of these items. Save the menus, dialog box, and so on with the getimage function prior to initializing the main interface screen.

Figure 9.1. Menus, dialog box, scroll bar, and buttons for the GUI demonstration

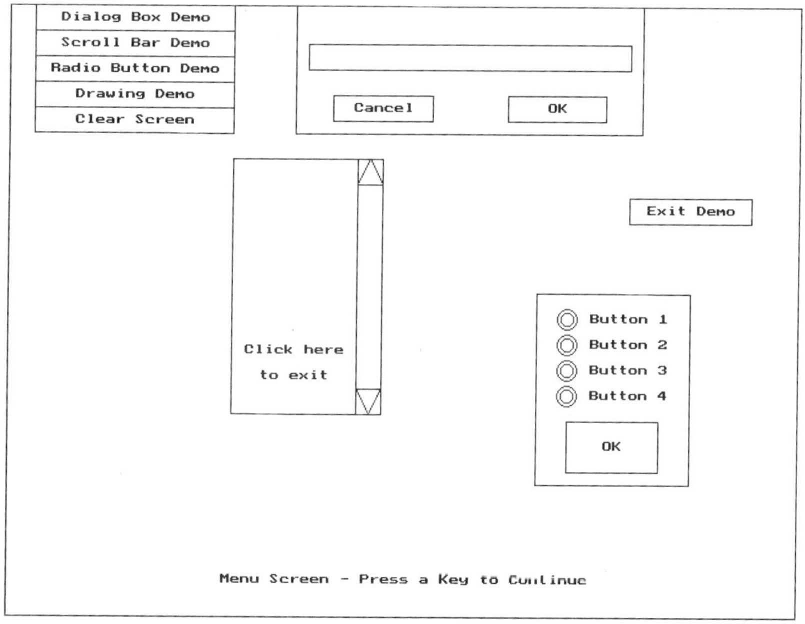

The main screen is created next. The mouse is then initialized and displayed. A menu bar with the options Demo Options and Exit is displayed at the top of the screen. The horizontal coordinate of the mouse cursor position is displayed in the lower left corner

of the screen. The vertical coordinate of the mouse cursor position is displayed in the lower right corner of the screen. Figure 9.2 provides the screen output of the user interface.

Figure 9.2. The main screen for the GUI demonstration

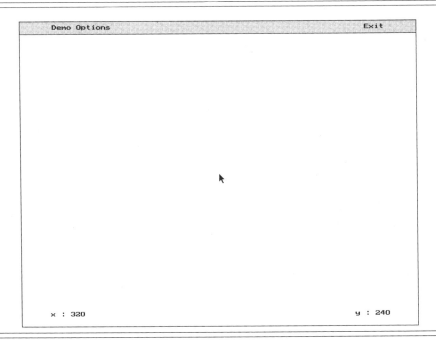

When the main screen has been initialized, the mouse buttons are monitored. When a mouse button at the main interface level is pressed, the mouse position is checked to see if the current position is within the constraints of the Demo Options menu or the Exit menu. If the mouse position is within the constraints of the Demo Options menu, the Demo Options menu will appear as shown in Figure 9.3.

When the Demo Options menu appears, you can select any one of the five options with another click of the mouse button. When you select an item, the working area (that portion of the screen not including the menu bar and position indicators) is cleared and the appropriate menu item is displayed. This demonstration does not use the `getimage` function to save the screen prior to bringing up the menu (as described in the procedure discussed previously in this chapter). Because this demonstration is simple, clearing the working area is sufficient. The first option of the Demo Options menu brings up a dialog box. The second option brings up a simple demonstration of a scrolling text field. The third option demonstrates a radio button. The fourth option selects a simple drawing tool. The last option simply clears the screen.

Figure 9.3. The Demo Options menu

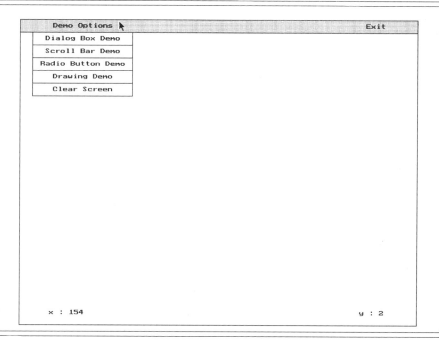

When you select Dialog Box Demo, the Demo Options menu is cleared from the screen and a dialog box appears (see Figure 9.4). Clicking on the text bar results in the appearance of a text string. Clicking on either the Cancel button or the OK button will remove the dialog box from the screen. You could easily modify the text bar to allow you to input text.

Selecting Scroll Bar Demo removes the Demo Options menu and displays the scrolling text field, which is shown in Figure 9.5. There are three active areas in this demonstration. The first active area is in the top right corner of the field. Clicking in this area will display the text string Text would scroll up. The second active area is in the lower right corner of the field. Clicking in this area will display the text string Text would scroll down. The third active area is the area where the text is displayed. Clicking anywhere in this area will result in the removal of the text field. You can add simple algorithms to scroll the text in the text field.

When you select Radio Button Demo from the Demo Options menu, the Demo Options menu is removed, and a button field with four radio buttons is displayed. The screen resulting from selecting Radio Button Demo is shown in Figure 9.6. Clicking on any of the radio buttons will change the state of the radio button. Clicking on the OK button will remove the radio button field from the screen.

Figure 9.4. The Dialog Box Demo option

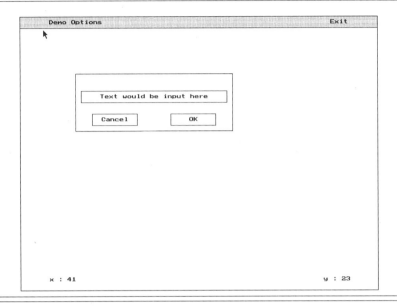

Figure 9.5. The Scroll Bar Demo option

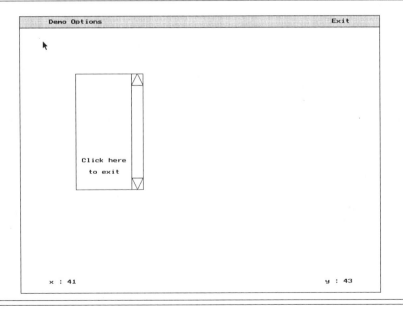

Figure 9.6. The Radio Button Demo option

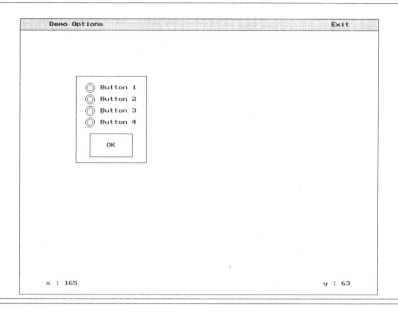

Figure 9.7. The Drawing Demo option

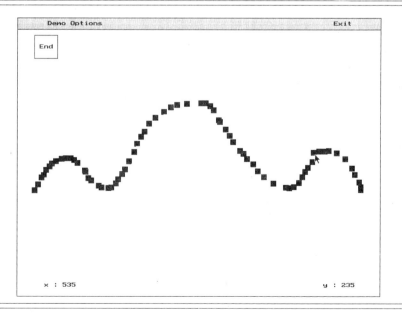

When you select the Drawing Demo option, it selects a simple drawing tool. Each time you click the mouse button in the predefined working area, a filled rectangle is drawn. Figure 9.7 shows the screen after the drawing tool has been used to draw several rectangles on the screen. Clicking on the End button will clear the screen and remove the drawing tool.

The last item in the Demo Options menu is the Clear Screen option. Selecting the Clear Screen option simply clears the working area.

If you do not select the Demo Options menu, the only other active area on the main screen is the Exit menu. Selecting the Exit menu puts the Exit menu on the screen. The only option under this menu is the Exit Demo option, shown in Figure 9.8. Selecting the Exit Demo option allows you to exit the demonstration.

Figure 9.8. The Exit Demo option

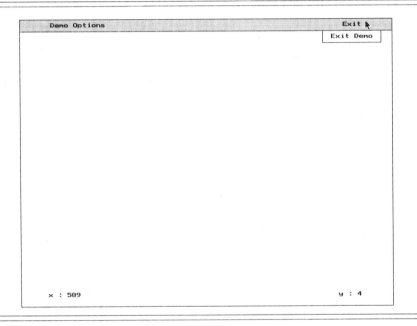

As mentioned previously, this demonstration is not perfect. However, the intent of this demonstration is to provide a stripped-down GUI that is coded simply enough so that you can easily understand and follow the basic steps and logic to creating GUIs. In order to make this GUI fully functional, you would need to add much more information. However, if this functionality was added, it would be very difficult to follow the structure and logic of the demonstration. Listing 9.1 contains the code used for the GUI demonstration.

Listing 9.1. Code for GUI demonstration

```c
#include <graphics.h>
#include <stdio.h>
#include <stdlib.h>
#include <conio.h>
#include <dos.h>

     /* mouse call prototype */

void mouse_call(int regax, int regbx, int regcx, int regdx);

     /* other function prototypes */

void get_demo_option(void);
void check_exit(void);
void monitor_dialog(void);
void monitor_scroll(void);
void monitor_radio(void);
void draw_tool (void);
void clear_screen(void);
void update_pos(void);

     /* global register values */

int globax, globbx, globcx, globdx;

     /* storage for menus, boxes, buttons, etc */

void *dialog_box;
void *demo_menu;
void *exit_menu;
void *radio_button;
void *scroll_bar;
unsigned int imsize;
int exit_status = 0;
char buffer [20];

int main ()
{
int gdriver = VGA;
int gmode = VGAHI;

     /* register EGAVGA_driver and sansserif_font */
     /* ... these have been added to graphics.lib */
     /* as described in UTIL.DOC                  */

registerbgidriver (EGAVGA_driver);
registerbgifont (sansserif_font);

     /* set VGA 16-color high resolution video mode   */

initgraph (&gdriver,&gmode,"");

     /* create the menus and dialog boxes         */
     /* ... this could be done on a hidden page */
```

Listing 9.1. *continues*

Listing 9.1. cont.   Code for GUI demonstration

```
setbkcolor (4);
clearviewport();
rectangle(0,0,639,479);
settextstyle (DEFAULT_FONT,HORIZ_DIR,1);
settextjustify(CENTER_TEXT,CENTER_TEXT);

      /* Demo Options Menu */

rectangle(20,0,180,20);
rectangle(20,20,180,40);
rectangle(20,40,180,60);
rectangle(20,60,180,80);
rectangle(20,80,180,100);
outtextxy(100,10,"Dialog Box Demo");
outtextxy(100,30,"Scroll Bar Demo");
outtextxy(100,50,"Radio Button Demo");
outtextxy(100,70,"Drawing Demo");
outtextxy(100,90,"Clear Screen");
imsize = imagesize(20,0,180,100);
demo_menu = malloc(imsize);
getimage(20,0,180,100,demo_menu);

      /* Dialog Box */

rectangle(230,0,510,100);
rectangle(240,30,500,50);
rectangle(260,70,340,90);
rectangle(400,70,480,90);
outtextxy(300,80,"Cancel");
outtextxy(440,80,"OK");
imsize = imagesize(230,0,510,100);
dialog_box = malloc(imsize);
getimage(230,0,510,100,dialog_box);

      /* Scroll Bar */

rectangle(180,120,300,320);
rectangle(280,120,300,320);
rectangle(280,120,300,140);
rectangle(280,300,300,320);
moveto(280,300);
lineto(290,320);
lineto(300,300);
moveto(280,140);
lineto(290,120);
lineto(300,140);
outtextxy(230,270,"Click here");
outtextxy(230,290,"to exit");
imsize = imagesize(180,120,300,320);
scroll_bar = malloc(imsize);
getimage(180,120,300,320,scroll_bar);
```

```
        /* Radio Buttons */

rectangle(425,225,550,375);
circle(450,245,8);
circle(450,245,5);
circle(450,265,8);
circle(450,265,5);
circle(450,285,8);
circle(450,285,5);
circle(450,305,8);
circle(450,305,5);
rectangle(450,325,525,365);
outtextxy(487,345,"OK");
outtextxy(500,245,"Button 1");
outtextxy(500,265,"Button 2");
outtextxy(500,285,"Button 3");
outtextxy(500,305,"Button 4");
imsize = imagesize(425,225,550,375);
radio_button = malloc(imsize);
getimage(425,225,550,375,radio_button);

        /* Exit Menu */

rectangle(500,150,600,170);
outtextxy(550,160,"Exit Demo");
imsize = imagesize(500,150,600,170);
exit_menu = malloc(imsize);
getimage(500,150,600,170,exit_menu);

        /* Delay before continuing */

outtextxy(320,450,"Menu Screen - Press a Key to Continue");
getch();

        /* start GUI demo */

clearviewport();
setbkcolor(1);
rectangle (0,0,639,479);

        /* reset the mouse status */

mouse_call(0,0,0,0);

        /* display the mouse */

mouse_call(1,0,0,0);

        /* get and display the mouse position */

mouse_call(3,0,0,0);
settextstyle (DEFAULT_FONT,HORIZ_DIR,1);
settextjustify (CENTER_TEXT,CENTER_TEXT);
sprintf (buffer,"x : %d",globcx);
outtextxy(75,460,buffer);
sprintf (buffer,"y : %d",globdx);
outtextxy(565,460,buffer);
```

Listing 9.1.   *continues*

231

Listing 9.1. cont.   Code for GUI demonstration

```
        /* create a menu bar */

setfillstyle(SOLID_FILL,4);
bar(1,1,638,20);
moveto(0,20);
lineto(639,20);
outtextxy(100,10,"Demo Options");
outtextxy(570,10,"Exit");

        /* main loop */

settextstyle(DEFAULT_FONT,HORIZ_DIR,1);
settextjustify(CENTER_TEXT,CENTER_TEXT);
setfillstyle(SOLID_FILL,1);

do
{
    /* display cursor positioning */

mouse_call(3,0,0,0);
bar(25,450,125,470);
sprintf(buffer,"x : %d",globcx);
outtextxy(75,460,buffer);
bar(515,450,615,470);
sprintf(buffer,"y : %d",globdx);
outtextxy(565,460,buffer);

    /* check for Demo Options box positioning */

if (globcx >= 25 && globcx <= 175 && globdx >= 0 && globdx <=20)
    {
    mouse_call(5,0,0,0);
    if (globbx >= 1)
        {
        putimage(20,20,demo_menu,COPY_PUT);
        get_demo_option();
        }
    }

    /* check for Exit box positioning */

if (globcx >=540 && globcx <= 620 && globdx >= 0 && globdx <= 20)
    {
    mouse_call(5,0,0,0);
    if (globbx >= 1)
        {
        putimage(520,20,exit_menu,COPY_PUT);
        check_exit();
        }
    }


} while (exit_status != 1);
```

```
    /* Delay and Exit */
closegraph();
return 0;
}


    /* This function is used to communicate with the */
    /* mouse via interrupt 0x33h.                     */
void mouse_call(regax, regbx, regcx, regdx)
{
union REGS inregs, outregs;

inregs.x.ax = regax;
inregs.x.bx = regbx;
inregs.x.cx = regcx;
inregs.x.dx = regdx;

int86(0x33,&inregs,&outregs);

globax = outregs.x.ax;
globbx = outregs.x.bx;
globcx = outregs.x.cx;
globdx = outregs.x.dx;
}

    /* this function gets the selection from the */
    /* demo options menu                         */
void get_demo_option (void)
{
do
{
    mouse_call(5,0,0,0);
    update_pos();
} while (globbx == 0);
bar(1,21,638,445);
if (globcx >= 20 && globcx <= 180 && globdx >= 20 && globdx <= 39)
    {
    putimage(100,100,dialog_box,COPY_PUT);
    monitor_dialog();
    }
if (globcx >= 20 && globcx <= 180 && globdx >= 40 && globdx <= 59)
    {
    putimage(100,100,scroll_bar,COPY_PUT);
    monitor_scroll();
    }
if (globcx >= 20 && globcx <= 18U && globdx >= 60 && globdx <= 79)
    {
    putimage(100,100,radio_button,COPY_PUT);
    monitor_radio();
    }
if (globcx >= 20 && globcx <= 180 && globdx >= 80 && globdx <= 99)
    {
    draw_tool();
    }
```

Listing 9.1. *continues*

Listing 9.1. cont.   Code for GUI demonstration

```
if (globcx >= 20 && globcx <= 180 && globdx > 100 && globdx <= 120)
    {
    clear_screen();
    }

}

    /* this option checks the exit menu */
void check_exit (void)
{
do
{
    mouse_call(5,0,0,0);
    update_pos();
} while (globbx == 0);
bar(1,21,638,445);
if (globcx >= 520 && globcx <= 620 && globdx >= 20 && globdx <= 40)
    {
    exit_status = 1;
    }
}

    /* this function monitors the dialog box */
void monitor_dialog(void)
{
int can_exit = 0;

do
{
do
{
    mouse_call(5,0,0,0);
    update_pos();
} while (globbx == 0);
if (globcx>=110 && globcx<=370 && globdx>=130 && globdx<=150)
    {
    outtextxy(240,140,"Text would be input here");
    }
if (globcx>=130 && globcx<=210 && globdx>=170 && globdx<=190)
    {
    bar(1,21,638,445);
    can_exit = 1;
    }
if (globcx>=270 && globcx<=350 && globdx>=170 && globdx<=190)
    {
    bar(1,21,638,445);
    can_exit = 1;
    }
} while (can_exit == 0);
}
```

```
        /* this function monitors the scroll bar demo */
void monitor_scroll(void)
{
int can_exit = 0;

do
{
do
{
    mouse_call(5,0,0,0);
    update_pos();
} while (globbx == 0);
if (globcx>=200 && globcx<=220 && globdx>=100 && globdx<=120)
    {
    bar(101,190,199,210);
    outtextxy(150,180,"Text would");
    outtextxy(150,200,"scroll up");
    }
if (globcx>=200 && globcx<=220 && globdx>=280 && globdx<=300)
    {
    bar(101,190,199,210);
    outtextxy(150,180,"Text would");
    outtextxy(150,200,"scroll down");
    }
if (globcx>=100 && globcx<=199 && globdx>=100 && globdx<=300)
    {
    clear_screen();
    can_exit = 1;
    }
} while (can_exit == 0);
}

        /* this function monitors the radio button demo */
void monitor_radio(void)
{
int can_exit = 0;
int button_1 = 1;
int button_2 = 1;
int button_3 = 1;
int button_4 = 1;

do
{
do
{
    mousc_call(5,0,0,0);
    update_pos();
} while (globbx == 0);
if (globcx>=116 && globcx<=132 && globdx>=112 && globdx<=128)
    {
    if (button_1 == 0)
        {
        button_1 = 1;
        setcolor(15);
        circle(125,120,5);
        }
```

Listing 9.1   *continues*

Listing 9.1. cont.   Code for GUI demonstration

```
        else
            {
            button_1 = 0;
            setcolor(1);
            circle(125,120,5);
            setcolor(15);
            }
        }
if (globcx>=116 && globcx<=132 && globdx>=132 && globdx<=148)
    {
    if (button_2 == 0)
        {
        button_2 = 1;
        setcolor(15);
        circle(125,140,5);
        }
        else
            {
            button_2 = 0;
            setcolor(1);
            circle(125,140,5);
            setcolor(15);
            }
    }
if (globcx>=116 && globcx<=132 && globdx>=152 && globdx<=168)
    {
    if (button_3 == 0)
        {
        button_3 = 1;
        setcolor(15);
        circle(125,160,5);
        }
        else
            {
            button_3 = 0;
            setcolor(1);
            circle(125,160,5);
            setcolor(15);
            }
    }

if (globcx>=116 && globcx<=132 && globdx>=172 && globdx<=188)
    {
    if (button_4 == 0)
        {
        button_4 = 1;
        setcolor(15);
        circle(125,180,5);
        }
        else
            {
            button_4 = 0;
            setcolor(1);
```

```
                  circle(125,180,5);
                  setcolor(15);
                  }
          }

     if(globcx>=125 && globcx<=200 && globdx>=200 && globdx<=240)
          {
          clear_screen();
          can_exit = 1;
          }
     } while (can_exit == 0);
}

     /* this function monitors the draw tool demo */

void draw_tool(void)
{
int can_exit = 0;

rectangle(30,30,70,70);
outtextxy(50,50,"End");

do
{
do
{
     mouse_call(5,0,0,0);
     update_pos();
} while (globbx == 0);
if (globcx>=30 && globcx<=70 && globdx>=30 && globdx<=70)
     {
     clear_screen();
     can_exit = 1;
     }
if (globcx>=10 && globcx<=630 && globdx>=80 && globdx<=430)
     {
     setfillstyle(SOLID_FILL,15);
     bar(globcx-10,globdx-10,globcx-1,globdx-1);
     setfillstyle(SOLID_FILL,1);
     }
} while (can_exit == 0);
}

     /* this function clears the working area */
     /* of the screen                        */

void clear_screen(void)
{
setfillstyle(SOLID_FILL,1);
bar(1,21,638,445);
}

     /* this function monitors and updates */
     /* the cursor position                */
```

Listing 9.1. *continues*

Listing 9.1. cont.   Code for GUI demonstration

```
void update_pos(void)
{
bar(25,450,125,470);
sprintf(buffer,"x : %d",globcx);
outtextxy(75,460,buffer);
bar(515,450,615,470);
sprintf(buffer,"y : %d",globdx);
outtextxy(565,460,buffer);
}
```

Summary

Graphical user interfaces provide relief from the tedious, manual selection and input of data. By properly designing the interface, the resulting application can be much easier and enjoyable to use.

II

Reference Guide

10

Video BIOS Services

T his chapter introduces alternate methods of accomplishing many of the functions provided by the Borland graphics library using the read-only memory (ROM) basic input/output system (BIOS). ROM BIOS provides services that permit low-level control over the hardware. This chapter discusses the ROM BIOS video services, with the intent of providing useful information about their capabilities. There is not much need to use these services because the graphics library provided by Borland is extensive and, in general, faster than these BIOS services.

Video Service 00H (Set Video Mode)

Input:
    AH = 00H
    AL = Video mode

Output:
    None

Description: Video service 00H is used to set the video configuration to one of the video modes listed in Table 10.1. The desired video mode is specified in the AL register. When you set the new video mode, the screen is cleared.

Table 10.1 *Video modes*

Mode	Screen Type	Resolution	Colors	Supported by
00H	Text	40x25	16	CGA,EGA,MCGA,VGA
01H	Text	40x25	16	CGA,EGA,MCGA,VGA
02H	Text	80x25	16	CGA,EGA,MCGA,VGA
03H	Text	80x25	16	CGA,EGA,MCGA,VGA
04H	Graphics	320x200	4	CGA,EGA,MCGA,VGA
05H	Graphics	320x200	4	CGA,EGA,MCGA,VGA
06H	Graphics	640x200	2	CGA,EGA,MCGA,VGA
07H	Text	80x25	Mono	EGA,VGA,MDA
0DH	Graphics	320x200	16	EGA,VGA,CGA
0EH	Graphics	640x200	16	EGA,VGA,CGA
0FH	Graphics	640x350	Mono	EGA,VGA
10H	Graphics	640x350	16	EGA,VGA
11H	Graphics	640x480	2	MCGA,VGA
12H	Graphics	640x480	16	VGA
13H	Graphics	320x200	256	MCGA,VGA

Video Service 01H (Set Cursor Size)

Input:
   AH = 01H
   CH = Starting scan line for cursor
   CL = Ending scan line for cursor

Output:
   None

Description: Video Service 01H is for use with text modes. The cursor, which is a line or set of lines in a character cell, blinks at the current character display position. This service defines the number of lines displayed. In CGA modes, eight scan lines (numbered 0-7) are used for the cursor. In EGA modes, 14 lines (numbered 0-13) are used. The MCGA and VGA adapters have a cursor height of 16 lines (numbered 0-15). The default settings are as follows:

CGA: CH = 6, CL = 7
EGA: CH = 11, CL = 12
MCGA and VGA: CH = 13, CL = 14.

Video Service 02H (Set Cursor Position)

Input:
AH = 02H
BH = Page number of cursor
DH = Row number of cursor
DL = Column number of cursor

Output:
None

Description: You can use Video Service 02H to move the cursor to the specified row and column position. This service can be used in both text and graphics modes; however, the cursor will be displayed only in text modes. The upper left corner of the screen is the origin of the row and column coordinate system, and has a value of (0,0). For text and graphics modes that support multiple pages, you must specify the page number to ensure that the correct cursor position is altered.

Video Service 03H (Read Cursor Position)

Input:
AH = 03H
BH = Page number

Output:
CH = Starting line for cursor
CL = Ending line for cursor
DH = Row number
DL = Column number

Description: You can use Video Service 03H to retrieve the cursor size and position of the specified page. The page number is specified in BH. The starting scan line of the cursor is returned in CH, while the ending scan line of the cursor is returned in CL. The row position is returned in DH, and the column position is returned in DL.

Video Service 04H (Read Light Pen Position)

Input:
AH = 04H

Output:
AH = 0: No trigger
= 1: Triggered
BX = Vertical pixel column number
CX = Horizontal pixel line number
DH = Character row number
DL = Character column number

Description: Video Service 04H is used to report the status of the light pen for CGA or EGA adapters. If the light pen has not been triggered, AH equals 0. If it has been triggered, AH equals 1, and the trigger position is returned. The character column and pixel row are initially determined by the hardware. The character row and pixel column are then determined and returned. The pixel column number is returned in BX. The horizontal pixel line number is returned in CH for modes 04H, 05H, and 06H, or returned in CX for all other EGA modes. The character row number is returned in DH; the character column number is returned in DL.

Video Service 05H (Set Active Display Page)

Input:
AH = 05H
AL = Active page number

Output:
None

Description: Video Service 05H is used to set the active display page number for text and graphics modes. The desired page number is specified in AL. For most text modes, page numbers range from 0 to 7. For EGA and VGA adapters with sufficient video memory, multiple pages of graphics can be supported. Page 0 is the default for all text and graphics modes.

Video Service 06H (Scroll Active Window Up)

Input:
AH = 06H
AL = Number of lines to scroll
BH = Attribute of blank lines
CH = Upper left row number
CL = Upper left column number
DH = Lower right row number
DL = Lower right column number

Output:
None

Description: Video Service 06H is used to create and scroll a text window. The upper left corner of the text window is defined in CH and CL. CH defines the upper left row number. CL defines the upper left column number. The lower right corner of the text window is defined in DH and DL. DH is used to define the lower right row number; DL is used to define the lower right column number. AL defines the number of lines to scroll up. If AL = 00H, the text window is blanked. When you scroll the window, the bottom line is blanked as defined by the display attribute in BH.

Video Service 07H (Scroll Active Window Down)

Input:
AH = 07H
AL = Number of lines to scroll
BH = Attribute for blank lines
CH = Upper left row number
CL = Upper left column number
DH = Lower right row number
DL = Lower right column number

Output:
None

Description: You can use Video Service 07H to create and scroll a text window. The upper left corner of the text window is defined in CH and CL. CH is used to define the upper left row number. CL is used to define the upper left column number. The lower right corner of the text window is defined in DH and DL. DH is used to define the lower right row number; DL is used to define the lower right column number. AL defines the number of lines to scroll down. If AL equals 00H, the text window is blanked. When you scroll the window down, the top line of the window is blanked, as defined by the display attribute in BH.

Video Service 08H (Read Character and Attribute)

Input:
> AH = 08H
> BH = Active page number

Output:
> AH = Character Attribute
> AL = ASCII character retrieved

Description: Video Service 08H is used to read the character at the current cursor location in either the text or video modes. In graphics mode, the retrieved character is compared with the character-generation table used with graphics modes. In text mode, the ASCII character code is retrieved. The attributes of the character are returned in AH; the ASCII code of the character is returned in AL. In graphics mode, the contents of AH are meaningless.

Video Service 09H (Write Character and Attribute)

Input:
> AH = 09H
> AL = ASCII character to write
> BL = Attribute of character to write
> BH = Active page number
> CX = Number of times to repeat character and attribute

Output:
> None

Description: Video Service 09H writes a character to the screen at the current cursor position. The ASCII character of the code to write is specified in AL. The character's attributes are specified in BL for text modes. BL specifies the foreground color for graphics mode. The specified character can be repeated. CX defines the number of times the character and attribute pair is to be written.

Video Service 0AH (Write Character)

Input:
> AH = 0AH
> AL = ASCII character to write
> BL = Attribute of character to write

BH = Active page number
CX = Number of times to repeat character

Output:
None

Description: Video Service 0AH is used to write a character to the screen. BL is not used in text modes, because the character attributes cannot be altered with this service. In graphics mode, BL defines the foreground color. For both text and graphics modes, AL specifies the ASCII character to write, and CX indicates the number of times to write the character.

Video Service 0BH (Set Color Palette)

Input:
AH = 0BH
BH = Color number
BL = Color value

Output:
None

Description: Video Service 0BH is used to set either the palette or the background/border color. When BH is set to 00H, you can set the border color in CGA text modes, or the background color in CGA graphics modes. BL specifies the color. When BH is 01H, one of two four-color palettes used in the 320-by-200 four-color mode can be selected. If BL is 1, the cyan-magenta-white palette is selected. If BL equals 0, the red-green-brown palette is selected.

Video Service 0CH (Write Pixel)

Input:
AH = 0CH
AL = Pixel color
BH = Display page
CX = Column number of pixel
DX = Row number of pixel

Output:
None

Description: Video Service 0CH is used to write a pixel on the screen at the specified location in a specified color. The AL register specifies the color and write mode of the pixel. The desired location of the pixel is defined in CX and DX. CX defines the column position of the pixel, while DX defines the row position.

Video Service 0DH (Read Pixel)

Input:
    AH = 0DH
    BH = Display page
    CX = Column number of pixel
    DX = Row number of pixel

Output:
    AL = Pixel color value

Description: Video Service 0DH is used to read the color of a pixel at a specified location. BH specifies the display page number. The position to read is defined by CX and DX. CX defines the column number of the pixel; DX defines the row number.

Video Service 0EH (Write TTY Character)

Input:
    AH = 0EH
    AL = ASCII character to write
    BH = Active display page
    BL = Foreground color (graphics mode only)

Output:
    None

Description: Video Service 0EH is used to write a character at the current position in teletype (TTY) mode. BL specifies the foreground color and works only in graphics modes. AL specifies the ASCII character to display. In teletype mode, ASCII characters 07H, 08H, 0AH, and 0DH are not written to the screen. Instead they are interpreted in the following manner:

07H - Beep from computer speaker
08H - Backspace one position
0AH - Do one line feed
0DH - Do one carriage return

Video Service 0FH (Get Current Video Mode)

Input:
AH = 0FH

Output:
AH = Number of characters per line
AL = Current display mode
BH = Active page number

Description: Video Service 0FH is used to retrieve the current video mode, the screen width in characters, and the active display page number. The video display mode is returned in AL. The screen width, in characters, is returned in AH. The active page number is returned in BH.

Video Service 10H, Subservice 00H (Set Palette Register—EGA and VGA Only)

Input:
AH = 10H
AL = 00H
BH = Color to be loaded
BL = Palette number

Output:
None

Description: Video Service 10H, Subservice 00H, is used to set the color for a specified palette register. The palette register number is described in BL. BH contains the color to be loaded.

Video Service 10H, Subservice 01H (Set EGA and VGA Overscan Register)

Input:
AH = 10H
AL = 01H
BH = Color code for overscan

Output:
None

Description: Video Service 10H, Subservice 01H, is used to set the border color (often called the *overscan border*) for EGA or VGA adapters. The color code is passed in BH.

Video Service 10H, Subservice 02H (Set Palette and Overscan Registers—EGA and VGA Only)

Input:
AH = 10H
AL = 02H
ES:DX = Pointer to 17-byte array of palette and overscan
colors

Output:
None

Description: Video Service 10H, Subservice 02H, is used to set all 16 palette registers and the overscan (or border) register. Before this subservice is called, the 17 values must be placed into a 17-byte table. The segment and offset (address) of the table is specified in ES and DX.

Video Service 10H, Subservice 03H (Toggle Blinking or Intensity—EGA and VGA Only)

Input:
AH = 10H
AL = 03H
BL = 0: Toggle intensity
= 1: Toggle blinking

Output:
None

Description: Video Service 10H, Subservice 03H, is used to enable or disable the blinking and intensity bits. The default settings of these bits are low intensity with no blinking. When this subservice is called with BL = 0, the intensity is toggled (if it is currently high it is set to low—if it is on low it is set to high). When this subservice is called with BL = 1, the blinking bit is toggled (if it is blinking, it is set to no blinking—if it is not blinking, it is set to blinking).

Video Service 10H, Subservice 07H (Read VGA Palette Register)

Input:
AH = 10H
AL = 07H
BL = Palette register number to read

Output:
BH = Palette register color value

Description: Video Service 10H, Subservice 07H, is used to read the color for a particular palette register. BL specifies the palette register to read. The color of the specified register is returned in BH.

Video Service 10H, Subservice 08H (Read Overscan Register—VGA only)

Input:
AH = 10H
AL = 08H

Output:
BH = Overscan register color value

Description: Video Service 10H, Subservice 08H, is used to read the color of the overscan, or border, register. The retrieved color is returned in BH.

Video Service 10H, Subservice 09H (Read VGA Palette and Overscan Registers)

Input:
AH = 10H
AL = 09H
ES:DX = Pointer to 17-byte array of palette and overscan
values

Output:
Retrieved information returned to 17-byte array at ES:DX

Description: Video Service 10H, Subservice 09H, is used to read all the VGA palette registers. These registers include the palette and overscan registers. The 17 bytes of register information are returned to the memory location pointed to by ES:DX.

251

Video Service 10H, Subservice 10H (Set Individual VGA Color Register)

Input:
AH = 10H
AL = 10H
BX = Color register to set
CH = Intensity of green
CL = Intensity of blue
DH = Intensity of red

Output:
None

Description: Video Service 10H, Subservice 10H, is used to set an individual digital-to-analog converter (DAC) register to a six-bit value for red, green, and blue. This subservice should be called with six-bit red, green, and blue values in registers DH, CH, and CL respectively. BX specifies the register to set.

Video Service 10H, Subservice 12H (Set Block of Color Registers—VGA Only)

Input:
AH = 10H
AL = 12H
BX = Number of first color register
CX = Number of color registers to set
ES:DX = Pointer to array of colors

Output:
None

Description: Video Service 10H, Subservice 12H, is used to set a block of digital-to-analog convertor (DAC) registers to the specified colors. BX specifies the first register to set; CX indicates the number of registers to set. The table that contains the three-byte red, green, and blue values for the registers is pointed to by ES and DX.

Video Service 10H, Subservice 13H (Select Color Page—VGA Only)

Input:
AH = 10H
AL = 13H

BL = 0: Select mode
= 1: Select page
BH = 0: Select four pages of 64-color when BL = 0
= 1: Select 16 pages of 16-color when BL = 0
= color page number when BL = 1

Output:
None

Description: Video Service 10H, Subservice 13H, is used with the VGA to select the color page or the color page mode. If BL = 0, you can select the color page mode. If BH = 0, four pages of 64 colors are selected. If BH = 1, 16 blocks of 16 colors are selected. When BL = 1, BH specifies the color page number.

Video Service 10H, Subservice 15H (Read Individual Color Register—VGA Only)

Input:
AH = 10H
AL = 15H
BX = Number of color register to read

Output:
CH = Intensity of green
CL = Intensity of blue
DH = Intensity of red

Description: Video Service 10H, Subservice 15H, is used to read the color values from a color register for VGA only. BX specifies the number of the color register to read. The red, green, and blue values of the specified register are returned in DH, CH, and CL, respectively.

Video Service 10H, Subservice 17H (Read Block of Color Registers—VGA Only)

Input:
AH = 10H
AL = 17H
BX = Number of first register to read
CX = Number of register
ES:DX = Pointer to array of color values

Output:
Color returned to array pointed to by ES:DX

Description: Video Service 10H, Subservice 17H, is used to read a block of color registers. BX specifies the number of the first register to read. CX defines the number of registers to read. The block of red, green, and blue values is returned to the table pointed to by ES:DX.

Video Service 10H, Subservice 1AH (Read Current Color Page Number—VGA Only)

Input:
AH = 10H
AL = 1AH

Output:
BH = Current color page
BL = Paging mode

Description: Video Service 10H, Subservice 1AH, is used to read the current color page and color paging mode. The current color page is returned in BH. The current color paging mode is returned in BL.

Video Service 10H, Subservice 1BH (Sum Color Values to Gray Scale—VGA Only)

Input:
AH = 10H
AL = 1BH
BX = First color register to convert
CX = Number of color registers to convert

Output:
None

Description: Video Service 10H, Subservice 1BH, is used to convert the color values in a block of consecutive video digital-to-analog convertor (DAC) color registers to their corresponding shades of gray. BX specifies the first color register to convert. CX defines the number of registers to convert.

Video Service 11H, Subservice 00H (Load Font—EGA and VGA Only)

Input:
> AH = 11H
> AL = 00H
> BL = Block to load
> BH = Number of bytes per character
> CX = Number of characters to load
> DX = Character offset
> ES:BP = Pointer to font buffer

Output:
> None

Description: Video Service 11H, Subservice 00H, is used to load a user character font into the loadable character generator. BL identifies the block to load. BH defines the number of bytes per character. CX contains the number of characters. The ASCII code of the first character is specified in DX. The address of the block (segment and offset) is specified in ES:BP.

Video Service 11H, Subservice 01H (Load ROM 8-by-14 Character Set—EGA and VGA Only)

Input:
> AH = 11H
> AL = 01H
> BL = Block to load

Output:
> None

Description: Video Service 11H, Subservice 01H, is used to load the ROM 8-by-14 monochrome character set. The block to load is specified in BL.

Video Service 11H, Subservice 02H (Load ROM 8-by-8 Character Set—EGA and VGA Only)

Input:
AH = 11H
AL = 02H
BL = Block to load

Output:
None

Description: Video Service 11H, Subservice 02H, is used to load the ROM 8-by-8 double dot character set. The block to load is specified in BL.

Video Service 11H, Subservice 03H (Set Block Specifier—EGA and VGA Only)

Input:
AH = 11H
AL = 03H
BL = Value to load into character map select register

Output:
None

Description: Video Service 11H, Subservice 03H, is used to select among text-mode character sets after they are loaded into the character generator RAM. The EGA has four tables; the VGA has eight tables. The BL register is used to specify one or two of these tables that will be used to display text-mode characters.

Video Service 11H, Subservice 04H (Load ROM 8-by-16 Character Set—EGA and VGA Only)

Input:
AH = 11H
AL = 04H
BL = Block number to load

Output:
None

Description: Video Service 11H, Subservice 04H, is used to load the ROM 8-by-16 character set. The block to load is specified in BL.

Video Service 11H, Subservice 10H (Load Font—EGA and VGA Only)

Input:
  AH = 11H
  AL = 10H
  BH = Number of bytes per character
  BL = Block to load
  CX = Number of characters
  DX = Character offset to memory block
  ES:BP = Pointer to font buffer

Output:
  None

Description: Video Service 11H, Subservice 10H, is used to load a user font. The address of the font to load is contained in ES:BP. The block to load is specified in BL. BH contains the number of bytes per character; CX is used to specify the number of characters to load.

Video Service 11H, Subservice 11H (Load ROM 8-by-14 Character Set—EGA and VGA Only)

Input:
  AH = 11H
  AL = 11H
  BL = Block to load

Output:
  None

Description: Video Service 11H, Subservice 11H, is used to load the ROM 8-by-14 character set. The block to load is specified in BL.

Video Service 11H, Subservice 12H (Load ROM 8-by-8 Character Set—EGA and VGA Only)

Input:
AH = 11H
AL = 12H
BL = Block to load

Output:
None

Description: Video Service 11H, Subservice 12H, is used to load the ROM 8-by-8 character set. The block to load is specified in BL.

Video Service 11H, Subservice 14H (Load ROM 8-by-16 Character Set)

Input:
AH = 11H
AL = 14H
BL = Target block

Output:
None

Description: Video Service 11H, Subservice 14H, is used to load the ROM 8-by-16 character set. The block to load is specified in BL.

Video Service 11H, Subservice 20H (Load Character Pointer—EGA and VGA Only)

Input:
AH = 11H
AL = 20H
ES:BP = Pointer to font buffer

Output:
None

Description: Video Service 11H, Subservice 20H, is used to store a pointer to the table of graphics characters represented by ASCII codes 128 to 255. The pointer is specified in ES:BP.

Video Service 11H, Subservice 21H (Load Character Pointer—EGA and VGA Only)

Input:

    AH = 11H
    AL = 21H
    BL = 01H: 14 screen rows
       = 02H: 25 screen rows
       = 03H: 43 screen rows
    CX = Number of bytes per character
    DL = Number of character rows
    ES:BP = Pointer to font buffer

Output:

    None

Description: Video Service 11H, Subservice 21H, is used to store a pointer to the table of all graphics characters. DL specifies the number of character rows. The contents of CX specify the number of bytes per character.

Video Service 11H, Subservice 22H (Load Graphics ROM 8-by-14 Character Set—EGA and VGA Only)

Input:

    AH = 11H
    AL = 22H
    BL = 01H: 14 screen rows
       = 02H: 25 screen rows
       = 03II. 43 screen rows
    DL = Number of character rows

Output:

    None

Description: Video Service 11H, Subservice 22H, is used to load the ROM 8-by-14 character set for graphics mode. DL is used to specify the number of character rows.

Video Service 11H, Subservice 23H (Load Graphics ROM 8-by-8 Character Set—EGA and VGA Only)

Input:
AH = 11H
AL = 23H
BL = 01H: 14 screen rows
= 02H: 25 screen rows
= 03H: 43 screen rows
DL = Number of character rows

Output:
None

Description: Video Service 11H, Subservice 23H, is used to load the ROM 8-by-8 character set for use in graphics mode. DL specifies the number of character rows.

Video Service 11H, Subservice 24H (Load Graphics ROM 8-by-16 Character Set—EGA and VGA Only)

Input:
AH = 11H
AL = 24H
BL = 01H: 14 screen rows
= 02H: 25 screen rows
= 03H: 43 screen rows
DL = Number of character rows

Output:
None

Description: Video Service 11H, Subservice 24H, is used to load the ROM 8-by-16 character set. The contents of DL specify the number of character rows.

Video Service 11H, Subservice 30H (Return Character Generator Data—EGA and VGA Only)

Input:
AH = 11H
AL = 30H
BH = 00H: INT 1FH pointer

= 01H: INT 43H pointer
= 02H: ROM 8-by-14 pointer
= 03H: ROM 8-by-8 pointer
= 04H: ROM 8-by-8 pointer
= 05H: ROM 9-by-14 pointer
= 06H: ROM 8-by-16 pointer
= 07H: ROM 9-by-16 pointer

Output:

CX = Bytes per character
DL = Number of rows in EGA
= Number of rows minus 1 in VGA
ES:BP = Pointer

Description: Video Service 11H, Subservice 30H, is used to retrieve information on the ROM BIOS character generator. The contents of BH determine the address returned in ES:BP. The bytes per character are returned in CX. The number of rows is returned in DL.

Video Service 12H, Subservice 10H (Get Video Information—EGA and VGA Only)

Input:

AH = 12H
BL = 10H

Output:

BH = 0: Color mode
= 1: Monochrome mode
BL = Memory size
= 00H: 64K
= 01H: 128K
= 02H: 192K
= 03H: 256K
CH = Feature control bits
CL = Video switch settings

Description: Video Service 12H, Subservice 10H, is used to retrieve information on the EGA or VGA configuration. The contents of BL indicate whether the current video mode is color (00H) or monochrome (01H). The video RAM size is indicated in BL as described above. CH indicates the status of the input from the feature connector. The contents of CL indicate the settings of the configuration switches.

Video Service 12H, Subservice 20H (Select Alternate Print Screen Routine—EGA and VGA Only)

Input:
AH = 12H
BL = 20H

Output:
None

Description: Video Service 12H, Subservice 20H, is used to change the print-screen routine from the motherboard ROM BIOS to the adapter ROM BIOS. The adapter ROM BIOS for EGA and VGA is capable of printing text-mode screens in excess of 25 rows.

Video Service 12H, Subservice 30H (Select Scan Lines for VGA Text Modes)

Input:
AH = 12H
BL = 30H
AL = 0: 200 scan lines
= 1: 350 scan lines
= 2: 400 scan lines

Output:
AL = 12H: Valid call
= Anything else: Call was invalid

Description: Video Service 12H, Subservice 30H, is used to set the number of scan lines and the default character set for alphanumeric modes. The contents of AL indicate the number of scan lines to set.

Video Service 12H, Subservice 31H (Default Palette Loading During Mode Set—VGA Only)

Input:
AH = 12H
BL = 31H
AL = 0: Enable palette loading
= 1: Disable palette loading

Output:
 AL = 12H: Valid call
     = Anything else: Call was invalid

Description: Video Service 12H, Subservice 31H, is used to enable or disable palette loading when a new VGA video mode is set. AL = 0 enables default palette loading; AL = 1 disables default palette loading.

Video Service 12H, Subservice 32H (Video Enable or Disable— VGA Only)

Input:
 AH = 12H
 BL = 32H
 AL = 0: Enable video
     = 1: Disable video

Output:
 AL = 12H: Valid call
     = Anything else: Call was invalid

Description: Video Service 12H, Subservice 32H, is used to enable or disable the video input port and buffer address decode. The contents of AL enable (00H) or disable (01H) the buffer and port addressing.

Video Service 12H, Subservice 33H (Sum to Gray Scale—VGA Only)

Input:
 AH = 12H
 BL = 33H
 AL = 0: Enable summing
     = 1: Disable summing

Output:
 AL = 12H: Valid call
     = Anything else: Call was invalid

Description: Video Service 12H, Subservice 33H, is used to enable or disable the gray-scale features of the VGA. AL = 00H enables gray-scaling; AL = 01H disables gray-scaling.

Video Service 12H, Subservice 34H (Cursor Emulation—VGA Only)

Input:
> AH = 12H
> BL = 34H
> AL = 0: Enable cursor emulation
>   = 1: Disable cursor emulation

Output:
> AL = 12H: Valid call
>   = Anything else: Call was invalid

Description: Video Service 12H, Subservice 34H, is used to enable or disable the cursor emulation for VGA in text modes. When AL = 00H, the cursor is emulated using CGA text mode cursor sizing when the video mode or cursor size is altered. When AL = 01H, the text mode cursor emulation is disabled.

Video Service 12H, Subservice 35H (Display switch—VGA Only)

Input:
> AH = 12H
> BL = 35H
> AL = 0: Switch off adapter
>   = 1: Switch on planar video
>   = 2: Switch off active video
>   = 3: Switch on inactive video
> ES:DX = Pointer to 128-byte buffer

Output:
> AL = 12H: Valid call
>   = Anything else: Call was invalid

Description: Video Service 12H, Subservice 35H, is used to select or deselect a video device. AL specifies the desired switching action. The options for AL arc described in the preceding list

Video Service 12H, Subservice 36H (Video Screen On or Off—VGA Only)

Input:
> AH = 12H

BL = 36H
AL = 0: Enable video output
    = 1: Disable video output

Output:
AL = 12H: Valid call
    = Anything else: Call was invalid

Description: Video Service 12H, Subservice 36H, is used to enable or disable the video output to the monitor display. When AL = 00H, video output, or video refresh, is enabled. When AL = 01H, video output is disabled. When the video output is disabled, the screen goes blank.

Video Service 13H, Subservice 00H (Write Character String—EGA and VGA Only)

Input:
AH = 13H
AL = 00H
BH = Page number
BL = Attribute
CX = Number of characters
DH = Row position
DL = Column position
ES:BP = Pointer to beginning of string

Output:
None

Description: Video Service 13H, Subservice 00H, is used to write a character string to the screen. The string is placed at the position specified in DH and DL. CX specifies the number of characters in the string. The string is written to the screen with the attributes defined in BL. ES:BP points to the character string. At the end of this service, the cursor remains at the beginning of the string.

Video Service 13H, Subservice 01H (Write Character String—EGA and VGA Only)

Input:
AH = 13H
AL = 01H

BH = Page number
BL = Attribute
CX = Number of characters
DH = Row position
DL = Column position
ES:BP = Pointer to beginning of string

Output:
None

Description: Video Service 13H, Subservice 01H, is used to write a character string to the screen. The string is placed at the position specified in DH and DL. CX specifies the number of characters in the string. The string is written to the screen with the attributes defined in BL. ES:BP points to the character string. At the end of this service, the cursor is positioned at the location following the last character in the string.

Video Service 13H, Subservice 02H (Write Character String—EGA and VGA Only)

Input:
AH = 13H
AL = 02H
BH = Page number
CX = Number of characters and attributes in string
DH = Row position
DL = Column position
ES:BP = Pointer to beginning of string

Output:
None

Description: Video Service 13H, Subservice 02H, is used to write a character string. ES:BP points to the beginning of the character string. The string is written to the screen beginning at the position specified in DH and DL. The string consists of alternate characters and attributes. The number of characters and attributes is defined in CX. The cursor position remains at DH, DL after the service is completed.

Video Service 13H, Subservice 03H (Write Character String—EGA and VGA Only)

Input:
AH = 13H

266

AL = 03H
BH = Page number
CX = Number of characters and attributes in string
DH = Row position
DL = Column position
ES:BP = Pointer to beginning of string

Output:
None

Description: Video Service 13H, Subservice 03H, is used to write a character string that consists of alternate characters and attributes. ES:BP points to the beginning of the character string. The string is written to the screen beginning at the position specified in DH, DL. The number of characters and attributes is defined in CX. The cursor is positioned at the location following the last character in the string when the service is ended.

Video Service 1AH (Read/Write Display Combination Code—VGA Only)

Input:
AH = 1AH
AL = 00H: Read DCC
    = 01H: Write DCC
BH = Inactive DCC
    = Active DCC

NOTE: DCC = Display Combination Code

Output:
AL = 1AH: Call is valid
    = Anything else: Call was invalid

Description: Video Service 1AH is used to read or write a two-byte display combination code. This service is a system function and, thus, is not ordinarily used.

Video Service 1BH (Return Functionality and State Data—VGA Only)

Input:
AH = 1BH
BX = 00H
ES:BP = Pointer to data buffer

Output:

AL = 1BH: Call is valid

= Anything else: Call was invalid

ES:BP = Data buffer updated

Description: Video Service 1BH is used to read the functionality and state table. This table contains information about the video mode and video hardware configuration.

Video Service 1CH (Save and Restore Video State—VGA Only)

Input:

AH = 1CH

AL = 00H: Return size of save and restore buffer

= 01H: Save video state

= 02H: Restore video state

CX = bit 0: Video hardware state

= bit 1: Video data areas

= bit 2: Video DAC state and color registers

ES:BP = Pointer to save and restore buffer

Output:

AL = 1CH: Call is valid

= Anything else: Call was invalid

BX = Block count for buffer size

Description: Video Service 1CH is used to save or restore video data to a designated buffer. When AL = 00H, the information that describes the status of the video BIOS and hardware is returned. When AL = 01H, the current video state information is saved in the buffer pointed to by ES:BP. When AL = 02H, the previous video state is restored.

Summary

The ROM BIOS video services allow you to directly control the video interface. These services can be used as an addition to or replacement for the run-time library graphics functions provided by Borland C++.

11

Borland C++ Graphics Reference

This chapter provides detailed information for all of the Borland C++ graphics functions. It provides a range of useful information and includes the syntax and an example for each function. Each heading used to describe each function is listed.

function_name

Syntax:
The syntax for each function is provided in this section. A brief description of each argument is also provided.

Function:
This section contains a very brief description of the function.

File(s) to Include:
The `include` file(s) needed for the function being described are listed in this section.

Description:
A full description of the function is contained in this section.

Value(s) Returned:
The return values of the function are described in this section.

Related Function(s):

This section describes some of the Turbo C++ functions that are used with, or similar to, the function being described.

Similar Microsoft C Function(s):

Microsoft C functions that are used for similar purposes are described in this section.

Example:

An example using the function is provided under this heading. A brief description, along with the code used to generate the example, is included.

arc

Syntax:

```
void far arc(int x, int y, int startangle, int endangle,
             int radius);

int x, y;              Center of arc
int startangle;        Starting angle
int endangle;          Ending angle
int radius;            Radius of arc
```

Function:

The arc function is used to create a circular arc on the screen.

File(s) to Include:

```
#include <graphics.h>
```

Description:

The arc function creates a circular arc. The arc is centered at the point specified by the x and y arguments, and it is drawn with the specified radius. The arc is not filled, but is drawn using the current color. The arc begins at the angle specified by the startangle argument and is drawn in a counterclockwise direction until it reaches the angle specified by the endangle argument. The arc function uses east (extending to the right of the arc's center in the horizontal direction) as its 0 degree point. The setlinestyle function can be used to set the width of the arc. The arc function will, however, ignore the pattern argument of the setlinestyle function. Figure 11.1 illustrates the use of the arc function.

Figure 11.1. The arc function

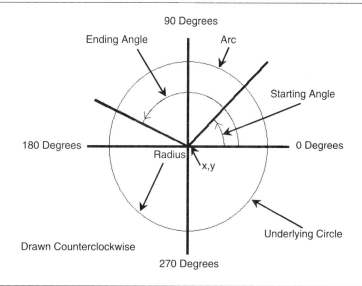

Value(s) Returned:
There is no return value.

Related Function(s):
getarccoords : gets coordinates of last call to arc
setcolor   : sets the current color

Similar Microsoft C Function(s):
_arc : draws an elliptical arc

```
short _far _arc(short x1, short y1, short x2, short y2,
                short x3, short y3, short x4, short y4);
```

Example:
Listing 11.1 (as shown in Figure 11.2) demonstrates the use of the arc function by creating a series of circular arcs. Each arc is centered in the display screen, while each subsequent arc has a decreasing radius.

Listing 11.1. The arc function

```
#include <graphics.h>
#include <stdio.h>
#include <stdlib.h>
#include <conio.h>

int main ()
{
int gdriver = EGA;
int gmode = EGAHI;
int radius;

     /* register EGAVGA_driver and sansserif_font */
     /* ... these have been added to graphics.lib  */
     /* as described in UTIL.DOC                    */

registerbgidriver (EGAVGA_driver);
registerbgifont (sansserif_font);

     /* set EGA video mode  */

initgraph (&gdriver,&gmode,"");
rectangle (0,0,639,349);

     /* Draw a series of arcs */

for (radius = 25; radius < 175; radius = radius + 25)
{
   arc (320,175,0,270,radius);
}

     /* Delay and Exit */

settextjustify(CENTER_TEXT,BOTTOM_TEXT);
outtextxy (320,320,"Press Any Key To Exit");
getch ();
closegraph();
return 0;
}
```

Figure 11.2. Screen output from Listing 11.1

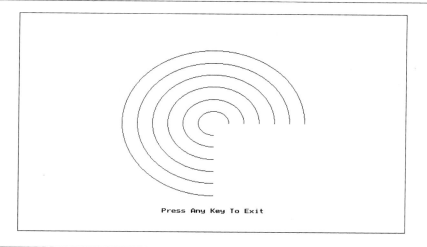

Press Any Key To Exit

bar

Syntax:
```
void far bar(int left, int top, int right, int bottom);

int left, top;              Upper left corner of bar
int right, bottom;          Lower right corner of bar
```

Function:
The bar function creates a filled, rectangular, two-dimensional bar.

File(s) to Include:
```
#include <graphics.h>
```

Description:
The bar function is used to draw a filled, rectangular, two-dimensional bar. The upper left-hand corner of the rectangular bar is defined by the left and top arguments. These arguments correspond to the x and y values of the top left corner. Similarly, the right and bottom arguments define the lower right corner of the bar. The bar is not outlined, but it is filled with the current fill pattern and fill color as set by the setfillstyle function. Figure 11.3 illustrates the use of the bar function.

Figure 11.3. The bar function

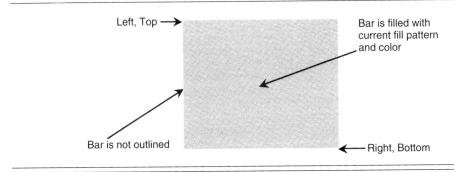

Left, Top →

Bar is filled with current fill pattern and color

Bar is not outlined

Right, Bottom ←

Value(s) Returned:

There is no return value.

Related Function(s):

setcolor   : sets the current color
rectangle   : generates a rectangle
setfillstyle : sets the current fill pattern

Similar Microsoft C Function(s):

_rectangle : draws a filled or unfilled rectangle

```
short _far _rectangle(short fillflag, short x1, short y1,
                      short x2, short y2);
```

Example:

Listing 11.2 and Figure 11.4 use the bar function to display a series of bars that extend from the left side of the screen to the right side of the screen. Each bar is drawn using a different fill pattern, color, and height.

Listing 11.2. The bar function

```
#include <graphics.h>
#include <stdio.h>
#include <stdlib.h>
#include <conio.h>

int main ()
{
int gdriver = EGA;
int gmode = EGAHI;
int x, y, color,fill;

    /* register EGAVGA_driver and sansserif_font */
    /* ... these have been added to graphics.lib */
    /* as described in UTIL.DOC                   */

registerbgidriver(EGAVGA_driver);
registerbgifont(sansserif_font);

    /* set EGA high-resolution 16-color mode */

initgraph (&gdriver,&gmode,"");
rectangle (0,0,639,349);

x = 20;
y = 20;
color = 1;
fill=1;

do
{
    setfillstyle (fill,color);
    bar (x,y,x+40,320);
    x = x+40;
    y = y+10;
    color = color+1;
    if (color > 15)
        color = 1;
    fill = fill+1;
    if (fill > 11)
        fill = 1;
} while (x < 620);

    /* Delay and Exit */

settextjustify(CENTER_TEXT,BOTTOM_TEXT);
outtextxy (330,345,"Press Any Key To Exit");

getch ();

closegraph();
return 0;
}
```

Figure 11.4. Screen output from Listing 11.2

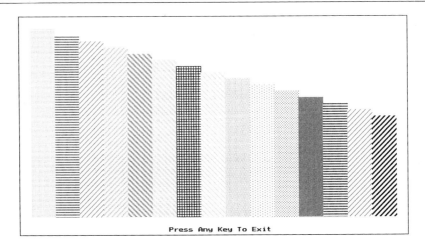

Press Any Key To Exit

bar3d

Syntax:

```
void far bar3d(int left, int top, int right, int bottom,
               int depth, int topflag);

int left, top;              Upper left corner of bar
int right, bottom;          Lower right corner of bar
int depth;                  Depth of 3D bar
int topflag;                0 - bar is topped, 1 - not topped
```

Function:

The bar3d function is used to create a three-dimensional rectangular bar.

File(s) to Include:

```
#include <graphics.h>
```

Description:

The bar3d function creates a three-dimensional rectangular bar. The left and top arguments define the upper left corner of the front-most rectangle. These arguments correspond to the x and y values of the corner. Similarly, the right and bottom arguments define the lower right corner of the frontmost rectangle. The depth argument defines the three-dimensional depth, in pixels, of the bar. The bar is outlined, in all three dimensions, in the current color and line style. The frontmost rectangle is filled using the current fill pattern and fill color. The topflag argument is used to specify whether or not it is possible to stack several bars on top of each other. If topflag is set to a nonzero value, a top is placed on the figure. If topflag is set to 0, no top is placed on the figure, allowing other bars to be stacked on top of the figure. Figure 11.5 illustrates the use of the bar3d function.

Figure 11.5. The bar3d function

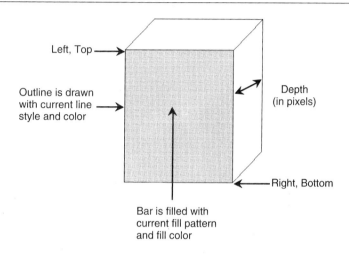

Value(s) Returned:
There is no return value.

Related Function(s):
bar   : creates a two-dimensional bar
setcolor : sets the current color
setfillstyle : sets the current fill pattern

Similar Microsoft C Function(s):
There are no similar Microsoft C functions.

Example:
The following example (Listing 11.3 and Figure 11.6) demonstrates the use of the bar3d function to create a filled, three-dimensional bar. The depth of the bar is 50 pixels.

Listing 11.3. The bar3d function

```
#include <graphics.h>
#include <stdio.h>
#include <stdlib.h>
#include <conio.h>

int main ()
{
int gdriver = EGA;
int gmode = EGAHI;
int pattern, color;

    /* register EGAVGA_driver and sansserif_font */
    /* ... these have been added to graphics.lib */
    /* as described in UTIL.DOC                   */

registerbgidriver(EGAVGA_driver);
registerbgifont(sansserif_font);

    /* set EGA high-resolution 16-color mode */

initgraph (&gdriver,&gmode,"");
rectangle (0,0,639,349);

    /* Draw 3d bar using white borders and fill  */
    /* pattern 11 - has depth of 50              */

pattern = 11;
color = 15;

setfillstyle (pattern,color);
bar3d (220,50,420,300,50,1);

    /* Delay and Exit */

settextjustify(CENTER_TEXT,BOTTOM_TEXT);
outtextxy (320,320,"Press Any Key To Exit");

getch ();
closegraph();
return 0;
}
```

Figure 11.6. Screen output from Listing 11.3

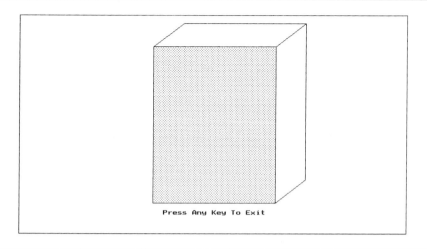

Press Any Key To Exit

circle

Syntax:
```
void far circle(int x, int y, int radius);

int x, y;          Center of circle
int radius;        Radius of circle
```

Function:
The `circle` function generates a circle centered at `(x,y)`.

File(s) to Include:
```
#include <graphics.h>
```

Description:
The `circle` function is used to draw a circle. The x and y arguments define the center of the circle, while the `radius` argument defines the radius of the circle. The circle is not filled but is drawn using the current color. The thickness of the circle's outline can be set by the `setlinestyle` function; however, the line style is ignored by the `circle` function. The aspect ratio for the current mode is taken into account when calculating the circle. Therefore, altering the default x and y aspect factors will affect the circle (it will no longer be round). Figure 11.7 illustrates the use of the `circle` function.

Figure 11.7. The `circle` function

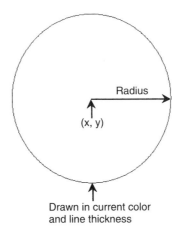

Radius

(x, y)

Drawn in current color
and line thickness

Value(s) Returned:
There is no return value.

Related Function(s):
`setcolor` : sets the current color
`ellipse` : draws an ellipse

Similar Microsoft C Function(s):
`_ellipse` : creates an ellipse in the defined rectangular region

```
short _far _ellipse(short fillflag, short x1, short y1,
                    short x2, short y2);
```

Example:
The `circle` function is used in the following example to create five series of concentric circles. One series is centered on the screen, while the others are displayed in the corners of the screen.(See Listing 11.4 and Figure 11.8.)

Listing 11.4. The `circle` function

```
#include <graphics.h>
#include <stdio.h>
#include <stdlib.h>
#include <conio.h>

int main ()
{
int gdriver = EGA;
int gmode = EGAHI;
int width, radius;
int style, pattern;

     /* register EGAVGA_driver and sansserif_font */
     /* ... these have been added to graphics.lib */
     /* as described in UTIL.DOC                  */

registerbgidriver(EGAVGA_driver);
registerbgifont(sansserif_font);

     /* set EGA high-resolution 16-color mode   */

initgraph (&gdriver,&gmode,"");
rectangle (0,0,639,349);

     /* Draw a series of concentric circles   */
     /* with wide line thickness              */

style = SOLID_LINE;
pattern = 1;
width = THICK_WIDTH;

for (radius = 150; radius != 0; radius = radius - 25)
     {
     setlinestyle (style,pattern,width);
     circle (320,175,radius);
     }

     /* Draw circles in the four corners using */
     /* normal width line thickness            */

width = NORM_WIDTH;

for (radius = 30; radius != 0; radius = radius - 5)
     {
     setlinestyle (style,pattern,width);
     circle (50,50,radius);
     circle (50,299,radius);
     circle (589,50,radius);
     circle (589,299,radius);
     }

     /* Delay and Exit */
```

Listing 11.4. *continues*

Listing 11.4. cont.   The `circle` function

```
settextjustify(CENTER_TEXT,BOTTOM_TEXT);
outtextxy (320,320,"Press Any Key To Exit");

getch ();

closegraph();
return 0;
}
```

Figure 11.8.   Screen output from Listing 11.4

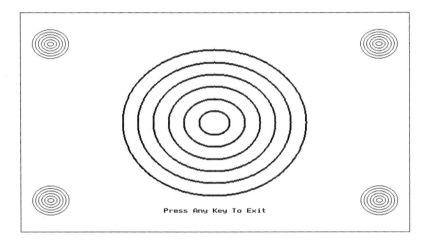

cleardevice

Syntax:
```
void far cleardevice(void);
```

Function:
The `cleardevice` function clears the graphics screen.

File(s) to Include:
```
#include <graphics.h>
```

Description:

The `cleardevice` function is used to clear a graphics screen. This function uses the current background color, as set by the `setbkcolor` function, to fill the screen. The position of the graphics cursor is the upper left corner of the screen—position `(0,0)`—after the screen has been cleared.

Value(s) Returned:

There is no return value.

Related Function(s):

```
clearviewport : clears the current viewport
setbkcolor    : sets the current background color
```

Similar Microsoft C Function(s):

`_clearscreen` : clears a specified area of the screen

```
void _far _clearscreen(short area);
```

Example:

The following example uses the `cleardevice` function to clear the screen with a different color each time a key is pressed. This continues until the <Esc> key is pressed.

Listing 11.5. The `cleardevice` function

```
#include <graphics.h>
#include <stdio.h>
#include <stdlib.h>
#include <conio.h>

int main ()
{
int gdriver = EGA;
int gmode = EGAHI;
int color;
int ch;

     /* register EGAVGA_driver and sansserif_font */
     /* ... these have been added to graphics.lib */
     /* as described in UTIL.DOC                   */

registerbgidriver(EGAVGA_driver);
registerbgifont(sansserif_font);

     /* set EGA high-resolution 16-color mode */
```

Listing 11.5. *continues*

283

Listing 11.5. cont. The `cleardevice` function

```
initgraph (&gdriver,&gmode,"");
rectangle (0,0,639,349);
color = 1;

        /* each time a key a pressed, the background */
        /* color is incremented and the screen is    */
        /* cleared - press ESC to exit                */

do
{
        setbkcolor (color);
        cleardevice();
        rectangle (0,0,639,349);

            /* Delay  */

        settextstyle (SANS_SERIF_FONT,HORIZ_DIR,2);
        settextjustify(CENTER_TEXT,BOTTOM_TEXT);
        outtextxy (320,320,"Press Any Key To Clear Screen -
                            ESC to Exit");
        ch = getch ();
        color = color + 1;
        if (color > 15)
            color = 0;
} while (ch != 27);

closegraph();
return 0;
}
```

clearviewport

Syntax:
```
void far clearviewport(void);
```

Function:
The `clearviewport` function clears the current viewport.

File(s) to Include:
```
#include <graphics.h>
```

Description:
The `clearviewport` function is used to fill the current viewport with the current background color. The background color can be set with the `setbkcolor` function. The current position of the graphics cursor is then set to the upper left corner of the current viewport. This position is (0,0), as seen by the viewport.

Value(s) Returned:
There is no return value.

Related Function(s):
cleardevice : clears the screen

Similar Microsoft C Function(s):
_clearscreen : clears a specified area of the screen

```
void _far _clearscreen(short area);
```

Example:
The clearviewport function is used in this example to clear the current viewport with a new color each time you press a key. This continues until you press the <Esc> key.

Listing 11.6.   The clearviewport function

```
#include <graphics.h>
#include <stdio.h>
#include <stdlib.h>
#include <conio.h>


int main ()
{
int gdriver = EGA;
int gmode = EGAHI;
int color;
int ch;

     /* register EGAVGA_driver and sansserif_font */
     /* ... these have been added to graphics.lib */
     /* as described in UTIL.DOC                   */

registerbgidriver(EGAVGA_driver);
registerbgifont(sansserif_font);

     /* set EGA high-resolution 16-color mode */

initgraph (&gdriver,&gmode,"");
rectangle (0,0,639,349);
rectangle (50,50,590,300);
color = 1;

     /* each time a key a pressed, the background */
     /* color is incremented and the viewport is  */
     /* cleared - press ESC to exit               */
```

Listing 11.6.   *continues*

Listing 11.6. cont. The `clearviewport` function

```
settextstyle (SANS_SERIF_FONT,HORIZ_DIR,2);
settextjustify(CENTER_TEXT,BOTTOM_TEXT);
outtextxy (320,330,"Press Any Key to Clear Viewport - ESC to
Exit");

setviewport (50,50,590,300,0);

do
{
    setbkcolor (color);
    clearviewport();
    rectangle (0,0,540,250);

        /* Delay  */

    ch = getch ();
    color = color + 1;
    if (color > 15)
        color = 0;
} while (ch != 27);


closegraph();
return 0;
}
```

closegraph

Syntax:
```
void far closegraph(void);
```

Function:
The `closegraph` function closes the graphics system.

File(s) to Include:
```
#include <graphics.h>
```

Description:
The `closegraph` function is used to close the graphics system as initiated by the `initgraph` function. The `closegraph` function frees all the memory used by the graphics system and then restores the video mode to the screen mode that was in use prior to the call to the `initgraph` function.

Value(s) Returned:
There is no return value.

Related Function(s):
initgraph : initializes the graphics system

Similar Microsoft C Function(s):
_setvideomode : initializes and closes the graphics system

```
short _far _setvideomode(short mode);
```

Example:
This example demonstrates the use of the closegraph function to shut down the graphics system and restore the screen mode.

Listing 11.7. The closegraph function

```
#include <graphics.h>
#include <stdio.h>
#include <stdlib.h>
#include <conio.h>

int main ()
{
int gdriver = EGA;
int gmode = EGAHI;

    /* register EGAVGA_driver and sansserif_font */
    /* ... these have been added to graphics.lib */
    /* as described in UTIL.DOC                  */

registerbgidriver(EGAVGA_driver);
registerbgifont(sansserif_font);

    /* set EGA high-resolution 16-color mode */

initgraph (&gdriver,&gmode,"");
setbkcolor (1);
rectangle (0,0,639,349);

setcolor (4);
circle (320,175,100);
setcolor (2);
rectangle(220,75,420,275);

    /* Delay and Exit */
```

Listing 11.7. *continues*

Listing 11.7. cont. The `closegraph` function

```
settextstyle (SANS_SERIF_FONT,HORIZ_DIR,2);
settextjustify(CENTER_TEXT,BOTTOM_TEXT);
outtextxy (320,330,"Press Any Key To Exit and Close Graphics
                    System");

getch ();
closegraph();
return 0;
}
```

detectgraph

Syntax:
```
void far detectgraph(int far *driver, int far *mode);

int far *driver;        Graphics driver
int far *mode;          Graphics mode
```

Function:
The `detectgraph` function determines the graphics driver and mode to use with the current graphics hardware.

File(s) to Include:
```
#include <graphics.h>
```

Description:
The `detectgraph` function is used to detect the graphics adapter and optimal mode to use for the computer system in use. If the `detectgraph` function cannot detect any graphics hardware, the `*driver` argument is set to `grNotDetected` `(-2)`. A call to `graphresult` will result in a return value of -2, or `grNotDetected`.

Table 11.1 lists the graphics drivers that can be used for the `*driver` argument. A value of 0, or `DETECT`, initiates the autodetection feature, which determines the optimal driver for use.

Table 11.2 lists the constants and values for the `*mode` argument. However, if the `*driver` argument is set to 0, or `DETECT`, the `*mode` argument is automatically set to the highest resolution mode for the driver.

Table 11.1. *Graphics drivers*

Constants	Values
DETECT	0
CGA	1
MCGA	2
EGA	3
EGA64	4
EGAMONO	5
IBM8514	6
HERCMONO	7
ATT400	8
VGA	9
PC3270	10

Table 11.2. *Graphics modes*

Driver	Mode	Value	Description
CGA	CGAC0	0	320x200–4-color
	CGAC1	1	320x200–4-color
	CGAC2	2	320x200–4-color
	CGAC3	3	320x200–4-color
	CGAHI	4	640x200–2-color
MCGA	MCGAC0	0	320x200–4-color
	MCGAC1	1	320x200–4-color
	MCGAC2	2	320x200–4-color
	MCGAC3	3	320x200–4-color
	MCGAMED	4	640x200–2-color
	MCGAHI	5	640x480–2-color
EGA	EGALO	0	640x200–16-color
	EGAHI	1	640x350–16-color
EGA64	EGA64LO	0	640x200–16-color
	EGA64HI	1	640x350–4-color
EGAMONO	EGAMONOHI	3	640x350–2-color
VGA	VGALO	0	640x200–16-color
	VGAMED	1	640x350–16-color
	VGAHI	2	640x480–16-color

Table 11.2. *continues*

Table 11.2. cont.   *Graphics modes*

Driver	Mode	Value	Description
ATT400	ATT400C0	0	320x200–4-color
	ATT400C1	1	320x200–4-color
	ATT400C2	2	320x200–4-color
	ATT400C3	3	320x200–4-color
	ATT400MED	4	640x200–2-color
	ATT400HI	5	640x400–2-color
HERC	HERCMONOHI	0	720x348–2-color
PC3270	PC3270HI	0	720x350–2-color
IBM8514	IBM8514LO	0	640x480–256-color
	IBM8514HI	1	1024x768–256-color

Value(s) Returned:

There is no return value.

Related Function(s):

`initgraph` : initializes the graphics system

Similar Microsoft C Function(s):

`_getvideoconfig` : gets the video configuration

```
struct videoconfig _far * _far _getvideoconfig(struct
videoconfig _far *configurationinfo);
```

Example:

This example (Listing 11.8 and Figure 11.9) uses the `detectgraph` function to determine the current graphics driver and mode. The retrieved information is then displayed on the screen.

Listing 11.8. The detectgraph function

```
#include <graphics.h>
#include <stdio.h>
#include <stdlib.h>
#include <conio.h>

int main ()
{
char buffer [40];
int gdriver;
int gmode;

    /* register EGAVGA_driver and sansserif_font */
    /* ... these have been added to graphics.lib */
    /* as described in UTIL.DOC                   */

registerbgidriver(EGAVGA_driver);
registerbgifont(sansserif_font);

    /* set EGA high-resolution 16-color mode */

detectgraph (&gdriver,&gmode);
initgraph(&gdriver,&gmode,"");
rectangle (0,0,639,349);

    /* get and display graphics driver and mode */

settextjustify (CENTER_TEXT,BOTTOM_TEXT);
sprintf (buffer,"Graphics Driver Value : %d",gdriver);
outtextxy(320,100,buffer);

sprintf (buffer,"Graphics Mode Value : %d",gmode);
outtextxy(320,200,buffer);

    /* Delay and Exit */

settextjustify(CENTER_TEXT,BOTTOM_TEXT);
outtextxy (320,320,"Press Any Key To Exit");

getch ();

closegraph();
return 0;
}
```

Figure 11.9. Screen output from Listing 11.8

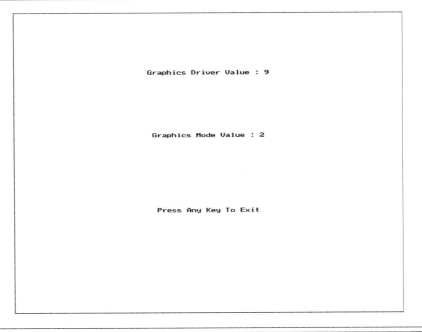

```
                    Graphics Driver Value : 9




                    Graphics Mode Value : 2




                    Press Any Key To Exit
```

drawpoly

Syntax:
```
void far drawpoly(int numpoints, int far *polypoints);

int numpoints;                    Number of points
int far *polypoints;              Points in polygon
```

Function:
The drawpoly function draws an unfilled polygon.

File(s) to Include:
```
#include <graphics.h>
```

Description:
The drawpoly function is used to create a polygon with a specified number of points. The numpoints argument is used to define the number of points in the polygon. For the drawpoly function, the number of points must be the actual number of points plus 1 in order to create a closed polygon. In other words, the first point must equal the last point. For example, numpoints would be equal to 4 for a triangle and 9 for an octagon. The

*polypoints argument points to an array of numbers of length numpoints multiplied by 2. The first two members of the array identify the x and y coordinates of the first point, respectively, while the next two specify the next point, and so forth. Therefore, the *polypoints array would be of length 8 for a triangle and of length 18 for an octagon. The drawpoly function draws the outline of the polygon with the current line style and color, but it does not fill the polygon. Figure 11.10 illustrates the use of the drawpoly function.

Figure 11.10. The drawpoly function

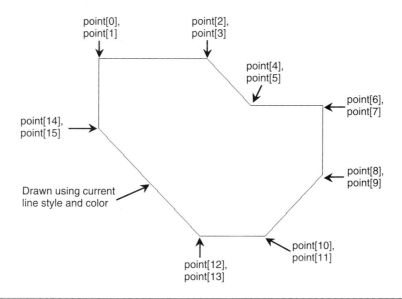

Value(s) Returned:
There is no return value.

Related Function(s):
fillpoly : draws a filled polygon
setcolor : sets the current color

Similar Microsoft C Function(s):
_polygon : creates a filled or unfilled polygon

```
short _far _polygon(short fillflag, struct xycoord
                    _far *points, short numpoints);
```

Example:

The drawpoly function is used in this example to create a nine-point polygon. Note that the last point is the same as the first. The drawpoly function does not automatically close the polygon. Therefore, if the polygon is to be closed, this is necessary. (See Listing 11.9 and Figure 11.11.)

Listing 11.9. The drawpoly function

```
#include <graphics.h>
#include <stdio.h>
#include <stdlib.h>
#include <conio.h>

int main ()
{
int gdriver = EGA;
int gmode = EGAHI;
int point[18];

     /* register EGAVGA_driver and sansserif_font */
     /* ... these have been added to graphics.lib */
     /* as described in UTIL.DOC                   */

registerbgidriver(EGAVGA_driver);
registerbgifont(sansserif_font);

     /* set EGA high-resolution 16-color mode */

initgraph (&gdriver,&gmode,"");
rectangle (0,0,639,349);

     /* define 9 point polygon - note that the last point */
     /* is equal to the first - the polygon is not        */
     /* automatically closed by the drawpoly function      */

point[0] = 50;
point[1] = 50;

point[2] = 320;
point[3] = 100;

point[4] = 590;
point[5] = 50;

point[6] - 370;
point[7] = 175;

point[8] = 590;
point[9] = 300;

point[10] = 320;
point[11] = 250;
```

```
point[12] = 50;
point[13] = 300;

point[14] = 270;
point[15] = 175;

point[16] = 50;
point[17] = 50;

drawpoly(9,point);

      /* Delay and Exit */

settextjustify(CENTER_TEXT,BOTTOM_TEXT);
outtextxy (320,320,"Press Any Key To Exit");

getch ();

closegraph();
return 0;
}
```

Figure 11.11. Screen output from Listing 11.9

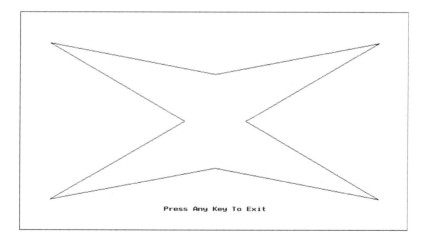

Press Any Key To Exit

ellipse

Syntax:
```
void far ellipse(int x, int y, int startangle, int endangle,
                 int xradius, int yradius);

int x, y;                    Center of ellipse
int startangle;              Starting angle
```

```
int endangle;          Ending angle
int xradius;           Radius in horizontal (x) direction
int yradius;           Radius in vertical (y) direction
```

Function:

The ellipse function generates an elliptical arc.

File(s) to Include:

```
#include <graphics.h>
```

Description:

The ellipse function is used to draw an elliptical arc in the current color. The elliptical arc is centered at the point specified by the x and y arguments. Because the arc is elliptical, the xradius argument specifies the horizontal radius and the yradius argument specifies the vertical radius. The elliptical arc begins at the angle specified by the startangle argument and extends in a counterclockwise direction to the angle specified by the endangle argument. The ellipse function considers east—the horizontal axis to the right of the ellipse center—to be 0 degrees. The elliptical arc is drawn with the current line thickness as set by the setlinestyle function. However, the line style is ignored by the ellipse function. Figure 11.12 illustrates the use of the ellipse function.

Figure 11.12. The ellipse function

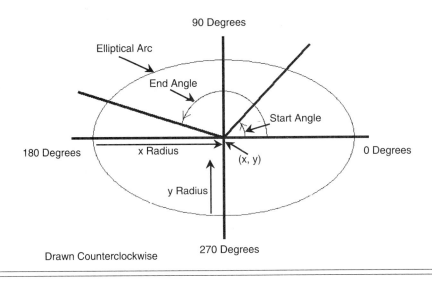

Value(s) Returned:

There is no return value.

Related Function(s):

circle   : generates a circle
arc   : generates a circular arc
setcolor : sets the current color

Similar Microsoft C Function(s):

_ellipse : draws an ellipse

```
short _far _ellipse(short fillflag, short x1, short y1,
                    short x2, short y2);
```

_arc : draws an elliptical arc

```
short _far _arc(short x1, short y1, short x2, short y2,
                short x3, short y3, short x4, short y4);
```

Example:

The ellipse function is used in the following example to display a set of elliptical arcs, each with a varying x and y radius. The starting point of each ellipse is 180 degrees from the endpoint of the previous ellipse. (See Listing 11.10 and Figure 11.13.)

Listing 11.10. The ellipse function

```
#include <graphics.h>
#include <stdio.h>
#include <stdlib.h>
#include <conio.h>

int main ()
{
int gdriver = EGA;
int gmode = EGAHI;
int xradius = 250;
int yradius = 150;
int angle = 0;

      /* register EGAVGA_driver and sansserif_font */
      /* ... these have been added to graphics.lib */
      /* as described in UTIL.DOC                   */

registerbgidriver(EGAVGA_driver);
registerbgifont(sansserif_font);

      /* set EGA high-resolution 16-color mode */
```

Listing 11.10. *continues*

297

Listing 11.10. cont. The ellipse function

```
initgraph (&gdriver,&gmode,"");
rectangle (0,0,639,349);

    /* draw concentric ellipses - each with a starting */
    /* and ending angle 90 degrees from the previous    */

do
{

ellipse (320,175,angle,angle + 270, xradius, yradius);
angle = angle + 90;
xradius = xradius - 25;
yradius = yradius - 25;

} while (yradius != 0);

    /* Delay and Exit */

settextjustify(CENTER_TEXT,BOTTOM_TEXT);
outtextxy (320,320,"Press Any Key To Exit");

getch ();

closegraph();
return 0;
}
```

Figure 11.13. Screen output from Listing 11.10

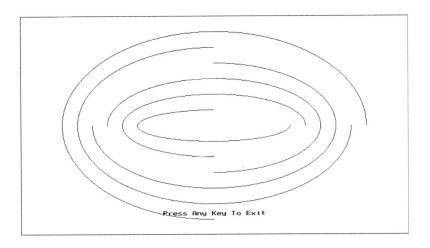

fillellipse

Syntax:

```
void far fillellipse(int x, int y, int xradius,
                     int yradius);

int x, y;            Center of ellipse
int xradius;         Radius in horizontal (x) direction
int yradius;         Radius in vertical (y) direction
```

Function:

The fillellipse function draws a filled ellipse.

File(s) to Include:

```
#include <graphics.h>
```

Description:

The fillellipse function is used to draw and fill an ellipse. The center of the ellipse is specified by the x and y arguments. The xradius argument identifies the radius of the ellipse in the horizontal direction, while the yradius argument identifies the radius of the ellipse in the vertical direction. The ellipse is outlined in the current color and filled with the current fill color and fill pattern. Figure 11.14 illustrates the use of the fillellipse function.

Figure 11.14.   The fillellipse function

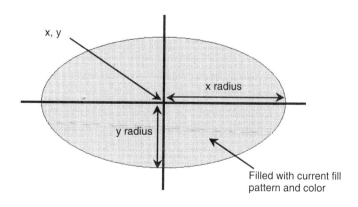

Value(s) Returned:
There is no return value.

Related Function(s):

ellipse   : draws an elliptical arc
circle   : draws a circle
arc   : draws a circular arc

Similar Microsoft C Function(s):
_ellipse : draws a filled or unfilled ellipse

```
short _far _ellipse(short fillflag, short x1, short y1,
                       short x2, short y2);
```

Example:
The fillellipse function is used in the following example to create two ellipses. The first is filled with a solid fill pattern, while the second uses an interleaving fill pattern. (See Listing 11.11 and Figure 11.15.)

Listing 11.11. The fillellipse function

```
#include <graphics.h>
#include <stdio.h>
#include <stdlib.h>
#include <conio.h>

int main ()
{
int gdriver = EGA;
int gmode = EGAHI;
int pattern, color;

     /* register EGAVGA_driver and sansserif_font */
     /* ... these have been added to graphics.lib */
     /* as described in UTIL.DOC                   */

registerbgidriver(EGAVGA_driver);
registerbgifont(sansserif_font);

     /* set EGA high-resolution 16-color mode */

initgraph (&gdriver,&gmode,"");
rectangle (0,0,639,349);

     /* draw two ellipses - solid, pattern */

pattern = SOLID_FILL;
color = 14;
setfillstyle (pattern,color);
```

```
fillellipse(180,175,100,150);

pattern = INTERLEAVE_FILL;
color = 1;
setfillstyle (pattern,color);
fillellipse(450,175,100,150);

    /* Delay and Exit */

settextjustify(CENTER_TEXT,BOTTOM_TEXT);
outtextxy (320,320,"Press Any Key To Exit");
getch ();
closegraph();
return 0;
}
```

Figure 11.15. Screen output from Listing 11.11

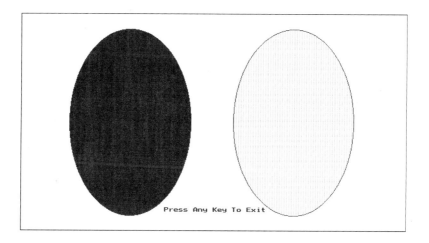

fillpoly

Syntax:

```
void far fillpoly(int numpoints, int far *polypoints);

int numpoints;                    Number of points
int far *polypoints;              Points describing the polygon
```

Function:

The fillpoly function generates a filled polygon.

File(s) to Include:

```
#include <graphics.h>
```

Description:

The `fillpoly` function is used to create a filled polygon. The `numpoints` argument is used to define the number of points in the polygon. Unlike the `drawpoly` function, the function closes the polygon automatically. Therefore, `numpoints` would be set to 3 for a triangle and 8 for an octagon. The `*polypoints` argument is a pointer to an array of length `numpoints` multiplied by 2. This array contains the x and y values of each point. The first two members of the array specify the location of the first point, while the next two members of the array specify the location of the next point, and so forth. The outline of the polygon is drawn first using the current color and line style. The polygon is then filled with the current fill pattern and fill color. Figure 11.16 illustrates the use of the `fillpoly` function.

Figure 11.16. The `fillpoly` function

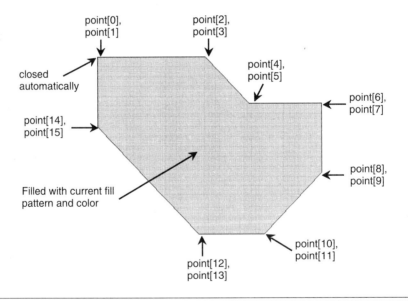

Value(s) Returned:

There is no return value.

Related Function(s):

drawpoly   : draws an unfilled polygon
setfillstyle : sets the current fill style

Similar Microsoft C Function(s):

_polygon : draws a filled or unfilled polygon

```
short _far _polygon(short fillflag, struct xycoord
                         _far *points, short numpoints);
```

Example:

The fillpoly function is used in this example to display an eight-point, filled polygon. The fillpoly function automatically closes the border of the polygon. Therefore, there is no need to make the first point equal to the last as with the drawpoly function. The polygon is filled with a red slash fill. (See Listing 11.12 and Figure 11.17.)

Listing 11.12.   The fillpoly function

```
#include <graphics.h>
#include <stdio.h>
#include <stdlib.h>
#include <conio.h>

int main ()
{
int gdriver = EGA;
int gmode = EGAHI;
int point[16];
int pattern, color;

      /* register EGAVGA_driver and sansserif_font */
      /* ... these have been added to graphics.lib */
      /* as described in UTIL.DOC                   */

registerbgidriver(EGAVGA_driver);
registerbgifont(sansserif_font);

      /* set EGA high-resolution 16-color mode */

initgraph (&gdriver,&gmode,"");
rectangle (0,0,639,349);

pattern = SLASH_FILL;
color = 4;

point[0] = 320;
point[1] = 50;

point[2] = 590;
point[3] = 100;
```

Listing 11.12.   *continues*

Listing 11.12. cont. The `fillpoly` function

```
point[4] = 370;
point[5] = 175;

point[6] = 590;
point[7] = 250;

point[8] = 320;
point[9] = 300;

point[10] = 50;
point[11] = 250;

point[12] = 270;
point[13] = 175;

point[14] = 50;
point[15] = 100;

setfillstyle (pattern,color);
fillpoly (8,point);

     /* Delay and Exit */

settextjustify(CENTER_TEXT,BOTTOM_TEXT);
outtextxy (320,320,"Press Any Key To Exit");

getch ();

closegraph();
return 0;
}
```

Figure 11.17. Screen output from Listing 11.12

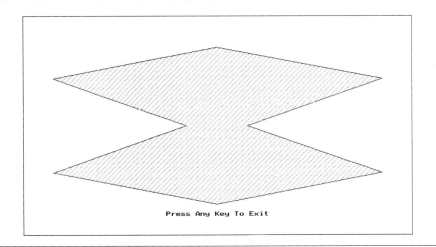

floodfill

Syntax:
```
void far floodfill(int x, int y, int border);

int x, y;                Starting point for fill
int border;              Border color;
```

Function:
The floodfill function fills a bound area with the current color.

File(s) to Include:
```
#include <graphics.h>
```

Description:
The floodfill function is used to fill a bound area with the current fill color and fill pattern. The x and y arguments specify the starting point for the filling algorithm. The border argument specifies the color value of the area's border. In order for the floodfill function to work as expected, the area to be filled must be surrounded by the color specified in the border argument. When the point specified by the x and y arguments lies within the area to be filled, the inside will be filled. If it lies outside the area, the outside will be filled. Figure 11.18 illustrates the use of the floodfill function. This function does not work with the IBM-8514 driver.

Figure 11.18. The floodfill function

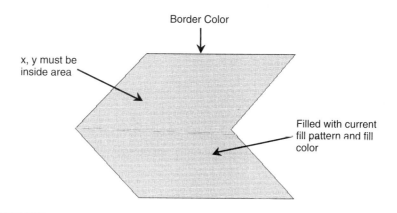

Value(s) Returned:

A value of -7 is returned via the `graphresult` function if an error occurs while filling a region.

Related Function(s):

`setcolor`   : sets the current color
`setfillstyle`   : sets the current fill style

Similar Microsoft C Function(s):

`_floodfill` : fills a bound area

```
short _far _floodfill(short x, short y, short bordercolor);
```

Example:

Listing 11.13 and Figure 11.19 use the `floodfill` function to fill a polygon with a blue, dotted fill pattern.

Listing 11.13.   The `floodfill` function

```
#include <graphics.h>
#include <stdio.h>
#include <stdlib.h>
#include <conio.h>


int main ()
{
int gdriver = EGA;
int gmode = EGAHI;
int point[18];
int pattern, color;

        /* register EGAVGA_driver and sansserif_font */
        /* ... these have been added to graphics.lib */
        /* as described in UTIL.DOC                   */

registerbgidriver(EGAVGA_driver);
registerbgifont(sansserif_font);

        /* set EGA high-resolution 16-color mode */

initgraph (&gdriver,&gmode,"");
rectangle (0,0,639,349);
```

```
         /* define 9 point polygon - note that the last point */
         /* is equal to the first - the polygon is not         */
         /* automatically closed by the drawpoly function  -   */
         /* then fill the polygon                              */

point[0] = 50;
point[1] = 50;

point[2] = 320;
point[3] = 100;

point[4] = 590;
point[5] = 50;

point[6] = 370;
point[7] = 175;

point[8] = 590;
point[9] = 300;

point[10] = 320;
point[11] = 250;

point[12] = 50;
point[13] = 300;

point[14] = 270;
point[15] = 175;

point[16] = 50;
point[17] = 50;

drawpoly(9,point);
pattern = 10;
color = 1;
setfillstyle (pattern, color);
floodfill (320,175,15);

      /* Delay and Exit */

settextjustify(CENTER_TEXT,BOTTOM_TEXT);
outtextxy (320,320,"Press Any Key To Exit");

getch ();

closegraph();
return 0;
}
```

Figure 11.19. Screen output from Listing 11.13

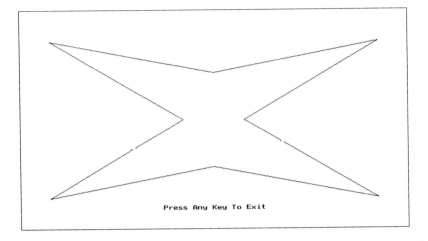

Press Any Key To Exit

getarccoords

Syntax:
```
void far getarccoords(struct arccoordstype far *arccoords);

struct arccoordstype far *arccoords;   Holds returned values
```

Function:
The `getarccoords` function retrieves the parameters used in the last call to the `arc` function.

File(s) to Include:
```
#include <graphics.h>
```

Description:
The `getarccoords` function is used to retrieve the coordinates of the center, starting, and ending points of the last successful call to the `arc` function. The `*arccoords` argument points to the structure of type `arccoordstype` that holds the retrieved information. The syntax for the `arccoordstype` structure is:

```
struct arccoordstype
       {
       int x, y;
       int xstart, ystart;
       int xend, yend;
       };
```

The x and y members define the center of the arc. The xstart and ystart members define the x and y coordinates of the starting point for the arc. Similarly, the xend and yend members define the x and y coordinates of the ending point of the arc.

Value(s) Returned:
There is no return value.

Related Function(s):
arc : draws a circular arc

Similar Microsoft C Function(s):
_getarcinfo : retrieves the arc coordinates

```
short _far _getarcinfo(struct xycoord _far *startpoint,
                       struct xycoord _far *endpoint,
                       struct xycoord _far *fillpoint);
```

Example:
The getarccoords function is used in this example to retrieve information about each arc drawn. This information is then used to draw a line from the starting point to the ending point for each arc. (See Listing 11.14 and Figure 11.20.)

Listing 11.14. The getarccoords function

```
#include <graphics.h>
#include <stdio.h>
#include <stdlib.h>
#include <conio.h>

int main ()
{
struct arccoordstype arcinfo;
int gdriver = EGA;
int gmode = EGAHI;
int radius;

     /* register EGAVGA_driver and sansserif_font */
     /* ... these have been added to graphics.lib */
     /* as described in UTIL.DOC                  */

registerbgidriver(EGAVGA_driver);
registerbgifont(sansserif_font);

     /* set EGA high-resolution 16-color mode */
```

Listing 11.14. *continues*

Listing 11.14. cont. The getarccoords function

```
initgraph (&gdriver,&gmode,"");
rectangle (0,0,639,349);

     /* Draw a series of arcs     */
     /* and connect the endpoints */

for (radius = 25; radius < 175; radius = radius + 25)
{
   arc (320,175,0,270,radius);
   getarccoords(&arcinfo);
   moveto(arcinfo.xstart,arcinfo.ystart);
   lineto(arcinfo.xend,arcinfo.yend);
}

     /* Delay and Exit */

settextjustify(CENTER_TEXT,BOTTOM_TEXT);
outtextxy (320,320,"Press Any Key To Exit");
getch ();
closegraph();
return 0;
}
```

Figure 11.20. Screen output from Listing 11.14

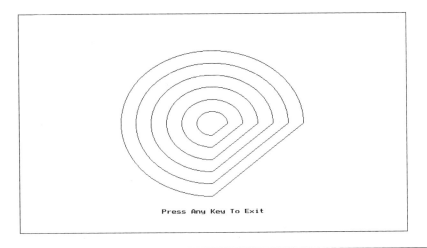

Press Any Key To Exit

getaspectratio

Syntax:
```
void far getaspectratio(int far *xaspect, int far *yaspect);

int far *xaspect;              Aspect ratio of x axis
int far *yaspect;              Aspect ratio of y axis
```

Function:
The getaspectratio function retrieves the aspect ratio of the current graphics mode.

File(s) to Include:
```
#include <graphics.h>
```

Description:
The getaspectratio function is used to retrieve the aspect ratio of the current graphics mode. The aspect ratio can be defined as the ratio of the width of the graphics mode's pixel to the height of the pixel. This ratio, using existing graphics modes, is always less than or equal to 1. The value for determining the aspect ratio with respect to the horizontal axis is returned in the *xaspect argument. Similarly, the value for the vertical axis is returned in the *yaspect argument. The *yaspect argument is set to 10,000, which is returned upon calling the getaspectratio function. The *xaspect argument is almost always less than the *yaspect value. This is due to the fact that most graphics modes have pixels that are taller than they are wide. The only exception is in VGA modes that produce square pixels (i.e. xaspect = yaspect).

Value(s) Returned:
There is no return value.

Related Function(s):
setaspectratio : changes the default aspect ratio

Similar Microsoft C Function(s):
There are no similar Microsoft C functions.

Example:
Listing 11.15 and Figure 11.21 use the getaspectratio function to retrieve the current screen aspect ratio. The x and y aspect ratios are then displayed.

Listing 11.15. The getaspectratio function

```c
#include <graphics.h>
#include <stdio.h>
#include <stdlib.h>
#include <conio.h>

int main ()
{
int gdriver = EGA;
int gmode = EGAHI;
int xaspect, yaspect;
char buffer[40];

        /* register EGAVGA_driver and sansserif_font */
        /* ... these have been added to graphics.lib */
        /* as described in UTIL.DOC                   */

registerbgidriver(EGAVGA_driver);
registerbgifont(sansserif_font);

        /* set EGA high-resolution 16-color mode */

initgraph (&gdriver,&gmode,"");
rectangle (0,0,639,349);

        /* get aspect ratios and display them */

getaspectratio (&xaspect,&yaspect);

settextjustify (CENTER_TEXT,CENTER_TEXT);
sprintf (buffer,"The x aspect ratio is : %d",xaspect);
outtextxy (320,100,buffer);

sprintf (buffer,"The y aspect ratio is : %d",yaspect);
outtextxy (320,200,buffer);

        /* Delay and Exit */

settextjustify(CENTER_TEXT,BOTTOM_TEXT);
outtextxy (320,320,"Press Any Key To Exit");
getch ();
closegraph();
return 0;
}
```

Figure 11.21. Screen output from Listing 11.15

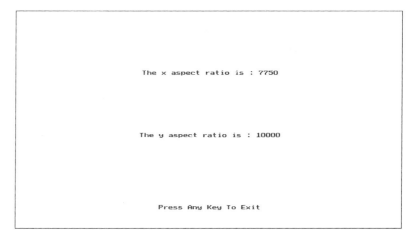

The x aspect ratio is : 7750

The y aspect ratio is : 10000

Press Any Key To Exit

getbkcolor

Syntax:
```
int far getbkcolor(void);
```

Function:
The getbkcolor function retrieves the current background color.

File(s) to Include:
```
#include <graphics.h>
```

Description:
The getbkcolor function is used to retrieve the color value of the current background color. The background color, by default, is color 0. However, this value can be changed by a call to the setbkcolor function. Table 11.3 lists the available background colors.

Table 11.3. *Background colors*

Constant	Value
BLACK	0
BLUE	1
GREEN	2
CYAN	3
RED	4
MAGENTA	5
BROWN	6
LIGHTGRAY	7
DARKGRAY	8
LIGHTBLUE	9
LIGHTGREEN	10
LIGHTCYAN	11
LIGHTRED	12
LIGHTMAGENTA	13
YELLOW	14
WHITE	15

Value(s) Returned:

The value of the current background color is returned.

Related Function(s):

setbkcolor : sets the background color

Similar Microsoft C Function(s):

_getbkcolor : retrieves the background color

```
long _far _getbkcolor(void);
```

Example:

This example uses the getbkcolor function to retrieve the value of the current background color. This value is then displayed on the screen.

Listing 11.16. The getbkcolor function

```
#include <graphics.h>
#include <stdio.h>
#include <stdlib.h>
#include <conio.h>

int main ()
{
int gdriver = EGA;
int gmode = EGAHI;
int background;
char buffer [40];

    /* register EGAVGA_driver and sansserif_font */
    /* ... these have been added to graphics.lib */
    /* as described in UTIL.DOC                   */

registerbgidriver(EGAVGA_driver);
registerbgifont(sansserif_font);

    /* set EGA high-resolution 16-color mode */

initgraph (&gdriver,&gmode,"");
rectangle (0,0,639,349);

    /* set, get, and display the background color */

setbkcolor (1);
background = getbkcolor();

sprintf (buffer,"The background color is : %d",background);
settextjustify (CENTER_TEXT,CENTER_TEXT);
outtextxy (320,175,buffer);

    /* Delay and Exit */

settextjustify(CENTER_TEXT,BOTTOM_TEXT);
outtextxy (320,320,"Press Any Key To Exit");

getch ();

closegraph();
return 0;
}
```

getcolor

Syntax:
```
int far getcolor(void);
```

Function:
The getcolor function retrieves the value of the current color.

File(s) to Include:
```
#include <graphics.h>
```

Description:
The getcolor function retrieves the value of the current color. The current color is the color used for drawing lines, arcs, etc. This color is not the same as the fill color. The retrieved color value is interpreted according to which mode is in use. For example, Color 1 varies in CGA modes depending on which palette is in use. Tables 11.4 and 11.5 will help to interpret the returned value according to the mode and palette in use.

Table 11.4. *Colors for 16-color modes*

Constant	Value
BLACK	0
BLUE	1
GREEN	2
CYAN	3
RED	4
MAGENTA	5
BROWN	6
LIGHTGRAY	7
DARKGRAY	8
LIGHTBLUE	9
LIGHTGREEN	11
LIGHTCYAN	11
LIGHTRED	12
LIGHTMAGENTA	13
YELLOW	14
WHITE	15

Table 11.5. *Color constants and values for CGA modes*

Palette Number	Color 1	Color 2	Color 3
0	CGA_LIGHTGREEN	CGA_LIGHTRED	CGA_YELLOW
1	CGA_LIGHTCYAN	CGA_LIGHTMAGENTA	CGA_WHITE
2	CGA_GREEN	CGA_RED	CGA_BROWN
3	CGA_CYAN	CGA_MAGENTA	CGA_LIGHTGRAY

NOTE: Color 0 is set with the setbkcolor function

Value(s) Returned:

The value of the current color is returned.

Related Function(s):

setcolor : sets the current color

Similar Microsoft C Function(s):

_getcolor : retrieves the current color

```
short _far _getcolor(void);
```

Example:

The getcolor function is used in this example to retrieve the value of the current color. In Listing 11.17 and Figure 11.22, three lines are drawn using three colors. The color value is retrieved after each line has been completed and then is displayed.

Listing 11.17. The getcolor function

```
#include <graphics.h>
#include <stdio.h>
#include <stdlib.h>
#include <conio.h>

int main ()
{
int gdriver = EGA;
int gmode = EGAHI;
int color;
char buffer [40];
int y, colnum;

     /* register EGAVGA_driver and sansserif_font */
     /* ... these have been added to graphics.lib */
```

Listing 11.17. *continues*

Listing 11.17. cont. The `getcolor` function

```
      /* as described in UTIL.DOC                    */

registerbgidriver(EGAVGA_driver);
registerbgifont(sansserif_font);

      /* set EGA high-resolution 16-color mode */

initgraph (&gdriver,&gmode,"");
rectangle (0,0,639,349);

      /* set, get, and display several colors */

colnum = 15;

settextjustify(LEFT_TEXT,CENTER_TEXT);

for (y = 75; y < 230; y = y + 75)
    {
    setcolor (colnum);
    line (20,y,400,y);
    color = getcolor();
    sprintf (buffer,"Color : %d",color);
    outtextxy (450,y,buffer);
    colnum = colnum - 5;
    }
    /* Delay and Exit */

settextjustify(CENTER_TEXT,BOTTOM_TEXT);
outtextxy (320,320,"Press Any Key To Exit");

getch ();

closegraph();
return 0;
}
```

Figure 11.22. Screen output from Listing 11.17

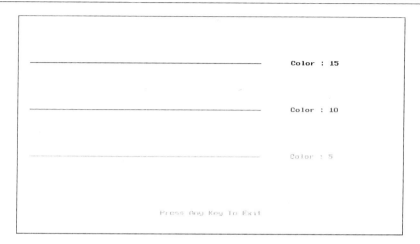

---

getdefaultpalette

Syntax:
```
struct palettetype *far getdefaultpalette(void);
```

Function:
The `getdefaultpalette` function is used to retrieve the structure that defines the palette.

File(s) to Include:
```
#include <graphics.h>
```

Description:
The `getdefaultpalette` function returns the pointer to the palette that was defined by the driver upon initialization. The pointer identifies a structure of type `palettetype`. The `palettetype` structure is defined in the following manner:

```
#define MAXCOLORS 15

struct palettetype
    {
    unsigned char size;
    signed char colors[MAXCOLORS + 1];
    };
```

Value(s) Returned:

The getdefaultpalette function returns a pointer to the palette that was initialized by the initgraph function.

Related Function(s):

initgraph : initializes the graphics environment

Similar Microsoft C Function(s):

There are no similar Microsoft C functions.

Example:

The getdefaultpalette function is used in this example to return the color values of the current palette in a structure of type palettetype. These color values are then displayed on the screen.

Listing 11.18. The getdefaultpalette function

```
#include <graphics.h>
#include <stdio.h>
#include <stdlib.h>
#include <conio.h>

int main ()
{
struct palettetype far *palette = NULL;
int gdriver = EGA;
int gmode = EGAHI;
int x, a, b;
char buffer[40];

        /* register EGAVGA_driver and sansserif_font */
        /* ... these have been added to graphics.lib */
        /* as described in UTIL.DOC                   */

registerbgidriver(EGAVGA_driver);
registerbgifont(sansserif_font);

        /* set EGA high-resolution 16-color mode */

initgraph (&gdriver,&gmode,"");
rectangle (0,0,639,349);

        /* get palette and print colors */

a = 5;
b = 5;
palette = getdefaultpalette();

for (x=0; x<palette->size; x = x + 1)
```

```
{
     gotoxy (a,b);
     printf("Color %d : %d", x, palette->colors[x]);
     b = b + 1;
}
     /* Delay and Exit */

settextjustify(CENTER_TEXT,BOTTOM_TEXT);
outtextxy (320,320,"Press Any Key To Exit");
getch ();
closegraph();
return 0;
}
```

getdrivername

Syntax:
```
char *far getdrivername(void);
```

Function:
The getdrivername function retrieves a pointer to the string that contains the name of the current graphics driver.

File(s) to Include:
```
#include <graphics.h>
```

Description:
The getdrivername function is used to return the pointer to a string that contains the name of the current graphics driver. This function should only be called after a driver has been defined and initialized (after the initgraph function).

Value(s) Returned:
The getdrivername function returns the pointer to the string that contains the current graphics driver.

Related Function(s):
initgraph : initializes the graphics environment

Similar Microsoft C Function(s):
There are no similar Microsoft C functions.

Example:

The getdrivername function is used in this example to return the pointer to the current driver name. The driver name is then displayed.

Listing 11.19. The getdrivername function

```
#include <graphics.h>
#include <stdio.h>
#include <stdlib.h>
#include <conio.h>

int main ()
{
char *driver;
int gdriver = EGA;
int gmode = EGAHI;

     /* register EGAVGA_driver and sansserif_font */
     /* ... these have been added to graphics.lib */
     /* as described in UTIL.DOC                   */

registerbgidriver(EGAVGA_driver);
registerbgifont(sansserif_font);

     /* set EGA high-resolution 16-color mode */

initgraph (&gdriver,&gmode,"");
rectangle (0,0,639,349);

     /* get the driver name and display */

driver = getdrivername();

settextstyle (SANS_SERIF_FONT,HORIZ_DIR,2);
settextjustify (CENTER_TEXT,CENTER_TEXT);
outtextxy(320,145,"The driver name is :");
outtextxy(320,175,driver);

     /* Delay and Exit */

settextjustify(CENTER_TEXT,BOTTOM_TEXT);
outtextxy (320,320,"Press Any Key To Exit");

getch ();

closegraph();
return 0;
}
```

getfillpattern

Syntax:

```
void far getfillpattern(char far *pattern);

char far *pattern;        Fill Pattern
```

Function:

The `getfillpattern` function copies a specified fill pattern into memory.

File(s) to Include:

```
#include <graphics.h>
```

Description:

The `getfillpattern` is used to retrieve a user-defined fill pattern, as defined by the `setfillpattern` function, and store it in memory. The `*pattern` argument is a pointer to an eight-byte series that represents an 8-by-8-bit fill pattern. Each byte represents an eight-bit row, where each bit is either on or off (1 or 0). A 1 bit indicates that the corresponding pixel is to be set to the current fill color. A 0 bit indicates that the corresponding pixel will not be changed.

Value(s) Returned:

There is no return value.

Related Function(s):

`setfillpattern` : sets the current fill pattern

Similar Microsoft C Function(s):

`_getfillmask` :   retrieves the current fill pattern

```
unsigned char _far * _far _getfillmask(unsigned char
                    _far *fillmask);
```

Example:

The example in Listing 11.20 and Figure 11.23 uses the `getfillpattern` function to store the default fill pattern. When stored, the fill pattern is changed twice, and rectangles are drawn with the new fill patterns. The fill pattern is then reset to the default, and a rectangle is filled with the default pattern.

Listing 11.20. The `getfillpattern` function

```c
#include <graphics.h>
#include <stdio.h>
#include <stdlib.h>
#include <conio.h>

int main ()
{
int gdriver = EGA;
int gmode = EGAHI;

        /* set 50% and 25% fill patterns        */
        /* also set a holder for the old pattern */

char pattern1[8] = {0x55,0xAA,0x55,0xAA,0x55,0xAA,0x55,0xAA};
char pattern2[8] = {0x44,0x11,0x44,0x11,0x44,0x11,0x44,0x11};
char patternhold[8] = {0x00,0x00,0x00,0x00,0x00,0x00,0x00,0x00};

        /* register EGAVGA_driver and sansserif_font */
        /* ... these have been added to graphics.lib */
        /* as described in UTIL.DOC                   */

registerbgidriver(EGAVGA_driver);
registerbgifont(sansserif_font);

        /* set EGA high-resolution 16-color mode */

initgraph (&gdriver,&gmode,"");
rectangle (0,0,639,349);

        /* first get the current fill pattern and save it   */
        /* in patternhold - next set the pattern to pattern1 */
        /* and fill the upper half of the screen - next      */
        /* fill the lower half of screen with pattern 2  -   */
        /* lastly get the old pattern and fill center square */

getfillpattern (patternhold);

setcolor (15);
rectangle (0,0,639,175);
setfillpattern(pattern1,1);
floodfill (1,1,15);

rectangle (0,175,639,349);
setfillpattern(pattern2,1);
floodfill (1,176,15);

rectangle (200,175,440,225);
setfillpattern(patternhold,0);
floodfill (201,176,15);

     /* Delay and Exit */

settextjustify(CENTER_TEXT,CENTER_TEXT);
outtextxy (320,200,"Press Any Key To Exit");

getch ();
```

```
closegraph();
return 0;
}
```

Figure 11.23. Screen output from Listing 11.20

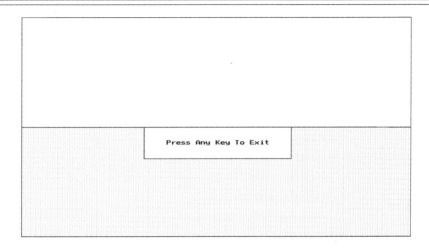

getfillsettings

Syntax:

```
void far getfillsettings(struct fillsettingstype far *info);

struct fillsettingstype far *info;     Fill Information
```

Function:

The getfillsettings function retrieves information concerning the current fill pattern and current fill color.

File(s) to Include:

```
#include <graphics.h>
```

Description:

The getfillsettings function is used to retrieve the current fill settings. The *info argument points to the structure of type fillsettingstype, which is updated when the getfillsettings function is called. This structure is:

```
struct fillsettingstype
    {
    int pattern;
    int color;
    };
```

Table 11.6 will assist in interpreting the returned pattern value. If the returned value is 12, a user-defined fill pattern is in use.

Table 11.6. *Predefined fill patterns*

Constant	Value	Meaning
EMPTY_FILL	0	Fill with background color
SOLID_FILL	1	Solid fill
LINE_FILL	2	Horizontal line fill
LTSLASH_FILL	3	Light slash fill
SLASH_FILL	4	Heavy slash fill
BKSLASH_FILL	5	Heavy backslash fill
LTBKSLASH_FILL	6	Light backslash fill
HATCH_FILL	7	Light hatch fill
XHATCH_FILL	8	Heavy hatch fill
INTERLEAVE_FILL	9	Interleaving fill
WIDE_DOT_FILL	10	Wide dot fill
CLOSE_DOT_FILL	11	Close dot fill
USER_FILL	12	User-defined pattern

Value(s) Returned:

There is no return value.

Related Function(s):

```
setfillpattern : sets a user-defined fill pattern
setfillstyle   : sets the current fill pattern and color
```

Similar Microsoft C Function(s):

```
_getfillmask : gets the current fill pattern

unsigned char _far * _far _getfillmask(unsigned char
                    _far *fillmask);
```

Example:

The getfillsettings function is used in this example to retrieve the current fill settings. These fill settings are then displayed on the screen. (See Listing 11.21 and Figure 11.24.)

Listing 11.21. The getfillsettings function

```
#include <graphics.h>
#include <stdio.h>
#include <stdlib.h>
#include <conio.h>

int main ()
{
struct fillsettingstype fillsettings;
int gdriver = EGA;
int gmode = EGAHI;
char buffer [40];

     /* register EGAVGA_driver and sansserif_font */
     /* ... these have been added to graphics.lib */
     /* as described in UTIL.DOC                   */

registerbgidriver(EGAVGA_driver);
registerbgifont(sansserif_font);

     /* set EGA high-resolution 16-color mode */

initgraph (&gdriver,&gmode,"");
rectangle (0,0,639,349);

     /* get fill settings and display information */

rectangle (200,150,440,250);
setfillstyle (SLASH_FILL,15);
floodfill (1,1,15);

getfillsettings (&fillsettings);

sprintf (buffer, "Fill Style : %d", fillsettings.pattern);
settextjustify (CENTER_TEXT,CENTER_TEXT);
outtextxy (320,175,buffer);

sprintf (buffer,"Fill Color : %d", fillsettings.color);
outtextxy (320,200,buffer);

     /* Delay and Exit */

outtextxy (320,225,"Press Any Key To Exit");

getch ();
closegraph();
return 0;
}
```

Figure 11.24. Screen output from Listing 11.21

getgraphmode

Syntax:
```
int far getgraphmode(void);
```

Function:
The getgraphmode function returns the current graphics mode.

File(s) to Include:
```
#include <graphics.h>
```

Description:
The getgraphmode function is used to retrieve the value of the current graphics mode. The current driver must be considered when interpreting the return value. This function should only be called after the graphics system has been initialized with the initgraph function. Table 11.7 is provided to assist in the interpretation of the returned value.

Table 11.7. *Graphics modes*

Driver	Mode	Value	Description
CGA	CGAC0	0	320x200–4-color
	CGAC1	1	320x200–4-color
	CGAC2	2	320x200–4-color
	CGAC3	3	320x200–4-color
	CGAHI	4	640x200–2-color
MCGA	MCGAC0	0	320x200–4-color
	MCGAC1	1	320x200–4-color
	MCGAC2	2	320x200–4-color
	MCGAC3	3	320x200–4-color
	MCGAMED	4	640x200–2-color
	MCGAHI	5	640x480–2-color
EGA	EGALO	0	640x200–16-color
	EGAHI	1	640x350–16-color
EGA64	EGA64LO	0	640x200–16-color
	EGA64HI	1	640x350–4-color
EGAMONO	EGAMONOHI	3	640x350–2-color
VGA	VGALO	0	640x200–16-color
	VGAMED	1	640x350–16-color
	VGAHI	2	640x480–16-color
ATT400	ATT400C0	0	320x200–4-color
	ATT400C1	1	320x200–4-color
	ATT400C2	2	320x200–4-color
	ATT400C3	3	320x200–4-color
	ATT400MED	4	640x200–2-color
	ATT400HI	5	640x400–2-color
HERC	HERCMONOHI	0	720x348–2-color
PC3270	PC3270HI	0	720x350–2-color
IBM8514	IBM8514LO	0	640x480–256-color
	IBM8514HI	1	1024x768–256-color

Value(s) Returned:

The graphics mode as set by the `initgraph` or `setgraphmode` functions is returned when the `getgraphmode` function is called.

Related Function(s):

setgraphmode : sets the graphics mode
initgraph   : initializes the graphics system

Similar Microsoft C Function(s):

_getvideoconfig : gets the current video configuration

```
struct videoconfig _far * _far _getvideoconfig(struct
                    videoconfig _far *configurationinfo);
```

Example:

This example uses the getgraphmode function to retrieve the current graphics mode. The mode is then displayed on the screen.

Listing 11.22. The getgraphmode function

```
#include <graphics.h>
#include <stdio.h>
#include <stdlib.h>
#include <conio.h>

int main ()
{
int gdriver = EGA;
int gmode = EGAHI;
char buffer [40];
int mode;

        /* register EGAVGA_driver and sansserif_font */
        /* ... these have been added to graphics.lib */
        /* as described in UTIL.DOC                   */

registerbgidriver(EGAVGA_driver);
registerbgifont(sansserif_font);

        /* set EGA high-resolution 16-color mode */

initgraph (&gdriver,&gmode,"");
rectangle (0,0,639,349);

        /* get mode and display */

mode = getgraphmode ();
sprintf (buffer,"The Mode Number is : %d",mode);
settextstyle (SANS_SERIF_FONT,HORIZ_DIR,2);
settextjustify (CENTER_TEXT,CENTER_TEXT);
outtextxy (320,175,buffer);
```

```
                /* Delay and Exit */

outtextxy (320,320,"Press Any Key To Exit");
getch ();
closegraph();
return 0;
}
```

getimage

Syntax:
```
void far getimage(int left, int top, int right, int bottom,
                  void far *image);

int left, top;              Upper left corner of image
int right, bottom;          Lower right corner of image
void far *image;            Image buffer
```

Function:
The getimage function stores a rectangular image in memory.

File(s) to Include:
```
#include <graphics.h>
```

Description:
The getimage function is used to store a rectangular portion of the screen for later use. The upper left corner of the rectangular area that is to be stored is defined by the left and top arguments. These arguments represent the x and y coordinates of the upper left corner, respectively. The right and bottom arguments define the lower right corner of the rectangular image. These arguments define the x and y values of the lower right corner. The *image argument points to the memory buffer where the image is stored. Figure 11.25 illustrates the use of the getimage function.

Figure 11.25. The getimage function

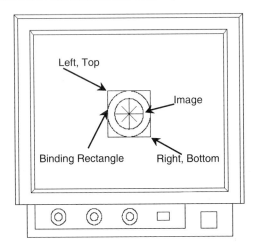

Value(s) Returned:
There is no return value.

Related Function(s):
imagesize : determines the required size of the image buffer
putimage   : places a stored image on the screen

Similar Microsoft C Function(s):
_getimage : stores a rectangular image in memory

```
void _far _getimage(short x1, short y1, short x2, short y2,
                    char _huge *image);
```

Example:
The getimage function is used in this example to store the rectangular image displayed in the center of the screen. This image is then placed in the four corners of the screen with the putimage function.(See Listing 11.23 and Figure 11.26.)

Listing 11.23. The get image function

```
#include <graphics.h>
#include <stdio.h>
#include <stdlib.h>
#include <conio.h>

int main ()
{
int gdriver = EGA;
int gmode = EGAHI;
void *image;
unsigned int imsize;

    /* register EGAVGA_driver and sansserif_font */
    /* ... these have been added to graphics.lib */
    /* as described in UTIL.DOC                   */

registerbgidriver(EGAVGA_driver);
registerbgifont(sansserif_font);

    /* set EGA high-resolution 16-color mode */

initgraph (&gdriver,&gmode,"");
rectangle (0,0,639,349);

    /* draw and store an image - then place it */
    /* in the four corners of the screen       */

setfillstyle(SOLID_FILL,2);
bar (280,135,360,215);
setfillstyle(SOLID_FILL,4);
fillellipse(320,175,40,40);

imsize = imagesize(280,135,360,215);
image = malloc(imsize);
getimage(280,135,360,215,image);

putimage (20,20,image,COPY_PUT);
putimage (540,20,image,COPY_PUT);
putimage (20,240,image,COPY_PUT);
putimage (540,240,image,COPY_PUT);

    /* Delay and Exit */

settextjustify(CENTER_TEXT,BOTTOM_TEXT);
outtextxy (320,320,"Press Any Key To Exit");

getch ();

closegraph();
return 0;
}
```

Figure 11.26. Screen output from Listing 11.23

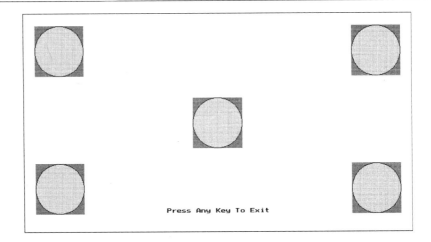

getlinesettings

Syntax:

```
void far getlinesettings(struct linesettingstype far *info);

struct linesettingstype far *info;    Line information
```

Function:

The `getlinesettings` function retrieves the current line style, line pattern, and line thickness.

File(s) to Include:

```
#include <graphics.h>
```

Description:

The `getlinesettings` function retrieves the current line settings. These settings are placed in a structure of type `linesettingstype` that is pointed to by the `*info` argument. The current line style, pattern, and thickness are placed in this structure. The syntax for the `linesettingstype` structure is:

```
struct linesettingstype
     {
     int linestyle;
     unsigned upattern;
     int thickness;
     };
```

The linestyle member of this structure specifies the style of the lines to be drawn. Table 11.8 lists the predefined line style constants and values. Table 11.9 lists the predefined line thickness constants and values.

Table 11.8. *Line styles*

Constant	Value	Meaning
SOLID_LINE	0	Solid line
DOTTED_LINE	1	Dotted line
CENTER_LINE	2	Centered line
DASHED_LINE	3	Dashed line
USERBIT_LINE	4	User-defined line

Table 11.9. *Line thicknesses*

Constant	Value	Meaning
NORM_WIDTH	1	Line width of 1 pixel
THICK_WIDTH	3	Line width of 3 pixels

The upattern member of the structure contains the user-defined line pattern only when the linestyle member is equal to USERBIT_LINE, or 4. When this is the case, the upattern member contains a 16-bit user-defined line pattern. A 1 bit in this line pattern indicates that the corresponding pixel will be set to the current color. A 0 bit indicates that the corresponding pixel will remain unchanged. For example, a user defined line pattern of 0001000100010001 binary, or 0x1111 hex, indicates that every fourth pixel on the line will be set to the current color.

Value(s) Returned:
There is no return value.

Related Function(s):
setlinestyle : sets the current line style

Similar Microsoft C Function(s):
_getlinestyle : gets the current line pattern

```
unsigned short _far _getlinestyle(void);
```

Example:

The example in Listing 11.24 and Figure 11.27 uses the `getlinesettings` function to retrieve the current line settings, including the current line style, user pattern, and line thickness. These settings are then displayed.

Listing 11.24. The `getlinesettings` function

```
#include <graphics.h>
#include <stdio.h>
#include <stdlib.h>
#include <conio.h>

int main ()
{
struct linesettingstype lineset;
int gdriver = EGA;
int gmode = EGAHI;
char buffer[40];

        /* register EGAVGA_driver and sansserif_font */
        /* ... these have been added to graphics.lib */
        /* as described in UTIL.DOC                   */

registerbgidriver(EGAVGA_driver);
registerbgifont(sansserif_font);

        /* set EGA high-resolution 16-color mode */

initgraph (&gdriver,&gmode,"");
rectangle (0,0,639,349);

        /* define, use, and retrieve line settings */

setlinestyle (DOTTED_LINE,0xFFFF,THICK_WIDTH);

getlinesettings (&lineset);

rectangle (50,50,590,300);
settextjustify(CENTER_TEXT,CENTER_TEXT);

sprintf (buffer,"The Line Style is : %d",lineset.linestyle);
outtextxy (320,75,buffer);

sprintf (buffer,"The User Pattern is : 0x%x",lineset.upattern);
outtextxy (320,150,buffer);

sprintf (buffer,"The Line Thickness is : %d",lineset.thickness);
outtextxy (320,225,buffer);

        /* Delay and Exit */
```

```
outtextxy (320,320,"Press Any Key To Exit");

getch ();

closegraph();
return 0;
}
```

Figure 11.27. Screen output from Listing 11.24

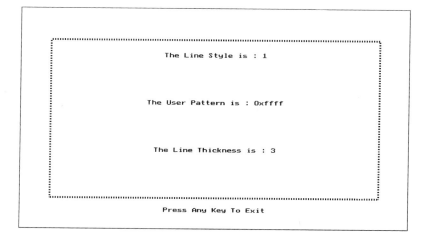

getmaxcolor

Syntax:
```
int far getmaxcolor(void);
```

Function:
The getmaxcolor function retrieves the value of the maximum color in the current palette.

File(s) to Include:
```
#include <graphics.h>
```

Description:
The getmaxcolor function is used to get the highest color value in the current palette. The palette in use depends upon the driver and mode initialized. For 16-color modes, the returned value is 15. Similarly, for two-color modes, the return value is 1.

Value(s) Returned:

The highest color value in the current palette is returned when the getmaxcolor function is called.

Related Function(s):

getcolor : gets the current color
setcolor : sets the current color

Similar Microsoft C Function(s):

There are no similar Microsoft C functions.

Example:

The getmaxcolor function is used in this example to retrieve the maximum color number in the current palette. The color number is then displayed.

Listing 11.25. The getmaxcolor function

```
#include <graphics.h>
#include <stdio.h>
#include <stdlib.h>
#include <conio.h>

int main ()
{
int gdriver = EGA;
int gmode = EGAHI;
int maxcolor;
char buffer[40];

        /* register EGAVGA_driver and sansserif_font */
        /* ... these have been added to graphics.lib */
        /* as described in UTIL.DOC                   */

registerbgidriver(EGAVGA_driver);
registerbgifont(sansserif_font);

        /* set EGA high-resolution 16-color mode */

initgraph (&gdriver,&gmode,"");
rectangle (0,0,639,349);

        /* get and display the maximum color number */

maxcolor = getmaxcolor();

settextstyle(SANS_SERIF_FONT,HORIZ_DIR,2);
settextjustify (CENTER_TEXT,CENTER_TEXT);
sprintf (buffer,"The Maximum Color Number is : %d",maxcolor);
outtextxy (320,175,buffer);
```

```
      /* Delay and Exit */

settextjustify(CENTER_TEXT,BOTTOM_TEXT);
outtextxy (320,320,"Press Any Key To Exit");

getch ();

closegraph();
return 0;
}
```

getmaxmode

Syntax:
```
int far getmaxmode(void);
```

Function:
The getmaxmode function returns the maximum mode number for the current driver.

File(s) to Include:
```
#include <graphics.h>
```

Description:
The getmaxmode function is used to determine the highest mode value for the current driver. The highest mode value generally represents the mode with the highest resolution. This function works with all drivers, including installed vendor-added drivers.

Value(s) Returned:
The maximum mode number for the current driver is returned when the getmaxmode function is called.

Related Function(s):
getmoderange : retrieves the range of modes for the driver
getmodename : returns the name of the graphics mode

Similar Microsoft C Function(s):
There are no similar Microsoft C functions.

Example:
The getmaxmode function is used in this example to retrieve the maximum mode number for the current driver. The maximum mode number is then displayed.

Listing 11.26. The getmaxmode function

```
#include <graphics.h>
#include <stdio.h>
#include <stdlib.h>
#include <conio.h>

int main ()
{
int gdriver = EGA;
int gmode = EGAHI;
int maxmode;
char buffer[40];

      /* register EGAVGA_driver and sansserif_font */
      /* ... these have been added to graphics.lib */
      /* as described in UTIL.DOC                   */

registerbgidriver(EGAVGA_driver);
registerbgifont(sansserif_font);

      /* set EGA high-resolution 16-color mode */

initgraph (&gdriver,&gmode,"");
rectangle (0,0,639,349);

      /* get and display the maximum mode */

maxmode = getmaxmode();

settextstyle (SANS_SERIF_FONT,HORIZ_DIR,2);
settextjustify (CENTER_TEXT,CENTER_TEXT);
sprintf (buffer,"The Maximum Mode Number is : %d", maxmode);
outtextxy(320,175,buffer);

      /* Delay and Exit */

outtextxy (320,320,"Press Any Key To Exit");

getch ();

closegraph();
return 0;
}
```

getmaxx

Syntax:
```
int far getmaxx(void);
```

Function:
The getmaxx function returns the maximum horizontal (x) screen coordinate.

File(s) to Include:

```
#include <graphics.h>
```

Description:

The `getmaxx` function is used to get the maximum screen coordinate in the horizontal direction. This value is usually the maximum horizontal resolution minus 1. For example, in EGA modes with 640 by 350 resolution, the returned value is 640 minus 1, or 639. This is due to the way the coordinates are numbered. The x axis begins at 0 and extends 640 pixels to 639. The y axis is numbered in a similar manner.

Value(s) Returned:

The maximum horizontal (x) screen coordinate is returned when the `getmaxx` function is called.

Related Function(s):

`getmaxy` : retrieves the maximum y coordinate

Similar Microsoft C Function(s):

`_getvideoconfig` : gets the current video configuration, including the number of pixels on the x axis

```
struct videoconfig _far * _far _getvideoconfig(struct
                    videoconfig _far *configurationinfo);
```

Example:

This example uses the `getmaxx` function to retrieve the maximum horizontal, or x, coordinate for the current screen mode. This x coordinate is then displayed on the screen.

Listing 11.27.   The `getmaxx` function

```
#include <graphics.h>
#include <stdio.h>
#include <stdlib.h>
#include <conio.h>

int main ()
{
int gdriver = EGA;
int gmode = EGAHI;
int maxx;
char buffer[40];
```

Listing 11.27.   *continues*

Listing 11.27. cont.   The getmaxx function

```
        /* register EGAVGA_driver and sansserif_font */
        /* ... these have been added to graphics.lib */
        /* as described in UTIL.DOC                  */

registerbgidriver(EGAVGA_driver);
registerbgifont(sansserif_font);

        /* set EGA high-resolution 16-color mode */

initgraph (&gdriver,&gmode,"");
rectangle (0,0,639,349);

        /* get and display the maximum x value for the mode */

maxx = getmaxx();

settextstyle (SANS_SERIF_FONT,HORIZ_DIR,2);
settextjustify(CENTER_TEXT,CENTER_TEXT);
sprintf (buffer,"The Maximum 'x' value is : %d",maxx);
outtextxy(320,175,buffer);

        /* Delay and Exit */

outtextxy (320,320,"Press Any Key To Exit");

getch ();

closegraph();
return 0;
}
```

getmaxy

Syntax:
```
int far getmaxy(void);
```

Function:
The getmaxy function returns the maximum vertical (y) screen coordinate.

File(s) to Include:
```
#include <graphics.h>
```

Description:
The getmaxy function is used to get the maximum screen coordinate in the vertical direction. This value is usually the maximum vertical resolution minus 1. For example, in

EGA modes with 640 by 350 resolution, the returned value is 350 minus 1, or 349. This is due to the way the coordinates are numbered. The y axis begins at 0 and extends 350 pixels to 349. The x axis is numbered in a similar manner.

Value(s) Returned:

The maximum vertical (y) screen coordinate is returned when the getmaxy function is called.

Related Function(s):

getmaxx : retrieves the maximum vertical (y) coordinate

Similar Microsoft C Function(s):

_getvideoconfig : gets the current video configuration, including the number of pixels on the y axis

```
struct videoconfig _far * _far _getvideoconfig(struct
                    videoconfig _far *configurationinfo);
```

Example:

The getmaxy function is used in this example to retrieve the maximum vertical, or y, coordinate for the current screen mode. This y coordinate is then displayed on the screen.

Listing 11.28. The getmaxy function

```
#include <graphics.h>
#include <stdio.h>
#include <stdlib.h>
#include <conio.h>

int main ()
{
int gdriver = EGA;
int gmode = EGAHI;
int maxy;
char buffer[40];

    /* register EGAVGA_driver and sansserif_font */
    /* ... these have been added to graphics.lib */
    /* as described in UTIL.DOC                   */

registerbgidriver(EGAVGA_driver);
registerbgifont(sansserif_font);

    /* set EGA high-resolution 16-color mode */
```

Listing 11.28. *continues*

Listing 11.28. cont. The getmaxy function

```
initgraph (&gdriver,&gmode,"");
rectangle (0,0,639,349);

     /* get and display the maximum y value for the mode */

maxy = getmaxy();

settextstyle (SANS_SERIF_FONT,HORIZ_DIR,2);
settextjustify(CENTER_TEXT,CENTER_TEXT);
sprintf (buffer,"The Maximum 'y' value is : %d",maxy);
outtextxy(320,175,buffer);

     /* Delay and Exit */

outtextxy (320,320,"Press Any Key To Exit");

getch ();

closegraph();
return 0;
}
```

getmodename

Syntax:
```
char *far getmodename(int modenumber);

int modenumber;              Graphics mode number
```

Function:
The getmodename function returns the pointer to the string that contains the name of the graphics mode.

File(s) to Include:
```
#include <graphics.h>
```

Description:
The getmodename function is used to retrieve the name of the graphics mode specified in the modenumber argument. The returned pointer indicates the string containing the mode name that is embedded in each driver.

Value(s) Returned:
The pointer is returned to the string that contains the name of the specified graphics mode when the getmodename function is called.

Related Function(s):

```
getmaxmode      : returns the maximum mode number
getmoderange    : returns the range of modes
```

Similar Microsoft C Function(s):

`_getvideoconfig` : gets the current video configuration including the mode

```
struct videoconfig _far * _far _getvideoconfig(struct
                    videoconfig _far *configurationinfo);
```

Example:

The following example uses the `getmodename` function to display the name of the retrieved mode. The mode and associated mode name are then displayed.

Listing 11.29. The `getmodename` function

```c
#include <graphics.h>
#include <stdio.h>
#include <stdlib.h>
#include <conio.h>

int main ()
{
int gdriver = EGA;
int gmode = EGAHI;
int mode;
char buffer[40];

    /* register EGAVGA_driver and sansserif_font */
    /* ... these have been added to graphics.lib */
    /* as described in UTIL.DOC                  */

registerbgidriver(EGAVGA_driver);
registerbgifont(sansserif_font);

    /* set EGA high-resolution 16-color mode */

initgraph (&gdriver,&gmode,"");
rectangle (0,0,639,349);

    /* get mode number and name - display them */

mode = getgraphmode();
settextstyle(SANS_SERIF_FONT,HORIZ_DIR,2);
settextjustify(CENTER_TEXT,CENTER_TEXT);

sprintf(buffer,"Current Mode Number : %d =>
            %s",mode,getmodename(mode));
outtextxy(320,175,buffer);
```

Listing 11.29. *continues*

Listing 11.29. cont. The `getmodename` function

```
    /* Delay and Exit */

outtextxy (320,320,"Press Any Key To Exit");

getch ();

closegraph();
return 0;
}
```

getmoderange

Syntax:
```
void far getmoderange(int driver, int far *lowmode,
                      int far *highmode);

int driver;              Graphics driver
int far *lowmode;        Lowest mode
int far *highmode;       Highest mode
```

Function:
The `getmoderange` function retrieves the range of modes for the specified graphics driver.

File(s) to Include:
```
#include <graphics.h>
```

Description:
The `getmoderange` function is used to retrieve the high and low mode values for the driver specified in the `driver` argument. The lowest mode value is returned in `*lowmode`, and the highest mode value is returned in `*highmode`. If the specified driver is invalid, a value of -1 is returned in both `*lowmode` and `*highmode`. However, if the `driver` argument is set to -1, the high and low modes for the current driver are returned.

Value(s) Returned:
There is no return value.

Related Function(s):
```
getmaxmode      : gets the highest mode number
getmodename     : gets the name of the graphics mode
```

Similar Microsoft C Function(s):

There are no similar Microsoft C functions.

Example:

The getmoderange function is used in this example to retrieve the minimum and maximum modes (the mode range) for the current screen mode. The mode range is then displayed.

Listing 11.30. The getmoderange function

```
#include <graphics.h>
#include <stdio.h>
#include <stdlib.h>
#include <conio.h>

int main ()
{
int gdriver = EGA;
int gmode = EGAHI;
int lowmode, highmode;
char buffer[40];

      /* register EGAVGA_driver and sansserif_font */
      /* ... these have been added to graphics.lib */
      /* as described in UTIL.DOC                   */

registerbgidriver(EGAVGA_driver);
registerbgifont(sansserif_font);

      /* set EGA high-resolution 16-color mode */
      /* assumes driver is in current directory */

initgraph (&gdriver,&gmode,"");
rectangle (0,0,639,349);

      /* get and display mode range */

getmoderange(gdriver,&lowmode,&highmode);

settextjustify (CENTER_TEXT,CENTER_TEXT);
sprintf (buffer,"The mode range is : %d to %d",lowmode,highmode);
outtextxy (320,175,buffer);

      /* Delay and Exit */

outtextxy (320,320,"Press Any Key To Exit");

getch ();

closegraph();
return 0;
}
```

getpalette

Syntax:

```
void far getpalette(struct palettetype far *palette)

struct palettetype far *palette;    Palette information
```

Function:

The getpalette function retrieves information on the current palette.

File(s) to Include:

```
#include <graphics.h>
```

Description:

The getpalette function is used to get the current palette settings. The *palette argument points to the structure of type palettetype where the palette information is stored. The syntax for the palettetype structure is:

```
#define MAXCOLORS 15

struct palettetype
    {
    unsigned char size;
    signed char colors[MAXCOLORS + 1];
    };
```

The size member of the structure indicates the number of color entries in the current palette. The colors array contains the color numbers for the palette entry.

Value(s) Returned:

There is no return value.

Related Function(s):

```
setpalette    : modifies one color in the current palette
setallpalette : modifies all colors in the palette
```

Similar Microsoft C Function(s):

There are no similar Microsoft C functions.

Example:

The getpalette function is used to retrieve the values of the current palette. These values are then displayed. (See Listing 11.31 and Figure 11.28.)

Listing 11.31. The getpalette function

```
#include <graphics.h>
#include <stdio.h>
#include <stdlib.h>
#include <conio.h>

int main ()
{
struct palettetype palette;
int gdriver = EGA;
int gmode = EGAHI;
int x, y;
char buffer[40];

     /* register EGAVGA_driver and sansserif_font */
     /* ... these have been added to graphics.lib */
     /* as described in UTIL.DOC               */

registerbgidriver(EGAVGA_driver);
registerbgifont(sansserif_font);

     /* set EGA high-resolution 16-color mode */

initgraph (&gdriver,&gmode,"");
rectangle (0,0,639,349);

     /* get and display palette information */

getpalette (&palette);
y = 50;

settextjustify (CENTER_TEXT,CENTER_TEXT);

sprintf (buffer,"Palette Size : %d",palette.size);
outtextxy (320,25,buffer);

for (x = 0; x < palette.size; x = x + 1)
     {
     sprintf (buffer,"Color [%02d] : 0x%02X",
                     x,palette.colors[x]);
     outtextxy (320,y,buffer);
     y = y + 15;
     }

     /* Delay and Exit */

settextjustify(CENTER_TEXT,CENTER_TEXT);
outtextxy (320,320,"Press Any Key To Exit");

getch ();

closegraph();
return 0;
}
```

Figure 11.28. Screen output from Listing 11.31

```
                    Palette Size : 16

                    Color [00] : 0x00
                    Color [01] : 0x01
                    Color [02] : 0x02
                    Color [03] : 0x03
                    Color [04] : 0x04
                    Color [05] : 0x05
                    Color [06] : 0x14
                    Color [07] : 0x07
                    Color [08] : 0x38
                    Color [09] : 0x39
                    Color [10] : 0x3A
                    Color [11] : 0x3B
                    Color [12] : 0x3C
                    Color [13] : 0x3D
                    Color [14] : 0x3E
                    Color [15] : 0x3F


                   Press Any Key To Exit
```

getpalettesize

Syntax:
```
int far getpalettesize(void);
```

Function:
The `getpalettesize` function returns the size of the current palette.

File(s) to Include:
```
#include <graphics.h>
```

Description:
The `getpalettesize` function is used to determine the number of valid palette entries for the current palette, considering the graphics mode in use. For 16-color modes, the `getpalettesize` function returns a 16.

Value(s) Returned:
The number of colors in the current palette is returned when `getpalettesize` is called.

Related Function(s):
```
setpalette      : modifies one color in the current palette
setallpalette : modifies all colors in the palette
```

Similar Microsoft C Function(s):

_getvideoconfig : gets the current video configuration, including the number of colors in the current palette

```
struct videoconfig _far * _far _getvideoconfig(struct
                            videoconfig _far *configurationinfo);
```

Example:

This example uses the getpalettesize function to retrieve the size of the current palette. The size is then displayed on the screen.

Listing 11.32. The getpalettesize function

```
#include <graphics.h>
#include <stdio.h>
#include <stdlib.h>
#include <conio.h>

int main ()
{
int gdriver = EGA;
int gmode = EGAHI;
int palsize;
char buffer[40];

      /* register EGAVGA_driver and sansserif_font */
      /* ... these have been added to graphics.lib */
      /* as described in UTIL.DOC                   */

registerbgidriver(EGAVGA_driver);
registerbgifont(sansserif_font);

      /* set EGA high-resolution 16-color mode */

initgraph (&gdriver,&gmode,"");
rectangle (0,0,639,349);

      /* get and display palette size */

palsize = getpalettesize ();

settextstyle (SANS_SERIF_FONT,HORIZ_DIR,2);
settextjustify (CENTER_TEXT,CENTER_TEXT);
sprintf (buffer,"The palette size is : %d",palsize);
outtextxy (320,175,buffer);

      /* Delay and Exit */

outtextxy (320,320,"Press Any Key To Exit");
```

Listing 11.32. *continues*

Listing 11.32. cont.   The `getpallettesize` function

```
getch ();

closegraph();
return 0;
}
```

getpixel

Syntax:
```
unsigned far getpixel(int x, int y);

int x, y;                    Coordinates of pixel
```

Function:
The `getpixel` function returns the color of the specified pixel.

File(s) to Include:
```
#include <graphics.h>
```

Description:
The `getpixel` function is used to retrieve the color value of the pixel specified by the x and y arguments. The x and y arguments specify the screen coordinates of the pixel to evaluate. When evaluating the returned color value, the graphics mode in use must be considered. Tables 11.10 and 11.11 are provided for the evaluation of the returned color value.

Table 11.10.   *Colors for 16-color modes*

Constant	Value
BLACK	0
BLUE	1
GREEN	2
CYAN	3
RED	4
MAGENTA	5
BROWN	6
LIGHTGRAY	7

Constant	Value
DARKGRAY	8
LIGHTBLUE	9
LIGHTGREEN	10
LIGHTCYAN	11
LIGHTRED	12
LIGHTMAGENTA	13
YELLOW	14
WHITE	15

Table 11.11. *Colors for CGA modes*

Palette Number	Color 1	Color 2	Color 3
0	CGA_LIGHTGREEN	CGA_LIGHTRED	CGA_YELLOW
1	CGA_LIGHTCYAN	CGA_LIGHTMAGENTA	CGA_WHITE
2	CGA_GREEN	CGA_RED	CGA_BROWN
3	CGA_CYAN	CGA_MAGENTA	CGA_LIGHTGRAY

NOTE: Color 0 is set to the background color

Value(s) Returned:

The color value of the specified pixel is returned when the `getpixel` function is called.

Related Function(s):

`putpixel` : sets the specified pixel to the specified color

Similar Microsoft C Function(s):

`_getpixel` : retrieves the color of a specified pixel

```
short _far _getpixel(short x, short y);
```

Example:

The `getpixel` function is used in this example to evaluate every pixel on the screen. If the pixel has a color value of 15 (white), that pixel is then set to color value 14 (yellow).

353

Listing 11.33. The get pixel function

```
#include <graphics.h>
#include <stdio.h>
#include <stdlib.h>
#include <conio.h>

int main ()
{
int gdriver = EGA;
int gmode = EGAHI;
int x,y;
int color;

        /* register EGAVGA_driver and sansserif_font */
        /* ... these have been added to graphics.lib */
        /* as described in UTIL.DOC                   */

registerbgidriver(EGAVGA_driver);
registerbgifont(sansserif_font);

        /* set EGA high-resolution 16-color mode */

initgraph (&gdriver,&gmode,"");
rectangle (0,0,639,349);
bar3d (50,50,590,300,25,1);

        /* evaluate each pixel on the screen */
        /* if the pixel is 15, set to 14      */

for (x = 0; x <640; x = x+1)
{
    for (y = 0; y < 350; y = y + 1)
        {
        color = getpixel (x,y);
        if (color == 15)
            putpixel (x,y,14);
        }
}
        /* Delay and Exit */

settextjustify(CENTER_TEXT,BOTTOM_TEXT);
outtextxy (320,320,"Press Any Key To Exit");
getch ();
closegraph();
return 0;
}
```

gettextsettings

Syntax:

```
void far gettextsettings(struct textsettingstype far *info);

struct textsettingstype far *info;              Text settings
```

Function:

The gettextsettings function retrieves information on the current graphics font.

File(s) to Include:

```
#include <graphics.h>
```

Description:

The gettextsettings function is used to get information about the current graphics font. This information is placed in a structure of type textsettingstype, which is pointed to by the *info argument. This structure contains information on the current font in use, the text direction, the character size, and horizontal and vertical text justification. The syntax for the textsettingstype structure is as follows:

```
struct textsettingstype
    {
    int font;
    int direction;
    int charsize;
    int horiz;
    int vert;
    };
```

Tables 11.12, 11.13, and 11.14 list the predefined constants, values, and meanings for the available fonts, text direction, and vertical and horizontal justifications. The charsize member contains the integer value that represents the magnification factor for the current font.

Table 11.12. *Text fonts*

Constant	Value	Meaning
DEFAULT_FONT	0	8-by-8 bit-mapped font
TRIPLEX_FONT	1	Triplex font
SMALL_FONT	2	Small font
SANS_SERIF_FONT	3	Sans serif font
GOTHIC_FONT	4	Gothic font

Table 11.13. *Text directions*

Constant	Value	Meaning
HORIZ_DIR	0	Horizontal text
VERT_DIR	1	Vertical text

Table 11.14. *Text Justifications*

Constant	Value	Meaning
Horizontal text justification		
LEFT_TEXT	0	Left justify
CENTER_TEXT	1	Center text
RIGHT_TEXT	2	Right justify
Vertical text justification		
BOTTOM_TEXT	0	Bottom justify
CENTER_TEXT	1	Center text
TOP_TEXT	2	Top justify

Value(s) Returned:

There is no return value.

Related Function(s):

`settextstyle` : sets the current font characteristics

Similar Microsoft C Function(s):

`_getfontinfo` : gets the characteristics of the current font

`short _far _getfontinfo(struct _fontinfo _far *fontinfo);`

Example:

The `gettextsettings` function is used to retrieve the current text settings, including the current font, text direction, character size, and vertical/horizontal justification. These text settings are then displayed on the screen.

Listing 11.34. The `gettextsettings` function

```
#include <graphics.h>
#include <stdio.h>
#include <stdlib.h>
#include <conio.h>

int main ()
{
struct textsettingstype textset;
int gdriver = EGA;
int gmode = EGAHI;
char buffer [40];
```

```
            /* register EGAVGA_driver and sansserif_font */
            /* ... these have been added to graphics.lib */
            /* as described in UTIL.DOC                  */

registerbgidriver (EGAVGA_driver);
registerbgifont (sansserif_font);

            /* set EGA 16-color high resolution video mode  */

initgraph (&gdriver,&gmode,"");
rectangle (0,0,639,349);

            /* set, get, and display text settings */

settextstyle(SANS_SERIF_FONT,HORIZ_DIR,2);
settextjustify(CENTER_TEXT,CENTER_TEXT);

gettextsettings(&textset);

sprintf (buffer,"Font Value : %d",textset.font);
outtextxy (320,75,buffer);

sprintf (buffer,"Text Direction : %d",textset.direction);
outtextxy (320,125,buffer);

sprintf (buffer,"Character Size : %d",textset.charsize);
outtextxy (320,175,buffer);

sprintf (buffer,"Horizontal Justification : %d",textset.horiz);
outtextxy (320,225,buffer);

sprintf (buffer,"Vertical Justification : %d",textset.vert);
outtextxy (320,275,buffer);

            /* Delay and Exit */

settextjustify(CENTER_TEXT,BOTTOM_TEXT);
outtextxy (320,320,"Press Any Key To Exit");

getch ();

closegraph();
return 0;
}
```

getviewsettings

Syntax:

```
void far getviewsettings(struct viewporttype far *viewport);

struct viewporttype far *viewport;      Viewport Information
```

Function:

The `getviewsettings` function retrieves information on the current viewport.

File(s) to Include:

```
#include <graphics.h>
```

Description:

The `getviewsettings` function is used to get information about the current viewport. This information is placed in a structure of type `viewporttype`, which is pointed to by the `*viewport` argument. This structure contains information about the upper left and lower right corners, as well as the setting of the viewport's clipping flag. The syntax for the `viewporttype` structure is:

```
struct viewportype
    {
    int left, top;
    int right, bottom;
    int clip;
    };
```

The `left` and `top` members of the structure define the x and y coordinates, respectively, of the upper left corner of the viewport. In the same manner, the `right` and `bottom` members define the lower right corner of the viewport. The `clip` member indicates whether or not graphics output that extends beyond the border of the viewport will be clipped. If the `clip` member is a nonzero value, graphics output is clipped at the borders of the viewport. If the `clip` member is 0, output can extend beyond the borders of the viewport.

Value(s) Returned:

There is no return value.

Related Function(s):

`setviewport` : sets the current viewport

Similar Microsoft C Function(s):

There are no similar Microsoft C functions.

Example:

This example uses the `getviewsettings` function to retrieve the parameters for the current viewport. These parameters are then displayed on the screen.

Listing 11.35. The getviewsettings function

```c
#include <graphics.h>
#include <stdio.h>
#include <stdlib.h>
#include <conio.h>

int main ()
{
struct viewporttype viewset;
int gdriver = EGA;
int gmode = EGAHI;
char buffer[40];

    /* register EGAVGA_driver and sansserif_font */
    /* ... these have been added to graphics.lib */
    /* as described in UTIL.DOC                   */

registerbgidriver (EGAVGA_driver);
registerbgifont (sansserif_font);

    /* set EGA 16-color high resolution video mode  */

initgraph (&gdriver,&gmode,"");
rectangle (0,0,639,349);

    /* get and display current viewport settings */

getviewsettings (&viewset);

settextjustify (CENTER_TEXT,CENTER_TEXT);

sprintf (buffer,"Upper left corner : %d,
%d",viewset.left,viewset.top);
outtextxy (320,100,buffer);

sprintf (buffer,"Lower right corner : %d,
%d",viewset.right,viewset.bottom);
outtextxy (320,150,buffer);

sprintf (buffer,"Clipping Value : %d",viewset.clip);
outtextxy (320,200,buffer);

    /* Delay and Exit */

settextjustify(CENTER_TEXT,BOTTOM_TEXT);
outtextxy (320,320,"Press Any Key To Exit");

getch ();

closegraph();
return 0;
}
```

getx

Syntax:
```
int far getx(void);
```

Function:
The `getx` function returns the horizontal (x) position of the graphics cursor.

File(s) to Include:
```
#include <graphics.h>
```

Description:
The `getx` function is used to retrieve the position, in the horizontal direction, of the graphics cursor. The returned value specifies the horizontal pixel location of the graphics cursor (the x coordinate), relative to the current viewport.

Value(s) Returned:
The horizontal (x) coordinate of the current graphics cursor position is returned when the `getx` function is called.

Related Function(s):
`gety` : returns the y position of the graphics cursor

Similar Microsoft C Function(s):
`_getcurrentposition` : gets the current position of the graphics cursor

```
struct xycoord _far _getcurrentposition(void);
```

Example:
This example uses the `getx` function to retrieve the current horizontal, or x, coordinate of the cursor position. This x coordinate is displayed along with the y coordinate.

Listing 11.36. The getx function

```
#include <graphics.h>
#include <stdio.h>
#include <stdlib.h>
#include <conio.h>

int main ()
{
int gdriver = EGA;
int gmode = EGAHI;
char buffer [40];

    /* register EGAVGA_driver and sansserif_font */
    /* ... these have been added to graphics.lib */
    /* as described in UTIL.DOC                   */

registerbgidriver (EGAVGA_driver);
registerbgifont (sansserif_font);

    /* set EGA 16-color high resolution video mode  */

initgraph (&gdriver,&gmode,"");
rectangle (0,0,639,349);

    /* set and display position of cursor */

moveto (320,175);
settextjustify (CENTER_TEXT,CENTER_TEXT);

sprintf (buffer,"The 'x' position of cursor is %d",getx());
outtextxy (320,175,buffer);

sprintf (buffer,"The 'y' position of cursor is %d",gety());
outtextxy (320,225,buffer);

    /* Delay and Exit */

settextjustify(CENTER_TEXT,BOTTOM_TEXT);
outtextxy (320,320,"Press Any Key To Exit");

getch ();
closegraph();
return 0;
}
```

gety

Syntax:
```
int far gety(void);
```

Function:

The `gety` function returns the vertical (y) coordinate of the current graphics cursor position.

File(s) to Include:

```
#include <graphics.h>
```

Description:

The `gety` function is used to retrieve the vertical position of the graphics cursor. The value returned by this function specifies the vertical pixel location (the y coordinate), relative to the current viewport, of the graphics cursor.

Value(s) Returned:

The vertical (y) coordinate of the current graphics cursor position is returned when the `gety` function is called.

Related Function(s):

`getx` : gets the x coordinate of the graphics cursor

Similar Microsoft C Function(s):

`_getcurrentposition` : gets the current position of the graphics cursor

```
struct xycoord _far _getcurrentposition(void);
```

Example:

The `gety` function is used in this example to retrieve the vertical, or y, coordinate of the current cursor position. The y coordinate is then displayed along with the x coordinate.

Listing 11.37. The `gety` function

```
#include <graphics.h>
#include <stdio.h>
#include <stdlib.h>
#include <conio.h>

int main ()
{
int gdriver = EGA;
int gmode = EGAHI;
char buffer [40];

        /* register EGAVGA_driver and sansserif_font */
```

```
        /* ... these have been added to graphics.lib */
        /* as described in UTIL.DOC                   */

registerbgidriver (EGAVGA_driver);
registerbgifont (sansserif_font);

        /* set EGA 16-color high resolution video mode  */

initgraph (&gdriver,&gmode,"");
rectangle (0,0,639,349);

        /* set and display position of cursor */

moveto (320,175);
settextjustify (CENTER_TEXT,CENTER_TEXT);

sprintf (buffer,"The 'x' position of cursor is %d",getx());
outtextxy (320,175,buffer);

sprintf (buffer,"The 'y' position of cursor is %d",gety());
outtextxy (320,225,buffer);

        /* Delay and Exit */

settextjustify(CENTER_TEXT,BOTTOM_TEXT);
outtextxy (320,320,"Press Any Key To Exit");

getch ();
closegraph();
return 0;
}
```

graphdefaults

Syntax:
```
void far graphdefaults(void);
```

Function:
The graphdefaults function resets all settings in the graphics environment to their default values.

File(s) to Include:
```
#include <graphics.h>
```

Description:
The graphdefaults function is used to reset all graphics settings to their original, or default, values. This function resets the viewport to cover the entire screen, moves the graphics cursor to position (0,0), and resets the current palette to its default colors.

It also resets the background color and current color to their default values, resets the fill style and pattern to their defaults, and resets the text font and justification.

Value(s) Returned:
There is no return value.

Related Function(s):
initgraph : initializes the graphics environment

Similar Microsoft C Function(s):
_setvideomode : initializes the graphics environment and is used to close the graphics environment

```
short _far _setvideomode(short mode);
```

Example:
The graphdefaults function is used in this example to reset all altered values to their default settings.

Listing 11.38. The graphdefaults function

```
#include <graphics.h>
#include <stdio.h>
#include <stdlib.h>
#include <conio.h>

int main ()
{
int gdriver = EGA;
int gmode = EGAHI;

     /* register EGAVGA_driver and sansserif_font */
     /* ... these have been added to graphics.lib */
     /* as described in UTIL.DOC                   */

registerbgidriver (EGAVGA_driver);
registerbgifont (sansserif_font);

     /* set EGA 16-color high resolution video mode  */

initgraph (&gdriver,&gmode,"");
rectangle (0,0,639,349);

     /* modify settings - call graphdefaults to reset */
     /* these to the defaults - use the defaults      */

setcolor (4);
setviewport (20,20,100,100,1);
```

```
settextstyle (SANS_SERIF_FONT,HORIZ_DIR,2);
settextjustify (CENTER_TEXT,CENTER_TEXT);

graphdefaults ();

line (0,0,639,349);
outtextxy(320,175,"EXAMPLE OF graphdefaults();");

    /* Delay and Exit */

settextjustify(CENTER_TEXT,BOTTOM_TEXT);
outtextxy (320,320,"Press Any Key To Exit");

getch ();
closegraph();
return 0;
}
```

grapherrormsg

Syntax:
```
char *far grapherrormsg(int errorcode);

int errorcode;          Error code
```

Function:
The grapherrormsg function returns the pointer to the error message string.

File(s) to Include:
```
#include <graphics.h>
```

Description:
The grapherrormsg function is used to get the pointer to the error message string for a specified error code. The errorcode argument specifies the value of the error code. The graphresult function must be used to retrieve the error code used for the errorcode argument.

Value(s) Returned:
The pointer is returned to the error message string when the grapherrormsg function is called.

Related Function(s):
graphresult : returns an error code

Similar Microsoft C Function(s):

_grstatus : determines if errors or warnings occurred during the last graphics call

```
short _far _grstatus(void);
```

Example:

The grapherrormsg function is used in this example to return the pointer to an error message string. This pointer is then used to display the error string.

Listing 11.39. The grapherrormsg function

```
#include <graphics.h>
#include <stdio.h>
#include <stdlib.h>
#include <conio.h>

int main ()
{
int gdriver = EGA;
int gmode = EGAHI;
int errorcode;
char buffer [40];

        /* register EGAVGA_driver and sansserif_font */
        /* ... these have been added to graphics.lib */
        /* as described in UTIL.DOC                   */

registerbgidriver (EGAVGA_driver);
registerbgifont (sansserif_font);

        /* set EGA 16-color high resolution video mode  */

initgraph (&gdriver,&gmode,"");
rectangle (0,0,639,349);

        /* draw rectangle - get error message - display code */

rectangle (50,50,590,200);
errorcode = graphresult ();

sprintf (buffer,"Error Message : %s",grapherrormsg(errorcode));
settextjustify (CENTER_TEXT,CENTER_TEXT);
outtextxy (320,175,buffer);

        /* Delay and Exit */

settextjustify(CENTER_TEXT,BOTTOM_TEXT);
outtextxy (320,320,"Press Any Key To Exit");
```

```
getch ();

closegraph();
return 0;
}
```

_graphfreemem

Syntax:
```
void far * far _graphfreemem(void far *ptr, unsigned size);

void far *ptr;              Pointer
unsigned size;             Size of buffer
```

Function:
The _graphfreemem function frees graphics memory.

File(s) to Include:
```
#include <graphics.h>
```

Description:
The _graphfreemem function is used by the graphics library to deallocate memory previously reserved by a call to the _graphgetmem function. Because this function is provided for use by the graphics library, no example is provided in this text. However, it is possible to control the graphics library memory management by declaring a function similar to the _graphfreemem function.

Value(s) Returned:
There is no return value.

Related Function(s):
_graphgetmem : allocates graphics memory

Similar Microsoft C Function(s):
There are no similar Microsoft C functions.

_graphgetmem

Syntax:
```
void far * far _graphgetmem(unsigned size);

unsigned size;                Size of buffer
```

Function:
The _graphgetmem function allocates graphics memory.

File(s) to Include:
```
#include <graphics.h>
```

Description:
The _graphgetmem function allocates graphics memory for internal buffers, graphics drivers, and fonts. This function is intended to be used by the graphics library; therefore, no example is provided. However, it is still possible to manage the graphics memory by creating a similar version of this function.

Value(s) Returned:
There is no return value.

Related Function(s):
_graphfreemem : deallocates graphics memory

Similar Microsoft C Function(s):
There are no similar Microsoft C functions.

---

graphresult

Syntax:
```
int far graphresult(void);
```

Function:
The graphresult function returns the error code for the latest unsuccessful graphics call.

File(s) to Include:
```
#include <graphics.h>
```

Description:

The `graphresult` function retrieves and returns the error code for the last unsuccessful graphics call. In addition, it resets the error level to 0, or `grOk`. Table 11.15 lists the possible return values and constants for the `graphresult` function.

Table 11.15. *Error codes*

Code	Constant	Meaning
0	grOK	No error
-1	grNoInitGraph	Graphics not initiated
-2	grNotDetected	No graphics hardware detected
-3	grFileNotFound	Driver file not found
-4	grInvalidDriver	Invalid driver file
-5	grNoLoadMem	No memory to load driver
-6	grNoScanMem	No memory in scan fill
-7	grNoFloodMem	No memory in floodfill
-8	grFontNotFound	Font file not found
-9	grNoFontMem	No memory to load font
-10	grInvalidMode	Invalid graphics mode
-11	grError	Graphics error
-12	grIOerror	Graphics IO error
-13	grInvalidFont	Invalid font file
-14	grInvalidFontNum	Invalid font number
-15	grInvalidDeviceNum	Invalid device number
-18	grInvalidVersion	Invalid version number

Value(s) Returned:

The current graphics error code is returned when the `graphresult` function is called.

Related Function(s):

`grapherrormsg` : returns the pointer to the error string

Similar Microsoft C Function(s):

_grstatus : determines if errors or warnings occurred during the last graphics function call

```
short _far _grstatus(void);
```

Example:

The graphresult function is used in this example to retrieve the status of the last graphics function. If an error occurs, an appropriate message is displayed. Similarly, a message is displayed if no error occurs.

Listing 11.40. The graphresult function

```
#include <graphics.h>
#include <stdio.h>
#include <stdlib.h>
#include <conio.h>

int main ()
{
int gdriver = EGA;
int gmode = EGAHI;
int errorcode;
char buffer [40];

        /* register EGAVGA_driver and sansserif_font */
        /* ... these have been added to graphics.lib */
        /* as described in UTIL.DOC                   */

registerbgidriver (EGAVGA_driver);
registerbgifont (sansserif_font);

        /* set EGA 16-color high resolution video mode  */

initgraph (&gdriver,&gmode,"");
rectangle (0,0,639,349);

        /* draw figure - get error message - display code */

rectangle (50,50,590,200);
ellipse (320,125,0,360,270,75);
errorcode = graphresult ();

if (errorcode == 0)
        sprintf (buffer,"No Error - Error Code : %d",errorcode);

if (errorcode != 0)
        sprintf (buffer,"Error - Error Code : %d",errorcode);

settextjustify (CENTER_TEXT,CENTER_TEXT);
outtextxy (320,175,buffer);
```

```
    /* Delay and Exit */

settextjustify(CENTER_TEXT,BOTTOM_TEXT);
outtextxy (320,320,"Press Any Key To Exit");

getch ();

closegraph();
return 0;
}
```

imagesize

Syntax:
```
unsigned far imagesize(int left, int top, int right,int bottom);

int left, top;          Upper left corner of image
int right, bottom;      Lower right corner of image
```

Function:
The imagesize function returns the required number of bytes to store the specified image.

File(s) to Include:
```
#include <graphics.h>
```

Description:
The imagesize function is used to determine the buffer size needed to store an image with the getimage function. The left and top arguments define the x and y coordinates of the upper left corner of the rectangular image. Similarly, the right and bottom arguments define the lower right corner of the image. The imagesize function returns the actual number of bytes needed if the required size is less than 64K minus 1 byte. If this is not the case, the returned value is 0xFFFF, or -1.

Value(s) Returned:
The number of bytes required to store the specified image is returned when the imagesize function is called.

Related Function(s):
getimage : stores an image to memory
putimage : places an image on the screen

Similar Microsoft C Function(s):

_imagesize : determines the number of bytes required to store a rectangular image

```
long _far _imagesize(short x1, short y1, short x2,
                     short y2);
```

Example:

The example in Listing 11.41 and Figure 11.29 uses the imagesize function to size the buffer used to store the rectangular image. This image is then placed on the screen several times in a diagonal fashion.

Listing 11.41. The imagesize function

```
#include <graphics.h>
#include <stdio.h>
#include <stdlib.h>
#include <conio.h>

int main ()
{
int gdriver = EGA;
int gmode = EGAHI;
void *image;
unsigned int imsize;
int x, y;

        /* register EGAVGA_driver and sansserif_font */
        /* ... these have been added to graphics.lib */
        /* as described in UTIL.DOC                   */

registerbgidriver(EGAVGA_driver);
registerbgifont(sansserif_font);

        /* set EGA high-resolution 16-color mode */

initgraph (&gdriver,&gmode,"");
rectangle (0,0,639,349);

        /* draw and store an image - then place it */
        /* in a diagonal fashion over the screen   */

setfillstyle(SOLID_FILL,14);
bar (280,135,360,215);
setfillstyle(SOLID_FILL,1);
fillellipse(320,175,40,40);

imsize = imagesize(280,135,360,215);
image = malloc(imsize);
getimage(280,135,360,215,image);

cleardevice ();
```

```
rectangle (0,0,639,349);
y = 20;

for (x=20; x<550; x=x+60)
{
    putimage (x,y,image,COPY_PUT);
    y = y + 25;
}

    /* Delay and Exit */

settextjustify(CENTER_TEXT,BOTTOM_TEXT);
outtextxy (320,320,"Press Any Key To Exit");

getch ();

closegraph();
return 0;
}
```

Figure 11.29.   Screen output from Listing 11.41

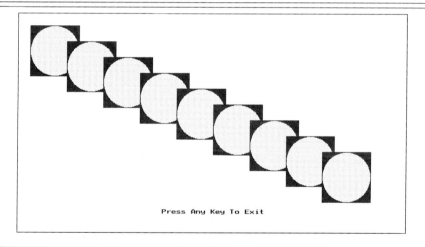

Press Any Key To Exit

initgraph

Syntax:

```
void far initgraph(int far *driver, int far *mode,
                   int far *path);

int far *driver;                Graphics driver
int far *mode;                  Graphics mode
int far *path;                  Path to the driver
```

Function:
The initgraph function initializes the graphics system.

File(s) to Include:
#include <graphics.h>

Description:
The initgraph function is used to load or validate a graphics driver and place the video system into graphics mode. This function must be called before any graphics functions that produce output are used. Table 11.16 lists the graphics drivers provided in the Borland environment. These constants and values are used for the *driver argument. If *driver is set to DETECT, or 0, the detectgraph function is called, and an appropriate driver and graphics mode are selected. Setting *driver to any other predefined value initiates the loading of the corresponding graphics driver.

Table 11.16. *Graphics drivers*

Constant	Value
DETECT	0
CGA	1
MCGA	2
EGA	3
EGA64	4
EGAMONO	5
IBM8514	6
HERCMONO	7
ATT400	8
VGA	9
PC3270	10

Table 11.17 lists the graphics modes associated with the drivers listed in Table 11.16. These values, or constants, are used for the *mode argument. These values should correspond to the driver specified in the *driver argument.

The *path argument specifies the directory path where the graphics drivers are located. The initgraph function will search this path for the driver first. If it is not found, the function will search the current directory. When the *path argument is NULL, only the current directory is searched.

One way to avoid having to load the driver from the disk each time the program is run is to "link" the appropriate driver into the executable program. The examples in this book use this format. However, the drivers must first be made into an .OBJ file, added to the graphics.lib file, and then registered in the current program. The UTIL.DOC file included in the distribution disks explains in detail how to create the driver object files and add them to the graphics.lib file.

Table 11.17. *Graphics modes*

Driver	Mode	Value	Description
CGA	CGAC0	0	320x200–4-color
	CGAC1	1	320x200–4-color
	CGAC2	2	320x200–4-color
	CGAC3	3	320x200–4-color
	CGAHI	4	640x200–2-color
MCGA	MCGAC0	0	320x200–4-color
	MCGAC1	1	320x200–4-color
	MCGAC2	2	320x200–4-color
	MCGAC3	3	320x200–4-color
	MCGAMED	4	640x200–2-color
	MCGAHI	5	640x480–2-color
EGA	EGALO	0	640x200–16-color
	EGAHI	1	640x350–16-color
EGA64	EGA64LO	0	640x200–16-color
	EGA64HI	1	640x350–4-color
EGAMONO	EGAMONOHI	3	640x350–2-color
VGA	VGALO	0	640x200–16-color
	VGAMED	1	640x350–16-color
	VGAHI	2	640x480–16-color
ATT400	ATT400C0	0	320x200–4-color
	ATT400C1	1	320x200–4-color
	ATT400C2	2	320x200–4-color
	ATT400C3	3	320x200–4-color
	ATT400MED	4	640x200–2-color
	ATT400HI	5	640x400–2-color
HERC	HERCMONOHI	0	720x348–2-color
PC3270	PC3270HI	0	720x350–2-color
IBM8514	IBM8514LO	0	640x480–256-color
	IBM8514HI	1	1024x768–256-color

Value(s) Returned:

When the `initgraph` function is called, the internal error code is set. If the `initgraph` function is successful, the code is set to 0. If not, the code is set as follows:

-2	grNotDetected	Graphics card not found
-3	grFileNotFound	Driver file not found
-4	grInvalidDriver	Driver file invalid
-5	grNoLoadMem	Not enough memory to load driver

Related Function(s):

`closegraph` : closes the graphics system

Similar Microsoft C Function(s):

`_setvideomode` : initializes and closes the graphics system

```
short _far _setvideomode(short mode);
```

Example:

The `initgraph` function is used in this example to initialize the graphics environment. The current mode and mode name are then displayed.

Listing 11.42. The `initgraph` function

```
#include <graphics.h>
#include <stdio.h>
#include <stdlib.h>
#include <conio.h>

int main ()
{
int gdriver = EGA;
int gmode = EGAHI;
int mode;
char buffer [40];

        /* register EGAVGA_driver and sansserif_font */
        /* ... these have been added to graphics.lib */
        /* as described in UTIL.DOC                   */

registerbgidriver(EGAVGA_driver);
registerbgifont(sansserif_font);

        /* set EGA high-resolution 16-color mode */

initgraph (&gdriver,&gmode,"");
setbkcolor (1);
rectangle (0,0,639,349);
```

```
        /* get and display the graphics mode */

settextjustify (CENTER_TEXT,CENTER_TEXT);
outtextxy (320,150,"Graphics System Intialized");
mode = getgraphmode();
sprintf (buffer,"Mode : %d",mode);
outtextxy (320,200,buffer);
sprintf (buffer,"Mode Name : %s",getmodename(mode));
outtextxy (320,250,buffer);

        /* Delay and Exit */

settextjustify(CENTER_TEXT,BOTTOM_TEXT);
outtextxy (320,330,"Press Any Key To Exit and Close Graphics
System");

getch ();
closegraph();
return 0;
}
```

installuserdriver

Syntax:
```
int far installuserdriver(char far *name, int huge (*detect)
                          (void));

char far *name;              New device driver file
int huge (*detect)(void));   Pointer to optional autodetect
```

Function:
The installuserdriver function installs a vendor-added device driver to the BGI device driver table.

File(s) to Include:
```
#include <graphics.h>
```

Description:
The installuserdriver function allows the user to add additional, third-party device drivers to the internal BGI device driver table. The *name argument defines the name of the new .BGI driver file. The *detect parameter is a pointer to an optional autodetect function that may or may not be provided with the new driver. The autodetect function is expected to receive no parameters and return an integer value. Because this function requires a third-party .BGI device driver, no example is provided.

Value(s) Returned:
The driver number parameter that would be passed to the initgraph function to select the new driver is returned when the installuserdriver function is called.

Related Function(s):
registerbgidriver : registers a driver file

Similar Microsoft C Function(s):
There are no similar Microsoft C functions.

installuserfont

Syntax:
```
int far installuserfont(char far *name);

char far *name;                Path to font file
```

Function:
The installuserfont function is used to load a font file that is not built into the BGI system.

File(s) to Include:
```
#include <graphics.h>
```

Description:
The installuserfont function loads a stroked font file that is not provided with the BGI system. The *name parameter specifies the name of the font file to load. The graphics system can have up to twenty fonts installed at any time. There is no example provided for this function since only BGI fonts are available for loading.

Value(s) Returned:
The font identification number that is used to select the new font through the settextstyle function is returned when the installuserfont function is called. If the internal font table is full, a value of -11 is returned, indicating an error.

Related Function(s):
settextstyle : sets the font characteristics

Similar Microsoft C Function(s):
There are no similar Microsoft C functions.

line

Syntax:
```
void far Line(int x1, int y1, int x2, int y2);

int x1, y1;             Starting point
int x2, y2;             Ending point
```

Function:
The line function draws a line between the two specified points.

File(s) to Include:
```
#include <graphics.h>
```

Description:
The line function is used to connect two points with a line. The first point is specified by the x1 and y1 arguments. The second point is specified by the x2 and y2 arguments. The connecting line is drawn using the current line style, thickness, and current color. The position of the graphics cursor is not affected by the line function. Figure 11.30 illustrates the use of the line function.

Figure 11.30. The line function

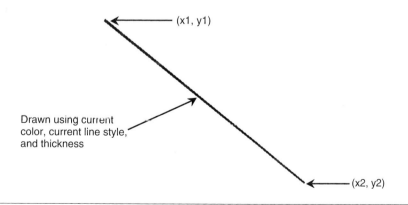

Value(s) Returned:

There is no return value.

Related Function(s):

lineto   : draws a line from the graphics cursor to a specified point

linerel : draws a line a specified distance relative to the graphics cursor

Similar Microsoft C Function(s):

_lineto : draws a line from the graphics cursor to a specified point

```
short _far _lineto(short x, short y);
```

Example:

The line function is used in this example to draw a line between two points that bounce around the screen. The color of the line changes every 500 iterations.

Listing 11.43.   The line function

```
#include <graphics.h>
#include <stdio.h>
#include <stdlib.h>
#include <conio.h>

int main ()
{
int gdriver = EGA;
int gmode = EGAHI;
int x1, y1;
int x2, y2;
int x1dir, y1dir;
int x2dir, y2dir;
int color;
int counter;

     /* register EGAVGA_driver and sansserif_font */
     /* ... these have been added to graphics.lib */
     /* as described in UTIL.DOC                   */

registerbgidriver (EGAVGA_driver);
registerbgifont (sansserif_font);

     /* set EGA 16-color high resolution video mode  */

initgraph (&gdriver,&gmode,"");
rectangle (0,0,639,349);

     /* draw line which bounces around on screen */
```

```
x1 = 300;
y1 = 175;
x2 = 300;
y2 = 200;

x1dir = 1;
y1dir = 1;
x2dir = 1;
y2dir = 1;

color = 1;
counter = 0;

do
{
    setcolor (color);
    line (x1,y1,x2,y2);
    if (x1 == 638)
        x1dir = -1;
    if (x1 == 1)
        x1dir = 1;
    if (x2 == 638)
        x2dir = -1;
    if (x2 == 1)
        x2dir = 1;
    if (y1 == 348)
        y1dir = -1;
    if (y1 == 1)
        y1dir = 1;
    if (y2 == 348)
        y2dir = -1;
    if (y2 == 1)
        y2dir = 1;

    x1 = x1 + x1dir;
    x2 = x1 + x2dir;
    y1 = y1 + y1dir;
    y2 = y2 + y2dir;

    counter = counter + 1;

    if (counter == 500)
        {
        counter = 0;
        color = color + 1;
        }

    if (color > 15)
        color = 1;

} while (!kbhit());

    /* Delay and Exit */

closegraph();
return 0;
}
```

linerel

Syntax:
```
void far linerel(int dx, int dy);

int dx, dy;              Relative distance to draw line
```

Function:
The linerel function draws a line a relative distance from the current graphics cursor position.

File(s) to Include:
```
#include <graphics.h>
```

Description:
The linerel function is used to draw a line a predetermined distance and direction from the current position of the graphics cursor. The dx argument specifies the relative number of pixels to travel in the horizontal direction. The dy argument specifies the relative number of pixels to travel in the vertical direction. These arguments can be either positive or negative values. The line is drawn in the current color, line style, and line thickness from the current graphics cursor position through the specified relative distance. When the line is finished, the cursor position is updated to the endpoint of the line. Figure 11.31 illustrates the use of the linerel function.

Figure 11.31. The linerel function

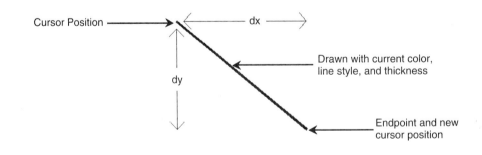

Value(s) Returned:
There is no return value.

Related Function(s):
line   : draws a line between two specified points
lineto   : draws a line from the cursor position to the specified point

Similar Microsoft C Function(s):
_lineto : draws a line from the current graphics cursor position to the specified
           point

```
short _far _lineto(short x, short y);
```

Example:
The linerel function is used to draw several lines (in the shape of an asterisk) relative
to a point that bounces around the screen. The current color changes each time the
asterisk is drawn.

Listing 11.44.   The linerel function

```
#include <graphics.h>
#include <stdio.h>
#include <stdlib.h>
#include <conio.h>

int main ()
{
int gdriver = EGA;
int gmode = EGAHI;
int x, y;
int xdir, ydir;
int color;

     /* register EGAVGA_driver and sansserif_font */
     /* ... these have been added to graphics.lib */
     /* as described in UTIL.DOC                   */

registerbgidriver (EGAVGA_driver);
registerbgifont (sansserif_font);

     /* set EGA 16-color high resolution video mode  */

initgraph (&gdriver,&gmode,"");
rectangle (0,0,639,349);

     /* draw asterisk which bounces around on screen */
```

Listing 11.44.   *continues*

Listing 11.44. cont. The `lineral` function

```
x = 320;
y = 175;

xdir = 1;
ydir = 1;
color = 1;

do
{
     setcolor (color);
     moveto (x,y);
     linerel (0,5);
     linerel (5,5);
     linerel (5,0);
     linerel (0,-5);
     linerel (-5,-5);
     linerel (-5,0);
     linerel (-5,5);
     linerel (5,-5);
     linerel (5,-5);

     if (x == 638)
          xdir = -1;
     if (x == 1)
          xdir = 1;
     if (y == 348)
          ydir = -1;
     if (y == 1)
          ydir = 1;

     x = x + xdir;
     y = y + ydir;

     color = color + 1;

     if (color > 15)
          color = 1;
} while (!kbhit());

     /* Delay and Exit */

closegraph();
return 0;
}
```

lineto

Syntax:
```
void far lineto(int x, int y);

int x, y;                    Endpoint of line
```

Function:

The lineto function draws a line from the current position of the graphics cursor to the point specified by (x, y).

File(s) to Include:

```
#include <graphics.h>
```

Description:

The lineto function is used to draw a line from the current position of the graphics cursor to the point specified by the x and y arguments. The line is drawn using the current color, line style, and line thickness. After the line has been drawn, the graphics cursor position is set to the position specified by the x and y arguments (the endpoint of the line). Figure 11.32 illustrates the use of the lineto function.

Figure 11.32. The lineto function

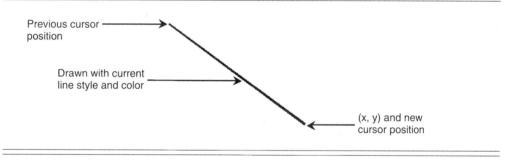

Value(s) Returned:

There is no return value.

Related Function(s):

line   : draws a line between two specified points
linerel : draws a line a relative distance from the graphics cursor

Similar Microsoft C Function(s):

_lineto : draws a line from the current position of the graphics cursor to the specified point

```
short _far _lineto(short x, short y);
```

Example:

The following example uses the `moveto` and `lineto` functions to draw a line between two points that bounce around the screen. The current color changes every 100 iterations.

Listing 11.45. The `lineto` function

```
#include <graphics.h>
#include <stdio.h>
#include <stdlib.h>
#include <conio.h>

int main ()
{
int gdriver = EGA;
int gmode = EGAHI;
int x1, y1;
int x2, y2;
int x1dir, y1dir;
int x2dir, y2dir;
int color;
int counter;

        /* register EGAVGA_driver and sansserif_font */
        /* ... these have been added to graphics.lib */
        /* as described in UTIL.DOC                   */

registerbgidriver (EGAVGA_driver);
registerbgifont (sansserif_font);

        /* set EGA 16-color high resolution video mode  */

initgraph (&gdriver,&gmode,"");
rectangle (0,0,639,349);

        /* draw line which bounces around on screen */

x1 = 100;
y1 = 1;
x2 = 1;
y2 = 130;

x1dir = 1;
y1dir = 1;
x2dir = 1;
y2dir = 1;
color = 1;
counter = 0;

do
{
        setcolor (color);
        moveto (x1,y1);
        lineto (x2,y2);
        if (x1 == 638)
                x1dir = -1;
```

```
        if (x1 == 1)
            x1dir = 1;
        if (x2 == 638)
            x2dir = -1;
        if (x2 == 1)
            x2dir = 1;
        if (y1 == 348)
            y1dir = -1;
        if (y1 == 1)
            y1dir = 1;
        if (y2 == 348)
            y2dir = -1;
        if (y2 == 1)
            y2dir = 1;

        x1 = x1 + x1dir;
        x2 = x1 + x2dir;
        y1 = y1 + y1dir;
        y2 = y2 + y2dir;

        counter = counter + 1;

        if (counter == 100)
            {
            color = color + 1;
            counter = 0;
            }

        if (color > 15)
            color = 1;

    } while (!kbhit());

        /* Delay and Exit */

closegraph();
return 0;
}
```

---

moverel

Syntax:

```
void far moverel(int dx, int dy);

int dx, dy;                     Distance to move cursor
```

Function:

The moverel function moves the graphics cursor a relative distance from the present location.

File(s) to Include:
`#include <graphics.h>`

Description:
The `moverel` function is used to move the position of the graphics cursor a relative distance as specified by the `dx` and `dy` arguments. The `dx` argument defines the relative distance to move in the horizontal direction, while the `dy` argument defines the relative distance to move in the vertical direction. These values can be either positive or negative. No drawing takes place as the cursor is moved. Figure 11.33 illustrates the use of the `moverel` function.

Figure 11.33. The `moverel` function

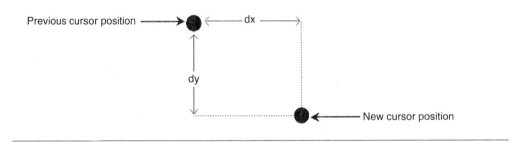

Value(s) Returned:
There is no return value.

Related Function(s):
`moveto` : moves the cursor to the specified point

Similar Microsoft C Function(s):
`_moveto` : moves the graphics cursor to the specified point

`struct xycoord _far _moveto(short x, short y);`

Example:
The following example uses the `moverel` function to move the cursor a relative distance for each iteration. The `lineto` function is used to draw a line from the new cursor position to the center of the screen. The current color changes every 50 iterations.

Listing 11.46. The moverel function

```
#include <graphics.h>
#include <stdio.h>
#include <stdlib.h>
#include <conio.h>

int main ()
{
int gdriver = EGA;
int gmode = EGAHI;
int x, y;
int xdir, ydir;
int color;
int counter;

    /* register EGAVGA_driver and sansserif_font */
    /* ... these have been added to graphics.lib */
    /* as described in UTIL.DOC                   */

registerbgidriver (EGAVGA_driver);
registerbgifont (sansserif_font);

    /* set EGA 16-color high resolution video mode  */

initgraph (&gdriver,&gmode,"");
rectangle (0,0,639,349);

    /* move cursor around screen - draw line to center */

moveto (1,175);

xdir = 1;
ydir = 1;
color = 1;

do
{
    setcolor (color);
    moverel (xdir,ydir);
    x = getx();
    y = gety();
    lineto (320,175);
    moveto (x,y);

    if (x == 638)
        xdir = -1;
    if (x == 1)
        xdir = 1;
    if (y == 348)
        ydir = -1;
    if (y == 1)
        ydir = 1;

    counter = counter + 1;
```

Listing 11.46. *continues*

Listing 11.46. cont.   The `moverel` function

```
        if (counter > 50)
               {
               counter = 0;
               color = color + 1;
               }

        if (color > 15)
               color = 1;

} while (!kbhit());

        /* Delay and Exit */

closegraph();
return 0;
}
```

moveto

Syntax:

```
void far moveto(int x, int y);

int x, y;                        Point to move cursor
```

Function:

The `moveto` function moves the graphics cursor to the specified point.

File(s) to Include:

```
#include <graphics.h>
```

Description:

The `moveto` function is used to place the graphics cursor at the point specified by the x and y arguments. As the cursor is moved from its previous position to the point specified by the x and y arguments, no drawing takes place. Figure 11.34 illustrates the use of the `moveto` function.

Figure 11.34. The moveto function

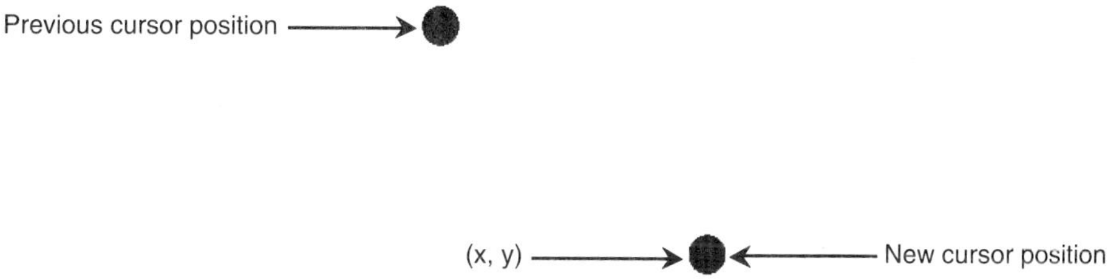

Previous cursor position ———→ ●

(x, y) ———→ ●← ——— New cursor position

Value(s) Returned:
There is no return value.

Related Function(s):
moverel : moves the cursor a relative distance

Similar Microsoft C Function(s):
_moveto : moves the cursor to the specified point

```
struct xycoord _far _moveto(short x, short y);
```

Example:
The moveto function is used in this example to move the cursor to a predetermined point that bounces around the screen. A line is then drawn to the center of the screen with the lineto function. The line color changes every 25 iterations.

Listing 11.47. The moveto function

```
#include <graphics.h>
#include <stdio.h>
#include <stdlib.h>
#include <conio.h>

int main ()
{
int gdriver = EGA;
int gmode = EGAHI;
int x, y;
int xdir, ydir;
int color;
int counter;
```

Listing 11.47. *continues*

Listing 11.47. cont. The move to function

```
        /* register EGAVGA_driver and sansserif_font */
        /* ... these have been added to graphics.lib */
        /* as described in UTIL.DOC                   */

registerbgidriver (EGAVGA_driver);
registerbgifont (sansserif_font);

        /* set EGA 16-color high resolution video mode  */

initgraph (&gdriver,&gmode,"");
rectangle (0,0,639,349);

        /* move cursor around screen - draw line to center */

x = 1;
y = 175;
xdir = 1;
ydir = 1;
color = 1;

do
{
    setcolor (color);
    moveto (x,y);
    lineto (320,175);

    if (x == 638)
        xdir = -1;
    if (x == 1)
        xdir = 1;
    if (y == 348)
        ydir = -1;
    if (y == 1)
        ydir = 1;

    x = x + xdir;
    y = y + ydir;

    counter = counter + 1;

    if (counter > 25)
        {
        counter = 0;
        color = color + 1;
        }

    if (color > 15)
        color = 1;

} while (!kbhit());

        /* Delay and Exit */

closegraph();
return 0;
}
```

outtext

Syntax:
```
void far outtext(char far *textstring);

char far *textstring;          String to Display
```

Function:
The outtext function displays a text string at the current graphics cursor position.

File(s) to Include:
```
#include <graphics.h>
```

Description:
The outtext function is used to display a text string. The *textstring argument defines the text string to display. The text string is displayed at the current graphics cursor position using the current color and text font, direction, settings, and justifications. The cursor position remains unchanged unless the current horizontal justification is LEFT_TEXT and the text direction is HORIZ_DIR. When this is the case, the cursor position is positioned horizontally the pixel width of the text string. In addition, when using the default font, any text that extends outside the current viewport is truncated.

Although the outtext function is designed for unformatted text, formatted text can be displayed through the use of a character buffer and the sprintf function. This method of displaying formatted text with the outtext and outtextxy functions is demonstrated in many of the examples in this chapter.

Value(s) Returned:
There is no return value.

Related Function(s):
outtextxy : displays a string at the specified location

Similar Microsoft C Function(s):
_outtext : displays a string at the text cursor position

```
void _far _outtext(unsigned char _far *text);
```

_outgtext : displays a string at the graphics cursor position

```
void _far _outgtext(unsigned char _far *text);
```

Example:

The outtext function is used in this example to display both vertical and horizontal text using the sans serif font.

Listing 11.48. The outtext function

```
#include <graphics.h>
#include <stdio.h>
#include <stdlib.h>
#include <conio.h>

int main ()
{
int gdriver = EGA;
int gmode = EGAHI;

        /* register EGAVGA_driver and sansserif_font */
        /* ... these have been added to graphics.lib */
        /* as described in UTIL.DOC                   */

registerbgidriver (EGAVGA_driver);
registerbgifont (sansserif_font);

        /* set EGA 16-color high resolution video mode  */

initgraph (&gdriver,&gmode,"");
rectangle (0,0,639,349);

        /* display text using outtext function */

settextstyle (SANS_SERIF_FONT,HORIZ_DIR,2);
settextjustify (CENTER_TEXT,CENTER_TEXT);

moveto (320,175);
outtext ("Horizontal Text");

settextstyle (SANS_SERIF_FONT,VERT_DIR,2);
moveto (20,175);
outtext ("Vertical Text");
moveto (619,175);
outtext ("Vertical Text");

        /* Delay and Exit */

settextstyle (SANS_SERIF_FONT,HORIZ_DIR,2);
settextjustify(CENTER_TEXT,BOTTOM_TEXT);
outtextxy (320,320,"Press Any Key To Exit");

getch ();
closegraph();
return 0;
}
```

outtextxy

Syntax:
```
void far outtextxy(int x, int y, char far *textstring);

int x, y;                  Location to place text
char far *textstring;      String to display
```

Function:
The outtextxy function is used to display a text string at the specified location.

File(s) to Include:
```
#include <graphics.h>
```

Description:
The outtextxy function is used to display a text string. The *textstring argument defines the text string to display. The text string is displayed at the position specified in the x and y arguments using the current color and text font, direction, settings, and justifications. When using the default font, any text that extends outside the current viewport is truncated.

Although the outtextxy function is designed for unformatted text, formatted text can be displayed through the use of a character buffer and the sprintf function. This method of displaying formatted text with the outtext and outtextxy functions is demonstrated in many of the examples in this chapter.

Value(s) Returned:
There is no return value.

Related Function(s):
outtext : displays text at the graphics cursor position

Similar Microsoft C Function(s):
_outtext : displays text at the text cursor position

```
void _far _outtext(unsigned char _far *text);
```

_outgtext : displays text at the graphics cursor position

```
void _far _outgtext(unsigned char _far *text);
```

Example:

This example uses the `outtextxy` function to display both vertical and horizontal text using the sans serif font.

Listing 11.49. The `outtextxy` function

```
#include <graphics.h>
#include <stdio.h>
#include <stdlib.h>
#include <conio.h>

int main ()
{
int gdriver = EGA;
int gmode = EGAHI;

    /* register EGAVGA_driver and sansserif_font */
    /* ... these have been added to graphics.lib */
    /* as described in UTIL.DOC                   */

registerbgidriver (EGAVGA_driver);
registerbgifont (sansserif_font);

    /* set EGA 16-color high resolution video mode   */

initgraph (&gdriver,&gmode,"");
rectangle (0,0,639,349);

    /* display text using outtextxy function */

settextstyle (SANS_SERIF_FONT,HORIZ_DIR,2);
settextjustify (CENTER_TEXT,CENTER_TEXT);
outtextxy (320,175,"Horizontal Text");

settextstyle (SANS_SERIF_FONT,VERT_DIR,2);
outtextxy (20,175,"Vertical Text");
outtextxy (619,175,"Vertical Text");

    /* Delay and Exit */

settextstyle (SANS_SERIF_FONT,HORIZ_DIR,2);
settextjustify(CENTER_TEXT,BOTTOM_TEXT);
outtextxy (320,320,"Press Any Key To Exit");

getch ();

closegraph();
return 0;
}
```

pieslice

Syntax:
```
void far pieslice(int x, int y, int startangle,
                  int endangle, int radius);

int x, y;                 Center of pie
int startangle;           Starting angle
int endangle;             Ending angle
int radius;               Radius of pie
```

Function:
The pieslice function draws a filled circular pie slice.

File(s) to Include:
```
#include <graphics.h>
```

Description:
The pieslice function is used to draw and fill a circular pic slice. The pie slice is centered at the point specified by the x and y arguments. The circular portion of the pie begins at the angle specified by the startangle argument and is drawn in a counterclockwise direction until it reaches the angle specified by the endangle argument. The pie slice is outlined in the current color and is filled with the current fill pattern and fill color. The pieslice function uses east (extending to the right of center in the horizontal direction) as its 0 degree reference point. Figure 11.35 illustrates the use of the pieslice function.

Value(s) Returned:
There is no return value.

Related Function(s):
```
arc     : draws a circular arc
sector  : draws a filled elliptical pie slice
```

Similar Microsoft C Function(s):
```
_pie : draws a pie-like wedge

short _far _pie(short fillflag, short x1, short y1,
                short x2, short y2, short x3,
                short y3, short x4, short y4);
```

Figure 11.35. The pieslice function

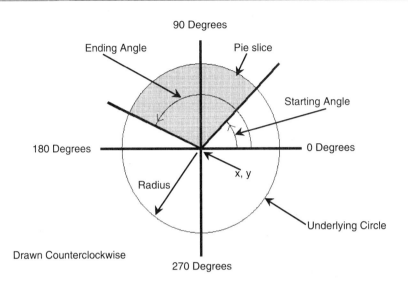

Example:

The pieslice function is used in this example to create a five-slice pie chart. Each wedge is filled with a different fill pattern. (See Listing 11.50 and Figure 11.36.)

Listing 11.50. The pieslice function

```
#include <graphics.h>
#include <stdio.h>
#include <stdlib.h>
#include <conio.h>

int main ()
{
int gdriver = EGA;
int gmode = EGAHI;

    /* register EGAVGA_driver and sansserif_font */
    /* ... these have been added to graphics.lib */
    /* as described in UTIL.DOC                   */

registerbgidriver (EGAVGA_driver);
registerbgifont (sansserif_font);

    /* set EGA 16-color high resolution video mode  */

initgraph (&gdriver,&gmode,"");
```

```
rectangle (0,0,639,349);

    /* draw a pie chart using various fill patterns */

setfillstyle (SOLID_FILL, 15);
pieslice (320,175,0,45,150);

setfillstyle (WIDE_DOT_FILL, 15);
pieslice (320,175,45,135,150);

setfillstyle (SLASH_FILL, 15);
pieslice (320,175,135,195,150);

setfillstyle (HATCH_FILL, 15);
pieslice (320,175,195,275,150);

setfillstyle (EMPTY_FILL, 15);
pieslice (320,175,275,360,150);

    /* Delay and Exit */

settextjustify(CENTER_TEXT,BOTTOM_TEXT);
outtextxy (320,320,"Press Any Key To Exit");

getch ();
closegraph();
return 0;
}
```

Figure 11.36. Screen output from Listing 11.50

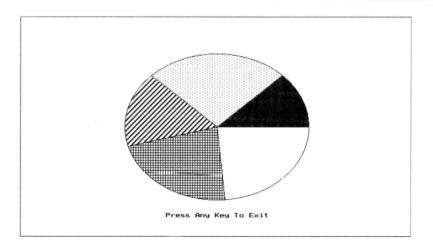

putimage

Syntax:
```
void far putimage(int left, int top, void far *image,
                  int action);

int left, top;          Upper left corner of image
void far *image;        Image buffer
int action;             Method used to place image
```

Function:
The putimage function places a stored image on the screen.

File(s) to Include:
```
#include <graphics.h>
```

Description:
The putimage function places an image that was previously stored by the getimage function onto the screen. The left and top arguments define the position to place the upper left corner of the image. The *image argument points to the memory where the image is stored. The image is placed on the screen with the action defined in the action argument. Table 11.18 describes the values and constants used for the action argument.

Table 11.18. *Operators for the putimage function*

Constant	Value	Meaning
COPY_PUT	0	Overwrite existing pixels
XOR_PUT	1	Exclusive OR pixels
OR_PUT	2	Inclusive OR pixels
AND_PUT	3	AND Pixels
NOT_PUT	4	Invert image

Value(s) Returned:
There is no return value.

Related Function(s):
getimage   : stores a rectangular image in memory
imagesize : determines the number of bytes required to store an image

Similar Microsoft C Function(s):

_putimage : places an image on the screen

```
void _far _putimage(short x, short y, char _huge *image,
                    short action);
```

Example:

The example in Listing 11.51 and Figure 11.37 uses the putimage function to place a stored rectangular image on the screen in three rows.

Listing 11.51. The putimage function

```
#include <graphics.h>
#include <stdio.h>
#include <stdlib.h>
#include <conio.h>

int main ()
{
int gdriver = EGA;
int gmode = EGAHI;
void *image;
unsigned int imsize;
int x;

    /* register EGAVGA_driver and sansserif_font */
    /* ... these have been added to graphics.lib */
    /* as described in UTIL.DOC                   */

registerbgidriver(EGAVGA_driver);
registerbgifont(sansserif_font);

    /* set EGA high-resolution 16-color mode */

initgraph (&gdriver,&gmode,"");
rectangle (0,0,639,349);

    /* draw and store an image - then place it */
    /* on the screen                           */

setfillstyle(SOLID_FILL,14);
bar (280,135,360,215);
setfillstyle(SOLID_FILL,1);
fillellipse(320,175,40,40);

imsize = imagesize(280,135,360,215);
image = malloc(imsize);
getimage(280,135,360,215,image);

cleardevice ();
rectangle (0,0,639,349);
```

Listing 11.51. *continues*

401

Listing 11.51. cont.   The `putimage` function

```
for (x=30; x<550; x=x+60)
{
     putimage (x,20,image,COPY_PUT);
     putimage (x,120,image,COPY_PUT);
     putimage (x,220,image,COPY_PUT);
}

     /* Delay and Exit */

settextjustify(CENTER_TEXT,BOTTOM_TEXT);
outtextxy (320,320,"Press Any Key To Exit");

getch ();

closegraph();
return 0;
}
```

Figure 11.37.   Screen output from Listing 11.51

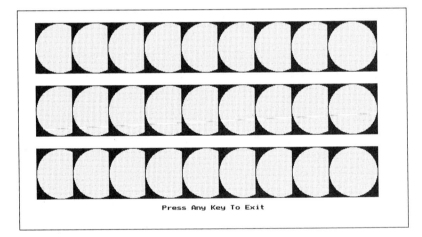

Press Any Key To Exit

putpixel

Syntax:
```
void far putpixel(int x, int y, int color);

int x, y;                    Coordinates of pixel
int color;                   Desired color
```

Function:

The `putpixel` function sets the specified pixel to the specified color.

File(s) to Include:

```
#include <graphics.h>
```

Description:

The `putpixel` function is uscd to set a particular pixel to a certain color. The position of the target pixel is specified by the x and y arguments. The `color` argument specifies the color value for the pixel.

Value(s) Returned:

There is no return value.

Related Function(s):

`getpixel` : gets the color of the specified pixel

Similar Microsoft C Function(s):

`_setpixel` : sets the specified pixel to the current color

```
short _far _setpixel(short x, short y);
```

Example:

This example uses the `getpixel` function to evaluate each pixel on the screen. If the pixel color is blue, the `putpixel` function is used to change it to red. Similarly, the `putpixel` function can be used to change red pixels to blue.

Listing 11.52. The `putpixel` function

```
#include <graphics.h>
#include <stdio.h>
#include <stdlib.h>
#include <conio.h>

int main ()
{
int gdriver = EGA;
int gmode = EGAHI;
int x,y;
int color;

    /* register EGAVGA_driver and sansserif_font */
    /* ... these have been added to graphics.lib */
    /* as described in UTIL.DOC                   */
```

Listing 11.52. *continues*

403

Listing 11.52. cont.   The `putpixel` function

```
registerbgidriver(EGAVGA_driver);
registerbgifont(sansserif_font);

      /* set EGA high-resolution 16-color mode */

initgraph (&gdriver,&gmode,"");
rectangle (0,0,639,349);

setfillstyle (SOLID_FILL,1);
bar (1,1,638,348);
setfillstyle (SOLID_FILL,4);
fillellipse (320,175,200,75);

      /* evaluate each pixel on the screen */
      /* switch pixel colors blue and red   */

for (x = 0;  x <640;  x = x+1)
      {
      for (y = 0;  y < 350;  y = y + 1)
          {
          color = getpixel (x,y);
          if (color == 1)
              putpixel (x,y,4);
          if (color == 4)
              putpixel (x,y,1);
          }
      }

      /* Delay and Exit */

settextjustify(CENTER_TEXT,BOTTOM_TEXT);
outtextxy (320,320,"Press Any Key To Exit");

getch ();
closegraph();
return 0;
}
```

rectangle

Syntax:
```
void far rectangle(int left, int top, int right,
                   int bottom);

int left, top;          Upper left corner of rectangle
int right, bottom;      Lower right corner of rectangle
```

Function:

The rectangle function draws a rectangle with the specified opposing corners.

File(s) to Include:

```
#include <graphics.h>
```

Description:

The rectangle function is used to create an unfilled rectangle using the current color. The upper left corner of the rectangle is specified by the left and top arguments. These arguments represent the x and y coordinates of the upper left corner. Similarly, the right and bottom arguments are used to specify the lower right corner of the rectangle. The borders of the rectangle are drawn using the current line style and thickness. Figure 11.38 illustrates the use of the rectangle function.

Figure 11.38. The rectangle function

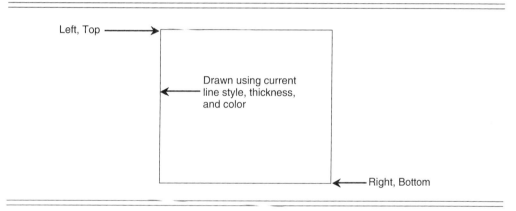

Value(s) Returned:

There is no return value.

Related Function(s):

```
bar    : draws a two-dimensional bar
bar3d  : draws a three-dimensional bar
```

Similar Microsoft C Function(s):

```
_rectangle : draws a rectangle

short _far _rectangle(short fillflag, short x1, short y1,
                      short x2, short y2);
```

Example:

The rectangle function is used in this example to create a series of rectangles with varying corner points.

Listing 11.53. The rectangle function

```
#include <graphics.h>
#include <stdio.h>
#include <stdlib.h>
#include <conio.h>

int main ()
{
int gdriver = EGA;
int gmode = EGAHI;
int x1,y1;
int x2,y2;
int color = 1;

        /* register EGAVGA_driver and sansserif_font */
        /* ... these have been added to graphics.lib */
        /* as described in UTIL.DOC                   */

registerbgidriver (EGAVGA_driver);
registerbgifont (sansserif_font);

        /* set EGA 16-color high resolution video mode   */

initgraph (&gdriver,&gmode,"");
rectangle (0,0,639,349);

        /* draw a series of multi-colored rectangles */

x1 = 0;
y1 = 0;
x2 = 639;
y2 = 349;

for (x1 = 0; x1 < x2; x1 = x1 + 1)
        {
        setcolor (color);
        rectangle (x1,y1,x2,y2);
        color = color + 1;
        if (color > 15)
                color = 1;
        x2 = x2 - 1;
        y1 = y1 + 1;
        y2 = y2 - 1;
        }

        /* Delay and Exit */

setcolor (0);
settextjustify(CENTER_TEXT,CENTER_TEXT);
outtextxy (320,320,"Press Any Key To Exit");
```

```
getch ();

closegraph();
return 0;
}
```

registerbgidriver

Syntax:
```
int registerbgidriver(void (*driver)(void));

void (*driver)(void);              Driver included during link
```

Function:
The `registerbgidriver` function registers a user-loaded or linked graphics driver code.

File(s) to Include:
```
#include <graphics.h>
```

Description:
The `registerbgidriver` function is used to load and register a graphics driver. The `*driver` argument points to the driver. A registered driver file can either be loaded from the disk or converted into `.OBJ` form and linked-in to the program. The examples in this chapter use the `registerbgidriver` function to register the `EGAVGA_driver`. However, before this could be done, the `EGAVGA.BGI` file had to be converted to `.OBJ` form and added to the `graphics.lib` file. This process is described in the `UTIL.DOC` file included with the Turbo C++ distribution disks. By registering the driver in this way, the `.EXE` file is not dependent on an external driver file to run.

Value(s) Returned:
The `registerbgidriver` function returns the driver number when it is successful. An error code, a negative number, is returned if the specified driver is invalid.

Related Function(s):
`installuserdriver` : installs a vendor-added device driver

Similar Microsoft C Function(s):
There are no similar Microsoft C functions.

Example:

The registerbgidriver function is used in this example to register the EGAVGA_driver. The driver name is then retrieved and displayed.

Listing 11.54. The registerbgidriver function

```
#include <graphics.h>
#include <stdio.h>
#include <stdlib.h>
#include <conio.h>

int main ()
{
int gdriver = EGA;
int gmode = EGAHI;
char *drivername;

      /* register EGAVGA_driver and sansserif_font */
      /* ... these have been added to graphics.lib */
      /* as described in UTIL.DOC                  */

registerbgidriver (EGAVGA_driver);
registerbgifont (sansserif_font);

      /* set EGA 16-color high resolution video mode  */

initgraph (&gdriver,&gmode,"");
rectangle (0,0,639,349);

      /* get and display the current driver */

drivername = getdrivername();

settextjustify (CENTER_TEXT,CENTER_TEXT);
outtextxy (320,125,"Driver Name Is :");
outtextxy (320,150,drivername);

      /* Delay and Exit */

settextjustify(CENTER_TEXT,BOTTOM_TEXT);
outtextxy (320,320,"Press Any Key To Exit");

getch ();

closegraph();
return 0;
}
```

registerbgifont

Syntax:
```
int registerbgifont(void (*font)(void));

void (*font)(void);           Font included during link
```

Function:
The `registerbgifont` function registers a linked font code.

File(s) to Include:
```
#include <graphics.h>
```

Description:
The `registerbgifont` is used to inform the system that the font pointed to by the `*font` argument was included during linking. The examples in this chapter use the `registerbgifont` function to register the `sansserif_font`. In order to do this, the `SANS.BGI` file had to be converted to `.OBJ` form and added to the `graphics.lib` file. This process is described in `UTIL.DOC`, which is included in the Borland C++ distribution disks. By registering the font file in this way, the `.EXE` file is not dependent on any outside files for proper execution.

Value(s) Returned:
If successful, the font number of the registered font is returned. If unsuccessful, an error code, a negative value, is returned.

Related Function(s):
`installuserfont` : loads a non-BGI font

Similar Microsoft C Function(s):
`_registerfont` : registers the font files specified

```
short _far _registerfonts(unsigned char _far *pathname);
```

Example:
The `registerbgifont` function is used in this example to register the `sansserif_font`. This font is then selected and used to display the various text settings.

Listing 11.55. The `registerbgifont` function

```c
#include <graphics.h>
#include <stdio.h>
#include <stdlib.h>
#include <conio.h>

int main ()
{
struct textsettingstype textset;
int gdriver = EGA;
int gmode = EGAHI;
char buffer [40];

     /* register EGAVGA_driver and sansserif_font */
     /* ... these have been added to graphics.lib */
     /* as described in UTIL.DOC                  */

registerbgidriver (EGAVGA_driver);
registerbgifont (sansserif_font);

     /* set EGA 16-color high resolution video mode  */

initgraph (&gdriver,&gmode,"");
rectangle (0,0,639,349);

     /* set, get, and display text settings */

settextstyle(SANS_SERIF_FONT,HORIZ_DIR,2);
settextjustify(CENTER_TEXT,CENTER_TEXT);

gettextsettings(&textset);

sprintf (buffer,"Font Value : %d",textset.font);
outtextxy (320,75,buffer);

sprintf (buffer,"Text Direction : %d",textset.direction);
outtextxy (320,125,buffer);

sprintf (buffer,"Character Size : %d",textset.charsize);
outtextxy (320,175,buffer);

sprintf (buffer,"Horizontal Justification : %d",textset.horiz);
outtextxy (320,225,buffer);

sprintf (buffer,"Vertical Justification : %d",textset.vert);
outtextxy (320,275,buffer);

     /* Delay and Exit */

settextjustify(CENTER_TEXT,BOTTOM_TEXT);
outtextxy (320,320,"Press Any Key To Exit");

getch ();

closegraph();
return 0;
}
```

restorecrtmode

Syntax:
```
void far restorecrtmode(void);
```

Function:
The restorecrtmode function restores the video system to the original mode set prior to the call of the initgraph function.

File(s) to Include:
```
#include <graphics.h>
```

Description:
The restorecrtmode function is used to reset the video graphics mode to the mode in use prior to the initialization of the graphics system. This function is often used with the setgraphmode function to switch between graphics and text modes as shown in the following example.

Value(s) Returned:
There is no return value.

Related Function(s):
initgraph : initializes the graphics environment

Similar Microsoft C Function(s):
_setvideomode : initializes and resets the video subsystem

```
short _far _setvideomode (short mode);
```

Example:
The restorecrtmode function is used in this example to set the video mode to the default text mode. The setgraphmode function is then used to restore the system to graphics mode.

Listing 11.56. The restorecrtmode function

```
#include <graphics.h>
#include <stdio.h>
#include <stdlib.h>
#include <conio.h>
```

Listing 11.56. *continues*

411

Listing 11.56. cont.   The `restorecrtmode` function

```
int main ()
{
int gdriver = EGA;
int gmode = EGAHI;

     /* register EGAVGA_driver and sansserif_font */
     /* ... these have been added to graphics.lib */
     /* as described in UTIL.DOC                   */

registerbgidriver (EGAVGA_driver);
registerbgifont (sansserif_font);

     /* set EGA 16-color high resolution video mode  */

initgraph (&gdriver,&gmode,"");
rectangle (0,0,639,349);

     /* press a key to go to text mode */

settextjustify (CENTER_TEXT,CENTER_TEXT);
outtextxy (320,175,"Press a key to go to text mode");
getch ();
restorecrtmode ();

     /* press another key to go back to graphics mode */

printf ("Press a key to go back to graphics mode");
getch ();
setgraphmode (gmode);
rectangle (0,0,639,349);

     /* Delay and Exit */

settextjustify(CENTER_TEXT,BOTTOM_TEXT);
outtextxy (320,320,"Press Any Key To Exit");

getch ();
closegraph();
return 0;
}
```

sector

Syntax:

```
void far sector (int x, int y, int startangle, int endangle,
                 int xradius, int yradius);
```

```
int x, y;                       Center of pie
int startangle;                 Starting angle
int endangle;                   Ending angle
int xradius;                    Radius about x axis
int yradius;                    Radius about y axis
```

Function:
The sector function draws a filled elliptical pie slice.

File(s) to Include:
#include <graphics.h>

Description:
The sector function is used to create an elliptical pie slice. The resulting pie slice is centered at the point specified by the x and y arguments. The elliptical arc of the pie slice begins at the angle specified by the startangle argument and is drawn in a counterclockwise direction until the angle specified by the endangle argument is reached. The radius of the elliptical arc is specified by the xradius argument for the horizontal radius and the yradius argument for the vertical radius. The pie slice is outlined using the current color and filled with the current fill pattern and fill color. Figure 11.39 illustrates the use of the sector function.

Figure 11.39. The sector function

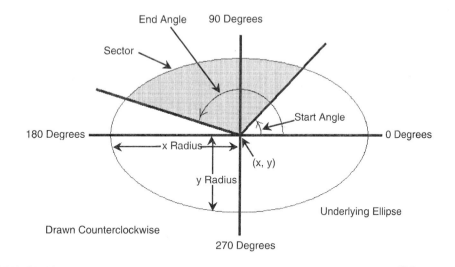

Value(s) Returned:
There is no return value.

Related Function(s):

ellipse : draws an elliptical arc
pieslice : draws a filled circular pie slice

Similar Microsoft C Function(s):

_pie : draws a wedge-like pie slice

```
short _far _pie(short fillflag, short x1, short y1,
                short x2, short y2, short x3,
                short y3, short x4, short y4);
```

Example:

The sector function is used in this example to create a five-wedge elliptical pie chart.
Each wedge is filled with a different fill pattern. (See Listing 11.57 and Figure 11.40.)

Listing 11.57. The sector function

```
#include <graphics.h>
#include <stdio.h>
#include <stdlib.h>
#include <conio.h>

int main ()
{
int gdriver = EGA;
int gmode = EGAHI;

        /* register EGAVGA_driver and sansserif_font */
        /* ... these have been added to graphics.lib */
        /* as described in UTIL.DOC                   */

registerbgidriver (EGAVGA_driver);
registerbgifont (sansserif_font);

        /* set EGA 16-color high resolution video mode  */

initgraph (&gdriver,&gmode,"");
rectangle (0,0,639,349);

        /* draw an elliptical pie chart  */
        /* using various fill patterns   */

setfillstyle (SOLID_FILL, 15);
sector (320,175,0,45,250,125);

setfillstyle (WIDE_DOT_FILL, 15);
sector (320,175,45,135,250,125);

setfillstyle (SLASH_FILL, 15);
sector (320,175,135,195,250,125);
```

```
setfillstyle (HATCH_FILL, 15);
sector (320,175,195,275,250,125);

setfillstyle (EMPTY_FILL, 15);
sector (320,175,275,360,250,125);

    /* Delay and Exit */

settextjustify(CENTER_TEXT,BOTTOM_TEXT);
outtextxy (320,320,"Press Any Key To Exit");

getch ();

closegraph();
return 0;
}
```

Figure 11.40. Screen output from Listing 11.57

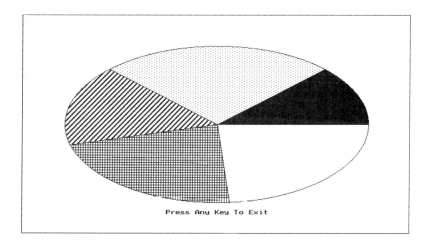

setactivepage

Syntax:
```
void far setactivepage(int page);

int page;                          Page number
```

Function:
The setactivepage function sets the *active page*, or section of memory, where all subsequent graphics output is sent.

File(s) to Include:

```
#include <graphics.h>
```

Description:

The `setactivepage` function is used to specify the page number that represents the section of video memory where all graphics output is sent. This section of memory is called the active page. The page argument specifies the active page number. In order to use this function effectively, your video adapter must be EGA or VGA and have sufficient memory to support multiple pages of graphics. This function is used with the `setvisualpage` function to draw on nonvisual pages and to create animation.

Value(s) Returned:

There is no return value.

Related Function(s):

`setvisualpage` : sets the visual page

Similar Microsoft C Function(s):

`_setactivepage` : sets the active page

```
short _far _setactivepage(short page);
```

Example:

The `setactivepage` function is used in this example to send all graphics output to a nonvisual page. The `setvisualpage` function is then used to display the page.

Listing 11.58. The `setactivepage` function

```
#include <graphics.h>
#include <stdio.h>
#include <stdlib.h>
#include <conio.h>

int main ()
{
int gdriver = EGA;
int gmode = EGAHI;
int activepage;
int visualpage;
int holder;
int ch;

    /* register EGAVGA_driver and sansserif_font */
    /* ... these have been added to graphics.lib */
    /* as described in UTIL.DOC                   */
```

```
registerbgidriver (EGAVGA_driver);
registerbgifont (sansserif_font);

    /* set EGA 16-color high resolution video mode  */

initgraph (&gdriver,&gmode,"");
rectangle (0,0,639,349);

    /* draw figure and message on two pages of EGA   */
    /* video memory - pressing a key will switch     */
    /* visual and active pages until ESC is presssed */

activepage = 1;
visualpage = 0;

setactivepage (activepage);
setvisualpage (visualpage);

setbkcolor (1);
cleardevice();
setfillstyle (SOLID_FILL,4);
bar (100,50,540,250);
settextjustify (CENTER_TEXT,CENTER_TEXT);
outtextxy (320,310,"PAGE ONE - PRESS ANY KEY TO CHANGE PAGE");
outtextxy (320,330,"PRESS ESC TO EXIT");

holder = activepage;
activepage = visualpage;
visualpage = holder;
setactivepage (activepage);
setvisualpage (visualpage);

cleardevice ();
fillellipse (320,150,220,100);
outtextxy (320,310,"PAGE ZERO - PRESS ANY KEY TO CHANGE PAGE");
outtextxy (320,330,"PRESS ESC TO EXIT");

do
{
    holder = activepage;
    activepage = visualpage;
    visualpage = holder;
    setactivepage (activepage);
    setvisualpage (visualpage);
    ch = getch ();
} while (ch != 27);

    /* Exit */

closegraph();
return 0;
}
```

setallpalette

Syntax:
```
void far setallpalette(struct palettetype far *palette);

struct palettetype far *palette;    New palette colors
```

Function:
The `setallpalette` function resets all the current palette colors to those specified.

File(s) to Include:
```
#include <graphics.h>
```

Description:
The `setallpalette` function is used to set the current palette to the palette defined in the structure of `palettetype` that is pointed to by the `*palette` argument. All the colors of the current palette are set to those defined in the `palettetype` structure. The syntax for the `palettetype` structure is:

```
#define MAXCOLORS 15

struct palettetype
    {
    unsigned char size;
    signed char color[MAXCOLORS + 1];
    };
```

The `size` member of the structure defines the number of colors in the current palette. The `colors` member is an array of color values for the palette. If the entry for any element of the array is set to -1, the color value of that element will not change. Note that all changes to the palette are immediately visible and that the `setallpalette` function should not be used with the IBM-8514 driver. Tables 11.19 and 11.20 list the predefined palettes for the CGA and EGA/VGA drivers.

Table 11.19.   *CGA color table*

Constant	Value
BLACK	0
BLUE	1
GREEN	2
CYAN	3
RED	4

Constant	Value
MAGENTA	5
BROWN	6
LIGHTGRAY	7
DARKGRAY	8
LIGHTBLUE	9
LIGHTGREEN	10
LIGHTCYAN	11
LIGHTRED	12
LIGHTMAGENTA	13
YELLOW	14
WHITE	15

Table 11.20. *EGA/VGA color table*

Constant	Value
EGA_BLACK	0
EGA_BLUE	1
EGA_GREEN	2
EGA_CYAN	3
EGA_RED	4
EGA_MAGENTA	5
EGA_LIGHTGRAY	7
EGA_BROWN	20
EGA_DARKGRAY	56
EGA_LIGHTBLUE	57
EGA_LIGHTGREEN	58
EGA_LIGHTCYAN	59
EGA_LIGHTRED	60
EGA_LIGHTMAGENTA	61
EGA_YELLOW	62
EGA_WHITE	63

Value(s) Returned:
If the passed values are invalid, a value of -11 is returned and the palette is unchanged.

Related Function(s):
setpalette : resets one color in the palette

Similar Microsoft C Function(s):
_remapallpalette : resets the entire palette

```
short _far _remapallpalette(long _far *colors);
```

Example:
This example uses the setallpalette function to invert the current palette. For example, colors 0 and 15 are switched, 1 and 14, etc.

Listing 11.59. The setallpalette function

```
#include <graphics.h>
#include <stdio.h>
#include <stdlib.h>
#include <conio.h>

int main ()
{
struct palettetype palette;
int gdriver = EGA;
int gmode = EGAHI;
int y, color;
char buffer[40];

      /* register EGAVGA_driver and sansserif_font */
      /* ... these have been added to graphics.lib */
      /* as described in UTIL.DOC               */

registerbgidriver(EGAVGA_driver);
registerbgifont(sansserif_font);

      /* set EGA high-resolution 16-color mode */

initgraph (&gdriver,&gmode,"");
rectangle (0,0,639,349);

      /* get and change palette information */

getpalette (&palette);
y = 20;

for (color = 1; color < 16; color = color + 1)
{
      setcolor (palette.colors[color]);
```

```
        line (20,y,620,y);
        y = y + 20;
}

settextjustify (CENTER_TEXT,CENTER_TEXT);
outtextxy (320,300,"PRESS ANY KEY TO MODIFY PALETTE");
getch ();

palette.colors[0] = EGA_WHITE;
palette.colors[1] = EGA_YELLOW;
palette.colors[2] = EGA_LIGHTMAGENTA;
palette.colors[3] = EGA_LIGHTRED;
palette.colors[4] = EGA_LIGHTCYAN;
palette.colors[5] = EGA_LIGHTGREEN;
palette.colors[6] = EGA_LIGHTBLUE;
palette.colors[7] = EGA_DARKGRAY;
palette.colors[8] = EGA_BROWN;
palette.colors[9] = EGA_LIGHTGRAY;
palette.colors[10] = EGA_MAGENTA;
palette.colors[11] = EGA_RED;
palette.colors[12] = EGA_CYAN;
palette.colors[13] = EGA_GREEN;
palette.colors[14] = EGA_BLUE;
palette.colors[15] = EGA_BLACK;

setallpalette(&palette);

    /* Delay and Exit */

settextjustify(CENTER_TEXT,CENTER_TEXT);
outtextxy (320,320,"Press Any Key To Exit");

getch ();

closegraph();
return 0;
}
```

setaspectratio

Syntax:
```
void far setaspectratio(int xaspect, int yaspect);

int xaspect;            Horizontal (x) aspect ratio
int yaspect;            Vertical (y) aspect ratio
```

Function:
The setaspectratio function modifies the default aspect ratio for the current mode.

File(s) to Include:
```
#include <graphics.h>
```

421

Description:

The setaspectratio function is used to modify the aspect ratio for the current screen mode. The aspect ratio is used by the graphics system to calculate circles and arcs. Therefore, the altering of the aspect ratio will affect the output of these functions. The getaspectratio function can be used to retrieve the default settings of the current mode prior to modifying them.

Value(s) Returned:

There is no return value.

Related Function(s):

getaspectratio : gets the current aspect ratio

Similar Microsoft C Function(s):

There are no similar Microsoft C functions.

Example:

The setaspectratio function is used in this example to modify the x and y aspect ratios of the screen. Therefore, the circles that are drawn are not circular. (See Listing 11.60 and Figure 11.41.)

Listing 11.60. The setaspectratio function

```
#include <graphics.h>
#include <stdio.h>
#include <stdlib.h>
#include <conio.h>

int main ()
{
int gdriver = EGA;
int gmode = EGAHI;
int width, radius;
int style, pattern;
int xaspect, yaspect;

        /* register EGAVGA_driver and sansserif_font */
        /* ... these have been added to graphics.lib */
        /* as described in UTIL.DOC                   */

registerbgidriver(EGAVGA_driver);
registerbgifont(sansserif_font);

        /* set EGA high-resolution 16-color mode   */
```

```
initgraph (&gdriver,&gmode,"");
rectangle (0,0,639,349);

     /* get old and set new aspect ratios */
     /* circles will not be round          */

getaspectratio (&xaspect,&yaspect);

setaspectratio ((xaspect * 2), yaspect);

     /* Draw a series of concentric circles  */
     /* with wide line thickness             */

style = SOLID_LINE;
pattern = 1;
width = THICK_WIDTH;

for (radius = 150; radius != 0; radius = radius - 25)
     {
     setlinestyle (style,pattern,width);
     circle (320,175,radius);
     }

     /* Draw circles in the four corners using */
     /* normal width line thickness            */

width = NORM_WIDTH;

for (radius = 30; radius != 0; radius = radius - 5)
     {
     setlinestyle (style,pattern,width);
     circle (50,50,radius);
     circle (50,299,radius);
     circle (589,50,radius);
     circle (589,299,radius);
     }

     /* Delay and Exit */

settextjustify(CENTER_TEXT,BOTTOM_TEXT);
outtextxy (320,320,"Press Any Key To Exit");

getch ();

closegraph();
return 0;
}
```

Figure 11.41. Screen output from Listing 11.60

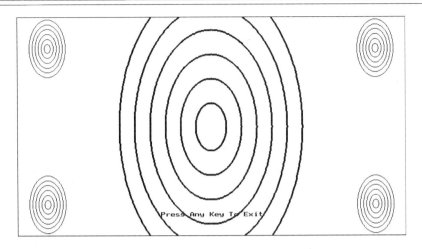

setbkcolor

Syntax:

```
void far setbkcolor(int color);

int color;                    Desired color
```

Function:

The setbkcolor function sets the background color to the specified color.

File(s) to Include:

```
#include <graphics.h>
```

Description:

The setbkcolor function sets the background color to the color value specified in the color argument. Table 11.21 lists the predefined constants and values available for the color argument.

Value(s) Returned:

There is no return value.

Table 11.21. *Background colors*

Constant	Value
BLACK	0
BLUE	1
GREEN	2
CYAN	3
RED	4
MAGENTA	5
BROWN	6
LIGHTGRAY	7
DARKGRAY	8
LIGHTBLUE	9
LIGHTGREEN	10
LIGHTCYAN	11
LIGHTRED	12
LIGHTMAGENTA	13
YELLOW	14
WHITE	15

Related Function(s):

`getbkcolor` : gets the current background color

Similar Microsoft C Function(s):

`_setbkcolor` : sets the background color

```
long _far _setbkcolor(long color);
```

Example:

This example uses the `setbkcolor` function to set the background color to blue. This background color is then retrieved and displayed on the screen.

Listing 11.61. The `setbkcolor` function

```c
#include <graphics.h>
#include <stdio.h>
#include <stdlib.h>
#include <conio.h>

int main ()
{
int gdriver = EGA;
int gmode = EGAHI;
int background;
char buffer [40];

        /* register EGAVGA_driver and sansserif_font */
        /* ... these have been added to graphics.lib */
        /* as described in UTIL.DOC                  */

registerbgidriver(EGAVGA_driver);
registerbgifont(sansserif_font);

        /* set EGA high-resolution 16-color mode */

initgraph (&gdriver,&gmode,"");
rectangle (0,0,639,349);

        /* set, get, and display the background color */

setbkcolor (1);
background = getbkcolor();

sprintf (buffer,"The background color is : %d",background);
settextjustify (CENTER_TEXT,CENTER_TEXT);
outtextxy (320,175,buffer);

        /* Delay and Exit */

settextjustify(CENTER_TEXT,BOTTOM_TEXT);
outtextxy (320,320,"Press Any Key To Exit");

getch ();

closegraph();
return 0;
}
```

setcolor

Syntax:

```c
void far setcolor(int color);

int color;                              Desired color
```

Function:
The setcolor function sets the current color to the specified color.

File(s) to Include:
#include <graphics.h>

Description:
The setcolor function is used to set the current color to the color value specified in the color argument. The current color is used for drawing lines, arcs, circles, text, etc. The predefined constants and values for 16-color modes and the CGA modes are listed in Tables 11.22 and 11.23.

Table 11.22. *Colors for 16-color modes*

Constant	Value
BLACK	0
BLUE	1
GREEN	2
CYAN	3
RED	4
MAGENTA	5
BROWN	6
LIGHTGRAY	7
DARKGRAY	8
LIGHTBLUE	9
LIGHTGREEN	10
LIGHTCYAN	11
LIGHTRED	12
LIGHTMAGENTA	13
YELLOW	14
WHITE	15

Table 11.23. *Colors for CGA modes*

Palette Number	Color 1	Color 2	Color 3
0	CGA_LIGHTGREEN	CGA_LIGHTRED	CGA_YELLOW
1	CGA_LIGHTCYAN	CGA_LIGHTMAGENTA	CGA_WHITE
2	CGA_GREEN	CGA_RED	CGA_BROWN
3	CGA_CYAN	CGA_MAGENTA	CGA_LIGHTGRAY

NOTE: Color 0 is set with the setbkcolor function

Value(s) Returned:

There is no return value.

Related Function(s):

getcolor : retrieves the current color

Similar Microsoft C Function(s):

_setcolor : sets the current color

short _far _setcolor(short color);

Example:

The setcolor function is used in this example to set the color of the line drawn between a point that bounces around the screen and the center of the screen.

Listing 11.62. The setcolor function

```
#include <graphics.h>
#include <stdio.h>
#include <stdlib.h>
#include <conio.h>

int main ()
{
int gdriver = EGA;
int gmode = EGAHI;
int x, y;
int xdir, ydir;
int color;
int counter;

    /* register EGAVGA_driver and sansserif_font */
    /* ... these have been added to graphics.lib */
    /* as described in UTIL.DOC                   */
```

```
registerbgidriver (EGAVGA_driver);
registerbgifont (sansserif_font);

    /* set EGA 16-color high resolution video mode   */

initgraph (&gdriver,&gmode,"");
rectangle (0,0,639,349);

    /* move cursor around screen - draw line to center */

x = 1;
y = 175;
xdir = 1;
ydir = 1;
color = 1;

do
{
    setcolor (color);
    moveto (x,y);
    lineto (320,175);

    if (x == 638)
        xdir = -1;
    if (x == 1)
        xdir = 1;
    if (y == 348)
        ydir = -1;
    if (y == 1)
        ydir = 1;

    x = x + xdir;
    y = y + ydir;

    counter = counter + 1;

    if (counter > 25)
        {
        counter = 0;
        color = color + 1;
        }

    if (color > 15)
        color = 1;
} while (!kbhit());

    /* Delay and Exit */

closegraph();
return 0;
}
```

setfillpattern

Syntax:
```
void far setfillpattern(char far *pattern, int color);

char far *pattern;                    Fill pattern
int color;                            Desired color
```

Function:
The `setfillpattern` function is used to specify the fill pattern.

File(s) to Include:
```
#include <graphics.h>
```

Description:
The `setfillpattern` function is used to select a user-defined fill pattern. The `*pattern` argument points to an eight-byte, 8-by-8 bit pattern that represents the fill pattern. Each byte represents an eight-bit row, where each bit describes the manner in which the fill pattern will behave. A 1 bit in the fill pattern indicates that the corresponding pixel will be set to the current fill color. A 0 bit indicates that the corresponding pixel will remain unchanged. For example, a fill pattern of

```
char pattern [8] = {0xFF,0xFF,0xFF,0xFF,0xFF,0xFF,0xFF,0xFF};
```

will generate a solid fill pattern where every pixel is set to the current fill color. The fill color is specified by the `color` argument.

Value(s) Returned:
There is no return value.

Related Function(s):
`getfillpattern` : copies a fill pattern into memory

Similar Microsoft C Function(s):
`_setfillmask` : sets the fill pattern

```
void _far _setfillmask(unsigned char _far *mask);
```

Example:
The `setfillpattern` function is used in this example to set the fill pattern to two user-defined fill patterns and then fill two rectangles using these fill patterns.

Listing 11.63. The `setfillpattern` function

```
#include <graphics.h>
#include <stdio.h>
#include <stdlib.h>
#include <conio.h>

int main ()
{
int gdriver = EGA;
int gmode = EGAHI;

     /* set 50% and 25% fill patterns       */
     /* also set a holder for the old pattern */

char pattern1[8] = {0x55,0xAA,0x55,0xAA,0x55,0xAA,0x55,0xAA};
char pattern2[8] = {0x44,0x11,0x44,0x11,0x44,0x11,0x44,0x11};
char patternhold[8] = {0x00,0x00,0x00,0x00,0x00,0x00,0x00,0x00};

     /* register EGAVGA_driver and sansserif_font */
     /* ... these have been added to graphics.lib */
     /* as described in UTIL.DOC                 */

registerbgidriver(EGAVGA_driver);
registerbgifont(sansserif_font);

     /* set EGA high-resolution 16-color mode */

initgraph (&gdriver,&gmode,"");
rectangle (0,0,639,349);

     /* first get the current fill pattern and save it   */
     /* in patternhold - next set the pattern to pattern1 */
     /* and fill the upper half of the screen - next      */
     /* fill the lower half of screen with pattern2   -   */
     /* lastly get the old pattern and fill center square */

getfillpattern (patternhold);

setcolor (15);
rectangle (0,0,639,175);
setfillpattern(pattern1,1);
floodfill (1,1,15);

rectangle (0,175,639,349);
setfillpattern(pattern2,1);
floodfill (1,176,15);

rectangle (200,175,440,225);
setfillpattern(patternhold,0);
floodfill (201,176,15);

     /* Delay and Exit */

settextjustify(CENTER_TEXT,CENTER_TEXT);
outtextxy (320,200,"Press Any Key To Exit");
```

Listing 11.63. *continues*

431

Listing 11.63. cont.   The `setfillpattern` function

```
getch ();

closegraph();
return 0;
}
```

setfillstyle

Syntax:
```
void far setfillstyle(int pattern, int color);

int pattern;              Predefined pattern
int color;               Desired color
```

Function:
The `setfillstyle` function selects a predefined fill pattern and a fill color.

File(s) to Include:
```
#include <graphics.h>
```

Description:
The `setfillstyle` function is used to select a predefined fill pattern and a fill color. The `pattern` argument specifies the predefined pattern, while the `color` argument specifies the fill color. Table 11.24 lists the predefined fill patterns. However, the `USER_FILL` (value 12) pattern should not be used to set a user-defined fill pattern. Instead, the `setfillpattern` function should be used.

Table 11.24.   *Predefined fill patterns*

Constant	Value	Meaning
EMPTY_FILL	0	Fill with background color
SOLID_FILL	1	Solid fill
LINE_FILL	2	Horizontal line fill
LTSLASH_FILL	3	Light slash fill
SLASH_FILL	4	Heavy slash fill
BKSLASH_FILL	5	Heavy backslash fill
LTBKSLASH_FILL	6	Light backslash fill

Constant	Value	Meaning
HATCH_FILL	7	Light hatch fill
XHATCH_FILL	8	Heavy hatch fill
INTERLEAVE_FILL	9	Interleaving fill
WIDE_DOT_FILL	10	Wide dot fill
CLOSE_DOT_FILL	11	Close dot fill
USER_FILL	12	User-defined pattern

Value(s) Returned:
There is no return value.

Related Function(s):
getfillsettings : gets the current fill pattern and color

Similar Microsoft C Function(s):
_setfillmask : sets the current fill pattern

```
void _far _setfillmask(unsigned char _far *mask);
```

Example:
The setfillstyle function is used in this example to select various fill patterns for use in displaying a five-wedge pie chart.

Listing 11.64.   The setfillstyle function

```
#include <graphics.h>
#include <stdio.h>
#include <stdlib.h>
#include <conio.h>

int main ()
{
int gdriver = EGA;
int gmode = EGAHI;

    /* register EGAVGA_driver and sansserif_font */
    /* ... these have been added to graphics.lib */
    /* as described in UTIL.DOC                  */

registerbgidriver (EGAVGA_driver);
registerbgifont (sansserif_font);
```

Listing 11.64.   *continues*

Listing 11.64. cont. The setfillstyle function

```
      /* set EGA 16-color high resolution video mode   */

initgraph (&gdriver,&gmode,"");
rectangle (0,0,639,349);

      /* draw a pie chart using various fill styles      */
      /* and colors as set by the setfillstyle function */

setfillstyle (SOLID_FILL, 1);
pieslice (320,175,0,45,150);

setfillstyle (WIDE_DOT_FILL, 15);
pieslice (320,175,45,135,150);

setfillstyle (SLASH_FILL, 4);
pieslice (320,175,135,195,150);

setfillstyle (HATCH_FILL, 14);
pieslice (320,175,195,275,150);

setfillstyle (EMPTY_FILL, 15);
pieslice (320,175,275,360,150);

   /* Delay and Exit */

settextjustify(CENTER_TEXT,BOTTOM_TEXT);
outtextxy (320,320,"Press Any Key To Exit");

getch ();

closegraph();
return 0;
}
```

setgraphbufsize

Syntax:
```
unsigned far setgraphbufsize(unsigned buffersize);

unsigned buffersize;              Buffer size
```

Function:
The setgraphbufsize function modifies the default size of the internal graphics buffer.

File(s) to Include:
```
#include <graphics.h>
```

Description:

The setgraphbufsize function is used to change the size of the internal graphics buffer as set by the initgraph function when the graphics system is initialized. The graphics buffer is used by several of the graphics functions; therefore, you should take extreme care when altering this buffer of default size 4,096. Note that the setgraphbufsize function should be called prior to calling the initgraph function.

Value(s) Returned:

The previous size of the internal graphics buffer is returned when the setgraphbufsize function is called.

Related Function(s):

_graphfreemem : deallocates graphics memory
_graphgetmem : allocates graphics memory

Similar Microsoft C Function(s):

There are no similar Microsoft C functions.

Example:

The setgraphbufsize function is used in this example to set a new graphics buffer size. The old and the new buffer sizes are then displayed.

Listing 11.65. The setgraphbufsize function

```
#include <graphics.h>
#include <stdio.h>
#include <stdlib.h>
#include <conio.h>

int main ()
{
int gdriver = EGA;
int gmode = EGAHI;
int originalsize, newsize;
char buffer [40];

        /* register EGAVGA_driver and sansserif_font */
        /* ... these have been added to graphics.lib */
        /* as described in UTIL.DOC                   */

registerbgidriver (EGAVGA_driver);
registerbgifont (sansserif_font);

        /* set EGA 16-color high resolution video mode */
```

Listing 11.65. *continues*

435

Listing 11.65. cont. The setgraphbufsize function

```
initgraph (&gdriver,&gmode,"");
rectangle (0,0,639,349);

     /* get old buffer size, set new size, display both */

newsize = 10000;

originalsize = setgraphbufsize(newsize);

sprintf (buffer,"The original buffer size was %d",originalsize);
settextjustify (CENTER_TEXT,CENTER_TEXT);
outtextxy (320,100,buffer);

sprintf (buffer,"The current buffer size is %d",newsize);
outtextxy (320,150,buffer);

setgraphbufsize(originalsize);

     /* Delay and Exit */

settextjustify(CENTER_TEXT,BOTTOM_TEXT);
outtextxy (320,320,"Press Any Key To Exit");

getch ();
closegraph();
return 0;
}
```

setgraphmode

Syntax:
```
void far setgraphmode(int mode);

int mode;                        Graphics mode
```

Function:
The setgraphmode function sets the graphics system to the specified video mode.

File(s) to Include:
```
#include <graphics.h>
```

Description:
The setgraphmode function is used to select a graphics mode only after the graphics system has been initialized by the initgraph function. The mode argument defines the desired mode given the current driver. In addition to setting a new mode, the setgraphmode

function clears the screen and resets all graphics settings to their default values. This function is often used with the restorecrtmode function to switch between text and graphics modes as in the following example.

Value(s) Returned:

A -10, for grInvalidMode, is returned when the specified video mode is invalid for the current device driver.

Related Function(s):

initgraph : initializes the graphics environment

Similar Microsoft C Function(s):

_setvideomode : sets the current video mode

```
short _far _setvideomode(short mode);
```

Example:

The setgraphmode function is used in this example to set the video mode to graphics mode after being placed in text mode with the restoremode function.

Listing 11.66. The setgraphmode function

```
#include <graphics.h>
#include <stdio.h>
#include <stdlib.h>
#include <conio.h>

int main ()
{
int gdriver = EGA;
int gmode = EGAHI;

    /* register EGAVGA_driver and sansserif_font */
    /* ... these have been added to graphics.lib */
    /* as described in UTIL.DOC                   */

registerbgidriver (EGAVGA_driver);
registerbgifont (sansserif_font);

    /* set EGA 16-color high resolution video mode  */

initgraph (&gdriver,&gmode,"");
rectangle (0,0,639,349);

    /* press a key to go to text mode */
```

Listing 11.66. *continues*

Listing 11.66. cont. The setgraphmode function

```
settextjustify (CENTER_TEXT,CENTER_TEXT);
outtextxy (320,175,"Press a key to go to text mode");
getch ();
restorecrtmode ();

     /* press another key to go back to graphics mode */

printf ("Press a key to go back to graphics mode");
getch ();
setgraphmode (gmode);
rectangle (0,0,639,349);

     /* Delay and Exit */

settextjustify(CENTER_TEXT,BOTTOM_TEXT);
outtextxy (320,320,"Press Any Key To Exit");

getch ();
closegraph();
return 0;
}
```

setlinestyle

Syntax:
```
void far setlinestyle(int linestyle, unsigned pattern,
                      int thickness);

int linestyle;             Line style
unsigned pattern;          User-defined line pattern
int thickness;             Thickness of line
```

Function:
The setlinestyle function sets the characteristics for straight lines, including the style and width of the lines.

File(s) to Include:
```
#include <graphics.h>
```

Description:
The setlinestyle function is used to define the line characteristics for straight lines. The linestyle parameter specifies the predefined line pattern to use. The predefined line styles are shown in Table 11.25. The thickness parameter defines the width of the line. The constants for the thickness argument are shown in Table 11.26.

438

Table 11.25. *Line styles*

Constant	Value	Meaning
SOLID_LINE	0	Solid line
DOTTED_LINE	1	Dotted line
CENTER_LINE	2	Centered line
DASHED_LINE	3	Dashed line
USERBIT_LINE	4	User defined line

Table 11.26. *Line thicknesses*

Constant	Value	Meaning
NORM_WIDTH	1	Line width of one pixel
THICK_WIDTH	3	Line width of three pixels

The pattern argument is a 16-bit pattern that describes the line style when the linestyle argument is USERBIT_LINE, or 4. This 16-bit pattern describes the line. A 1 bit in the pattern indicates that the corresponding pixel on the line will be set to the current color. A 0 bit indicates that the corresponding pixel will remain unchanged. For example, a pattern of 1111111111111111 binary or 0xFFFF hex indicates that all pixels on the line will be set to the current color; therefore, 0xFFFF represents a solid line.

Value(s) Returned:
If an invalid parameter is passed to the setlinestyle function, a -11 is returned via the graphresult function.

Related Function(s):
getlinesettings : gets the current line style, pattern, and thickness

Similar Microsoft C Function(s):
_setlinestyle : sets the pattern for line drawing

```
void _far _setlinestyle(unsigned short linepattern);
```

Example:
This example uses the setlinestyle function to set the current line style. These line settings are then retrieved and displayed.

Listing 11.67. The setlinestyle function

```c
#include <graphics.h>
#include <stdio.h>
#include <stdlib.h>
#include <conio.h>

int main ()
{
struct linesettingstype lineset;
int gdriver = EGA;
int gmode = EGAHI;
char buffer[40];

    /* register EGAVGA_driver and sansserif_font */
    /* ... these have been added to graphics.lib */
    /* as described in UTIL.DOC                  */

registerbgidriver(EGAVGA_driver);
registerbgifont(sansserif_font);

    /* set EGA high-resolution 16-color mode */

initgraph (&gdriver,&gmode,"");
rectangle (0,0,639,349);

    /* define, use, and retrieve line settings */

setlinestyle (DOTTED_LINE,0xFFFF,THICK_WIDTH);

getlinesettings (&lineset);

rectangle (50,50,590,300);
settextjustify(CENTER_TEXT,CENTER_TEXT);

sprintf (buffer,"The Line Style is : %d",lineset.linestyle);
outtextxy (320,75,buffer);

sprintf (buffer,"The User Pattern is : 0x%x",lineset.upattern);
outtextxy (320,150,buffer);

sprintf (buffer,"The Line Thickness is : %d",lineset.thickness);
outtextxy (320,225,buffer);

    /* Delay and Exit */

outtextxy (320,320,"Press Any Key To Exit");

getch ();
closegraph();
return 0;
}
```

setpalette

Syntax:
```
void far setpalette(int palettenumber, int color);

int palettenumber;              Palette number to change
int color;                      New color
```

Function:
The setpalette function modifies one entry in the current palette.

File(s) to Include:
```
#include <graphics.h>
```

Description:
The setpalette function is used to modify a single entry in the current palette. The palettenumber argument specifies the palette member to change. The color argument specifies the new color value for the palette member. Note that all changes made to the palette are immediately visible, and that the setpalette function cannot be used with the IBM-8514 driver. Tables 11.27 and 11.28 show the predefined color values and constants for the CGA and EGA/VGA.

Table 11.27. *CGA Color table*

Constant	Value
BLACK	0
BLUE	1
GREEN	2
CYAN	3
RED	4
MAGENTA	5
BROWN	6
LIGHTGRAY	7
DARKGRAY	8
LIGHTBLUE	9
LIGHTGREEN	10

Table 11.27. *continues*

Table 11.27. cont.   *CGA Color table*

Constant	Value
LIGHTCYAN	11
LIGHTRED	12
LIGHTMAGENTA	13
YELLOW	14
WHITE	15

Table 11.28.   *EGA/VGA Color table*

Constant	Value
EGA_BLACK	0
EGA_BLUE	1
EGA_GREEN	2
EGA_CYAN	3
EGA_RED	4
EGA_MAGENTA	5
EGA_LIGHTGRAY	7
EGA_BROWN	20
EGA_DARKGRAY	56
EGA_LIGHTBLUE	57
EGA_LIGHTGREEN	58
EGA_LIGHTCYAN	59
EGA_LIGHTRED	60
EGA_LIGHTMAGENTA	61
EGA_YELLOW	62
EGA_WHITE	63

Value(s) Returned:

If an invalid parameter is passed to the `setpalette` function, a -11 is returned via the `graphresult` function.

Related Function(s):

`setallpalette` : resets the entire palette

442

Similar Microsoft C Function(s):

_remappalette : modifies one entry in the palette

```
long _far _remappalette(short paletteindex, long color);
```

Example:

The setpalette function is used in this example to invert two colors, one pair at a time, each time a key is pressed. The <Esc> key can be pressed to exit the program.

Listing 11.68.   The setpalette function

```
#include <graphics.h>
#include <stdio.h>
#include <stdlib.h>
#include <conio.h>

int col[16] = {EGA_WHITE,EGA_YELLOW,EGA_LIGHTMAGENTA,EGA_LIGHTRED,
               EGA_LIGHTCYAN,EGA_LIGHTGREEN,EGA_LIGHTBLUE,
               EGA_DARKGRAY,EGA_BROWN,EGA_LIGHTGRAY,EGA_MAGENTA,
               EGA_RED,EGA_CYAN,EGA_GREEN,EGA_BLUE,EGA_BLACK};

int main ()
{
struct palettetype palette;
int gdriver = EGA;
int gmode = EGAHI;
int y, color;
char buffer[40];
int ch;

     /* register EGAVGA_driver and sansserif_font */
     /* ... these have been added to graphics.lib */
     /* as described in UTIL.DOC                   */

registerbgidriver(EGAVGA_driver);
registerbgifont(sansserif_font);

     /* set EGA high-resolution 16-color mode */

initgraph (&gdriver,&gmode,"");
rectangle (0,0,639,349);

     /* change one palette color with each key stroke */

getpalette (&palette);
color = 1;

for (y = 10; y < 160; y = y + 10)
{
     setcolor (color);
     line (20,y,620,y);
     color = color + 1;
}
```

Listing 11.68.   *continues*

Listing 11.68. cont. The setpallette function

```
color = 0;
settextjustify (CENTER_TEXT,CENTER_TEXT);
outtextxy (320,320,"Press ESC to Exit");

do
{
    ch =  getch ();
    setpalette (color,col[color]);
    color = color + 1;
} while (ch != 27);
    /* Exit */
closegraph();
return 0;
}
```

setrgbpalette

Syntax:
```
void far setrgbpalette(int palettenum, int red, int green,
                       int blue);
```

```
int palettenum;              Palette entry to modify
int red;                     Red component
int green;                   Green component
int blue;                    Blue component
```

Function:
The setrgbpalette function is used to define colors for the IBM 8514.

File(s) to Include:
```
#include <graphics.h>
```

Description:
The setrgbpalette function is for use with the IBM 8514 and VGA drivers. The palettenum argument specifies the palette entry to be modified. For the IBM 8514, the palette range is 0 to 255. For VGA modes, the palette range is 0 to 15. The red, green, and blue arguments define the color intensity of the palette entry.

Value(s) Returned:
There is no return value.

Related Function(s):
```
setpalette    : modifies one color in the current palette
setallpalette : modifies all colors in the current palette
```

444

Similar Microsoft C Function(s):

There are no similar Microsoft C functions.

Example:

The following example modifies one member of the VGA palette.

Listing 11.69. The setrgbpalette function

```
#include <graphics.h>
#include <stdio.h>
#include <stdlib.h>
#include <conio.h>

int main ()
{
struct palettetype palette;
int gdriver = VGA;
int gmode = VGAHI;

    /* register EGAVGA_driver and sansserif_font */
    /* ... these have been added to graphics.lib */
    /* as described in UTIL.DOC                   */

registerbgidriver (EGAVGA_driver);
registerbgifont (sansserif_font);

    /* set VGA high resolution video mode  */

initgraph (&gdriver,&gmode,"");
rectangle (0,0,639,349);

    /* get palette and modify a palette entry */

getpalette (&palette);

setrgbpalette (palette.colors[3],6,4,1);


    /* Delay and Exit */

settextjustify(CENTER_TEXT,BOTTOM_TEXT);
outtextxy (320,320,"Press Any Key To Exit");

getch ();

closegraph();
return 0;
}
```

settextjustify

Syntax:

```
void far settextjustify(int horizontal, int vertical);

int horizontal;                    Horizontal justification
int vertical;                      Vertical justification
```

Function:

The `settextjustify` function sets the text justification for the graphics functions.

File(s) to Include:

```
#include <graphics.h>
```

Description:

The `settextjustify` function is used to specify the method in which the text is placed on the screen relative to the cursor position. The `horizontal` argument is used to specify the horizontal justification, while the `vertical` argument is used to specify the vertical justification. The predefined constants and values for the `horizontal` and `vertical` justifications are shown in Table 11.29. The default settings for the text justifications are `LEFT_TEXT` for horizontal and `TOP_TEXT` for vertical.

Table 11.29. *Text justifications*

Constant	Value	Meaning
Horizontal text justification		
LEFT_TEXT	0	Left justify
CENTER_TEXT	1	Center text
RIGHT_TEXT	2	Right justify
Vertical text justification		
BOTTOM_TEXT	0	Bottom justify
CENTER_TEXT	1	Center text
TOP_TEXT	2	Top justify

Value(s) Returned:

If an invalid parameter is passed to the `settextjustify` function, a -11 is returned via the `graphresult` function.

Related Function(s):

outtext : used to display text in graphics mode

Similar Microsoft C Function(s):

There are no similar Microsoft C functions.

Example:

The settextjustify function is used in this example to display text using different vertical and horizontal justifications.

Listing 11.70. The settextjustify function

```
#include <graphics.h>
#include <stdio.h>
#include <stdlib.h>
#include <conio.h>

int main ()
{
struct textsettingstype textset;
int gdriver = EGA;
int gmode = EGAHI;
char buffer [40];

    /* register EGAVGA_driver and sansserif_font */
    /* ... these have been added to graphics.lib */
    /* as described in UTIL.DOC              */

registerbgidriver (EGAVGA_driver);
registerbgifont (sansserif_font);

    /* set EGA 16-color high resolution video mode  */

initgraph (&gdriver,&gmode,"");
rectangle (0,0,639,349);

    /* display text with different justifications */

settextjustify (LEFT_TEXT,BOTTOM_TEXT);
outtextxy (320,175,"LEFT_TEXT - BOTTOM_TEXT");

settextjustify (RIGHT_TEXT,TOP_TEXT);
outtextxy (320,175,"RIGHT_TEXT - TOP_TEXT");

    /* Delay and Exit */

settextjustify(CENTER_TEXT,BOTTOM_TEXT);
outtextxy (320,320,"Press Any Key To Exit");

getch ();
```

Listing 11.70. *continues*

447

Listing 11.70. cont. The `settextjustify` function

```
closegraph();
return 0;
}
```

settextstyle

Syntax:
```
void far settextstyle(int font, int direction,
                      int charsize);
```

```
int font;                    Font to use
int direction;               Direction to display text
int charsize;                Character size
```

Function:
The `settextstyle` function sets the graphics font output characteristics.

File(s) to Include:
```
#include <graphics.h>
```

Description:
The `settextstyle` function is used to specify the characteristics for font text output. The `font` argument specifies the registered font to use. The font should be registered for predictable results (see `registerbgifont`). The `direction` argument specifics the direction in which text will be displayed. Tables 11.30 and 11.31 list the available fonts and directions. The default direction is `HORIZ_DIR`. The `charsize` argument defines the factor by which the current font will be multiplied. A nonzero `charsize` argument can be used with bit-mapped or stroked fonts. However, a `charsize` of 0, which selects the user-defined character size as defined in the `setusercharsize` function, only works with stroked fonts. The `charsize` argument can magnify the size of the font up to 10 times its normal size.

Table 11.30. *Text fonts*

Constant	Value	Meaning
DEFAULT_FONT	0	8-by-8 bit-mapped font
TRIPLEX_FONT	1	Triplex font
SMALL_FONT	2	Small font
SANS_SERIF_FONT	3	Sans serif font
GOTHIC_FONT	4	Gothic font

Table 11.31. *Text directions*

Constant	Value	Meaning
HORIZ_DIR	0	Horizontal text
VERT_DIR	1	Vertical text

Value(s) Returned:

There is no return value.

Related Function(s):

gettextsettings : gets information on the current text characteristics

Similar Microsoft C Function(s):

_setfont : selects the current font with the specified characteristics

```
short _far _setfont(unsigned char _far *options);
```

Example:

The settextstyle function is used in this example to select the sans serif font in the horizontal direction with a character size of 2. The text settings are then retrieved and displayed.

Listing 11.71. The settextstyle function

```
#include <graphics.h>
#include <stdio.h>
#include <stdlib.h>
#include <conio.h>

int main ()
{
struct textsettingstype textset;
int gdriver = EGA;
int gmode = EGAHI;
char buffer [40];

    /* register EGAVGA_driver and sansserif_font */
    /* ... these have been added to graphics.lib */
    /* as described in UTIL.DOC                   */

registerbgidriver (EGAVGA_driver);
registerbgifont (sansserif_font);
```

Listing 11.71. *continues*

449

Listing 11.71. cont. The `settextstyle` function

```
        /* set EGA 16-color high resolution video mode  */

initgraph (&gdriver,&gmode,"");
rectangle (0,0,639,349);

        /* set, get, and display text settings */

settextstyle(SANS_SERIF_FONT,HORIZ_DIR,2);
settextjustify(CENTER_TEXT,CENTER_TEXT);

gettextsettings(&textset);

sprintf (buffer,"Font Value : %d",textset.font);
outtextxy (320,75,buffer);

sprintf (buffer,"Text Direction : %d",textset.direction);
outtextxy (320,125,buffer);

sprintf (buffer,"Character Size : %d",textset.charsize);
outtextxy (320,175,buffer);

sprintf (buffer,"Horizontal Justification : %d",textset.horiz);
outtextxy (320,225,buffer);

sprintf (buffer,"Vertical Justification : %d",textset.vert);
outtextxy (320,275,buffer);

        /* Delay and Exit */

settextjustify(CENTER_TEXT,BOTTOM_TEXT);
outtextxy (320,320,"Press Any Key To Exit");

getch ();

closegraph();
return 0;
}
```

setusercharsize

Syntax:

```
void far setusercharsize(int multx, int divx, int multy,
                         int divy);

int multx, divx;              Set ratio for character width
int multy, divy;              Set ratio for character height
```

Function:
The setusercharsize function is used to set the character width and height for stroked fonts.

File(s) to Include:
```
#include <graphics.h>
```

Description:
The setusercharsize function sets the size characteristics for stroked fonts. In order for this function to affect the character size, the charsize argument of the settextstyle function must be set to 0. The width of the character is set by the multx and divx arguments. For example, in order to double the size of the character, multx could be set to 2, while divx could be set to 1. The resulting width is 2/1 or 2 times the default width. Similarly, the multy and divy arguments specify the height of the character.

Value(s) Returned:
There is no return value.

Related Function(s):
gettextsettings : gets the characteristics of the current font

Similar Microsoft C Function(s):
_setfont : selects the font with the specified characteristics

```
short _far _setfont(unsigned char _far *options);
```

Example:
The setusercharsize function is used in this example to set the character size to 50 percent height and 33 percent width. The height and width ratios are then displayed.

Listing 11.72. The setusercharsize function

```
#include <graphics.h>
#include <stdio.h>
#include <stdlib.h>
#include <conio.h>

int main ()
{
int gdriver = EGA;
```

Listing 11.72. *continues*

Listing 11.72. cont. The s e t u s e r c h a r s i z e function

```
int gmode = EGAHI;
int multx, divx;
int multy, divy;
char buffer[40];

        /* register EGAVGA_driver and sansserif_font */
        /* ... these have been added to graphics.lib */
        /* as described in UTIL.DOC                   */

registerbgidriver (EGAVGA_driver);
registerbgifont (sansserif_font);

        /* set EGA 16-color high resolution video mode  */

initgraph (&gdriver,&gmode,"");
rectangle (0,0,639,349);

        /* set font and character size */

multx = 1;
divx = 2;
multy = 1;
divy = 3;

settextstyle (SANS_SERIF_FONT,HORIZ_DIR,0);

setusercharsize (multx,divx,multy,divy);

settextjustify (CENTER_TEXT,CENTER_TEXT);
sprintf (buffer,"The Width Ratio is %d to %d",multx,divx);
outtextxy (320,150,buffer);

sprintf (buffer,"The Height Ratio is %d to %d",multy,divy);
outtextxy (320,200,buffer);

    /* Delay and Exit */

settextjustify(CENTER_TEXT,BOTTOM_TEXT);
outtextxy (320,320,"Press Any Key To Exit");

getch ();

closegraph();
return 0;
}
```

setviewport

Syntax:
```
void far setviewport(int left, int top, int right,
                     int bottom, int clip);
```

```
int left, top;              Upper left corner of viewport
int right, bottom;          Lower right corner of viewport
int clip;                   Clip flag;
```

Function:
The setviewport function specifies the current viewport and its characteristics.

File(s) to Include:
```
#include <graphics.h>
```

Description:
The setviewport function is used to define the current viewport. The left and top arguments define the upper left corner of the viewport. The left and top arguments correspond to the x and y coordinates of this corner respectively. Similarly, the right and bottom arguments define the lower right corner of the viewport. The clip argument defines whether or not subsequent graphics output will be clipped at the viewport's border. A clip value of 0 indicates that the output will not be clipped, while a nonzero value indicates that output will be clipped. When the viewport is initialized, the cursor position is moved to position (0,0) (the upper left corner). All output after the viewport is initialized is relative to this point. The default viewport covers the entire screen.

Value(s) Returned:
A -11 is returned via the graphresult function when an invalid parameter is passed to the setviewport function.

Related Function(s):
```
getviewsettings   : gets the settings of the current viewport
clearviewport     : clears the current viewport
```

Similar Microsoft C Function(s):
```
_setviewport : defines a viewport while clipping output at the border and
               redefining the view origin
```

```
void _far _setviewport(short x1, short y1, short x2, short y2);
```

```
_setcliprgn : defines a clipping region without modifying the view origin
```

```
void _far _setcliprgn(short x1, short y1, short x2, short y2);
```

Example:

The setviewport function is used in this example to create a viewport that clips output at its border. The example then attempts to draw a line outside the border of the viewport.

Listing 11.73. The setviewport function

```
#include <graphics.h>
#include <stdio.h>
#include <stdlib.h>
#include <conio.h>

int main ()
{
int gdriver = EGA;
int gmode = EGAHI;

        /* register EGAVGA_driver and sansserif_font */
        /* ... these have been added to graphics.lib */
        /* as described in UTIL.DOC                   */

registerbgidriver(EGAVGA_driver);
registerbgifont(sansserif_font);

        /* set EGA high-resolution 16-color mode */

initgraph (&gdriver,&gmode,"");
rectangle (0,0,639,349);

        /* highlight and create viewport --    */
        /* attempt to draw outside of viewport */
        /* reset viewport to entire screen     */

rectangle (50,50,590,300);
setviewport (50,50,590,300,1);

line (0,0,639,349);

setviewport (0,0,639,349,1);

     /* Delay and Exit */

settextjustify (CENTER_TEXT,CENTER_TEXT);
outtextxy (320,330,"Press Any Key to Exit");
getch ();

closegraph();
return 0;
}
```

setvisualpage

Syntax:
```
void far setvisualpage(int page);

int page;               Page number
```

Function:
The setvisualpage function sets the visual page (or display page) to the specified page number.

File(s) to Include:
```
#include <graphics.h>
```

Description:
The setvisualpage function is used to set the visual page as specified in the page argument. A page is a section of memory where video information is stored. When used with a system (EGA or VGA) with sufficient video memory to support multiple pages of graphics, the setvisualpage (in conjunction with the setactivepage function) allows the programmer to create graphics on hidden pages and flip between multiple pages of graphics information.

Value(s) Returned:
There is no return value.

Related Function(s):
setactivepage : sets the active page

Similar Microsoft C Function(s):
_setvisualpage : sets the visual, or display, page

```
short _far _setvisualpage(short page);
```

Example:
This example uses the setvisualpage function to set the current active page to the visual page when all output to that page is finished.

Listing 11.74. The setvisualpage function

```
#include <graphics.h>
#include <stdio.h>
#include <stdlib.h>
#include <conio.h>

int main ()
{
int gdriver = EGA;
int gmode = EGAHI;
int activepage;
int visualpage;
int holder;
int ch;

        /* register EGAVGA_driver and sansserif_font */
        /* ... these have been added to graphics.lib */
        /* as described in UTIL.DOC                   */

registerbgidriver (EGAVGA_driver);
registerbgifont (sansserif_font);

        /* set EGA 16-color high resolution video mode  */

initgraph (&gdriver,&gmode,"");
rectangle (0,0,639,349);

        /* draw figure and message on two pages of EGA    */
        /* video memory - pressing a key will switch      */
        /* visual and active pages until ESC is presssed */

activepage = 1;
visualpage = 0;

setactivepage (activepage);
setvisualpage (visualpage);

setbkcolor (1);
cleardevice();
setfillstyle (SOLID_FILL,4);
bar (100,50,540,250);
rectangle (100,50,540,250);
settextjustify (CENTER_TEXT,CENTER_TEXT);
outtextxy (320,310,"PAGE ONE - PRESS ANY KEY TO CHANGE PAGE");
outtextxy (320,330,"PRESS ESC TO EXIT");

holder = activepage;
activepage = visualpage;
visualpage = holder;
setactivepage (activepage);
setvisualpage (visualpage);
```

```
cleardevice ();
fillellipse (320,150,220,100);
outtextxy (320,310,"PAGE ZERO - PRESS ANY KEY TO CHANGE PAGE");
outtextxy (320,330,"PRESS ESC TO EXIT");

do
{
    holder = activepage;
    activepage = visualpage;
    visualpage = holder;
    setactivepage (activepage);
    setvisualpage (visualpage);
    ch = getch ();
} while (ch != 27);

    /* Exit */

closegraph();
return 0;
}
```

setwritemode

Syntax:
```
void far setwritemode(int mode);

int mode;                    Write mode
```

Function:
The setwritemode function sets the writing mode for drawing straight lines in graphics mode.

File(s) to Include:
```
#include <graphics.h>
```

Description:
The setwritemode function is used to set the logical writing mode for straight lines. The mode argument is used to specify the writing mode. The writing mode determines the interaction between existing pixel values and the pixel values on the line. Table 11.32 lists the values and constants for the mode argument.

Table 11.32. *Write modes*

Constant	Value	Meaning
COPY_PUT	0	Line pixels overwrite existing pixels
XOR_PUT	1	Screen pixels are the exclusive OR of line and existing pixels

Value(s) Returned:

There is no return value.

Related Function(s):

```
drawpoly    : uses the write mode to draw the polygon
line        : uses the write mode to draw lines
linerel     : uses the write mode to draw lines
lineto      : uses the write mode to draw lines
rectangle   : uses the write mode to draw the rectangle
```

Similar Microsoft C Function(s):

```
_setwritemode : sets the write mode for straight lines

short _far _setwritemode(short action);
```

Example:

This example uses the setwritemode function to set the logical line writing mode. A line is then drawn using the two write modes.

Listing 11.75. The setwritemode function

```
#include <graphics.h>
#include <stdio.h>
#include <stdlib.h>
#include <conio.h>

int main ()
{
int gdriver - EGA;
int gmode = EGAHI;

    /* register EGAVGA_driver and sansserif_font */
    /* ... these have been added to graphics.lib */
    /* as described in UTIL.DOC                   */

registerbgidriver (EGAVGA_driver);
registerbgifont (sansserif_font);
```

```
        /* set EGA 16-color high resolution video mode  */

initgraph (&gdriver,&gmode,"");
rectangle (0,0,639,349);
setfillstyle (SOLID_FILL,1);
bar (1,1,638,348);

        /* draw lines using the write modes */

setcolor (14);
setwritemode (COPY_PUT);
line (20,40,620,40);
settextjustify (CENTER_TEXT,CENTER_TEXT);
outtextxy (320,80,"COPY_PUT Line");

setwritemode (XOR_PUT);
line (20,150,620,150);
outtextxy (320,190,"XOR_PUT Line");

        /* Delay and Exit */

settextjustify(CENTER_TEXT,BOTTOM_TEXT);
outtextxy (320,320,"Press Any Key To Exit");

getch ();
closegraph();
return 0;
}
```

textheight

Syntax:
```
int far textheight(char far *textstring);

char far *textstring;                     Text string to evaluate
```

Function:
The textheight function determines and returns the height, in pixels, of the specified text string.

File(s) to Include:
```
#include <graphics.h>
```

Description:
The textheight function is used to determine the height, in pixels, of the text string specified by the *textstring argument. The text height is determined using the current font and character size.

Value(s) Returned:

The height, in pixels, of the specified text string is returned when the `textheight` function is called.

Related Function(s):

`textwidth` : returns the width of a text string

Similar Microsoft C Function(s):

`_getfontinfo` : gets the current font characteristics, including the character height

```
short _far _getfontinfo(struct _fontinfo _far *fontbuffer);
```

Example:

The `textheight` function is used in this example to determine the height, in pixels, of the current font. The width and height of the specified string are then displayed.

Listing 11.76. The `textheight` function

```
#include <graphics.h>
#include <stdio.h>
#include <stdlib.h>
#include <conio.h>

int main ()
{
int gdriver = EGA;
int gmode = EGAHI;
int multx, divx;
int multy, divy;
char buffer[40];
int textht;
int textwid;

        /* register EGAVGA_driver and sansserif_font */
        /* ... these have been added to graphics.lib */
        /* as described in UTIL.DOC                   */

registerbgidriver (EGAVGA_driver);
registerbgifont (sansserif_font);

        /* set EGA 16-color high resolution video mode   */

initgraph (&gdriver,&gmode,"");
rectangle (0,0,639,349);

        /* set font and get character size */
```

```
    multx = 1;
    divx = 2;
    multy = 1;
    divy = 3;

    settextstyle (SANS_SERIF_FONT,HORIZ_DIR,2);
    setusercharsize (multx,divx,multy,divy);

    textht = textheight ("X");

    textwid = textwidth ("Width : xxx - Height : xx");

    settextjustify (CENTER_TEXT,CENTER_TEXT);
    sprintf (buffer,"Width Ratio : %d - Height: %d",textwid,textht);
    outtextxy (320,150,buffer);

        /* Delay and Exit */

    settextjustify(CENTER_TEXT,BOTTOM_TEXT);
    outtextxy (320,320,"Press Any Key To Exit");

    getch ();

    closegraph();
    return 0;
    }
```

textwidth

Syntax:
```
int far textwidth(char far *textstring);

char far *textstring;              Text string to evaluate
```

Function:
The textwidth function determines and returns the width, in pixels, of the specified text string.

File(s) to Include:
```
#include <graphics.h>
```

Description:
The textwidth function is used to determine the width of the text string specified by the *textstring argument. The current font and character size are used in determining the width of the string.

Value(s) Returned:

The width, in pixels, of the specified text string is returned when the textwidth function is called.

Related Function(s):

textheight : determines the height of a text string

Similar Microsoft C Function(s):

_getgtextextent : determines the width of a text string

short _far _getgtextextent(unsigned char _far *text);

Example:

The width of the specified text string is determined by the textwidth function. The height and width of this string are then displayed.

Listing 11.77. The textwidth function

```
#include <graphics.h>
#include <stdio.h>
#include <stdlib.h>
#include <conio.h>

int main ()
{
int gdriver = EGA;
int gmode = EGAHI;
int multx, divx;
int multy, divy;
char buffer[40];
int textht;
int textwid;

        /* register EGAVGA_driver and sansserif_font */
        /* ... these have been added to graphics.lib */
        /* as described in UTIL.DOC                   */

registerbgidriver (EGAVGA_driver);
registerbgifont (sansserif_font);

        /* set EGA 16-color high resolution video mode   */

initgraph (&gdriver,&gmode,"");
rectangle (0,0,639,349);

        /* set font and get character size */

multx = 1;
divx = 2;
```

```
multy = 1;
divy = 3;

settextstyle (SANS_SERIF_FONT,HORIZ_DIR,2);
setusercharsize (multx,divx,multy,divy);

textht = textheight ("X");

textwid = textwidth ("Width : xxx - Height : xx");

settextjustify (CENTER_TEXT,CENTER_TEXT);
sprintf (buffer,"Width Ratio : %d - Height: %d",textwid,textht);
outtextxy (320,150,buffer);

    /* Delay and Exit */

settextjustify(CENTER_TEXT,BOTTOM_TEXT);
outtextxy (320,320,"Press Any Key To Exit");

getch ();
closegraph();
return 0;
}
```

A
Line Patterns

The following 28 line patterns are provided for demonstration and use. These samples reflect a wide range of patterns, including dashed patterns, dotted patterns, and patterns that combine dashes and dots. Although these line patterns by no means cover the range of possible line pattern combinations, they do represent the most commonly used patterns. Chapter 4 explains the method for deriving the line pattern and its binary and hexidecimal values.

Figure A.1. Line pattern 0x8000

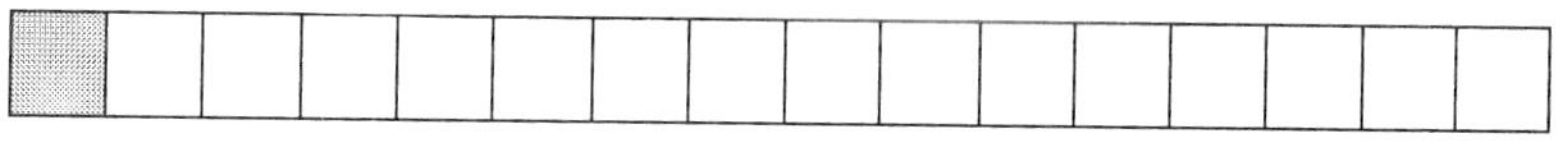

Figure A.2. Line pattern 0xC000

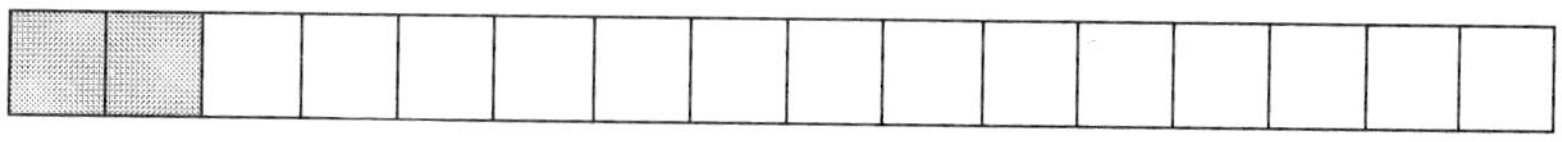

Figure A.3. Line pattern 0xE000

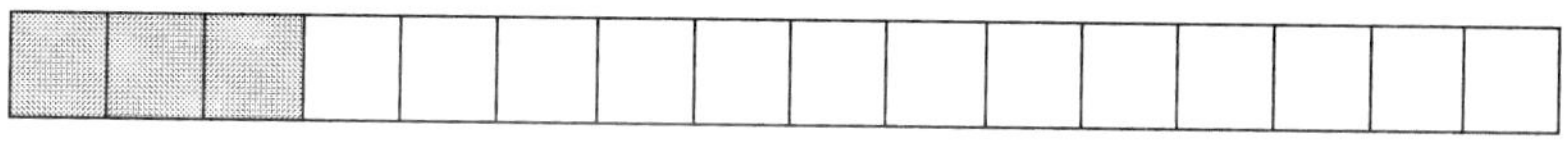

Figure A.4. Line pattern 0xF000

Figure A.5. Line pattern 0xF800

Figure A.6. Line pattern 0xFC00

Figure A.7. Line pattern 0xFE00

Figure A.8. Line pattern 0xFF00

Figure A.9. Line pattern 0xFF80

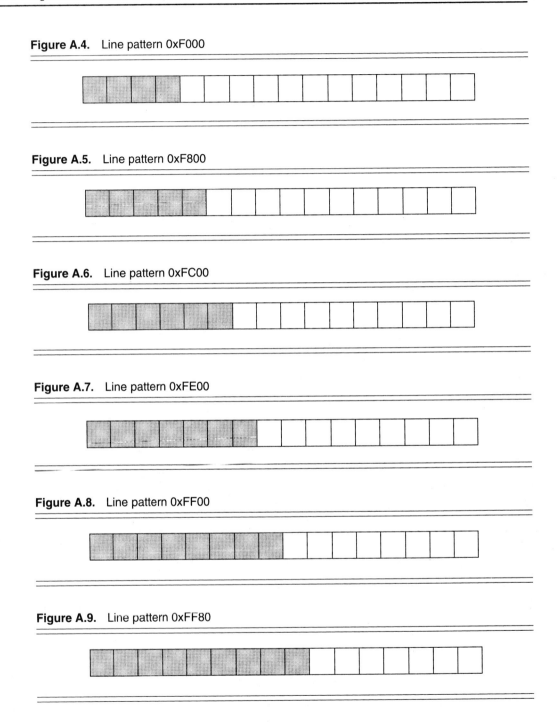

Figure A.10. Line pattern 0xFFC0

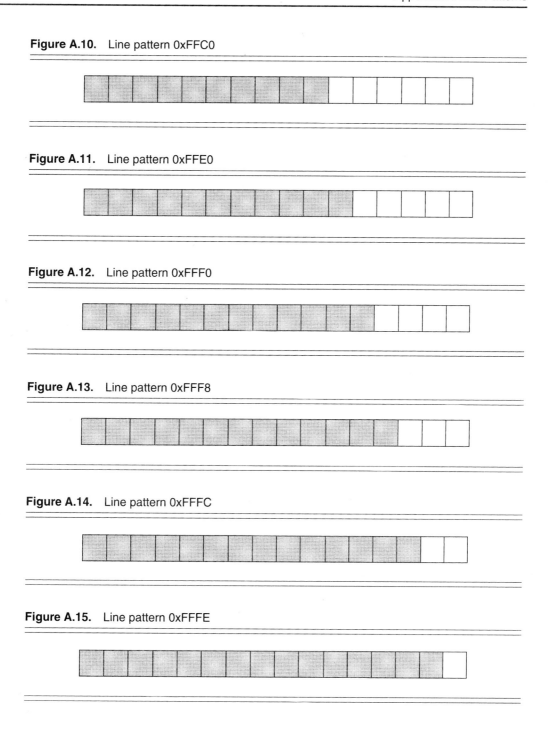

Figure A.11. Line pattern 0xFFE0

Figure A.12. Line pattern 0xFFF0

Figure A.13. Line pattern 0xFFF8

Figure A.14. Line pattern 0xFFFC

Figure A.15. Line pattern 0xFFFE

Figure A.16. Line pattern 0xFFFF

Figure A.17. Line pattern 0x8080

Figure A.18. Line pattern 0xC0C0

Figure A.19. Line pattern 0xE0E0

Figure A.20. Line pattern 0xF0F0

Figure A.21. Line pattern 0xF8F8

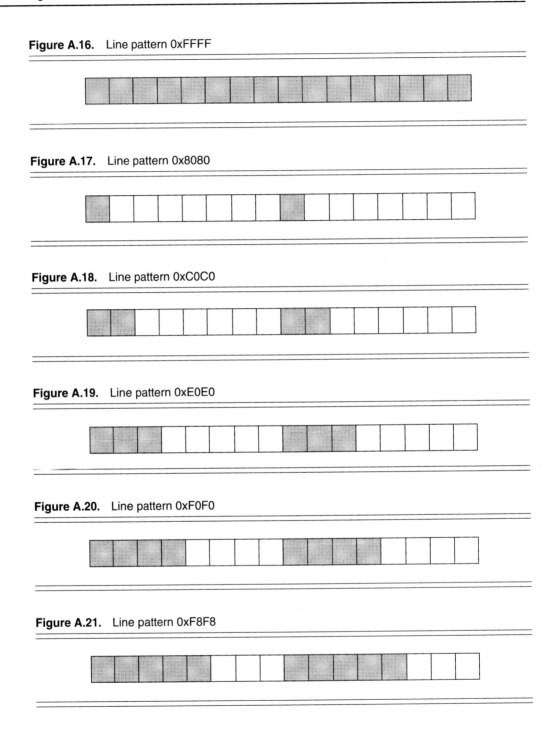

Figure A.22. Line pattern 0xFCFC

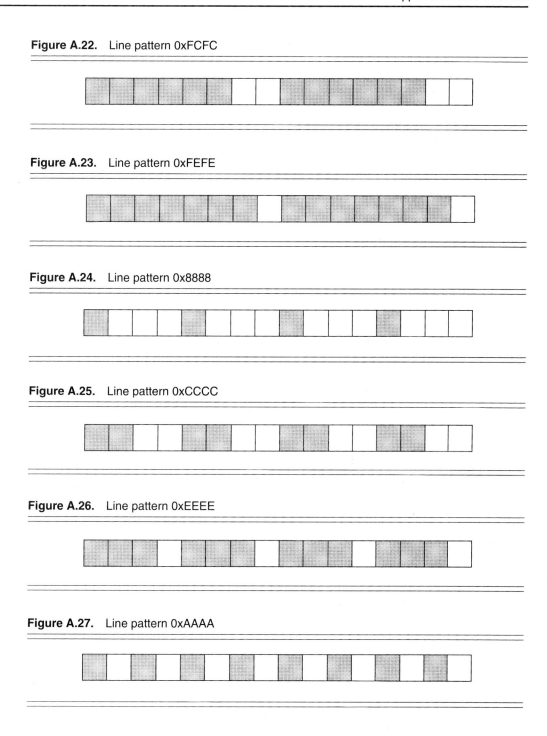

Figure A.23. Line pattern 0xFEFE

Figure A.24. Line pattern 0x8888

Figure A.25. Line pattern 0xCCCC

Figure A.26. Line pattern 0xEEEE

Figure A.27. Line pattern 0xAAAA

Figure A.28. Line pattern 0xF6F6

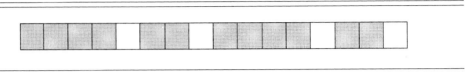

B

Fill Patterns

The following 12 fill patterns are provided for demonstration and use. Although these fill patterns by no means cover the range of possible fill patterns, they do represent the most commonly used fill patterns. Chapter 4 explains the method for developing and deriving a fill pattern and its binary and hexidecimal values.

Figure B.1. Three percent fill pattern
\x00\x20\x00\x00\x00\x20\x00\x00

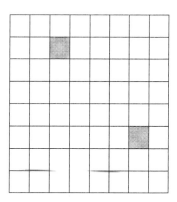

Figure B.2. Six percent fill pattern
\x20\x00\x02\x00\x80\x00\x08\x00

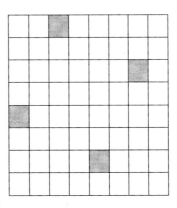

Figure B.3. 12.5 percent fill pattern
\x20\x02\x80\x08\x20\x02\x80\x08

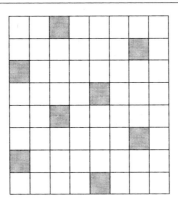

Figure B.4.   25 percent fill pattern
\x44\x11\x44\x11\x44\x11\x44\x11

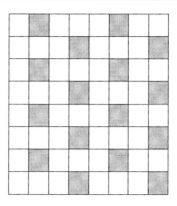

Figure B.5.   37.5 percent fill pattern
\xAA\x44\xAA\x11\xAA\x44\xAA\x11

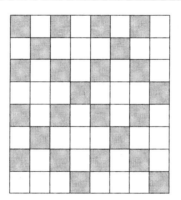

Figure B.6. 50 percent fill pattern
\x55\xAA\x55\xAA\x55\xAA\x55\xAA

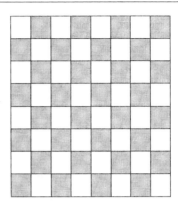

Figure B.7. 62.5 percent fill pattern
\x55\xBB\x55\xEE\x55\xBB\x55\xEE

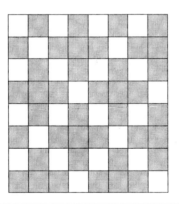

Figure B.8.   75 percent fill pattern
\xBB\xEE\xBB\xEE\xBB\xEE\xBB\xEE

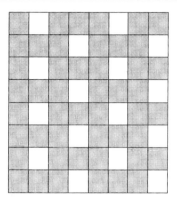

Figure B.9.   87.5 percent fill pattern
\xDF\xFD\x7F\xF7\xDF\xFD\x7F\xF7

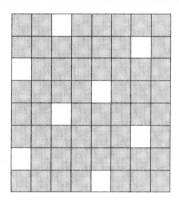

Figure B.10. 94 percent fill pattern

\xDF\xFF\xFD\xFF\x7F\xFF\xF7\xFF

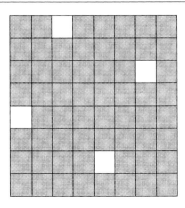

Figure B.11. 97 percent fill pattern

\xFF\xDF\xFF\xFF\xFF\xFD\xFF\xFF

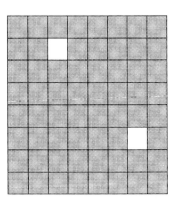

Figure B.12. 100 percent fill pattern
\xFF\xFF\xFF\xFF\xFF\xFF\xFF\xFF

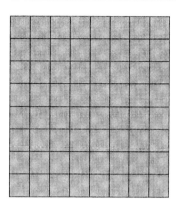

C
Character Set

The following character set was developed with the character creation techniques described in Chapter 5. The character model and code are provided for each character.

Figure C.1.   A

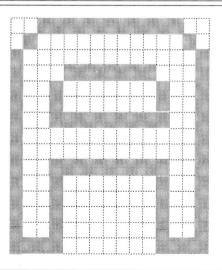

```
void a ()
{
    moveto (x+fraction[2],y);
    lineto (x+fraction[12],y);
    lineto (x+fraction[14],y+fraction[2]);
    lineto (x+fraction[14],y+fraction[14]);
    lineto (x+fraction[11],y+fraction[14]);
    lineto (x+fraction[11],y+fraction[9]);
    lineto (x+fraction[3],y+fraction[9]);
    lineto (x+fraction[3],y+fraction[14]);
    lineto (x,y+fraction[14]);
    lineto (x,y+fraction[2]);
    lineto (x+fraction[2],y);
    moveto (x+fraction[4],y+fraction[3]);
    lineto (x+fraction[10],y+fraction[3]);
    lineto (x+fraction[11],y+fraction[4]);
    lineto (x+fraction[11],y+fraction[6]);
    lineto (x+fraction[3],y+fraction[6]);
    lineto (x+fraction[3],y+fraction[4]);
    lineto (x+fraction[4],y+fraction[3]);
}
```

Figure C.2.   B

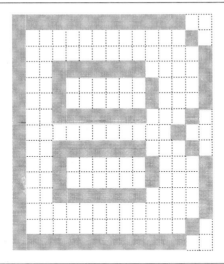

```
void b ()
{
    moveto (x,y);
    lineto (x+fraction[12],y);
    lineto (x+fraction[14],y+fraction[2]);
    lineto (x+fraction[14],y+fraction[5]);
    lineto (x+fraction[12],y+fraction[7]);
    lineto (x+fraction[14],y+fraction[9]);
    lineto (x+fraction[14],y+fraction[12]);
    lineto (x+fraction[12],y+fraction[14]);
    lineto (x,y+fraction[14]);
    lineto (x,y);
    moveto (x+fraction[3],y+fraction[3]);
    lineto (x+fraction[9],y+fraction[3]);
    lineto (x+fraction[10],y+fraction[4]);
    lineto (x+fraction[10],y+fraction[5]);
    lineto (x+fraction[9],y+fraction[6]);
    lineto (x+fraction[3],y+fraction[6]);
    lineto (x+fraction[3],y+fraction[3]);
    moveto (x+fraction[3],y+fraction[8]);
    lineto (x+fraction[9],y+fraction[8]);
    lineto (x+fraction[10],y+fraction[9]);
    lineto (x+fraction[10],y+fraction[10]);
    lineto (x+fraction[9],y+fraction[11]);
    lineto (x+fraction[3],y+fraction[11]);
    lineto (x+fraction[3],y+fraction[8]);
}
```

Figure C.3.   C

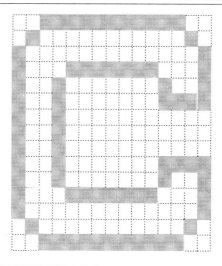

```
void c ()
{
    moveto (x+fraction[2],y);
    lineto (x+fraction[12],y);
    lineto (x+fraction[14],y+fraction[2]);
    lineto (x+fraction[14],y+fraction[5]);
    lineto (x+fraction[11],y+fraction[5]);
    lineto (x+fraction[11],y+fraction[4]);
    lineto (x+fraction[10],y+fraction[3]);
    lineto (x+fraction[4],y+fraction[3]);
    lineto (x+fraction[3],y+fraction[4]);
    lineto (x+fraction[3],y+fraction[10]);
    lineto (x+fraction[4],y+fraction[11]);
    lineto (x+fraction[10],y+fraction[11]);
    lineto (x+fraction[11],y+fraction[10]);
    lineto (x+fraction[11],y+fraction[9]);
    lineto (x+fraction[14],y+fraction[9]);
    lineto (x+fraction[14],y+fraction[12]);
    lineto (x+fraction[12],y+fraction[14]);
    lineto (x+fraction[2],y+fraction[14]);
    lineto (x,y+fraction[12]);
    lineto (x,y+fraction[2]);
    lineto (x+fraction[2],y);
}
```

Figure C.4. D

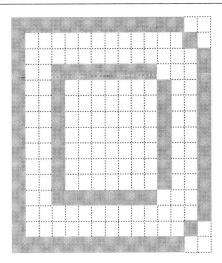

```
void d ()
{
    moveto (x,y);
    lineto (x+fraction[12],y);
    lineto (x+fraction[14],y+fraction[2]);
    lineto (x+fraction[14],y+fraction[12]);
    lineto (x+fraction[12],y+fraction[14]);
    lineto (x,y+fraction[14]);
    lineto (x,y);
    moveto (x+fraction[3],y+fraction[3]);
    lineto (x+fraction[10],y+fraction[3]);
    lineto (x+fraction[11],y+fraction[4]);
    lineto (x+fraction[11],y+fraction[10]);
    lineto (x+fraction[10],y+fraction[11]);
    lineto (x+fraction[3],y+fraction[11]);
    lineto (x+fraction[3],y+fraction[3]);
}
```

Figure C.5. E

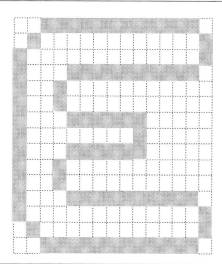

```
void e ()
{
    moveto (x+fraction[2],y);
    lineto (x+fraction[13],y);
    lineto (x+fraction[14],y+fraction[1]);
    lineto (x+fraction[14],y+fraction[2]);
    lineto (x+fraction[13],y+fraction[3]);
    lineto (x+fraction[4],y+fraction[3]);
    lineto (x+fraction[3],y+fraction[4]);
    lineto (x+fraction[3],y+fraction[5]);
    lineto (x+fraction[4],y+fraction[6]);
    lineto (x+fraction[9],y+fraction[6]);
    lineto (x+fraction[9],y+fraction[8]);
    lineto (x+fraction[4],y+fraction[8]);
    lineto (x+fraction[3],y+fraction[9]);
    lineto (x+fraction[3],y+fraction[10]);
    lineto (x+fraction[4],y+fraction[11]);
    lineto (x+fraction[13],y+fraction[11]);
    lineto (x+fraction[14],y+fraction[12]);
    lineto (x+fraction[14],y+fraction[13]);
    lineto (x+fraction[13],y+fraction[14]);
    lineto (x+fraction[2],y+fraction[14]);
    lineto (x,y+fraction[12]);
    lineto (x,y+fraction[2]);
    lineto (x+fraction[2],y);
}
```

Figure C.6. F

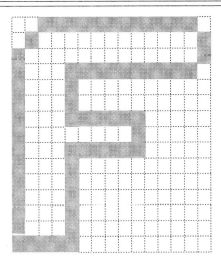

```
void f ()
{
    moveto (x+fraction[2],y);
    lineto (x+fraction[13],y);
    lineto (x+fraction[14],y+fraction[1]);
    lineto (x+fraction[14],y+fraction[2]);
    lineto (x+fraction[13],y+fraction[3]);
    lineto (x+fraction[4],y+fraction[3]);
    lineto (x+fraction[3],y+fraction[4]);
    lineto (x+fraction[3],y+fraction[6]);
    lineto (x+fraction[9],y+fraction[6]);
    lineto (x+fraction[9],y+fraction[8]);
    lineto (x+fraction[3],y+fraction[8]);
    lineto (x+fraction[3],y+fraction[14]);
    lineto (x,y+fraction[14]);
    lineto (x,y+fraction[2]);
    lineto (x+fraction[2],y);
}
```

Figure C.7.   G

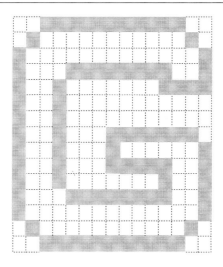

485

```
void g ()
{
    moveto (x+fraction[2],y);
    lineto (x+fraction[12],y);
    lineto (x+fraction[14],y+fraction[2]);
    lineto (x+fraction[14],y+fraction[4]);
    lineto (x+fraction[11],y+fraction[4]);
    lineto (x+fraction[11],y+fraction[3]);
    lineto (x+fraction[4],y+fraction[3]);
    lineto (x+fraction[3],y+fraction[4]);
    lineto (x+fraction[3],y+fraction[10]);
    lineto (x+fraction[4],y+fraction[11]);
    lineto (x+fraction[11],y+fraction[11]);
    lineto (x+fraction[11],y+fraction[9]);
    lineto (x+fraction[7],y+fraction[9]);
    lineto (x+fraction[7],y+fraction[7]);
    lineto (x+fraction[13],y+fraction[7]);
    lineto (x+fraction[14],y+fraction[8]);
    lineto (x+fraction[14],y+fraction[12]);
    lineto (x+fraction[12],y+fraction[14]);
    lineto (x+fraction[2],y+fraction[14]);
    lineto (x,y+fraction[12]);
    lineto (x,y+fraction[2]);
    lineto (x+fraction[2],y);
}
```

Figure C.8.   H

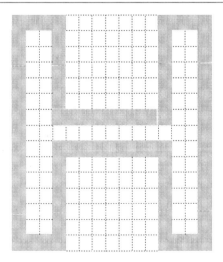

486

```
void h ()
{
    moveto (x,y);
    lineto (x+fraction[3],y);
    lineto (x+fraction[3],y+fraction[6]);
    lineto (x+fraction[11],y+fraction[6]);
    lineto (x+fraction[11],y);
    lineto (x+fraction[14],y);
    lineto (x+fraction[14],y+fraction[14]);
    lineto (x+fraction[11],y+fraction[14]);
    lineto (x+fraction[11],y+fraction[8]);
    lineto (x+fraction[3],y+fraction[8]);
    lineto (x+fraction[3],y+fraction[14]);
    lineto (x,y+fraction[14]);
    lineto (x,y);
}
```

Figure C.9. I

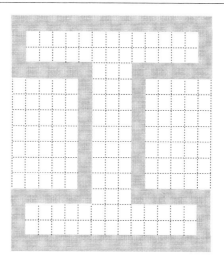

```
void i ()
{
  moveto (x,y);
    lineto (x+fraction[14],y);
    lineto (x+fraction[14],y+fraction[3]);
    lineto (x+fraction[9],y+fraction[3]);
    lineto (x+fraction[9],y+fraction[11]);
    lineto (x+fraction[14],y+fraction[11]);
    lineto (x+fraction[14],y+fraction[14]);
    lineto (x,y+fraction[14]);
    lineto (x,y+fraction[11]);
    lineto (x+fraction[5],y+fraction[11]);
    lineto (x+fraction[5],y+fraction[3]);
    lineto (x,y+fraction[3]);
    lineto (x,y);
}
```

Figure C.10.   J

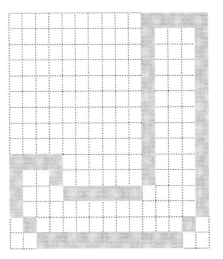

```
void j ()
{
    moveto (x+fraction[10],y);
    lineto (x+fraction[14],y);
    lineto (x+fraction[14],y+fraction[12]);
    lineto (x+fraction[12],y+fraction[14]);
    lineto (x+fraction[2],y+fraction[14]);
    lineto (x,y+fraction[12]);
    lineto (x,y+fraction[9]);
    lineto (x+fraction[3],y+fraction[9]);
    lineto (x+fraction[3],y+fraction[10]);
    lineto (x+fraction[4],y+fraction[11]);
    lineto (x+fraction[9],y+fraction[11]);
    lineto (x+fraction[10],y+fraction[10]);
    lineto (x+fraction[10],y);
}
```

Figure C.11.   K

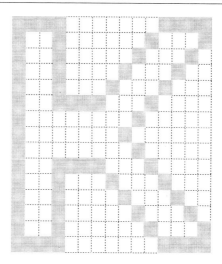

```
void k ()
{
    moveto (x,y);
    lineto (x+fraction[3],y);
    lineto (x+fraction[3],y+fraction[5]);
    lineto (x+fraction[6],y+fraction[5]);
    lineto (x+fraction[11],y);
    lineto (x+fraction[14],y);
    lineto (x+fraction[14],y+fraction[1]);
    lineto (x+fraction[8],y+fraction[7]);
    lineto (x+fraction[14],y+fraction[13]);
    lineto (x+fraction[14],y+fraction[14]);
    lineto (x+fraction[11],y+fraction[14]);
    lineto (x+fraction[6],y+fraction[9]);
    lineto (x+fraction[3],y+fraction[9]);
    lineto (x+fraction[3],y+fraction[14]);
    lineto (x,y+fraction[14]);
  lineto (x,y);
}
```

Figure C.12. L

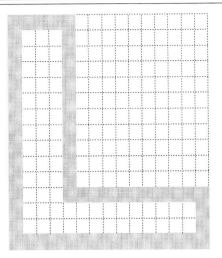

```
void L ()
{
    moveto (x,y);
    lineto (x+fraction[4],y);
    lineto (x+fraction[4],y+fraction[11]);
    lineto (x+fraction[14],y+fraction[11]);
    lineto (x+fraction[14],y+fraction[14]);
    lineto (x,y+fraction[14]);
    lineto (x,y);
}
```

Figure C.13. M

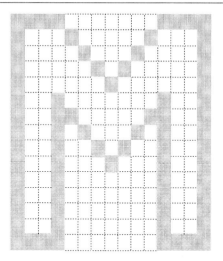

```
void m ()
{
    moveto (x,y);
    lineto (x+fraction[3],y);
    lineto (x+fraction[7],y+fraction[4]);
    lineto (x+fraction[11],y);
    lineto (x+fraction[14],y);
    lineto (x+fraction[14],y+fraction[14]);
    lineto (x+fraction[11],y+fraction[14]);
    lineto (x+fraction[11],y+fraction[5]);
    lineto (x+fraction[7],y+fraction[9]);
    lineto (x+fraction[3],y+fraction[5]);
    lineto (x+fraction[3],y+fraction[14]);
    lineto (x,y+fraction[14]);
    lineto (x,y);
}
```

Figure C.14. N

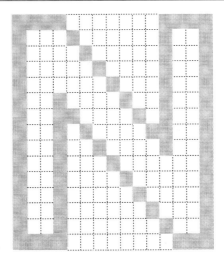

```
void n ()
{
    moveto (x,y);
    lineto (x+fraction[3],y);
    lineto (x+fraction[11],y+fraction[8]);
    lineto (x+fraction[11],y);
    lineto (x+fraction[14],y);
    lineto (x+fraction[14],y+fraction[14]);
    lineto (x+fraction[12],y+fraction[14]);
    lineto (x+fraction[3],y+fraction[5]);
    lineto (x+fraction[3],y+fraction[14]);
    lineto (x,y+fraction[14]);
    lineto (x,y);
}
```

Figure C.15. O

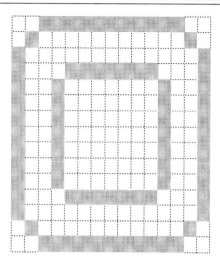

```
void o ()
{
    moveto (x+fraction[2],y);
    lineto (x+fraction[12],y);
    lineto (x+fraction[14],y+fraction[2]);
    lineto (x+fraction[14],y+fraction[12]);
    lineto (x+fraction[12],y+fraction[14]);
    lineto (x+fraction[2],y+fraction[14]);
    lineto (x,y+fraction[12]);
    lineto (x,y+fraction[2]);
    lineto (x+fraction[2],y);
    moveto (x+fraction[4],y+fraction[3]);
    lineto (x+fraction[10],y+fraction[3]);
    lineto (x+fraction[11],y+fraction[4]);
    lineto (x+fraction[11],y+fraction[10]);
    lineto (x+fraction[10],y+fraction[11]);
    lineto (x+fraction[4],y+fraction[11]);
    lineto (x+fraction[3],y+fraction[10]);
    lineto (x+fraction[3],y+fraction[4]);
    lineto (x+fraction[4],y+fraction[3]);
}
```

493

Figure C.16. P

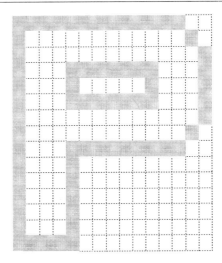

```
void p ()
{
    moveto (x,y);
    lineto (x+fraction[12],y);
    lineto (x+fraction[14],y+fraction[2]);
    lineto (x+fraction[14],y+fraction[6]);
    lineto (x+fraction[12],y+fraction[8]);
    lineto (x+fraction[4],y+fraction[8]);
    lineto (x+fraction[4],y+fraction[14]);
    lineto (x,y+fraction[14]);
    lineto (x,y);
    moveto (x+fraction[4],y+fraction[3]);
    lineto (x+fraction[10],y+fraction[3]);
    lineto (x+fraction[10],y+fraction[5]);
    lineto (x+fraction[4],y+fraction[5]);
  lineto (x+fraction[4],y+fraction[3]);
}
```

Figure C.17.   Q

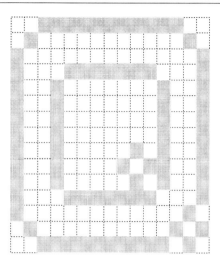

```
void q ()
{
    moveto (x+fraction[2],y);
  lineto (x+fraction[12],y);
    lineto (x+fraction[14],y+fraction[2]);
    lineto (x+fraction[14],y+fraction[11]);
    lineto (x+fraction[13],y+fraction[12]);
    lineto (x+fraction[14],y+fraction[13]);
    lineto (x+fraction[13],y+fraction[14]);
    lineto (x+fraction[12],y+fraction[13]);
    lineto (x+fraction[11],y+fraction[14]);
    lineto (x+fraction[2],y+fraction[14]);
    lineto (x,y+fraction[12]);
    lineto (x,y+fraction[2]);
    lineto (x+fraction[2],y);
    moveto (x+fraction[4],y+fraction[3]);
    lineto (x+fraction[10],y+fraction[3]);
    lineto (x+fraction[11],y+fraction[4]);
    lineto (x+fraction[11],y+fraction[10]);
    lineto (x+fraction[9],y+fraction[8]);
    lineto (x+fraction[8],y+fraction[9]);
    lineto (x+fraction[10],y+fraction[11]);
    lineto (x+fraction[4],y+fraction[11]);
    lineto (x+fraction[3],y+fraction[10]);
    lineto (x+fraction[3],y+fraction[4]);
    lineto (x+fraction[4],y+fraction[3]);
}
```

Figure C.18.   R

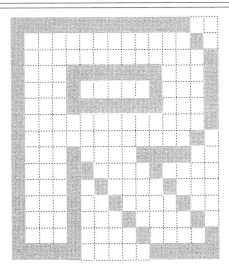

```
void r ()
{
  moveto (x,y);
    lineto (x+fraction[12],y);
    lineto (x+fraction[14],y+fraction[2]);
    lineto (x+fraction[14],y+fraction[6]);
    lineto (x+fraction[12],y+fraction[8]);
    lineto (x+fraction[9],y+fraction[8]);
    lineto (x+fraction[14],y+fraction[13]);
    lineto (x+fraction[14],y+fraction[14]);
    lineto (x+fraction[10],y+fraction[14]);
    lineto (x+fraction[4],y+fraction[8]);
    lineto (x+fraction[4],y+fraction[14]);
    lineto (x,y+fraction[14]);
    lineto (x,y);
    moveto (x+fraction[4],y+fraction[3]);
    lineto (x+fraction[10],y+fraction[3]);
    lineto (x+fraction[10],y+fraction[5]);
    lineto (x+fraction[4],y+fraction[5]);
    lineto (x+fraction[4],y+fraction[3]);
}
```

Figure C.19. S

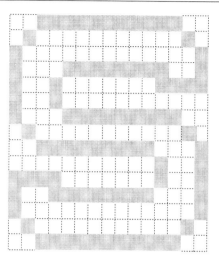

```
void s ()
{
    moveto (x+fraction[2],y);
    lineto (x+fraction[12],y);
    lineto (x+fraction[14],y+fraction[2]);
    lineto (x+fraction[14],y+fraction[4]);
    lineto (x+fraction[11],y+fraction[4]);
    lineto (x+fraction[11],y+fraction[3]);
    lineto (x+fraction[4],y+fraction[3]);
    lineto (x+fraction[3],y+fraction[4]);
    lineto (x+fraction[3],y+fraction[5]);
    lineto (x+fraction[4],y+fraction[6]);
    lineto (x+fraction[13],y+fraction[6]);
    lineto (x+fraction[14],y+fraction[7]);
    lineto (x+fraction[14],y+fraction[12]);
    lineto (x+fraction[12],y+fraction[14]);
    lineto (x+fraction[2],y+fraction[14]);
    lineto (x,y+fraction[12]);
    lineto (x,y+fraction[10]);
    lineto (x+fraction[3],y+fraction[10]);
    lineto (x+fraction[3],y+fraction[11]);
    lineto (x+fraction[10],y+fraction[11]);
    lineto (x+fraction[11],y+fraction[10]);
    lineto (x+fraction[11],y+fraction[9]);
    lineto (x+fraction[10],y+fraction[8]);
    lineto (x+fraction[2],y+fraction[8]);
    lineto (x,y+fraction[6]);
    lineto (x,y+fraction[2]);
    lineto (x+fraction[2],y);
}
```

Figure C.20. T

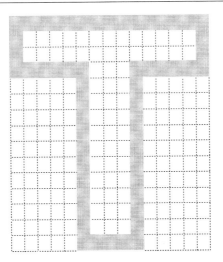

```
void t ()
{
    moveto (x,y);
    lineto (x+fraction[14],y);
    lineto (x+fraction[14],y+fraction[3]);
    lineto (x+fraction[9],y+fraction[3]);
    lineto (x+fraction[9],y+fraction[14]);
    lineto (x+fraction[5],y+fraction[14]);
    lineto (x+fraction[5],y+fraction[3]);
    lineto (x,y+fraction[3]);
    lineto (x,y);
}
```

Figure C.21. U

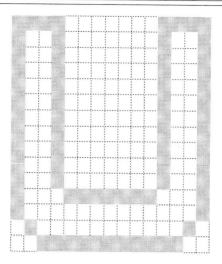

```
void u ()
{
    moveto (x,y);
    lineto (x+fraction[3],y);
    lineto (x+fraction[3],y+fraction[10]);
    lineto (x+fraction[4],y+fraction[11]);
    lineto (x+fraction[10],y+fraction[11]);
    lineto (x+fraction[11],y+fraction[10]);
    lineto (x+fraction[11],y);
    lineto (x+fraction[14],y);
    lineto (x+fraction[14],y+fraction[12]);
    lineto (x+fraction[12],y+fraction[14]);
    lineto (x+fraction[2],y+fraction[14]);
    lineto (x,y+fraction[12]);
    lineto (x,y);
}
```

Figure C.22. V

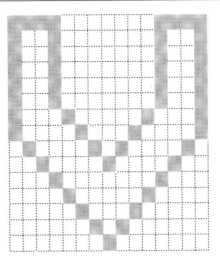

```
void v ()
{
    moveto (x,y);
    lineto (x+fraction[3],y);
    lineto (x+fraction[3],y+fraction[5]);
    lineto (x+fraction[7],y+fraction[9]);
    lineto (x+fraction[11],y+fraction[5]);
    lineto (x+fraction[11],y);
    lineto (x+fraction[14],y);
    lineto (x+fraction[14],y+fraction[7]);
    lineto (x+fraction[7],y+fraction[14]);
    lineto (x,y+fraction[7]);
    lineto (x,y);
}
```

Figure C.23. W

```
void w ()
{
    moveto (x,y);
    lineto (x+fraction[3],y);
    lineto (x+fraction[3],y+fraction[9]);
    lineto (x+fraction[7],y+fraction[5]);
    lineto (x+fraction[11],y+fraction[9]);
    lineto (x+fraction[11],y);
    lineto (x+fraction[14],y);
    lineto (x+fraction[14],y+fraction[14]);
    lineto (x+fraction[11],y+fraction[14]);
    lineto (x+fraction[7],y+fraction[10]);
    lineto (x+fraction[3],y+fraction[14]);
    lineto (x,y+fraction[14]);
    lineto (x,y);
}
```

Figure C.24. X

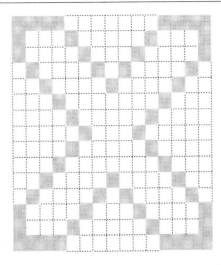

```
void x ()
{
    moveto (x,y);
    lineto (x+fraction[3],y);
    lineto (x+fraction[7],y+fraction[4]);
    lineto (x+fraction[11],y);
    lineto (x+fraction[14],y);
    lineto (x+fraction[14],y+fraction[2]);
    lineto (x+fraction[9],y+fraction[7]);
    lineto (x+fraction[14],y+fraction[12]);
    lineto (x+fraction[14],y+fraction[14]);
    lineto (x+fraction[11],y+fraction[14]);
    lineto (x+fraction[7],y+fraction[10]);
    lineto (x+fraction[3],y+fraction[14]);
    lineto (x,y+fraction[14]);
    lineto (x,y+fraction[12]);
    lineto (x+fraction[5],y+fraction[7]);
    lineto (x,y+fraction[2]);
    lineto (x,y);
}
```

Figure C.25. Y

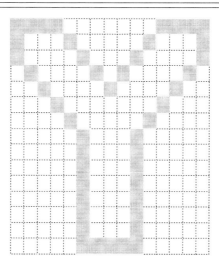

```
void y ()
{
    moveto (x,y);
    lineto (x+fraction[3],y);
    lineto (x+fraction[7],y+fraction[4]);
    lineto (x+fraction[11],y);
    lineto (x+fraction[14],y);
    lineto (x+fraction[14],y+fraction[2]);
    lineto (x+fraction[9],y+fraction[7]);
    lineto (x+fraction[9],y+fraction[14]);
    lineto (x+fraction[5],y+fraction[14]);
    lineto (x+fraction[5],y+fraction[7]);
    lineto (x,y+fraction[2]);
    lineto (x,y);
}
```

Figure C.26. Z

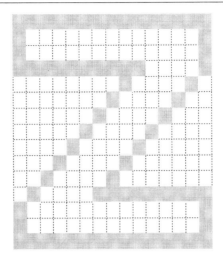

```
void z ()
{
    moveto (x,y);
    lineto (x+fraction[14],y);
    lineto (x+fraction[14],y+fraction[2]);
    lineto (x+fraction[5],y+fraction[11]);
    lineto (x+fraction[14],y+fraction[11]);
    lineto (x+fraction[14],y+fraction[14]);
    lineto (x,y+fraction[14]);
    lineto (x,y+fraction[12]);
    lineto (x+fraction[9],y+fraction[3]);
    lineto (x,y+fraction[3]);
    lineto (x,y);
}
```

Bibliography

Adams, Lee. *High Performance CAD GRAPHICS IN C*. Blue Ridge Summit, Pennsylvania: Windcrest Books, 1989.

Adams, Lee. *High-Speed Animation and Simulation for Microcomputers*. Blue Ridge Summit, Pennsylvania: TAB Books, Inc., 1987.

Campbell, John L. *Inside OS/2: The Complete Programmer's Reference*. Blue Ridge Summit, Pennsylvania: TAB Books, Inc., 1988.

Charette, Robert N. *Software Engineering Environments: Concepts and Technology*. New York: Intertext Publications, Inc., 1986.

Ferraro, Richard F. *Programmer's Guide to the EGA and VGA Cards*. Reading, Massachusetts: Addison-Wesley Publishing Company, 1988.

Howard, Bill. "Supplementing the Keyboard: Point and Shoot Devices," *PC Magazine*, August 1987, 95-96.

Hsu, Jeffrey. *Microcomputer Programming Languages*. Hasbrouck Heights, New Jersey: Hayden Book Company, 1986.

Norton, Peter and Richard Wilton. *The New Peter Norton Programmer's Guide to the IBM PC and PS/2*. Redmond, Washington: Microsoft Press, 1988.

Norton, Peter and John Socha. *Peter Norton's Assembly Language Book for the IBM PC*. New York: Brady Books, 1986.

Petzold, Charles. "Understanding and Using Bézier Splines in OS/2 Graphics," *PC Magazine*, November 14, 1989, 409-420.

Rosch, Winn L. "Digitizing Tablets Pointing the Way to Easier Input," *PC Magazine*, November 28, 1989, 227-234.

Stevens, Roger T. *Graphics Programming in C*. Redwood City, California: M&T Books, 1989.

Turbo C++: Reference Guide, Borland International, 1990.

Index

Symbols

G

H

Sams—Covering The Latest In Computer And Technical Topics!